Toradora!

VOL. 4

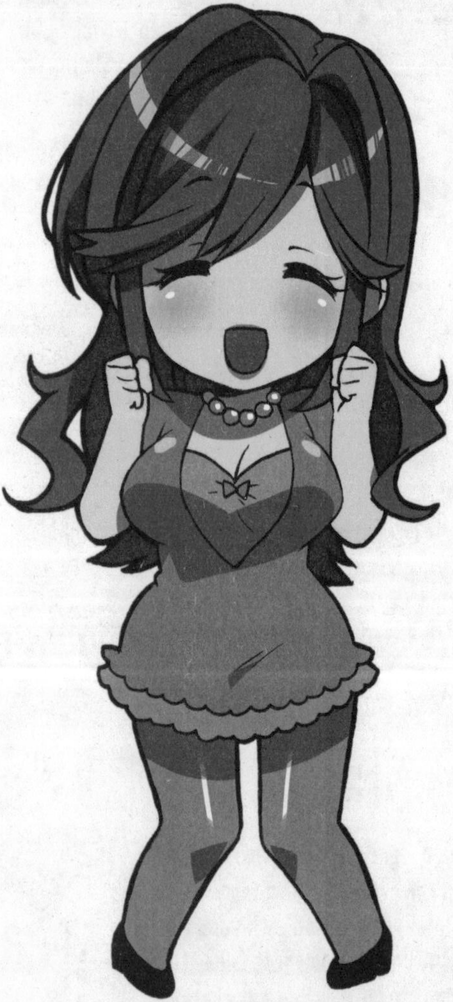

Based on the novels by Yuyuko Tak
Manga artwork by Ze
Original character design by

ra do ra

VOLUME 4

story by **Yuyuko Takemiya**

art by **Zekkyou**

character design by **Yasu**

STAFF CREDITS

translation	Adrienne Beck
adaptation	Bambi Eloriaga-Amago
lettering	Roland Amago
layout	Mheeya Wok
cover design	Nicky Lim
copy editor	Shanti Whitesides
editor	Adam Arnold
publisher	Jason DeAngelis
	Seven Seas Entertainment

TORADORA! VOL. 4
Copyright © 2011 Yukuko Takemiya / Zekkyou
First published in 2011 by ASCII MEDIA WORKS., Tokyo, Japan.
English translation rights arranged with ASCII MEDIA WORKS.

ISBN: 978-1-935934-17-2

Printed in Canada

First Printing: April 2012

10 9 8 7 6 5 4 3

Seven Seas

FOLLOW US ONLINE: *www.gomanga.com*

READING DIRECTIONS

This book reads from *right to left*, Japanese style.
If this is your first time reading manga, you start
reading from the top right panel on each page and
take it from there. If you get lost, just follow the
numbered diagram here. It may seem backwards
at first, but you'll get the hang of it! Have fun!!

Chapter 25
HEY, DID YOU KNOW THE MOST POPULAR LINING COLOR FOR SCHOOL SWIMSUITS ISN'T WHITE BUT BEIGE?

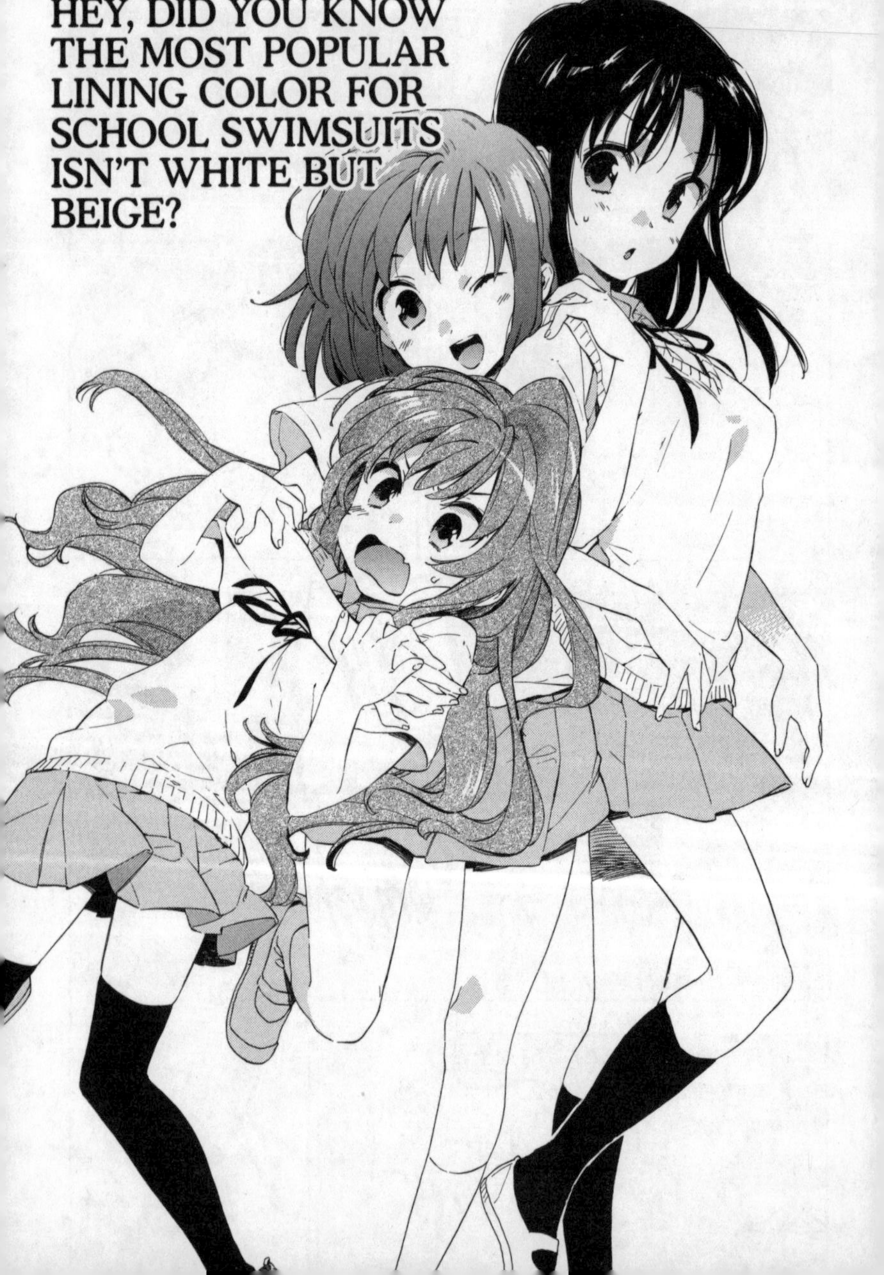

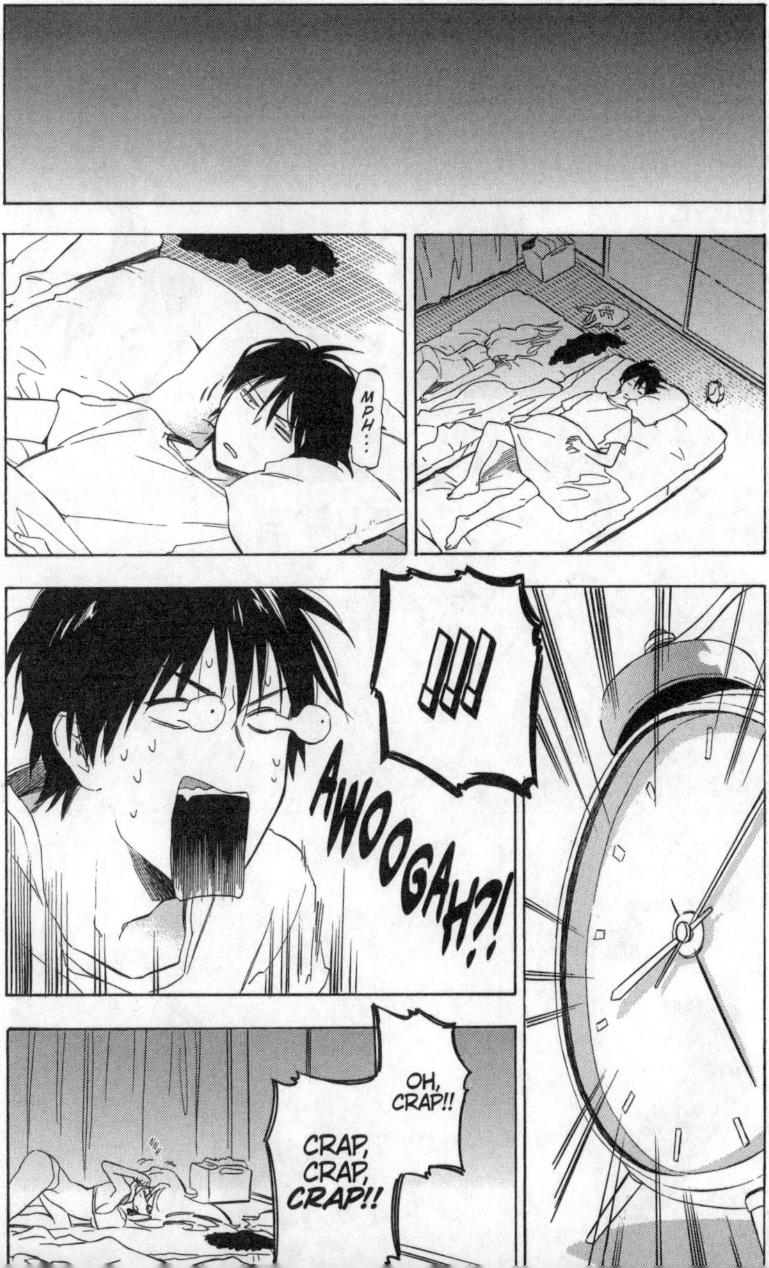
MPH...
!!!
AWOOGAH?!
OH, CRAP!!
CRAP, CRAP, CRAP!!

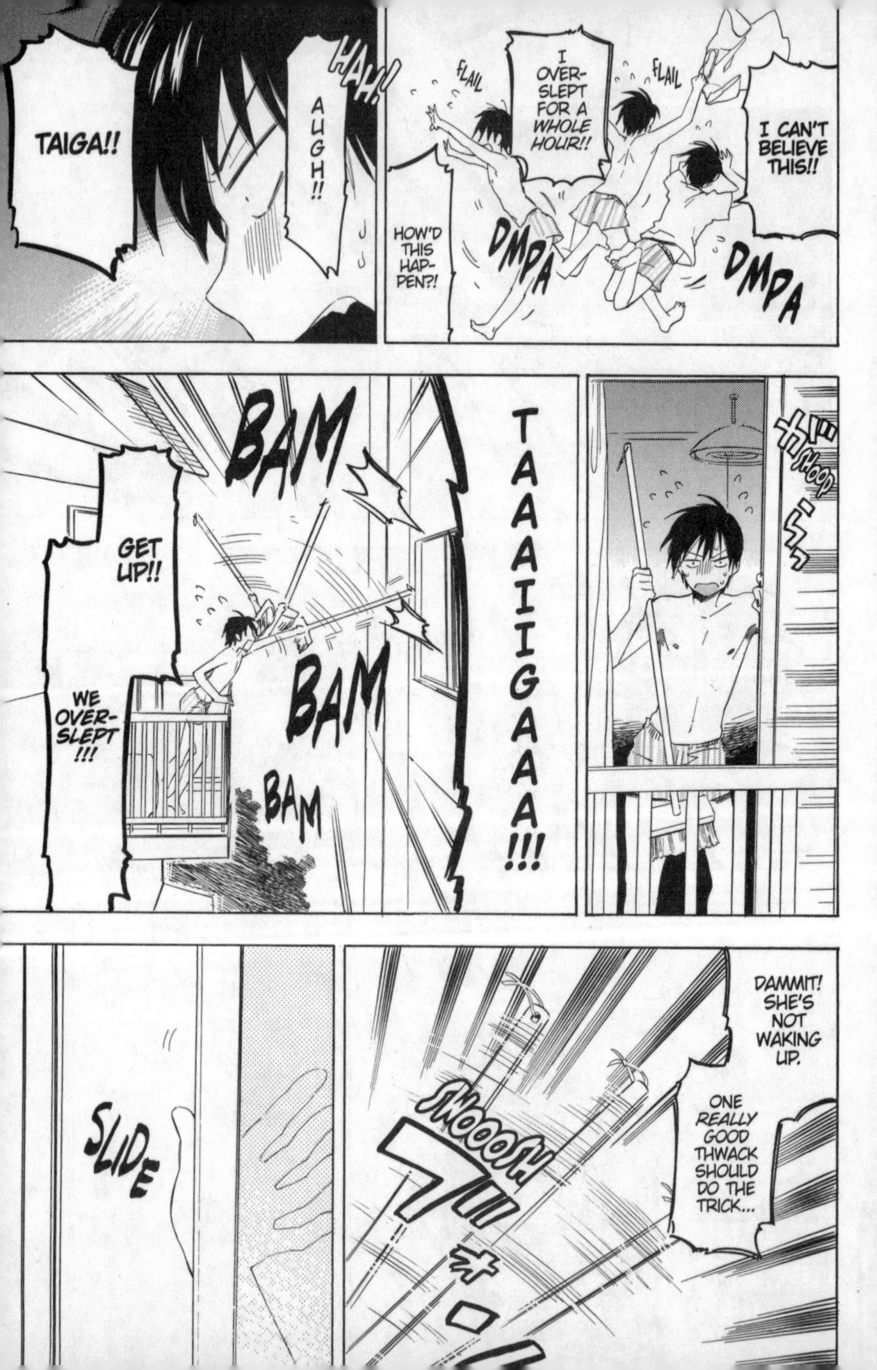
I CAN'T BELIEVE THIS!!
FLAIL
I OVER-SLEPT FOR A WHOLE HOUR!!
FLAIL
DMPA
HOW'D THIS HAP-PEN?!
DMPA
HAH!
AUGH!!
TAIGA!!
SHOOP
TAAAAIIGAAAA!!!
BAM
BAM
BAM
GET UP!!
WE OVER-SLEPT!!!
DAMMIT! SHE'S NOT WAKING UP.
ONE REALLY GOOD THWACK SHOULD DO THE TRICK...
SWOOOSH
SLIDE

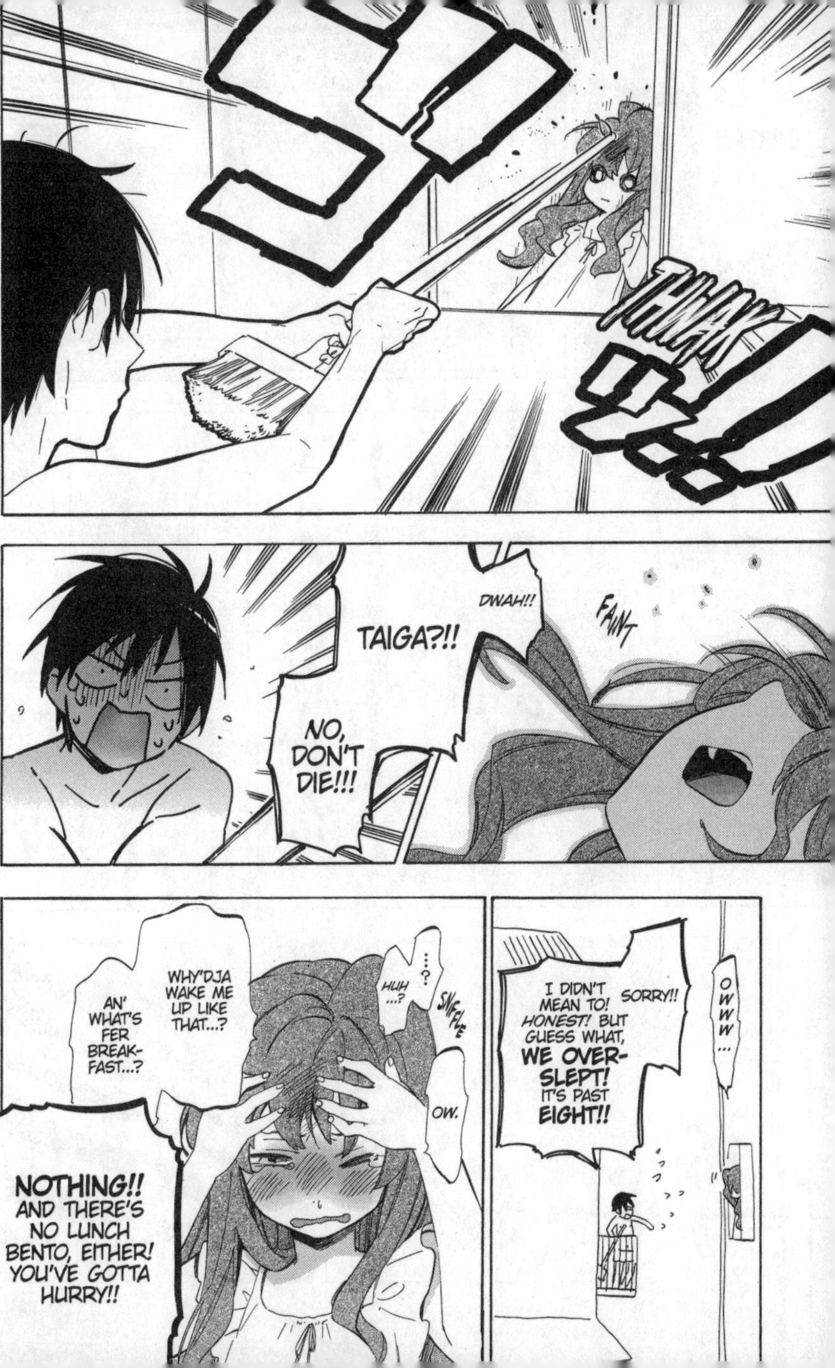
THWAK
FAINT
DWAH!!
TAIGA?!!
NO, DON'T DIE!!!
OWWW...
SORRY!!
I DIDN'T MEAN TO! HONEST! BUT GUESS WHAT, WE OVER-SLEPT! IT'S PAST EIGHT!!
SNIFFLE
...?
HUH ...?
OW.
WHY'DJA WAKE ME UP LIKE THAT...?
AN' WHAT'S FER BREAK-FAST...?
NOTHING!! AND THERE'S NO LUNCH BENTO, EITHER! YOU'VE GOTTA HURRY!!

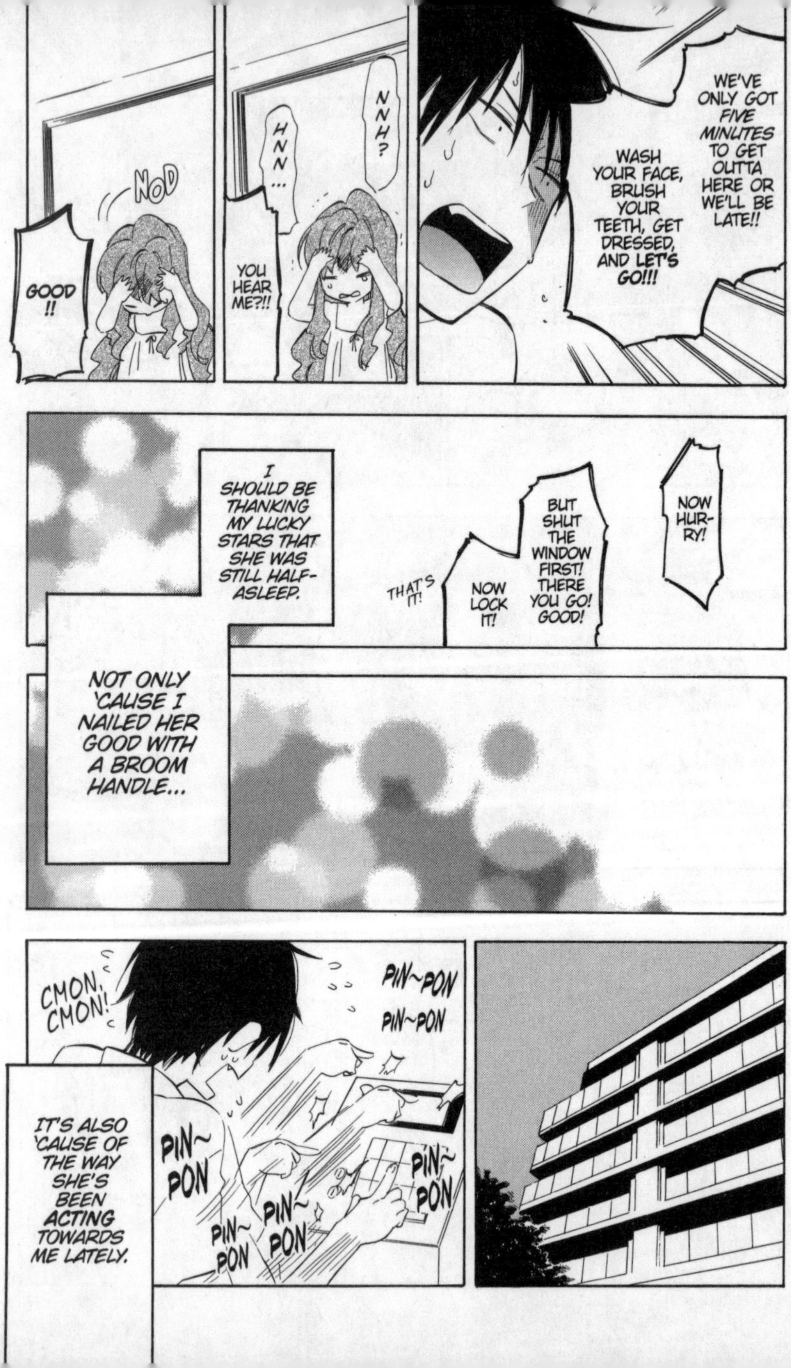
WE'VE ONLY GOT FIVE MINUTES TO GET OUTTA HERE OR WE'LL BE LATE!!
WASH YOUR FACE, BRUSH YOUR TEETH, GET DRESSED, AND LET'S GO!!!
NNH?
HNN...
YOU HEAR ME?!!
NOD
GOOD!!
NOW HURRY!
BUT SHUT THE WINDOW FIRST! THERE YOU GO! GOOD!
NOW LOCK IT!
THAT'S IT!
I SHOULD BE THANKING MY LUCKY STARS THAT SHE WAS STILL HALF-ASLEEP.
NOT ONLY 'CAUSE I NAILED HER GOOD WITH A BROOM HANDLE...
PIN~PON
PIN~PON
CMON, CMON!
PIN~PON
PIN~PON
PIN~PON
PIN~PON
IT'S ALSO 'CAUSE OF THE WAY SHE'S BEEN ACTING TOWARDS ME LATELY.

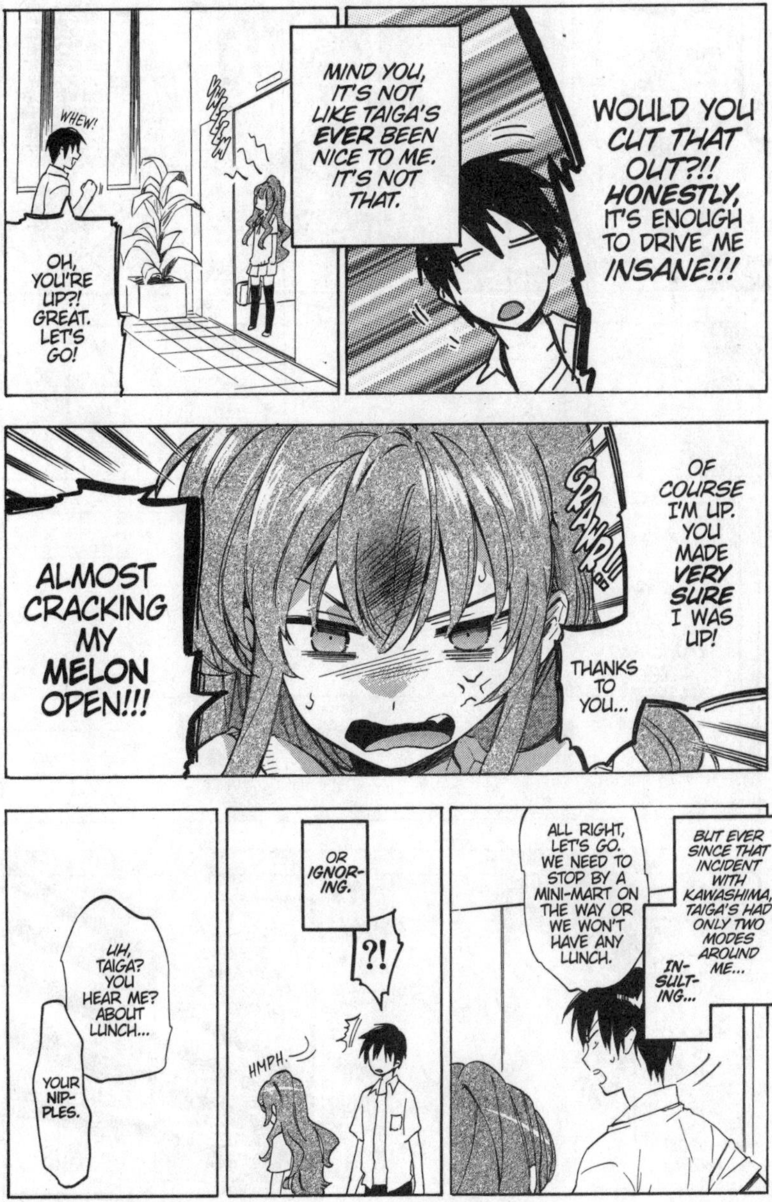
WOULD YOU CUT THAT OUT?!! HONESTLY, IT'S ENOUGH TO DRIVE ME INSANE!!!
MIND YOU, IT'S NOT LIKE TAIGA'S EVER BEEN NICE TO ME. IT'S NOT THAT.
WHEW!
OH, YOU'RE UP?! GREAT. LET'S GO!
GRAWR!!
OF COURSE I'M UP. YOU MADE VERY SURE I WAS UP!
THANKS TO YOU...
ALMOST CRACKING MY MELON OPEN!!!
BUT EVER SINCE THAT INCIDENT WITH KAWASHIMA, TAIGA'S HAD ONLY TWO MODES AROUND ME...
ALL RIGHT, LET'S GO. WE NEED TO STOP BY A MINI-MART ON THE WAY OR WE WON'T HAVE ANY LUNCH.
IN-SULT-ING...
OR IGNOR-ING.
?!
HMPH.
UH, TAIGA? YOU HEAR ME? ABOUT LUNCH...
YOUR NIP-PLES.

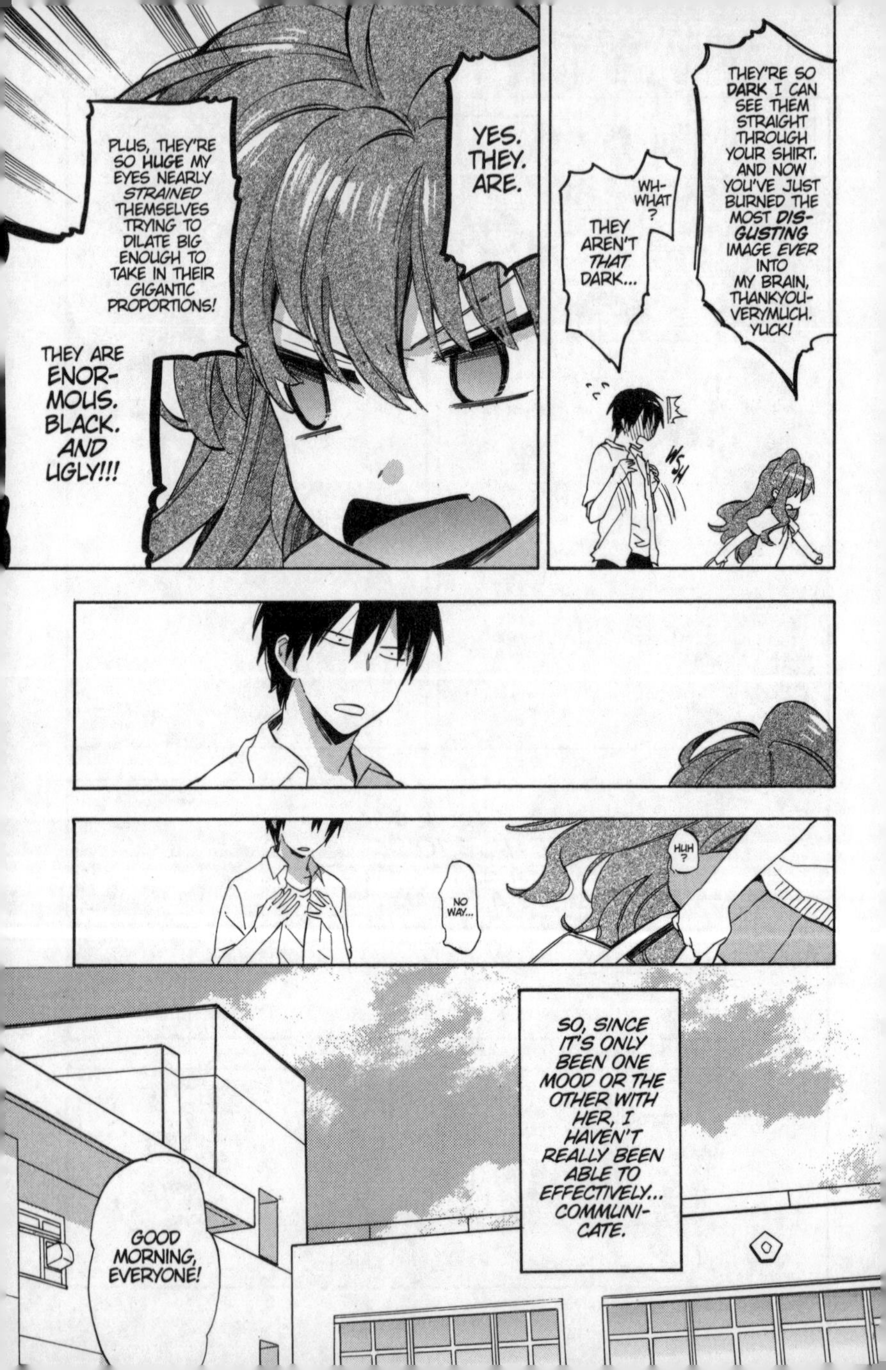
THEY'RE SO DARK I CAN SEE THEM STRAIGHT THROUGH YOUR SHIRT. AND NOW YOU'VE JUST BURNED THE MOST DISGUSTING IMAGE EVER INTO MY BRAIN, THANKYOU-VERYMUCH. YUCK!
WH-WHAT? THEY AREN'T THAT DARK...
WSH
YES. THEY. ARE.
PLUS, THEY'RE SO HUGE MY EYES NEARLY STRAINED THEMSELVES TRYING TO DILATE BIG ENOUGH TO TAKE IN THEIR GIGANTIC PROPORTIONS!
THEY ARE ENORMOUS. BLACK. AND UGLY!!!
HUH?
NO WAY...
SO, SINCE IT'S ONLY BEEN ONE MOOD OR THE OTHER WITH HER, I HAVEN'T REALLY BEEN ABLE TO EFFECTIVELY... COMMUNICATE.
GOOD MORNING, EVERYONE!

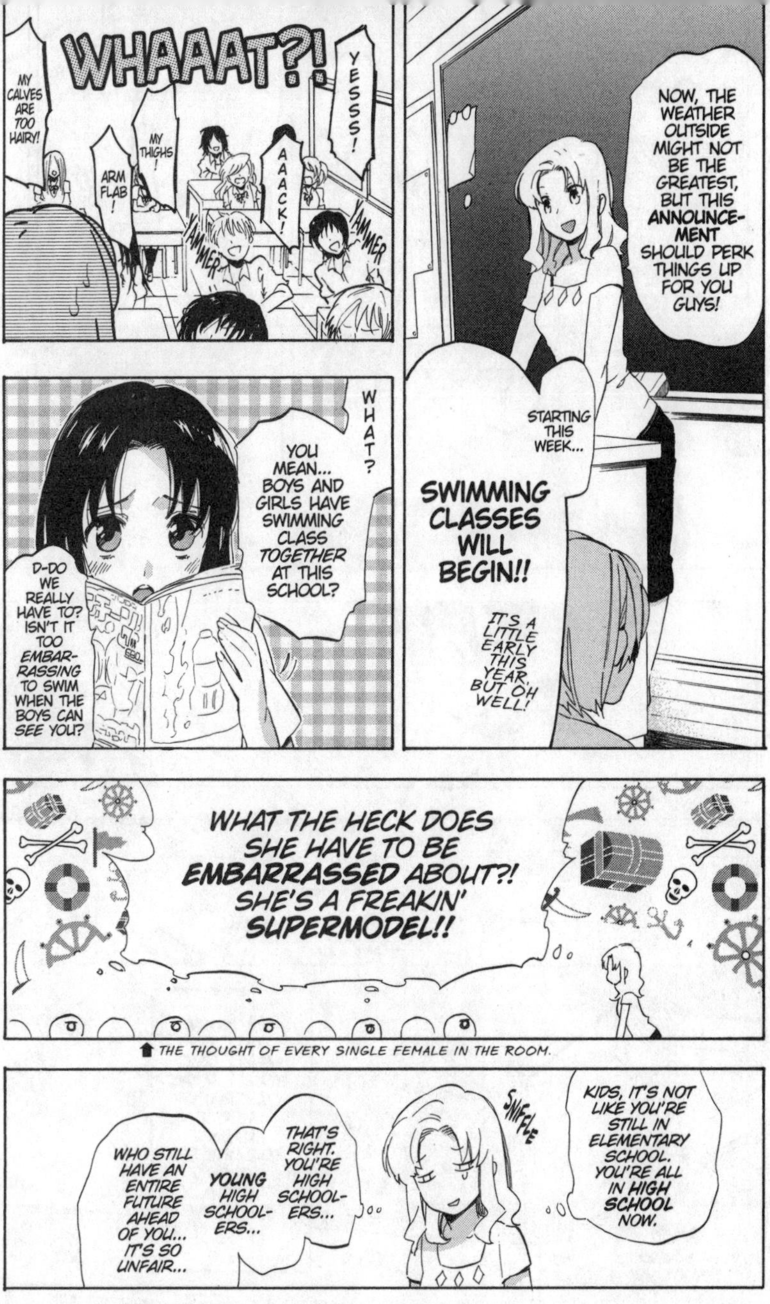
NOW, THE WEATHER OUTSIDE MIGHT NOT BE THE GREATEST, BUT THIS ANNOUNCEMENT SHOULD PERK THINGS UP FOR YOU GUYS!
STARTING THIS WEEK...
SWIMMING CLASSES WILL BEGIN!!
IT'S A LITTLE EARLY THIS YEAR, BUT OH WELL!
WHAAAT?!
YESSS!
AAAACK!
YAMMER
MY THIGHS!
MY CALVES ARE TOO HAIRY!
ARM FLAB!
YAMMER
WHAT?
YOU MEAN... BOYS AND GIRLS HAVE SWIMMING CLASS TOGETHER AT THIS SCHOOL?
D-DO WE REALLY HAVE TO? ISN'T IT TOO EMBARRASSING TO SWIM WHEN THE BOYS CAN SEE YOU?
WHAT THE HECK DOES SHE HAVE TO BE EMBARRASSED ABOUT?! SHE'S A FREAKIN' SUPERMODEL!!
THE THOUGHT OF EVERY SINGLE FEMALE IN THE ROOM.
KIDS, IT'S NOT LIKE YOU'RE STILL IN ELEMENTARY SCHOOL. YOU'RE ALL IN HIGH SCHOOL NOW.
SNIFFLE
THAT'S RIGHT. YOU'RE HIGH SCHOOLERS...
YOUNG HIGH SCHOOLERS...
WHO STILL HAVE AN ENTIRE FUTURE AHEAD OF YOU... IT'S SO UNFAIR...

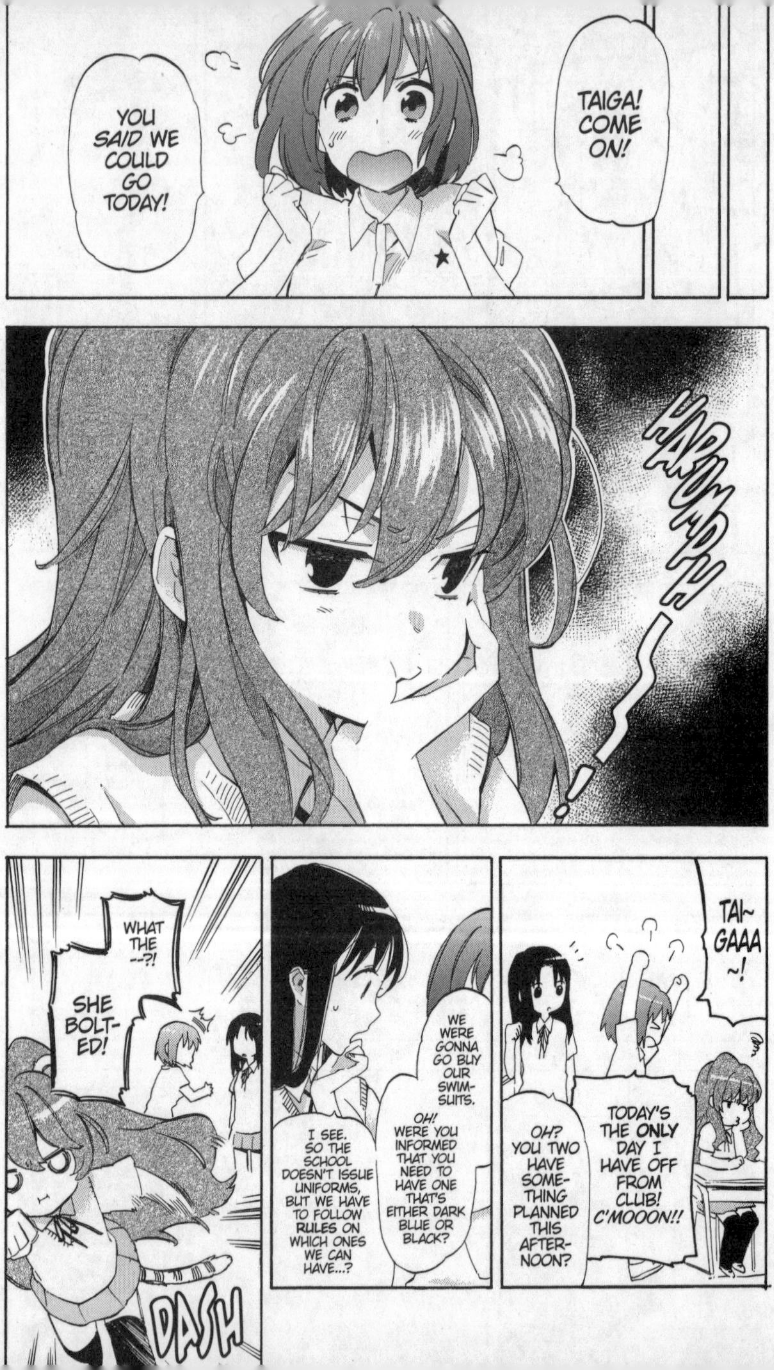
TAIGA! COME ON!
YOU SAID WE COULD GO TODAY!
HARUMPH~~!
TAI~GAAA~!
TODAY'S THE ONLY DAY I HAVE OFF FROM CLUB! C'MOOON!!
OH? YOU TWO HAVE SOMETHING PLANNED THIS AFTERNOON?
WE WERE GONNA GO BUY OUR SWIMSUITS.
OH! WERE YOU INFORMED THAT YOU NEED TO HAVE ONE THAT'S EITHER DARK BLUE OR BLACK?
I SEE. SO THE SCHOOL DOESN'T ISSUE UNIFORMS, BUT WE HAVE TO FOLLOW RULES ON WHICH ONES WE CAN HAVE...?
WHAT THE --?!
SHE BOLTED!
DASH

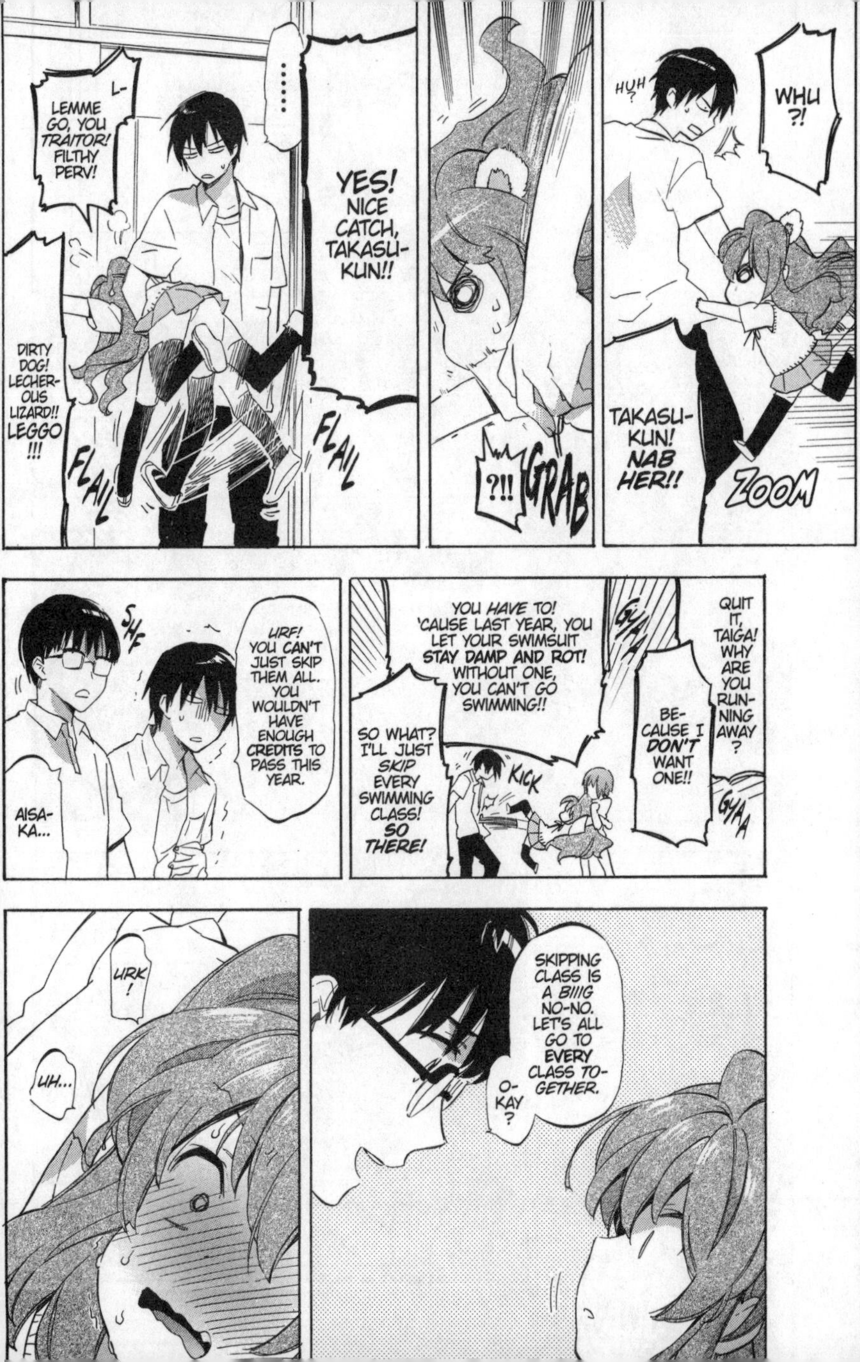
WHU ?!
HUH ?
TAKASU-KUN! NAB HER!!
ZOOM
?!!
GRAB
......
YES! NICE CATCH, TAKASU-KUN!!
L- LEMME GO, YOU TRAITOR! FILTHY PERV!
DIRTY DOG! LECHEROUS LIZARD!! LEGGO !!!
FLAIL
FLAIL
QUIT IT, TAIGA! WHY ARE YOU RUNNING AWAY?
GYAA
BECAUSE I DON'T WANT ONE!!
YOU HAVE TO! 'CAUSE LAST YEAR, YOU LET YOUR SWIMSUIT STAY DAMP AND ROT! WITHOUT ONE, YOU CAN'T GO SWIMMING!!
SO WHAT? I'LL JUST SKIP EVERY SWIMMING CLASS! SO THERE!
KICK
GYAA
SHF
URF! YOU CAN'T JUST SKIP THEM ALL. YOU WOULDN'T HAVE ENOUGH CREDITS TO PASS THIS YEAR.
AISAKA...
SKIPPING CLASS IS A BIIIG NO-NO. LET'S ALL GO TO EVERY CLASS TOGETHER.
O-KAY?
URK!
UH...

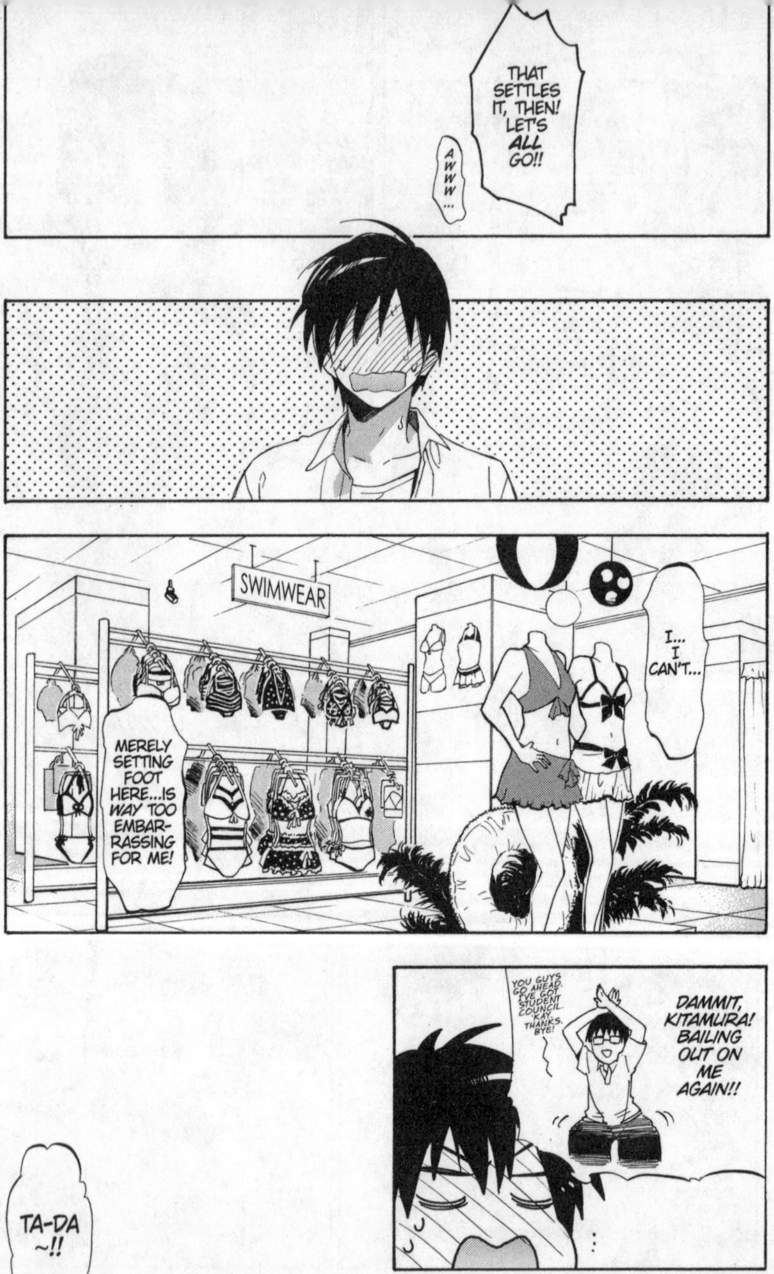
THAT SETTLES IT, THEN! LET'S ALL GO!!
AWWW...
I... I CAN'T...
MERELY SETTING FOOT HERE...IS WAY TOO EMBARRASSING FOR ME!
DAMMIT, KITAMURA! BAILING OUT ON ME AGAIN!!
YOU GUYS GO AHEAD. I'VE GOT STUDENT COUNCIL. 'KAY, THANKS, BYE!
...
TA-DA~!!

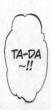

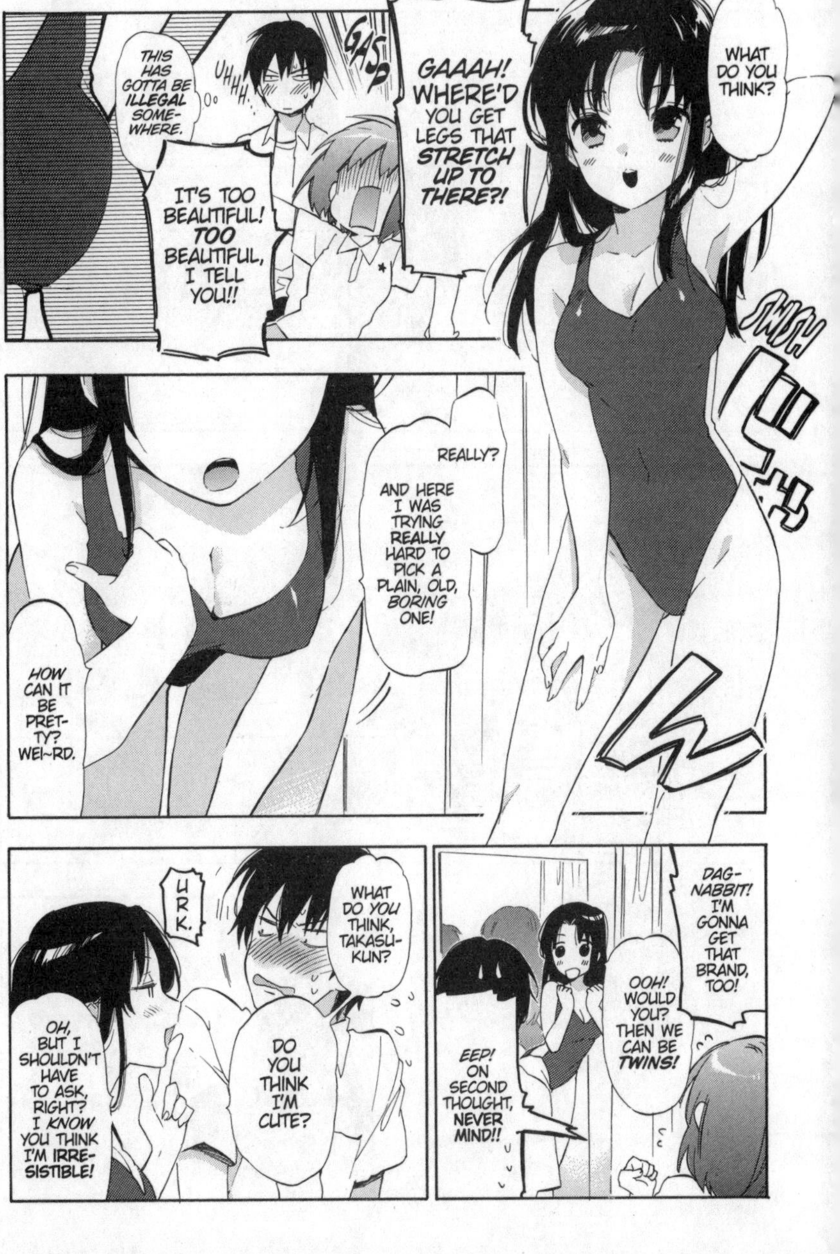
WHAT DO YOU THINK?
GAAAH! WHERE'D YOU GET LEGS THAT STRETCH UP TO THERE?!
GASP
THIS HAS GOTTA BE ILLEGAL SOMEWHERE.
UHHH...
IT'S TOO BEAUTIFUL! TOO BEAUTIFUL, I TELL YOU!!
REALLY?
AND HERE I WAS TRYING REALLY HARD TO PICK A PLAIN, OLD, BORING ONE!
HOW CAN IT BE PRETTY? WEI~RD.
DAG-NABBIT! I'M GONNA GET THAT BRAND, TOO!
OOH! WOULD YOU? THEN WE CAN BE TWINS!
EEP! ON SECOND THOUGHT, NEVER MIND!!
URK.
WHAT DO YOU THINK, TAKASU-KUN?
DO YOU THINK I'M CUTE?
OH, BUT I SHOULDN'T HAVE TO ASK, RIGHT? I KNOW YOU THINK I'M IRRESISTIBLE!

*A gradol (or gravure idol) models swimsuits and lingerie for men's magazines, DVDs, etc.

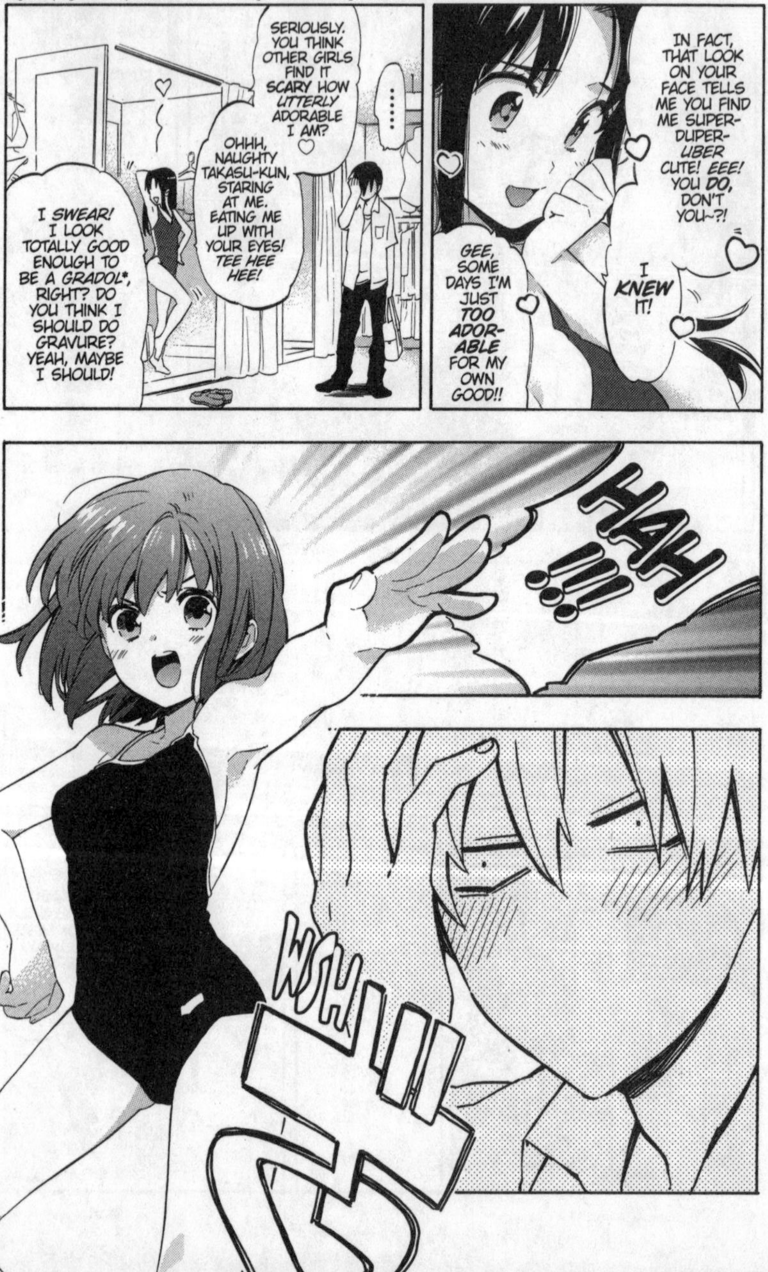
IN FACT, THAT LOOK ON YOUR FACE TELLS ME YOU FIND ME SUPER-DUPER-*UBER* CUTE! *EEE!* YOU **DO,** DON'T YOU~?!
I **KNEW** IT!
GEE, SOME DAYS I'M JUST ***TOO ADORABLE*** FOR MY OWN GOOD!!
SERIOUSLY. YOU THINK OTHER GIRLS FIND IT **SCARY** HOW *UTTERLY* ADORABLE I AM?
......
OHHH, NAUGHTY TAKASU-KUN, STARING AT ME. EATING ME UP WITH YOUR EYES! *TEE HEE HEE!*
I *SWEAR!* I LOOK TOTALLY GOOD ENOUGH TO BE A *GRADOL**, RIGHT? DO YOU THINK I SHOULD DO GRAVURE? YEAH, MAYBE I SHOULD!
HAH!!!
WSH!!

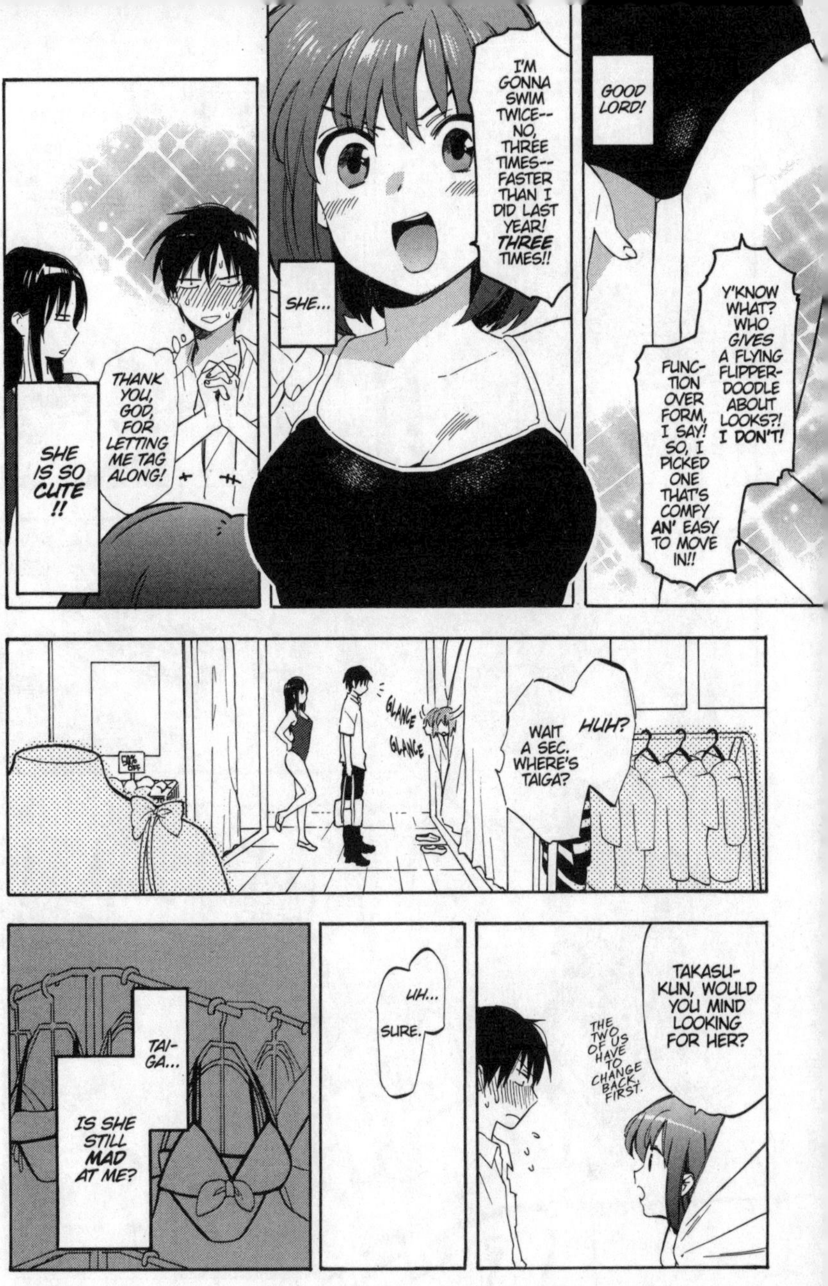
GOOD LORD!
Y'KNOW WHAT? WHO GIVES A FLYING FLIPPER-DOODLE ABOUT LOOKS?! I DON'T!
FUNCTION OVER FORM, I SAY! SO, I PICKED ONE THAT'S COMFY AN' EASY TO MOVE IN!!
I'M GONNA SWIM TWICE--NO, THREE TIMES--FASTER THAN I DID LAST YEAR! THREE TIMES!!
SHE...
THANK YOU, GOD, FOR LETTING ME TAG ALONG!
SHE IS SO CUTE !!
HUH?
WAIT A SEC. WHERE'S TAIGA?
GLANCE
GLANCE
TAKASU-KUN, WOULD YOU MIND LOOKING FOR HER?
THE TWO OF US HAVE TO CHANGE BACK, FIRST.
UH...
SURE.
TAI-GA...
IS SHE STILL MAD AT ME?

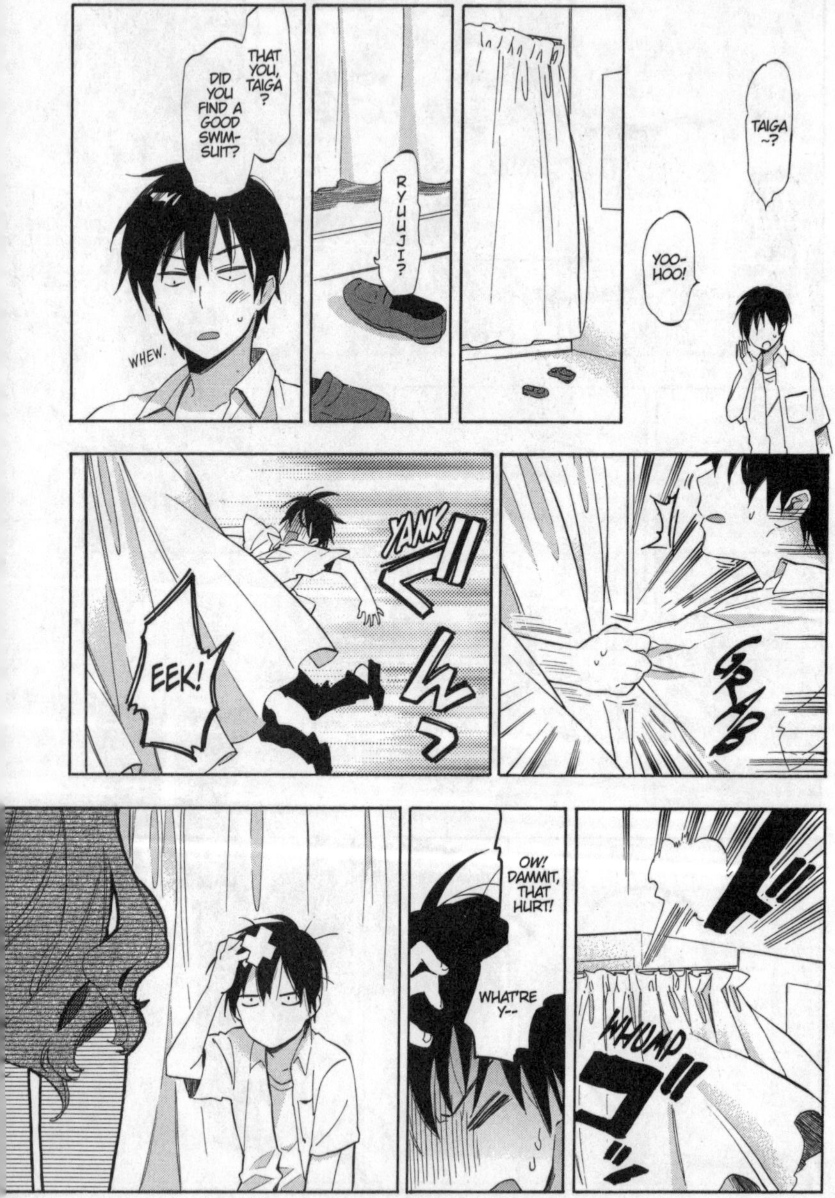
TAIGA ~?
YOO-HOO!
RYUUJI?
THAT YOU, TAIGA?
DID YOU FIND A GOOD SWIM-SUIT?
WHEW.
GRAB
YANK
EEK!
WHUMP
OW! DAMMIT, THAT HURT!
WHAT'RE Y--

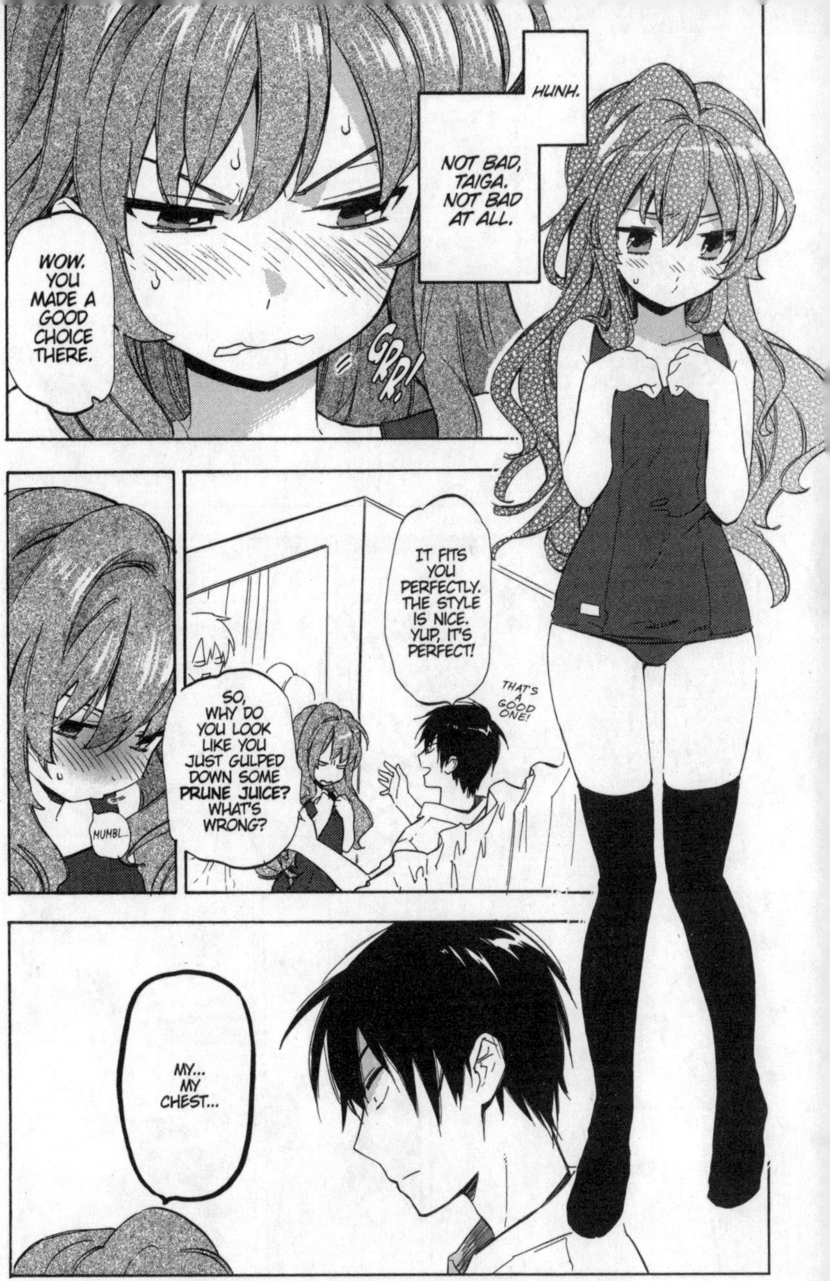
HUNH.
NOT BAD, TAIGA. NOT BAD AT ALL.
GRR!
WOW. YOU MADE A GOOD CHOICE THERE.
IT FITS YOU PERFECTLY. THE STYLE IS NICE. YUP, IT'S PERFECT!
THAT'S A GOOD ONE!
SO, WHY DO YOU LOOK LIKE YOU JUST GULPED DOWN SOME PRUNE JUICE? WHAT'S WRONG?
MUMBL...
MY... MY CHEST...

Chapter 26 BOOBS, BOOBS, EVERYWHERE BOOBS

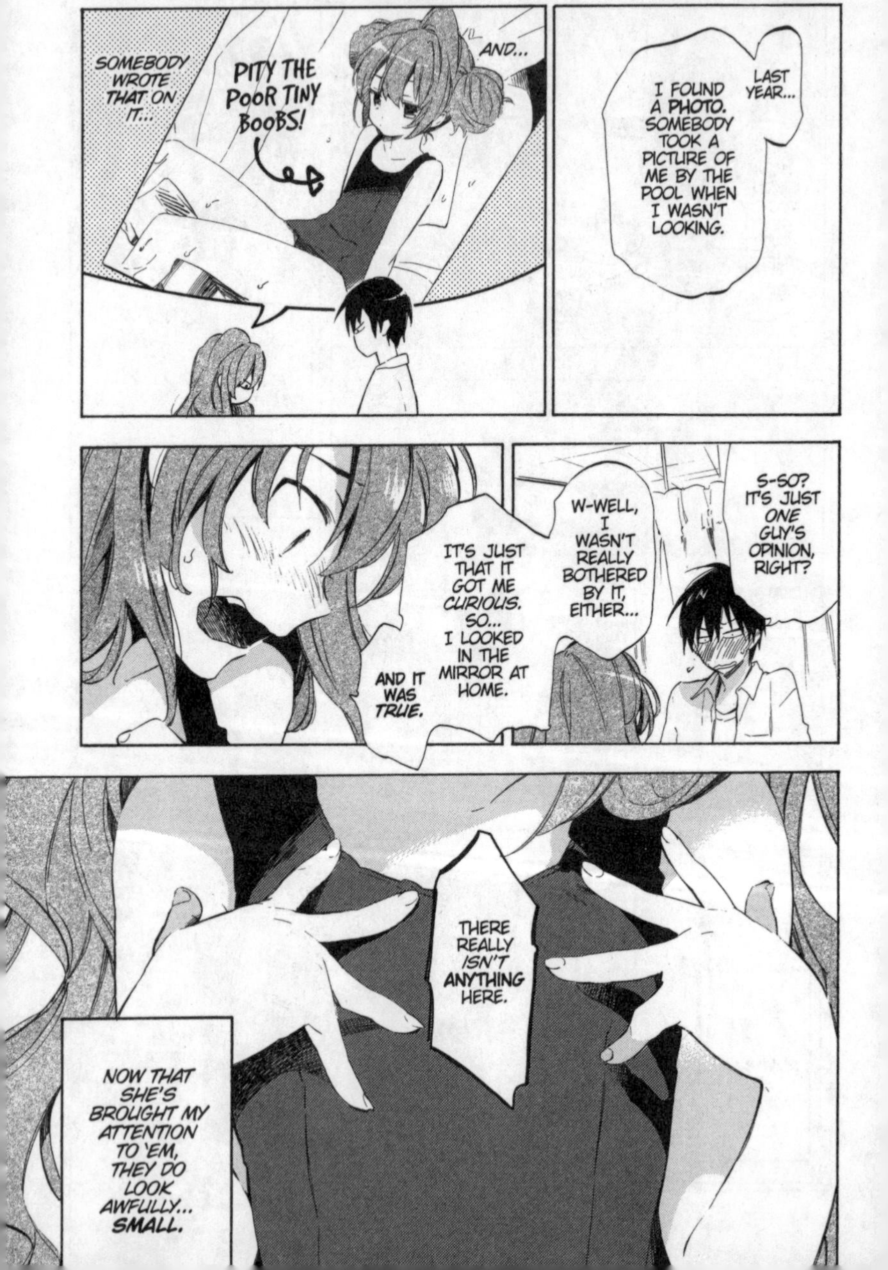
LAST YEAR...
I FOUND A PHOTO. SOMEBODY TOOK A PICTURE OF ME BY THE POOL WHEN I WASN'T LOOKING.
AND...
PITY THE POOR TINY BOOBS!
SOMEBODY WROTE THAT ON IT...
S-SO? IT'S JUST ONE GUY'S OPINION, RIGHT?
W-WELL, I WASN'T REALLY BOTHERED BY IT, EITHER...
IT'S JUST THAT IT GOT ME CURIOUS. SO... I LOOKED IN THE MIRROR AT HOME.
AND IT WAS TRUE.
THERE REALLY ISN'T ANYTHING HERE.
NOW THAT SHE'S BROUGHT MY ATTENTION TO 'EM, THEY DO LOOK AWFULLY... SMALL.

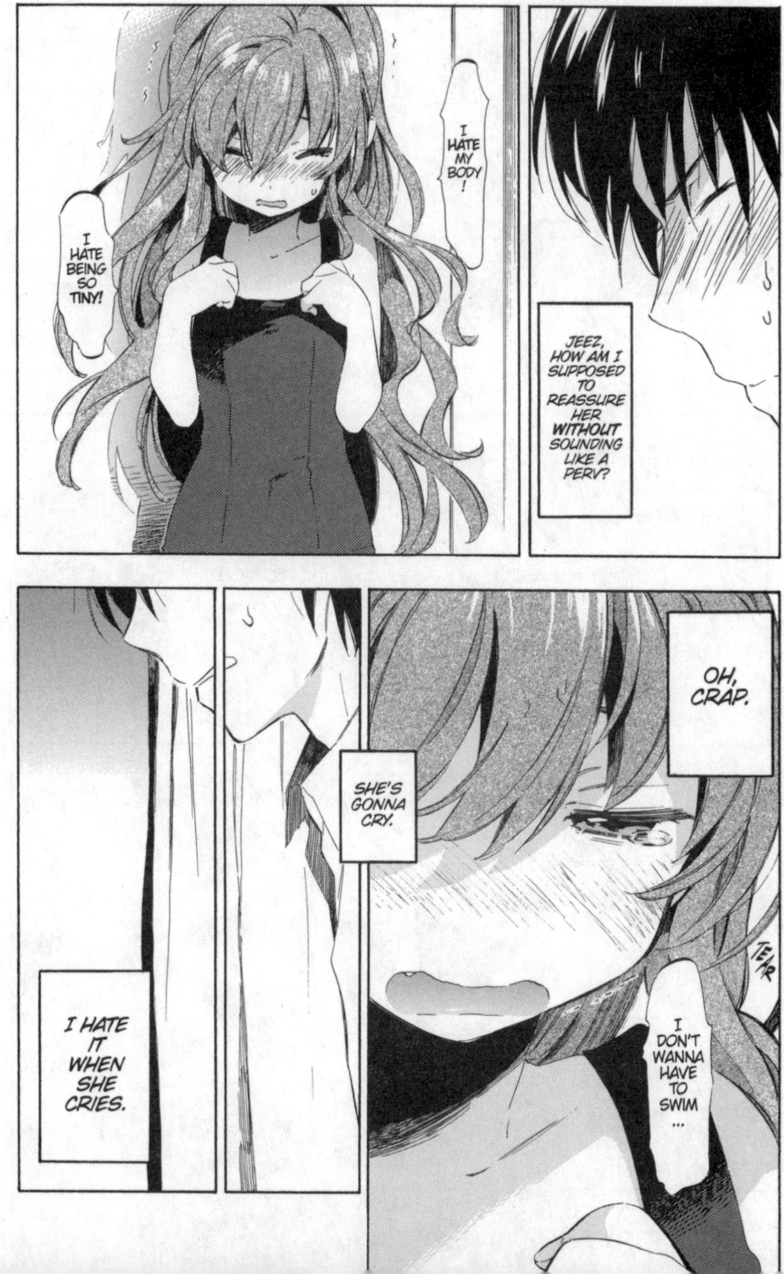
JEEZ, HOW AM I SUPPOSED TO REASSURE HER WITHOUT SOUNDING LIKE A PERV?
I HATE MY BODY!
I HATE BEING SO TINY!
OH, CRAP.
SHE'S GONNA CRY.
TEAR
I DON'T WANNA HAVE TO SWIM ...
I HATE IT WHEN SHE CRIES.

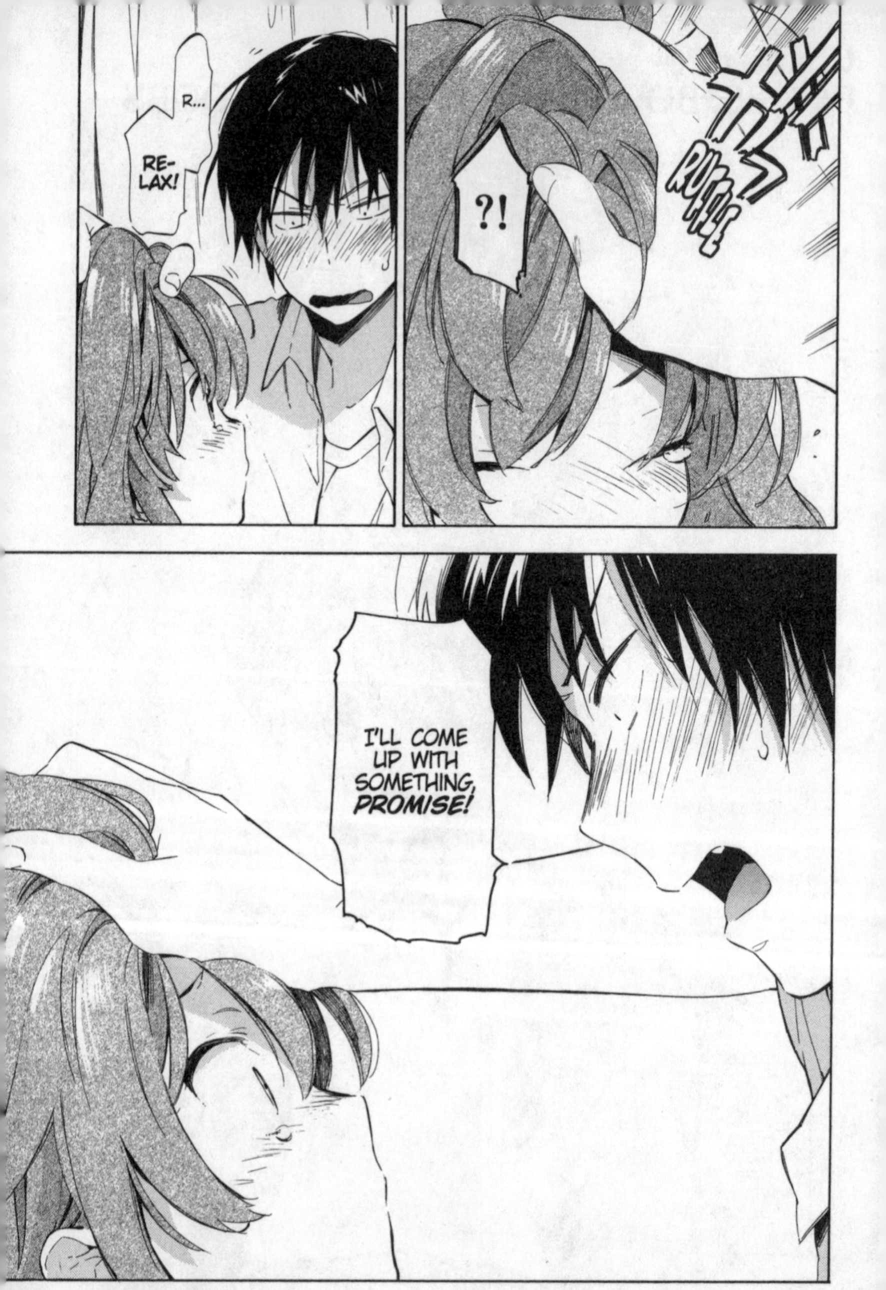
RUFFLE
?!
R...
RE-
LAX!
I'LL COME UP WITH SOMETHING, PROMISE!

Chapter 26
BOOBS, BOOBS, EVERYWHERE BOOBS

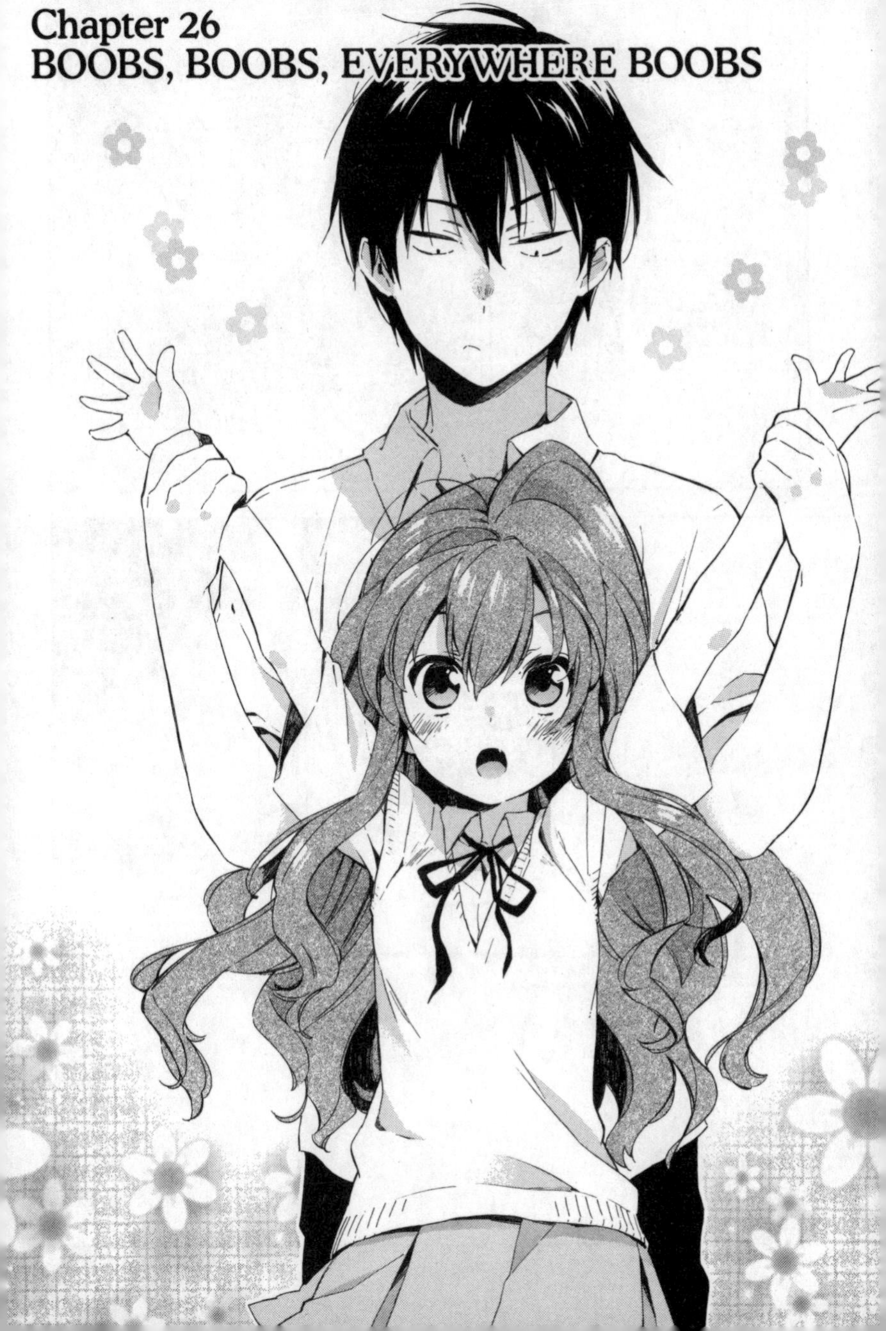

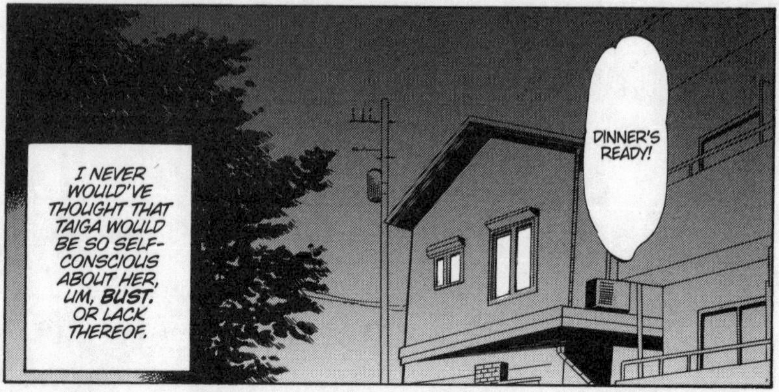
DINNER'S READY!
I NEVER WOULD'VE THOUGHT THAT TAIGA WOULD BE SO SELF-CONSCIOUS ABOUT HER, UM, **BUST.** OR LACK THEREOF.

*Chicken Nanban is fried chicken topped with a mixture of tartar sauce and vinegar.

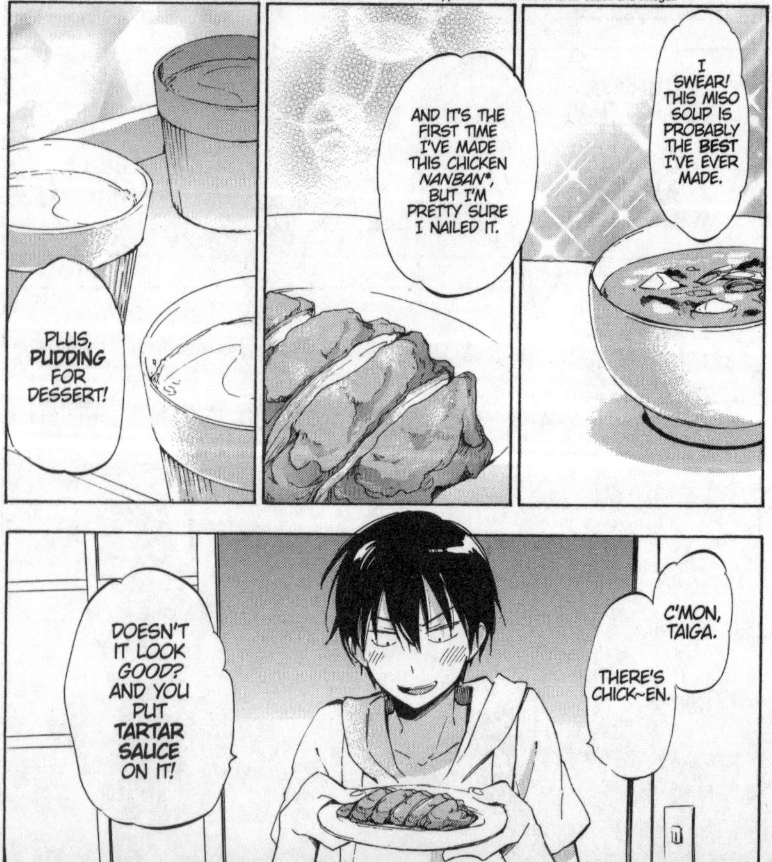
I SWEAR! THIS MISO SOUP IS PROBABLY THE BEST I'VE EVER MADE.
AND IT'S THE FIRST TIME I'VE MADE THIS CHICKEN *NANBAN**, BUT I'M PRETTY SURE I NAILED IT.
PLUS, **PUDDING** FOR DESSERT!
C'MON, TAIGA.
THERE'S CHICK~EN.
DOESN'T IT LOOK GOOD? AND YOU PUT **TARTAR SAUCE** ON IT!

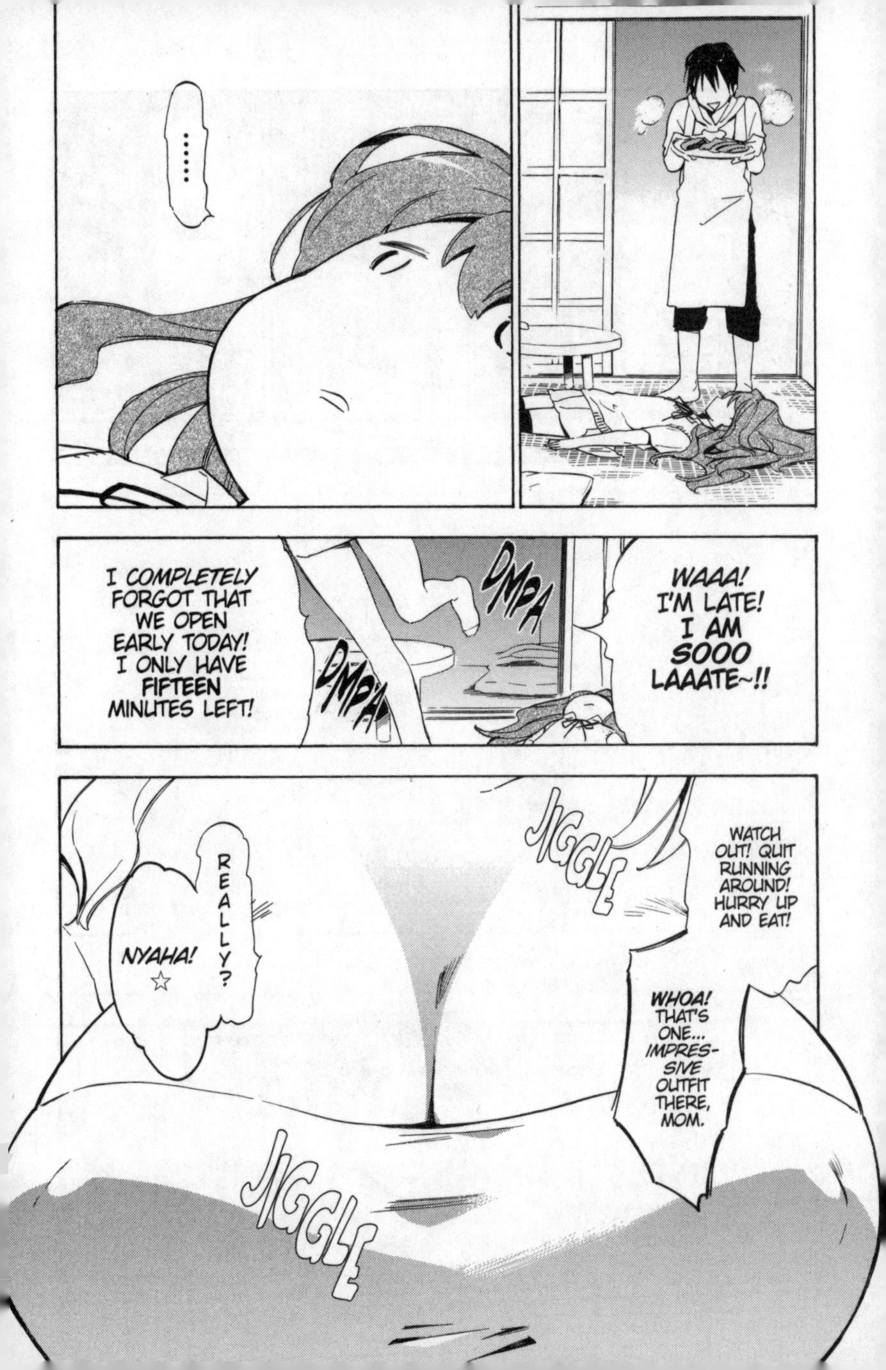
......
WAAA! I'M LATE! I AM SOOO LAAATE~!!
DMPA
DMPA
I COMPLETELY FORGOT THAT WE OPEN EARLY TODAY! I ONLY HAVE FIFTEEN MINUTES LEFT!
WATCH OUT! QUIT RUNNING AROUND! HURRY UP AND EAT!
JIGGLE
REALLY?
NYAHA! ☆
WHOA! THAT'S ONE... IMPRESSIVE OUTFIT THERE, MOM.
JIGGLE

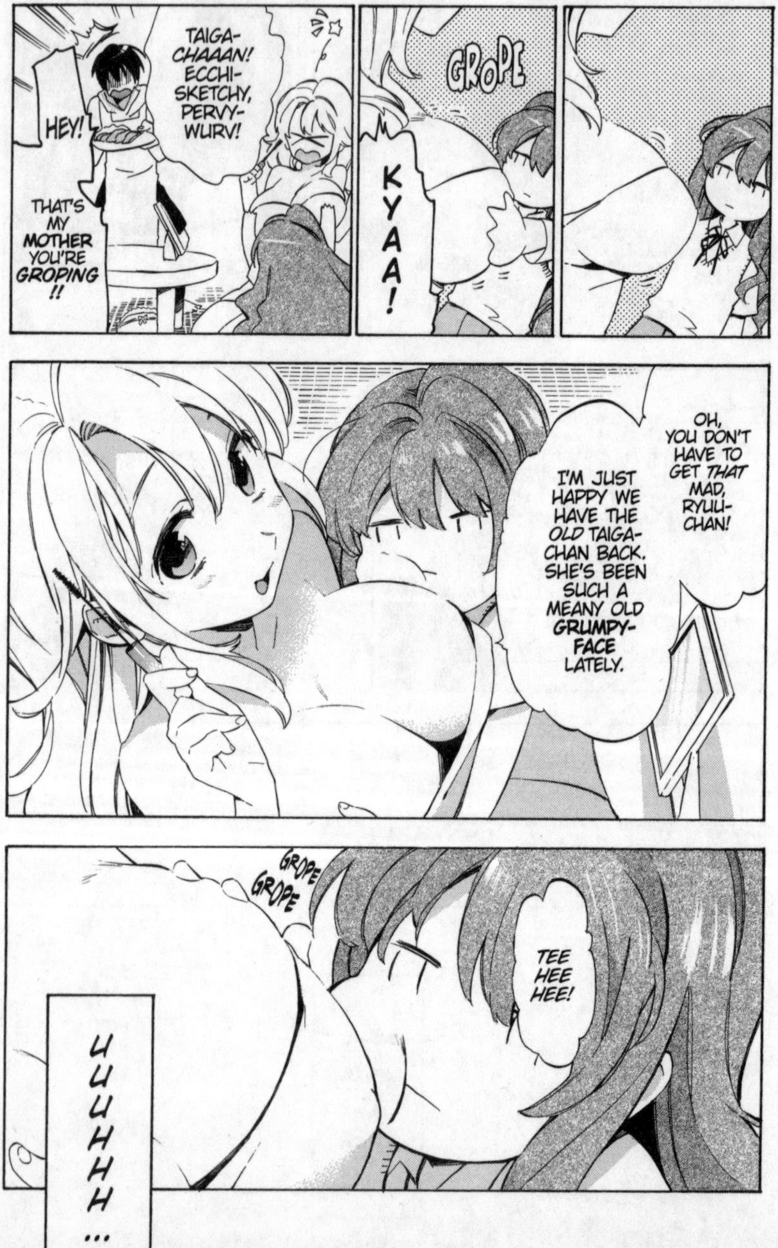
GROPE
KYAA!
TAIGA-CHAAAN! ECCHI-SKETCHY, PERVY-WURV!
HEY!
THAT'S MY MOTHER YOU'RE GROPING!!
OH, YOU DON'T HAVE TO GET THAT MAD, RYUU-CHAN!
I'M JUST HAPPY WE HAVE THE OLD TAIGA-CHAN BACK. SHE'S BEEN SUCH A MEANY OLD GRUMPY-FACE LATELY.
GROPE GROPE
TEE HEE HEE!
UUUHHH...

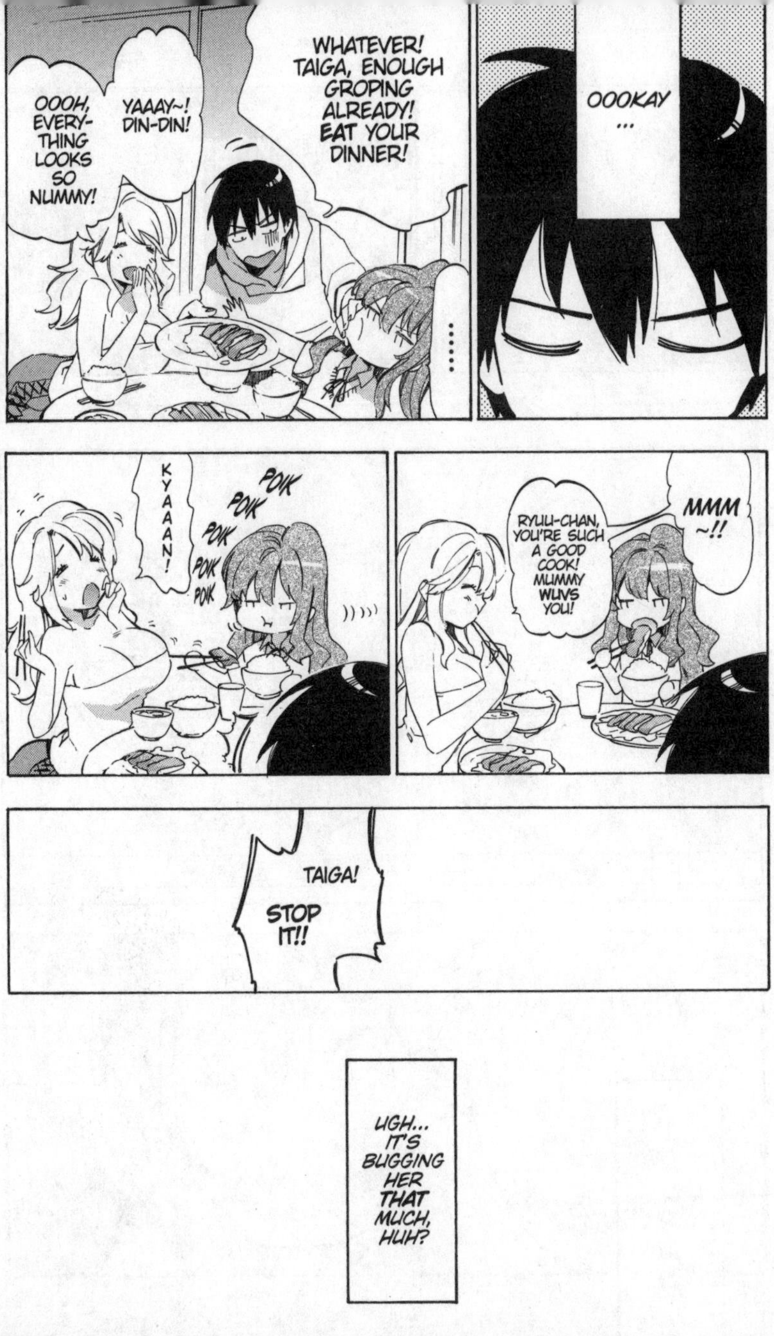
OOOKAY ...
WHATEVER! TAIGA, ENOUGH GROPING ALREADY! EAT YOUR DINNER!
YAAAY~! DIN-DIN!
OOOH, EVERY-THING LOOKS SO NUMMY!
MMM ~!!
RYUU-CHAN, YOU'RE SUCH A GOOD COOK! MUMMY WUVS YOU!
POIK POIK POIK POIK POIK
KYAAAN!
TAIGA!
STOP IT!!
UGH... IT'S BUGGING HER THAT MUCH, HUH?

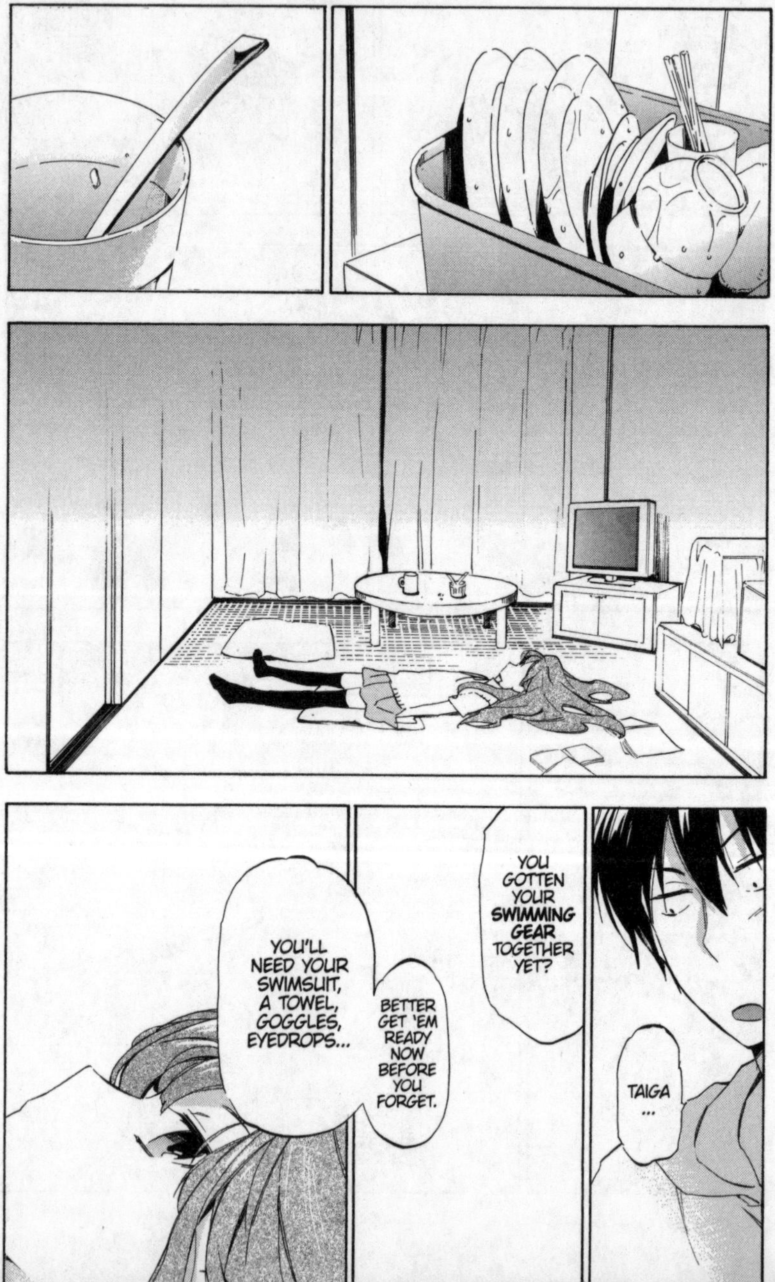
TAIGA ...
YOU GOTTEN YOUR SWIMMING GEAR TOGETHER YET?
YOU'LL NEED YOUR SWIMSUIT, A TOWEL, GOGGLES, EYEDROPS...
BETTER GET 'EM READY NOW BEFORE YOU FORGET.

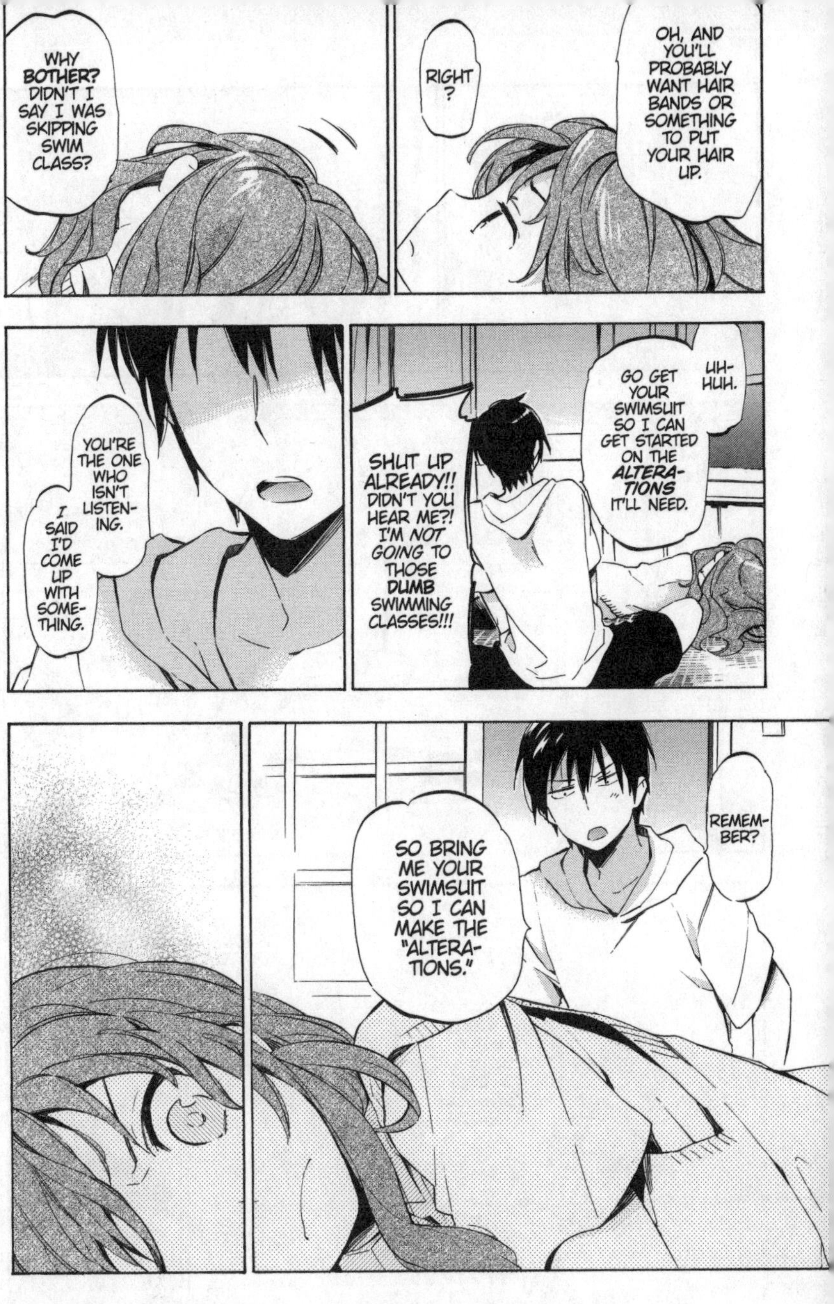
OH, AND YOU'LL PROBABLY WANT HAIR BANDS OR SOMETHING TO PUT YOUR HAIR UP.
RIGHT?
WHY BOTHER? DIDN'T I SAY I WAS SKIPPING SWIM CLASS?
UH-HUH.
GO GET YOUR SWIMSUIT SO I CAN GET STARTED ON THE ALTERATIONS IT'LL NEED.
SHUT UP ALREADY!! DIDN'T YOU HEAR ME?! I'M NOT GOING TO THOSE DUMB SWIMMING CLASSES!!!
YOU'RE THE ONE WHO ISN'T LISTENING.
I SAID I'D COME UP WITH SOMETHING.
REMEMBER?
SO BRING ME YOUR SWIMSUIT SO I CAN MAKE THE "ALTERATIONS."

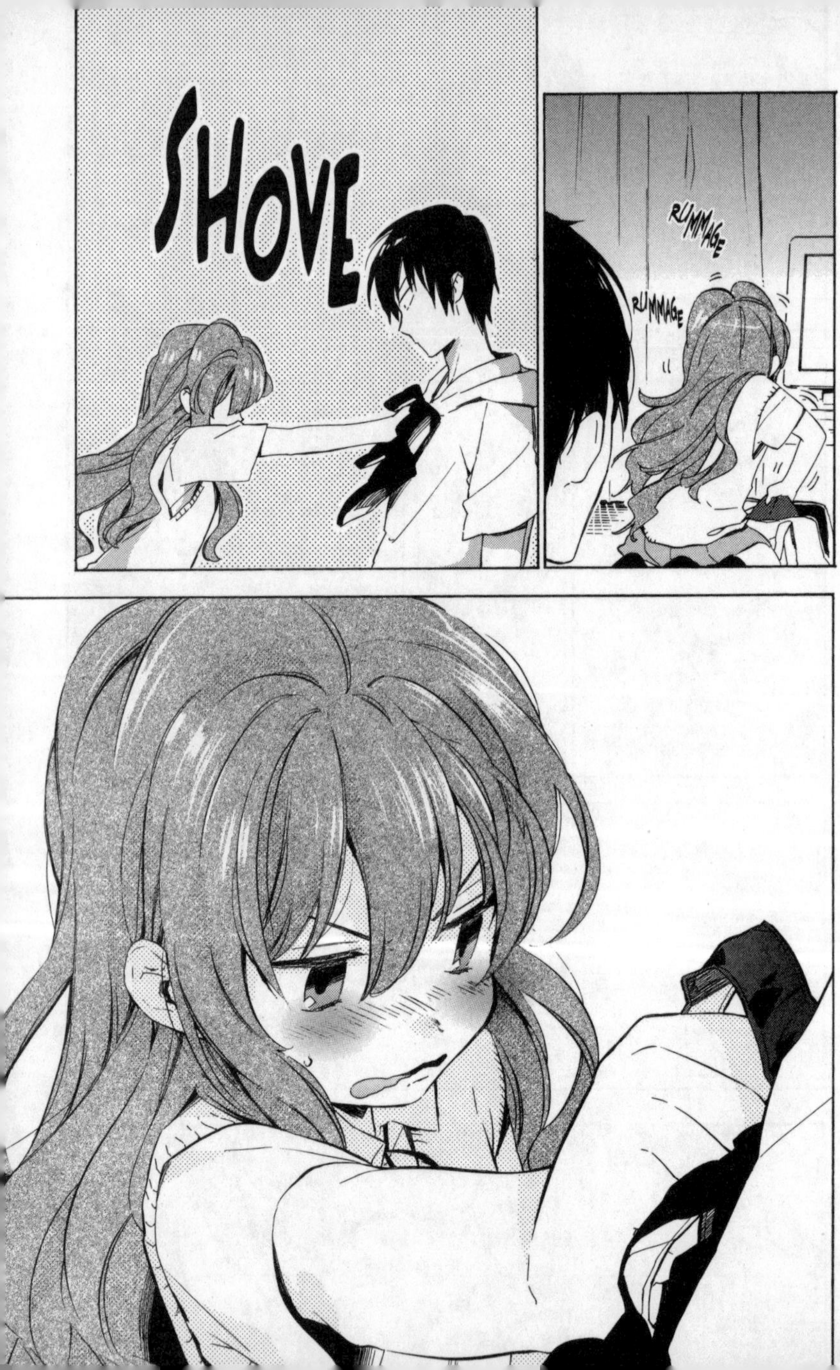
RUMMAGE
RUMMAGE
SHOVE

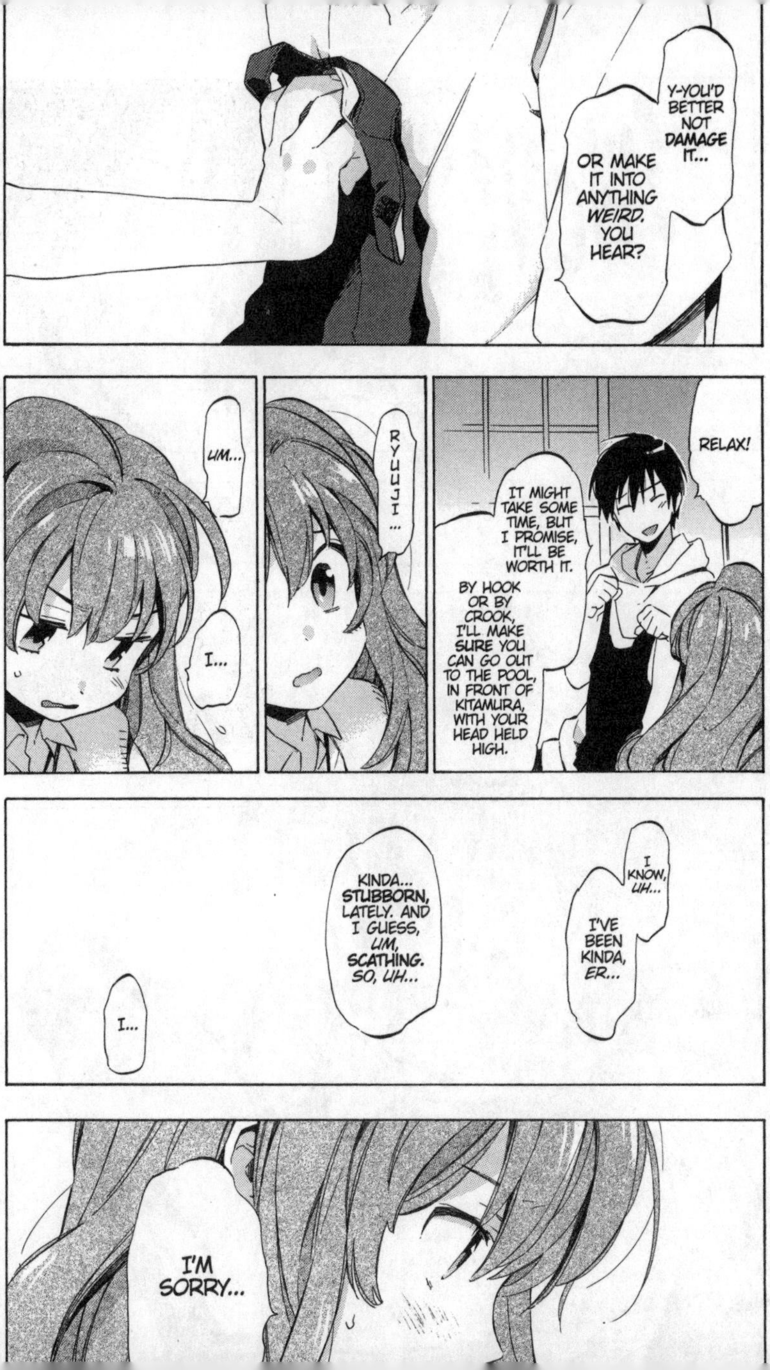
Y-YOU'D BETTER NOT DAMAGE IT...
OR MAKE IT INTO ANYTHING *WEIRD.* YOU HEAR?
RELAX!
IT MIGHT TAKE SOME TIME, BUT I PROMISE, IT'LL BE WORTH IT.
BY HOOK OR BY CROOK, I'LL MAKE SURE YOU CAN GO OUT TO THE POOL, IN FRONT OF KITAMURA, WITH YOUR HEAD HELD HIGH.
RYUUJI...
UM...
I...
I KNOW, *UH...*
I'VE BEEN KINDA, *ER...*
KINDA... STUBBORN, LATELY. AND I GUESS, *UM,* SCATHING. *SO, UH...*
I...
I'M SORRY...

HUNH.

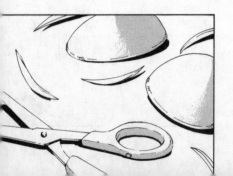

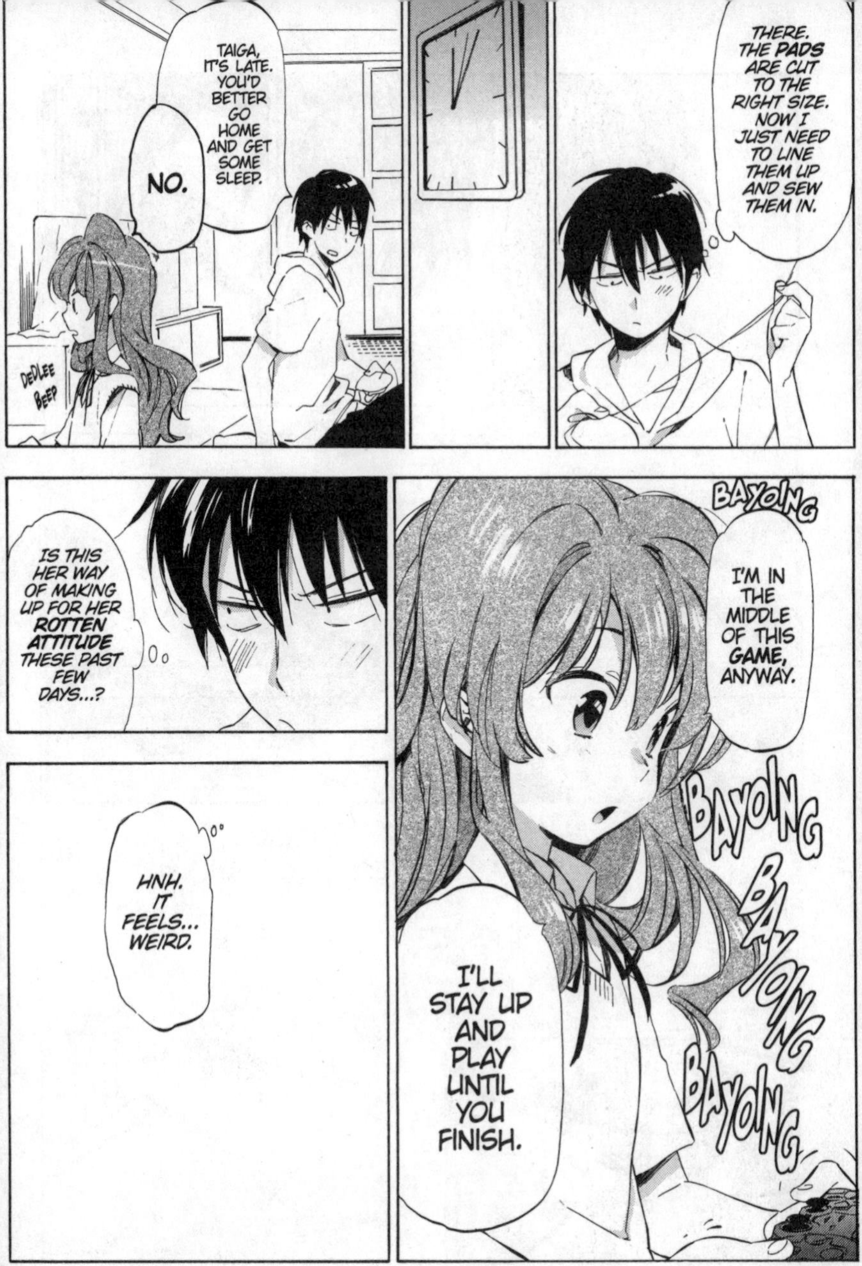
THERE. THE PADS ARE CUT TO THE RIGHT SIZE. NOW I JUST NEED TO LINE THEM UP AND SEW THEM IN.
TAIGA, IT'S LATE. YOU'D BETTER GO HOME AND GET SOME SLEEP.
NO.
DEDLEE BEEP
BAYOING
I'M IN THE MIDDLE OF THIS GAME, ANYWAY.
BAYOING
BAYOING
BAYOING
I'LL STAY UP AND PLAY UNTIL YOU FINISH.
IS THIS HER WAY OF MAKING UP FOR HER ROTTEN ATTITUDE THESE PAST FEW DAYS...?
HNH. IT FEELS... WEIRD.

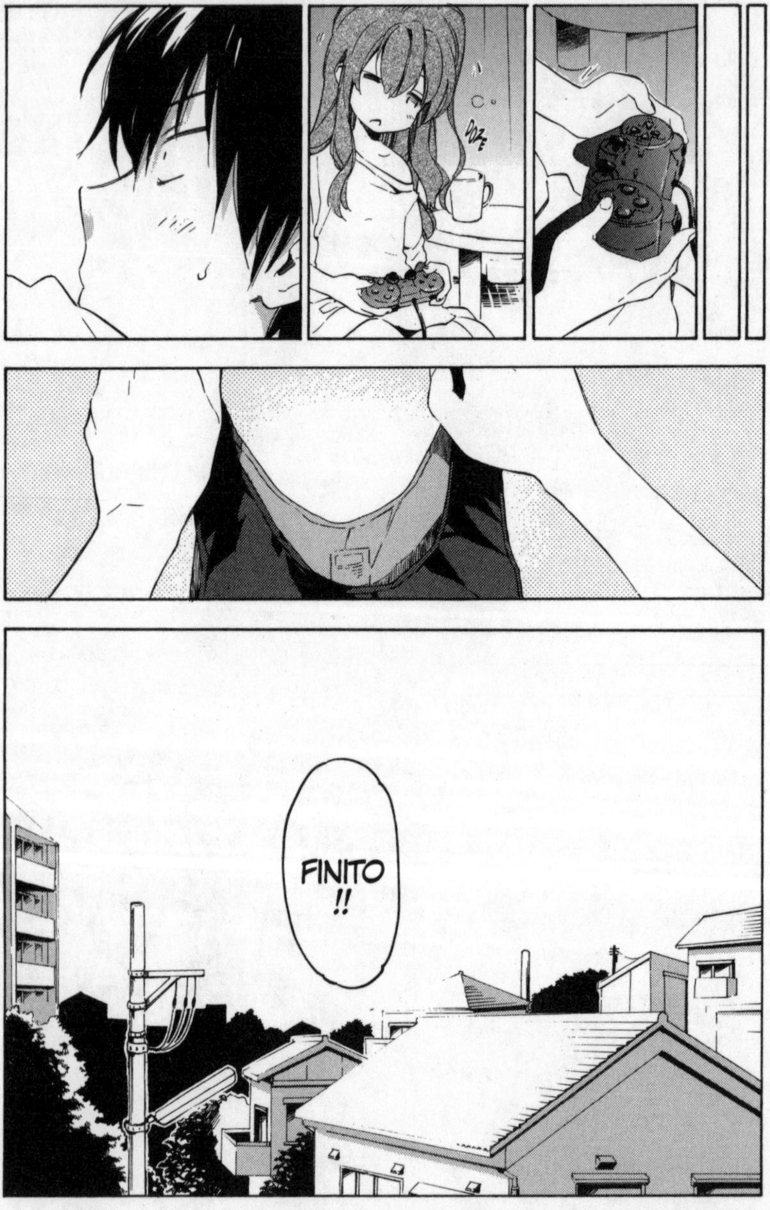
DOZE
FINITO !!

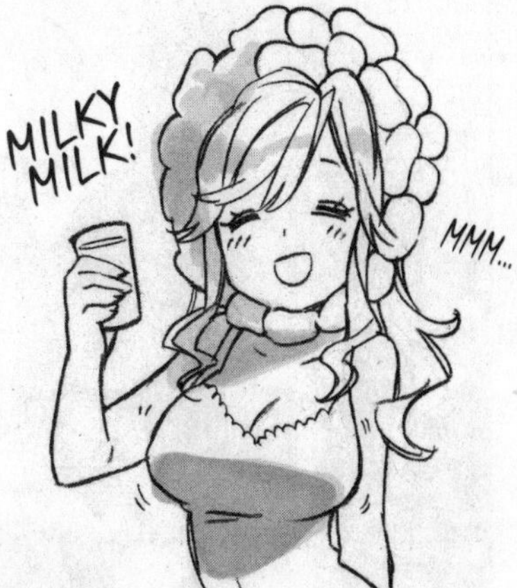
MILKY MILK!
MMM...

Chapter 27 TORA TORA TORA

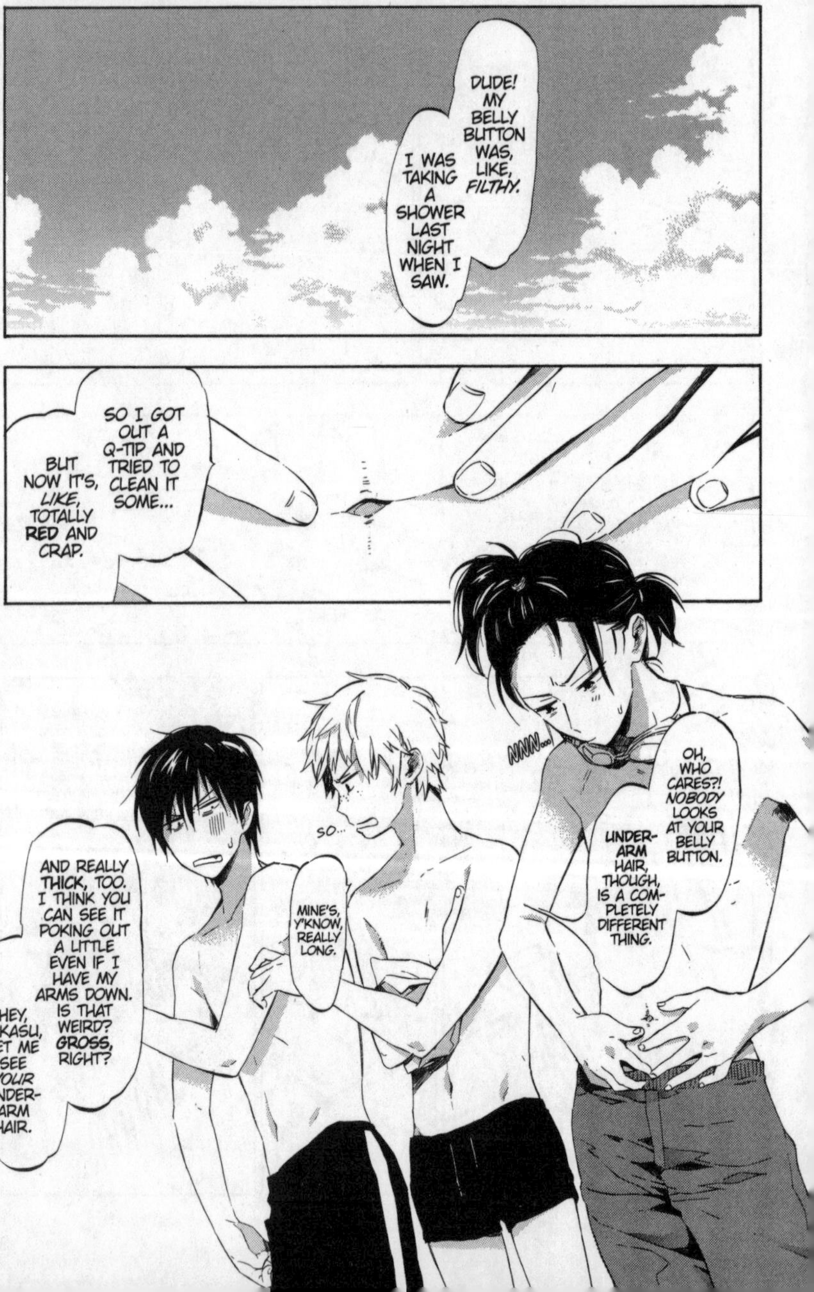

DUDE! MY BELLY BUTTON WAS, LIKE, *FILTHY.*
I WAS TAKING A SHOWER LAST NIGHT WHEN I SAW.
SO I GOT OUT A Q-TIP AND TRIED TO CLEAN IT SOME...
BUT NOW IT'S, *LIKE,* TOTALLY **RED** AND CRAP.
OH, WHO CARES?! NOBODY LOOKS AT YOUR BELLY BUTTON.
UNDERARM HAIR, THOUGH, IS A COMPLETELY DIFFERENT THING.
NNN...
SO...
MINE'S, Y'KNOW, REALLY LONG.
AND REALLY **THICK,** TOO. I THINK YOU CAN SEE IT POKING OUT A LITTLE EVEN IF I HAVE MY ARMS DOWN. IS THAT WEIRD? **GROSS,** RIGHT?
HEY, TAKASU, LET ME SEE *YOUR* UNDERARM HAIR.

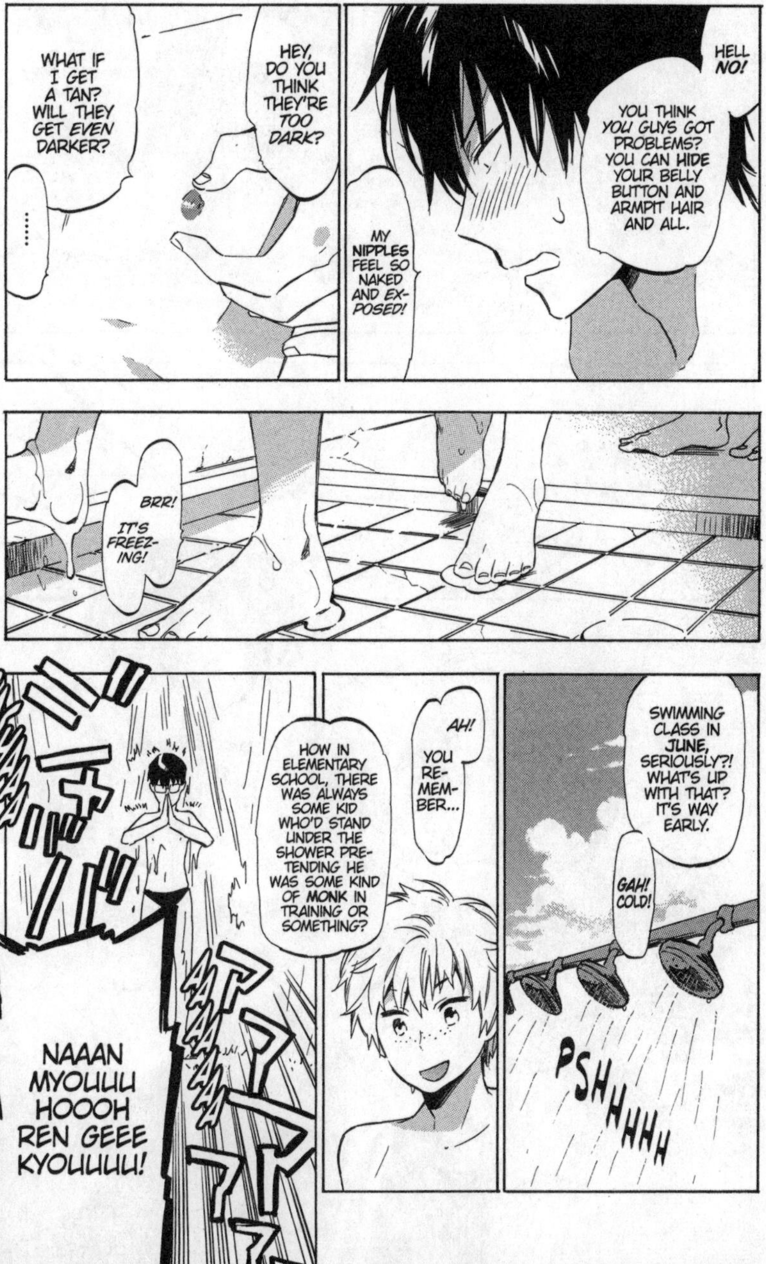
HELL NO!
YOU THINK YOU GUYS GOT PROBLEMS? YOU CAN HIDE YOUR BELLY BUTTON AND ARMPIT HAIR AND ALL.
MY NIPPLES FEEL SO NAKED AND EX-POSED!
HEY, DO YOU THINK THEY'RE TOO DARK?
WHAT IF I GET A TAN? WILL THEY GET EVEN DARKER?
......
BRR! IT'S FREEZ-ING!
SWIMMING CLASS IN JUNE, SERIOUSLY?! WHAT'S UP WITH THAT? IT'S WAY EARLY.
GAH! COLD!
PSHHHHH
AH!
YOU RE-MEM-BER...
HOW IN ELEMENTARY SCHOOL, THERE WAS ALWAYS SOME KID WHO'D STAND UNDER THE SHOWER PRE-TENDING HE WAS SOME KIND OF MONK IN TRAINING OR SOMETHING?
NAAAN MYOUUUU HOOOH REN GEEE KYOUUUU!

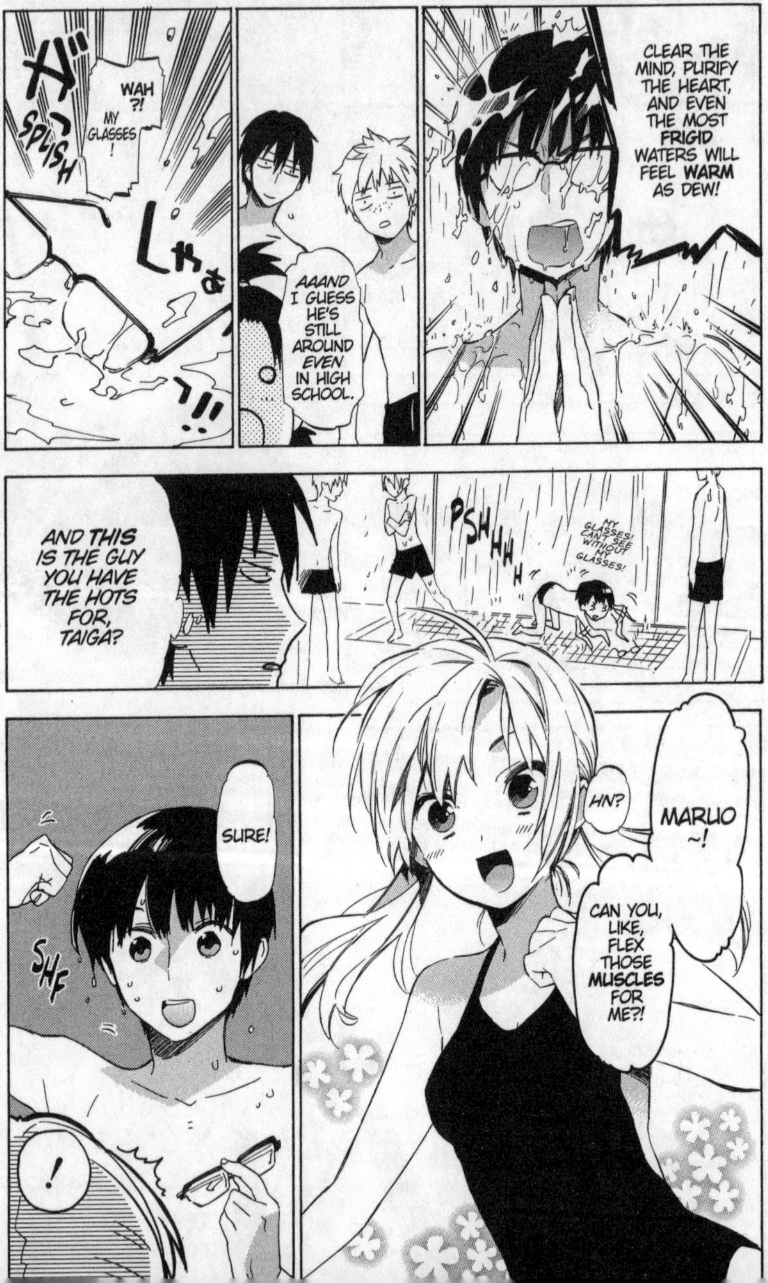
CLEAR THE MIND, PURIFY THE HEART, AND EVEN THE MOST FRIGID WATERS WILL FEEL WARM AS DEW!
AAAND I GUESS HE'S STILL AROUND EVEN IN HIGH SCHOOL.
WAH ?!
MY GLASSES !
SPLISH
MY GLASSES! CAN'T SEE WITHOUT MY GLASSES!
PSHHHH
AND THIS IS THE GUY YOU HAVE THE HOTS FOR, TAIGA?
MARUO ~!
HN?
CAN YOU, LIKE, FLEX THOSE MUSCLES FOR ME?!
SURE!
SHF
!

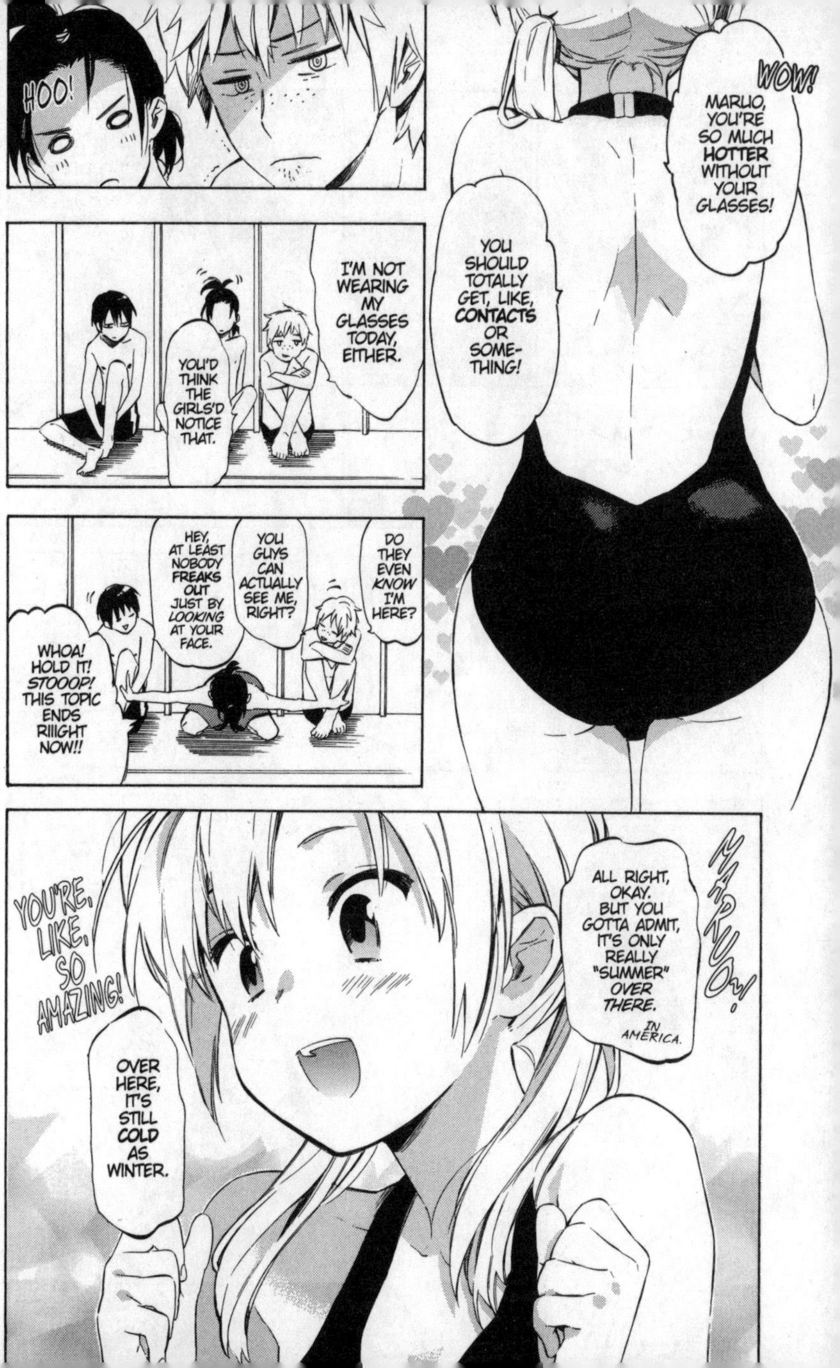
WOW!
MARUO, YOU'RE SO MUCH HOTTER WITHOUT YOUR GLASSES!
YOU SHOULD TOTALLY GET, LIKE, CONTACTS OR SOME-THING!
HOO!
I'M NOT WEARING MY GLASSES TODAY, EITHER.
YOU'D THINK THE GIRLS'D NOTICE THAT.
DO THEY EVEN KNOW I'M HERE?
YOU GUYS CAN ACTUALLY SEE ME, RIGHT?
HEY, AT LEAST NOBODY FREAKS OUT JUST BY LOOKING AT YOUR FACE.
WHOA! HOLD IT! STOOOP! THIS TOPIC ENDS RIIGHT NOW!!
MARUO~!
ALL RIGHT, OKAY. BUT YOU GOTTA ADMIT, IT'S ONLY REALLY "SUMMER" OVER THERE.
IN AMERICA.
YOU'RE, LIKE, SO AMAZING!
OVER HERE, IT'S STILL COLD AS WINTER.

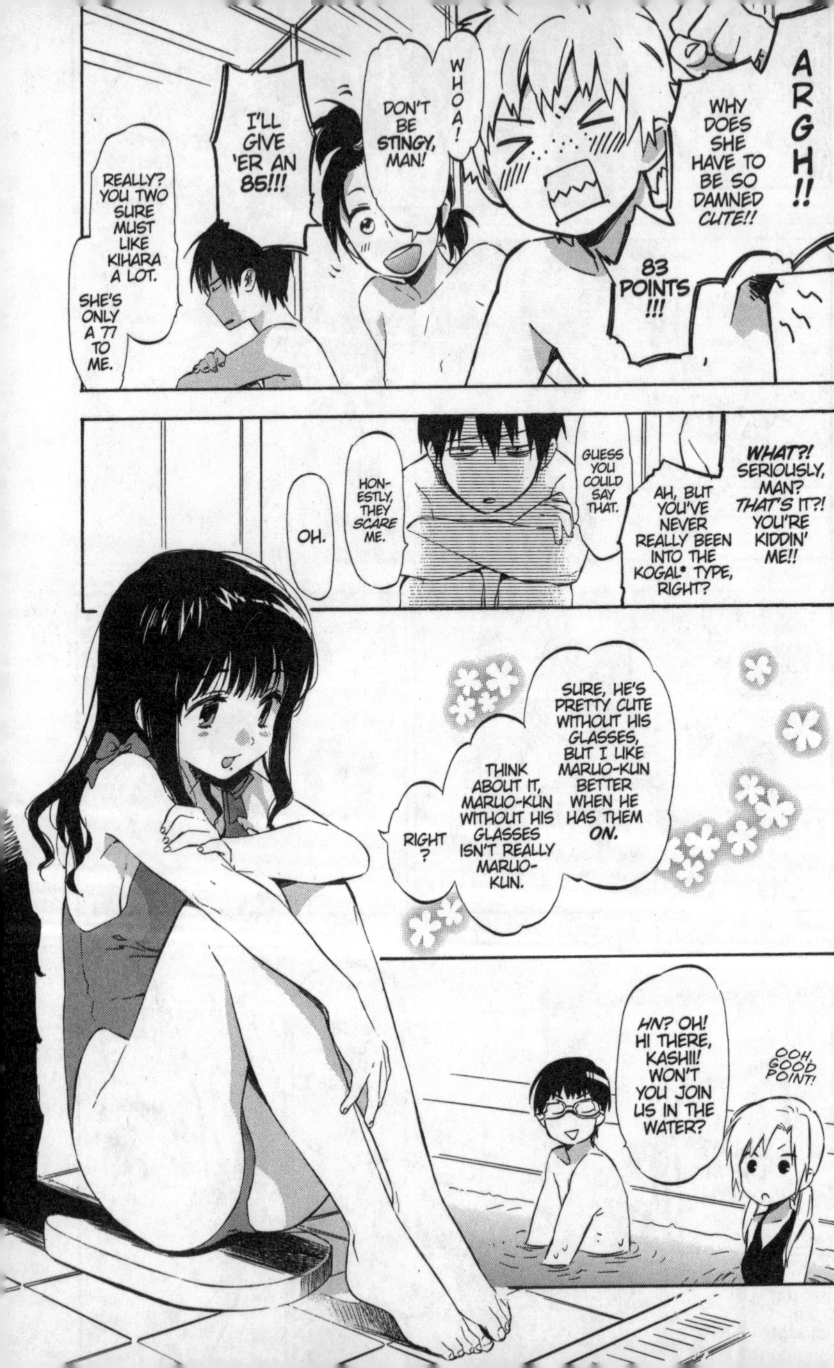
ARGH!!
WHY DOES SHE HAVE TO BE SO DAMNED CUTE!!
83 POINTS!!!
WHOA!
DON'T BE STINGY, MAN!
I'LL GIVE 'ER AN 85!!!
REALLY? YOU TWO SURE MUST LIKE KIHARA A LOT.
SHE'S ONLY A 77 TO ME.
WHAT?! SERIOUSLY, MAN? THAT'S IT?! YOU'RE KIDDIN' ME!!
AH, BUT YOU'VE NEVER REALLY BEEN INTO THE KOGAL* TYPE, RIGHT?
GUESS YOU COULD SAY THAT.
HON-ESTLY, THEY SCARE ME.
OH.
SURE, HE'S PRETTY CUTE WITHOUT HIS GLASSES, BUT I LIKE MARUO-KUN BETTER WHEN HE HAS THEM ON.
THINK ABOUT IT, MARUO-KUN WITHOUT HIS GLASSES ISN'T REALLY MARUO-KUN.
RIGHT?
HN? OH! HI THERE, KASHII! WON'T YOU JOIN US IN THE WATER?
OOH, GOOD POINT!

*The Japanese equivalent of a "valley girl." They speak in distinctive slang peppered with English words and sport fashion based on a Japanese school uniform. Loose socks and short skirts are a must. Dyed hair optional.

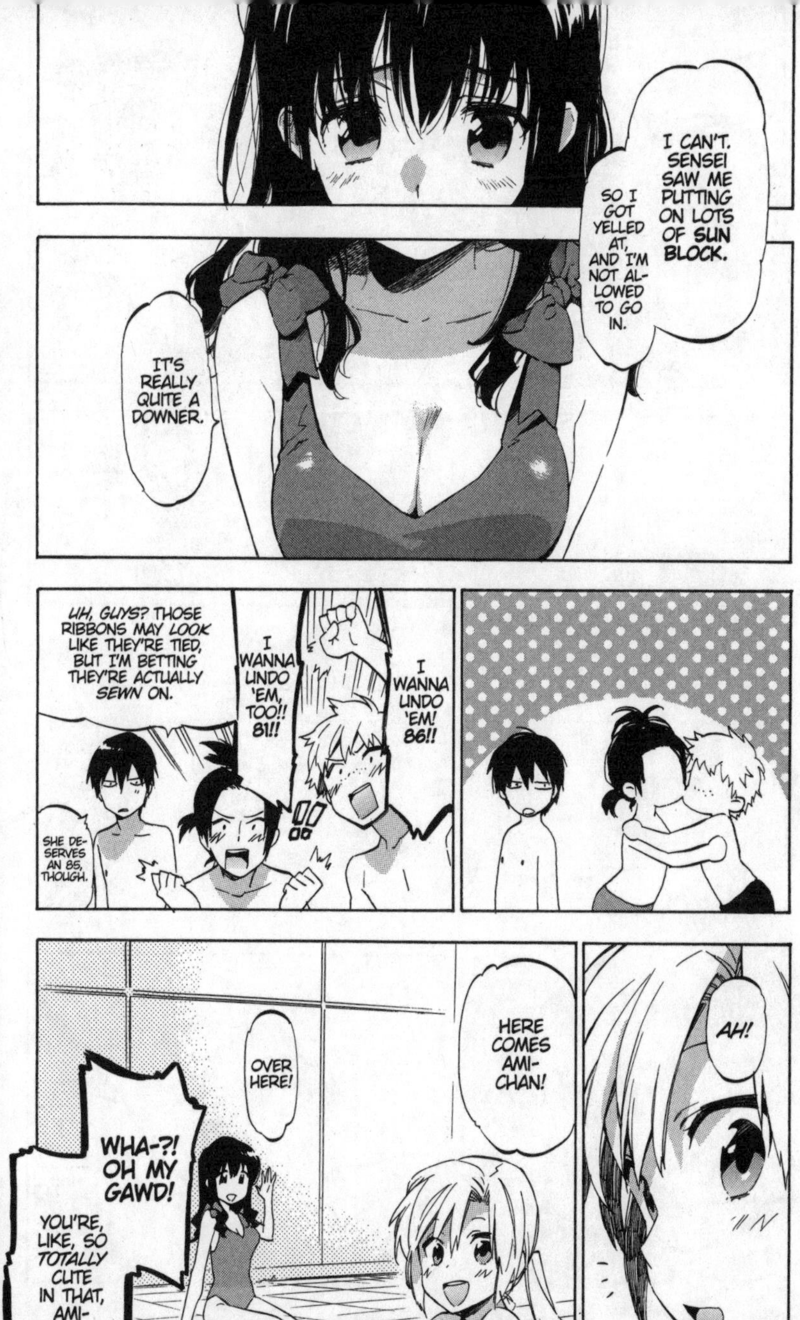
I CAN'T. SENSEI SAW ME PUTTING ON LOTS OF SUN BLOCK.
SO I GOT YELLED AT, AND I'M NOT ALLOWED TO GO IN.
IT'S REALLY QUITE A DOWNER.
I WANNA UNDO 'EM! 86!!
I WANNA UNDO 'EM, TOO!! 81!!
UH, GUYS? THOSE RIBBONS MAY LOOK LIKE THEY'RE TIED, BUT I'M BETTING THEY'RE ACTUALLY SEWN ON.
SHE DESERVES AN 85, THOUGH.
AH!
HERE COMES AMI-CHAN!
OVER HERE!
WHA-?! OH MY GAWD!
YOU'RE, LIKE, SO TOTALLY CUTE IN THAT, AMI-CHAN!!

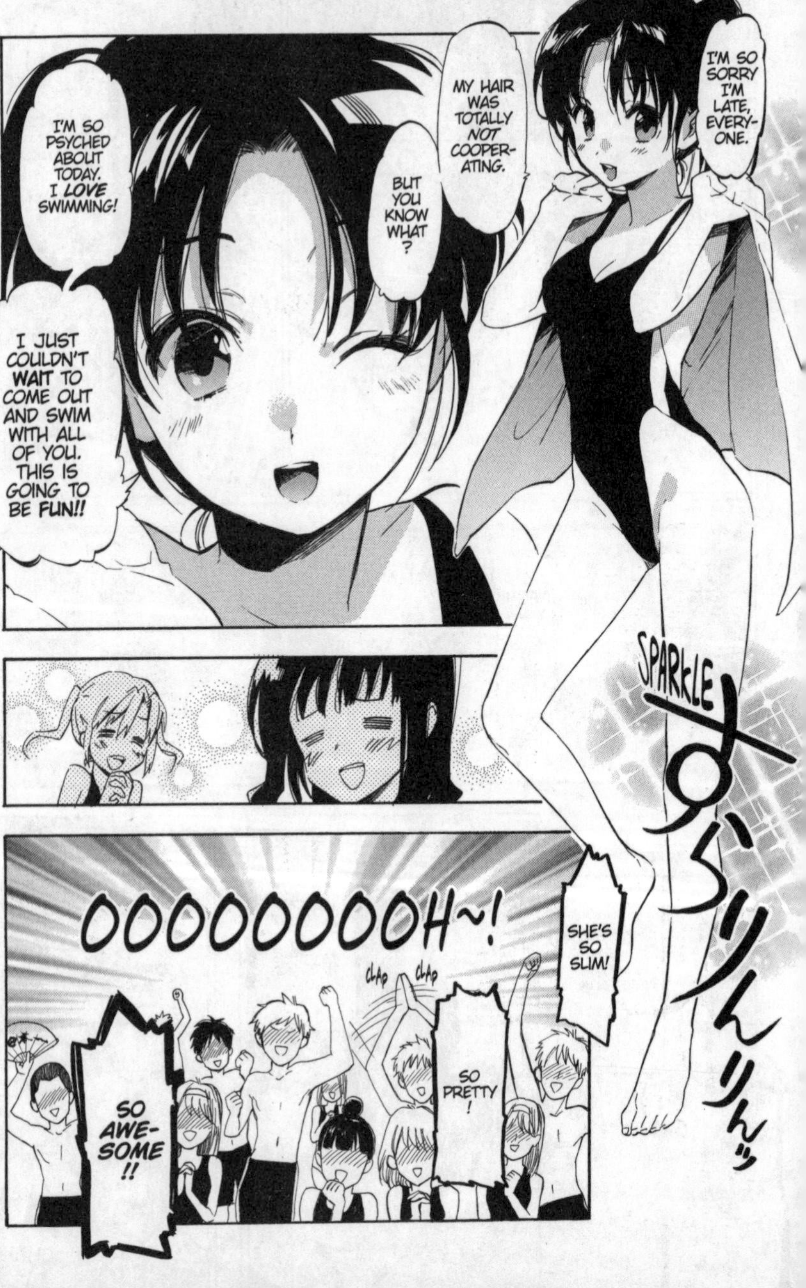

I'M SO SORRY I'M LATE, EVERYONE.
MY HAIR WAS TOTALLY NOT COOPERATING.
BUT YOU KNOW WHAT?
I'M SO PSYCHED ABOUT TODAY. I LOVE SWIMMING!
I JUST COULDN'T WAIT TO COME OUT AND SWIM WITH ALL OF YOU. THIS IS GOING TO BE FUN!!
SPARKLE
すらりんりんッ
SHE'S SO SLIM!
OOOOOOOOH~!
CLAP CLAP
SO PRETTY!
SO AWESOME!!

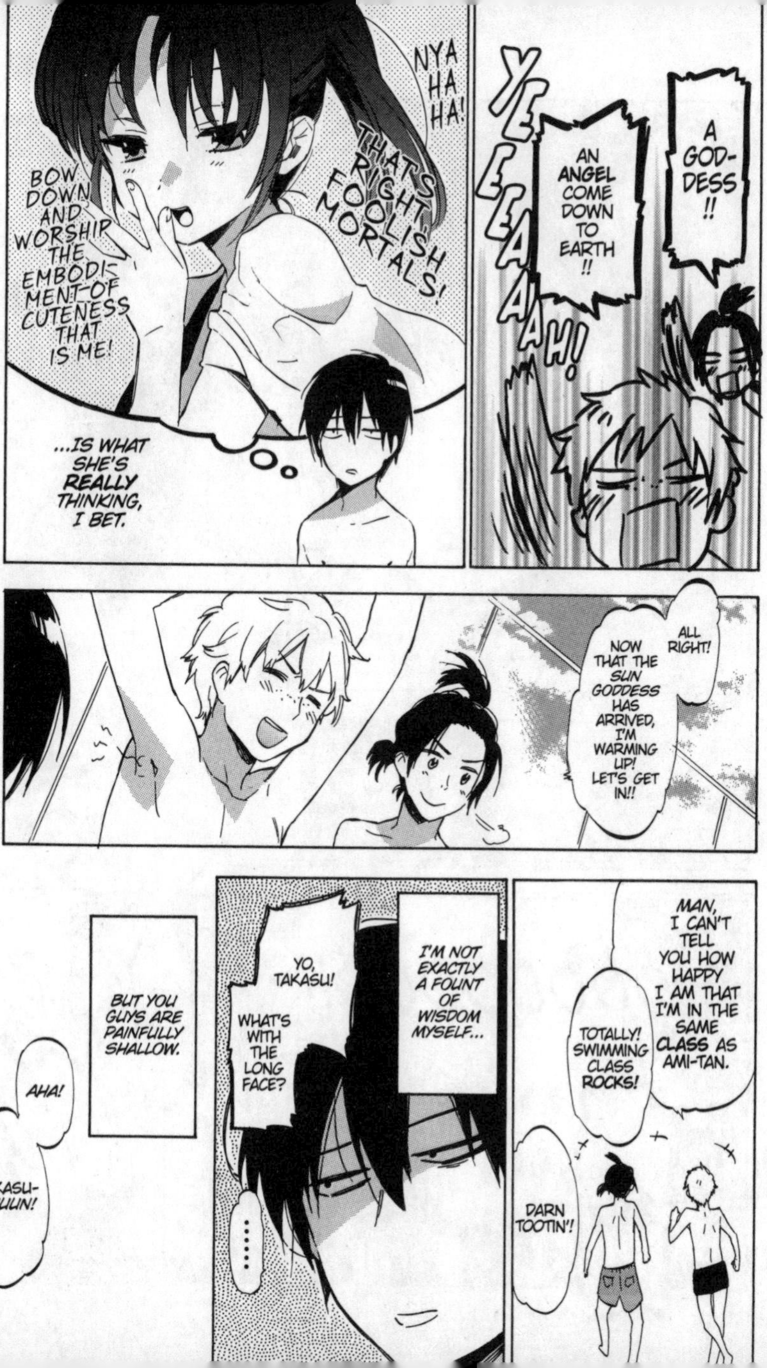

A GODDESS!!
AN ANGEL COME DOWN TO EARTH!!
YEEEAAAAH!
NYA HA HA!
THAT'S RIGHT, FOOLISH MORTALS!
BOW DOWN AND WORSHIP THE EMBODIMENT OF CUTENESS THAT IS ME!
...IS WHAT SHE'S REALLY THINKING, I BET.
ALL RIGHT!
NOW THAT THE SUN GODDESS HAS ARRIVED, I'M WARMING UP! LET'S GET IN!!
MAN, I CAN'T TELL YOU HOW HAPPY I AM THAT I'M IN THE SAME CLASS AS AMI-TAN.
TOTALLY! SWIMMING CLASS ROCKS!
DARN TOOTIN'!
I'M NOT EXACTLY A FOUNT OF WISDOM MYSELF...
YO, TAKASU!
WHAT'S WITH THE LONG FACE?
......
BUT YOU GUYS ARE PAINFULLY SHALLOW.
AHA!
TAKASU-KUUUN!

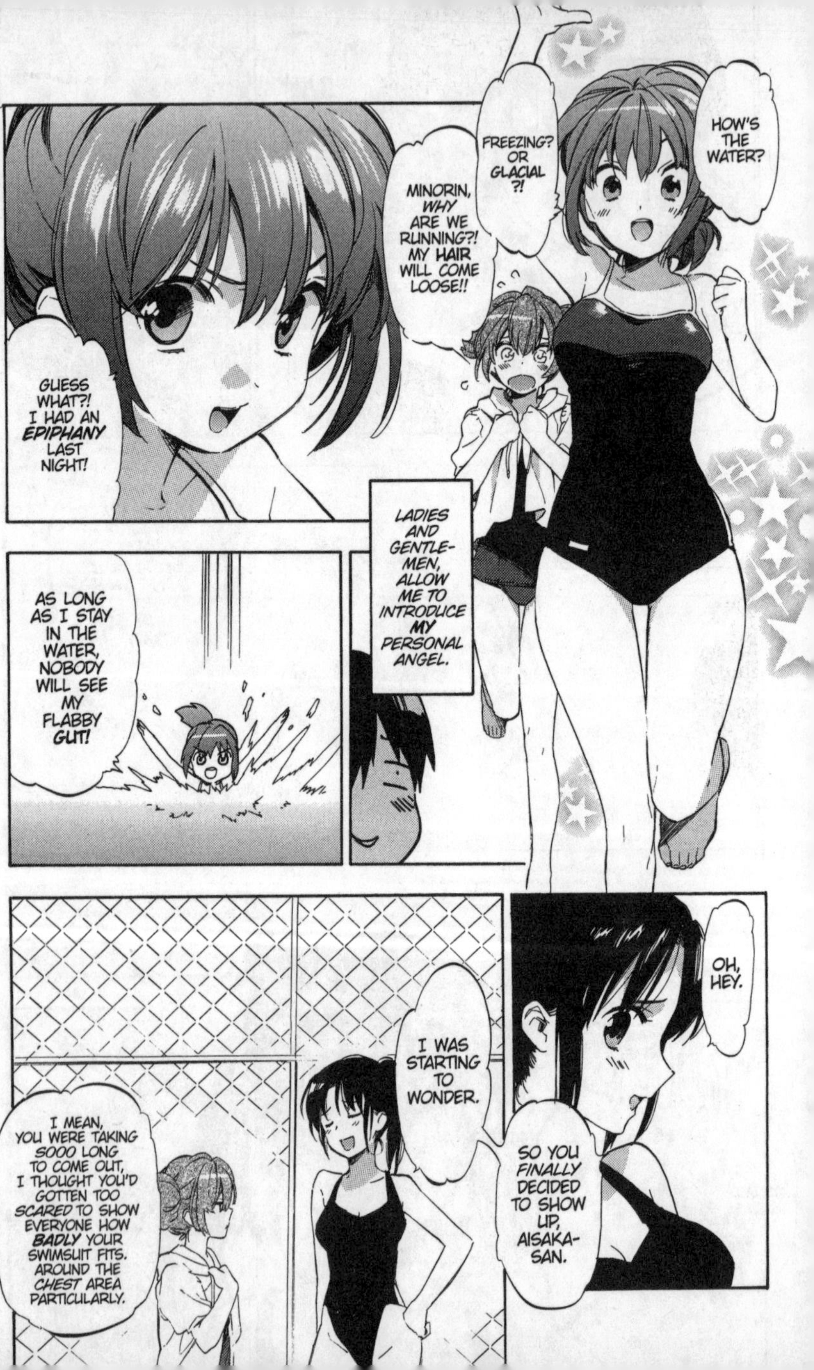
HOW'S THE WATER?
FREEZING? OR GLACIAL?!
MINORIN, WHY ARE WE RUNNING?! MY HAIR WILL COME LOOSE!!
GUESS WHAT?! I HAD AN EPIPHANY LAST NIGHT!
LADIES AND GENTLE-MEN, ALLOW ME TO INTRODUCE MY PERSONAL ANGEL.
AS LONG AS I STAY IN THE WATER, NOBODY WILL SEE MY FLABBY GUT!
OH, HEY.
SO YOU FINALLY DECIDED TO SHOW UP, AISAKA-SAN.
I WAS STARTING TO WONDER.
I MEAN, YOU WERE TAKING SOOO LONG TO COME OUT, I THOUGHT YOU'D GOTTEN TOO SCARED TO SHOW EVERYONE HOW BADLY YOUR SWIMSUIT FITS. AROUND THE CHEST AREA PARTICULARLY.

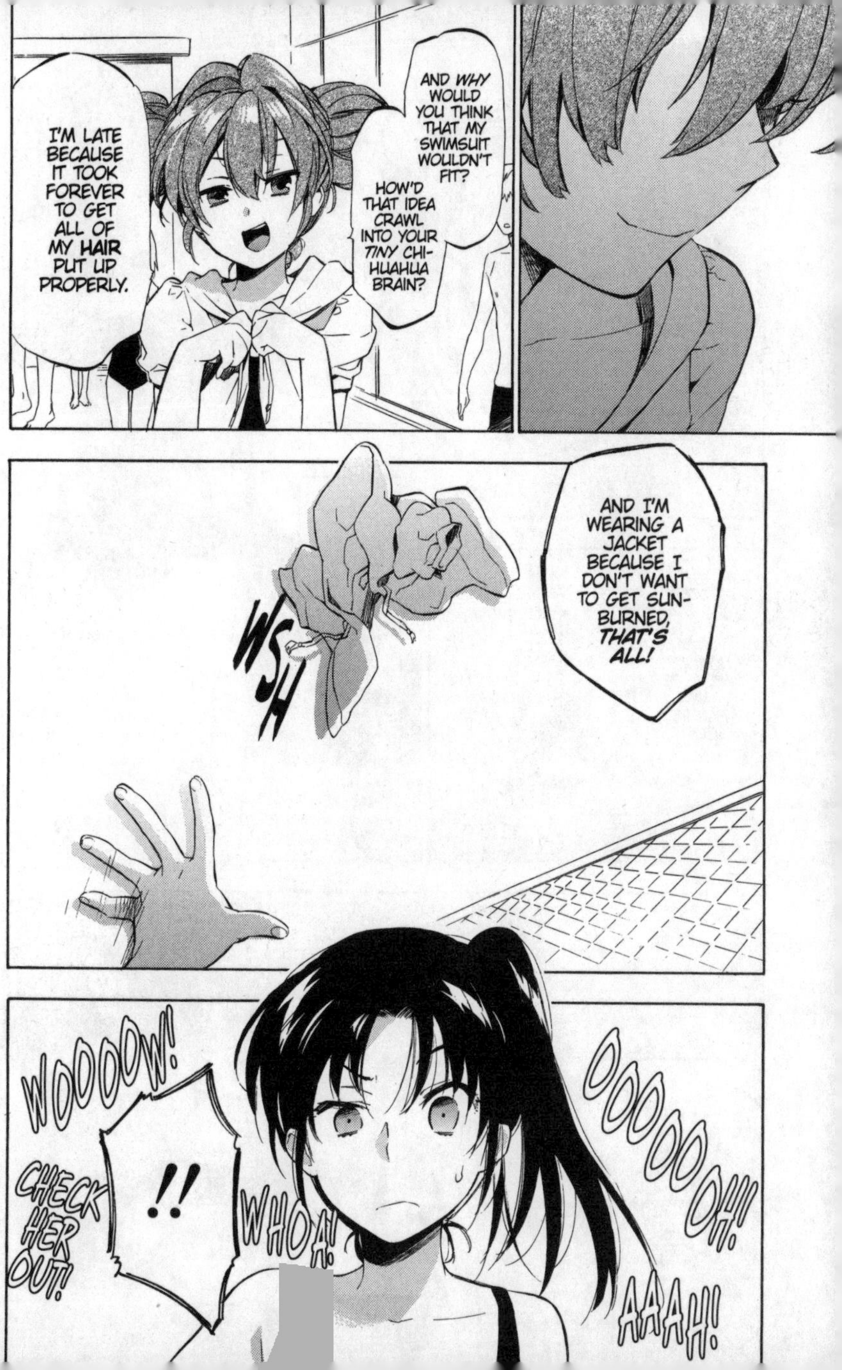
AND WHY WOULD YOU THINK THAT MY SWIMSUIT WOULDN'T FIT?
HOW'D THAT IDEA CRAWL INTO YOUR TINY CHI-HUAHUA BRAIN?
I'M LATE BECAUSE IT TOOK FOREVER TO GET ALL OF MY HAIR PUT UP PROPERLY.
AND I'M WEARING A JACKET BECAUSE I DON'T WANT TO GET SUN-BURNED, THAT'S ALL!
WSH
OOOOOOH!
AAAH!
WHOA!
!!
WOOOOW!
CHECK HER OUT!

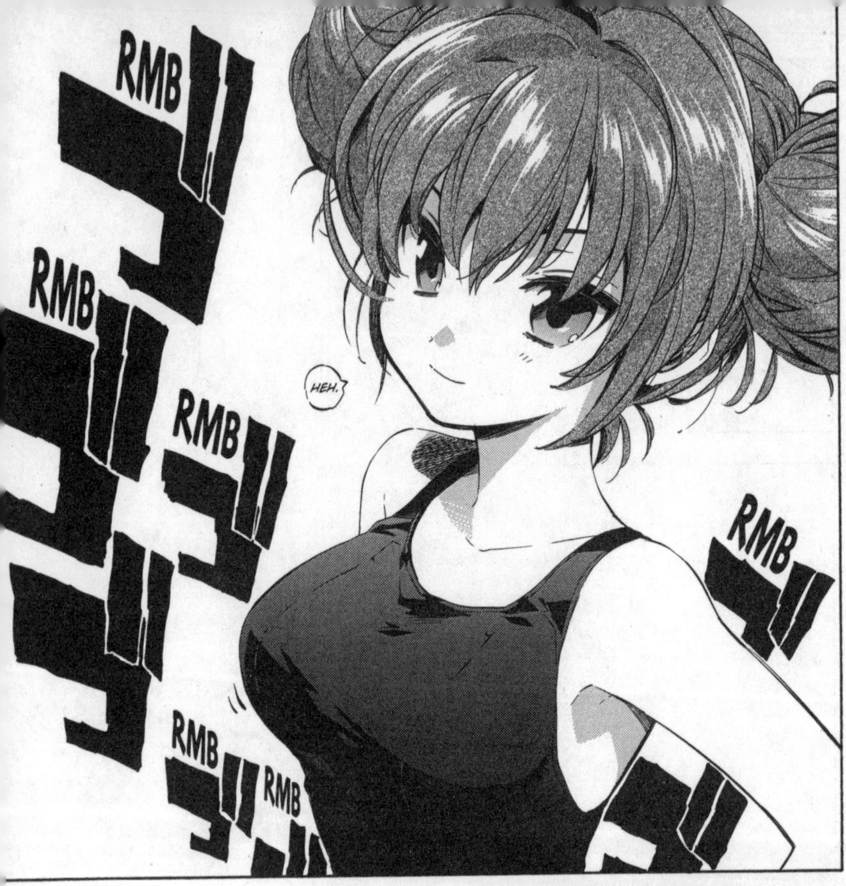
RMB
RMB
HEH.
RMB
RMB
RMB
RMB
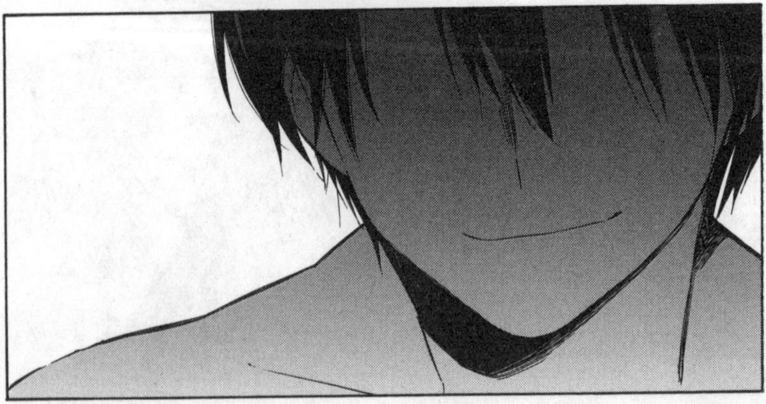

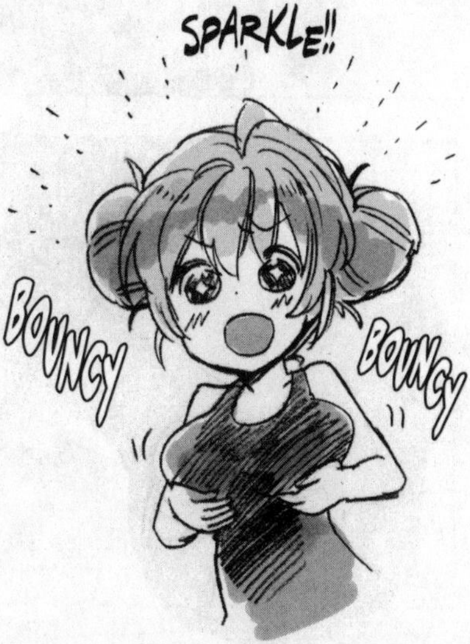
SPARKLE!!
BOUNCY
BOUNCY

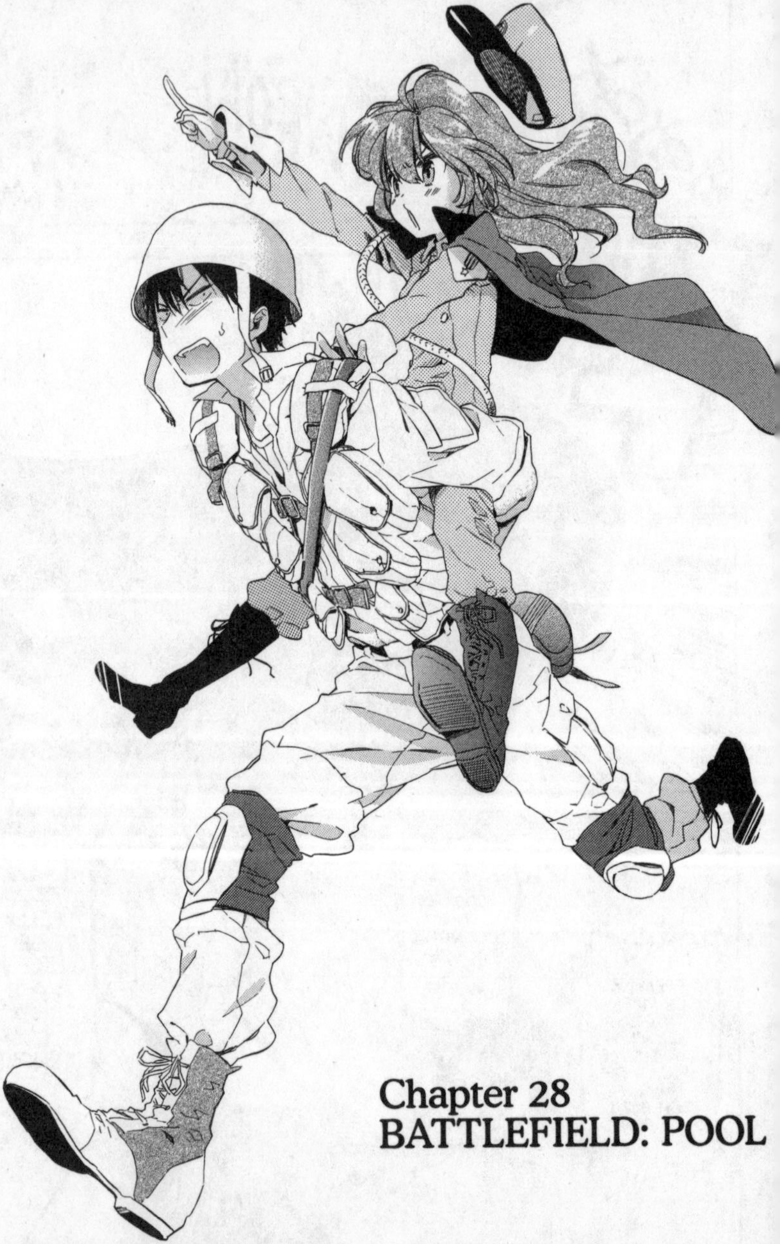

Chapter 28
BATTLEFIELD: POOL

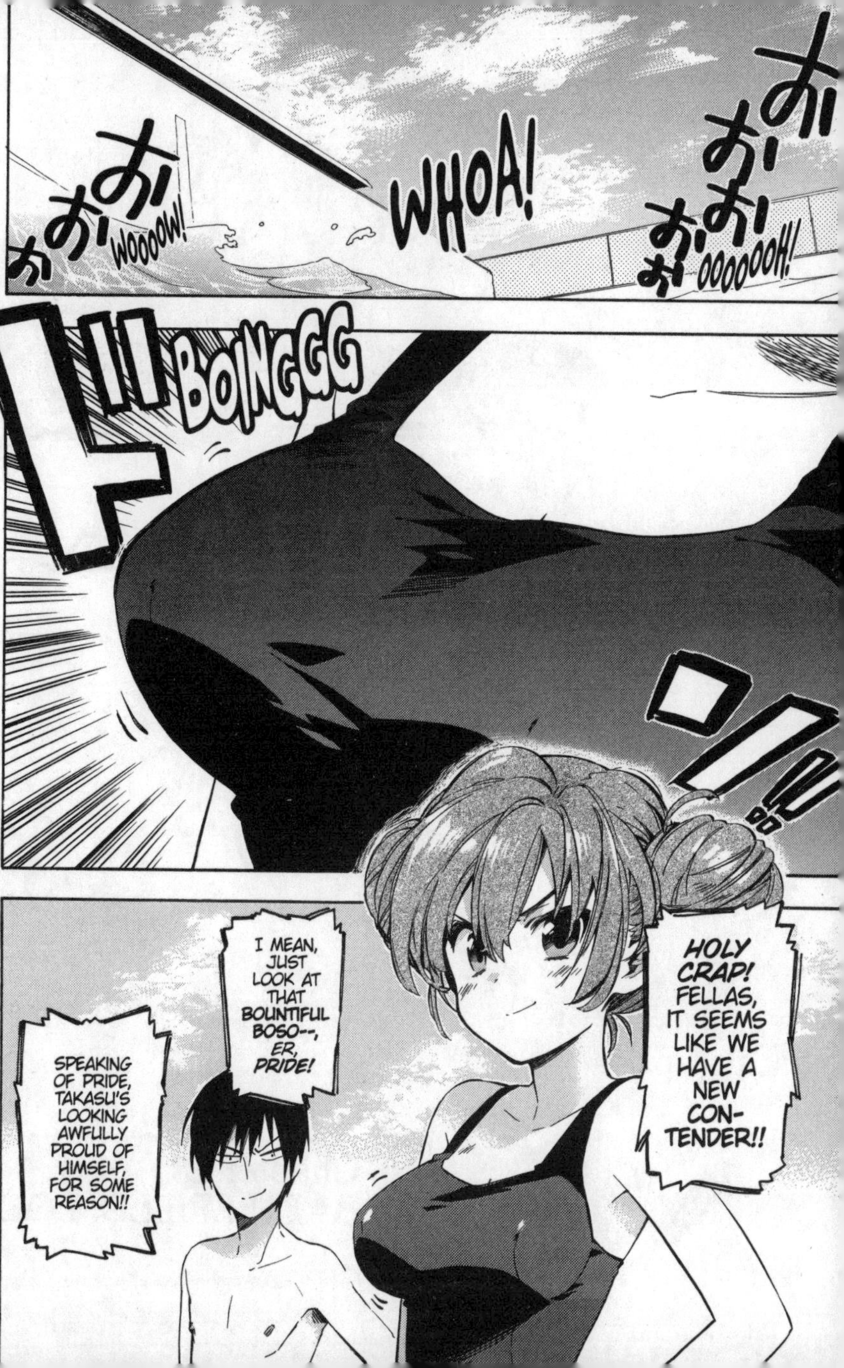
OOOOOOH!
WHOA!
WOOOOW!
BOINGGG
HOLY CRAP! FELLAS, IT SEEMS LIKE WE HAVE A NEW CON-TENDER!!
I MEAN, JUST LOOK AT THAT BOUNTIFUL BOSO--, ER, PRIDE!
SPEAKING OF PRIDE, TAKASU'S LOOKING AWFULLY PROUD OF HIMSELF, FOR SOME REASON!!

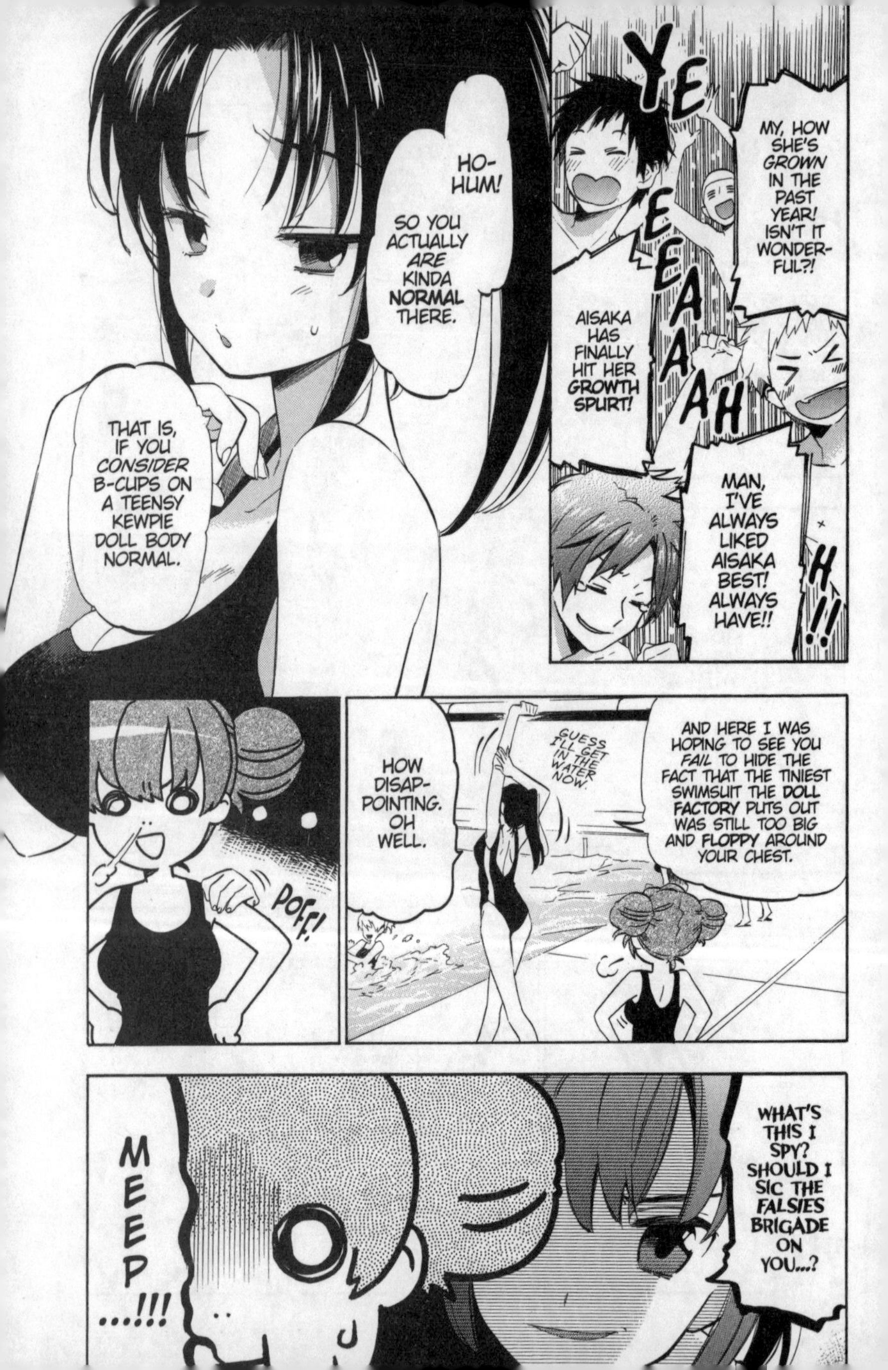
YEEEAAAHH!!
MY, HOW SHE'S GROWN IN THE PAST YEAR! ISN'T IT WONDERFUL?!
AISAKA HAS FINALLY HIT HER GROWTH SPURT!
MAN, I'VE ALWAYS LIKED AISAKA BEST! ALWAYS HAVE!!
HO-HUM!
SO YOU ACTUALLY ARE KINDA NORMAL THERE.
THAT IS, IF YOU CONSIDER B-CUPS ON A TEENSY KEWPIE DOLL BODY NORMAL.
AND HERE I WAS HOPING TO SEE YOU FAIL TO HIDE THE FACT THAT THE TINIEST SWIMSUIT THE DOLL FACTORY PUTS OUT WAS STILL TOO BIG AND FLOPPY AROUND YOUR CHEST.
GUESS I'LL GET IN THE WATER NOW.
HOW DISAPPOINTING. OH WELL.
POFF!
WHAT'S THIS I SPY? SHOULD I SIC THE FALSIES BRIGADE ON YOU...?
MEEP ...!!!

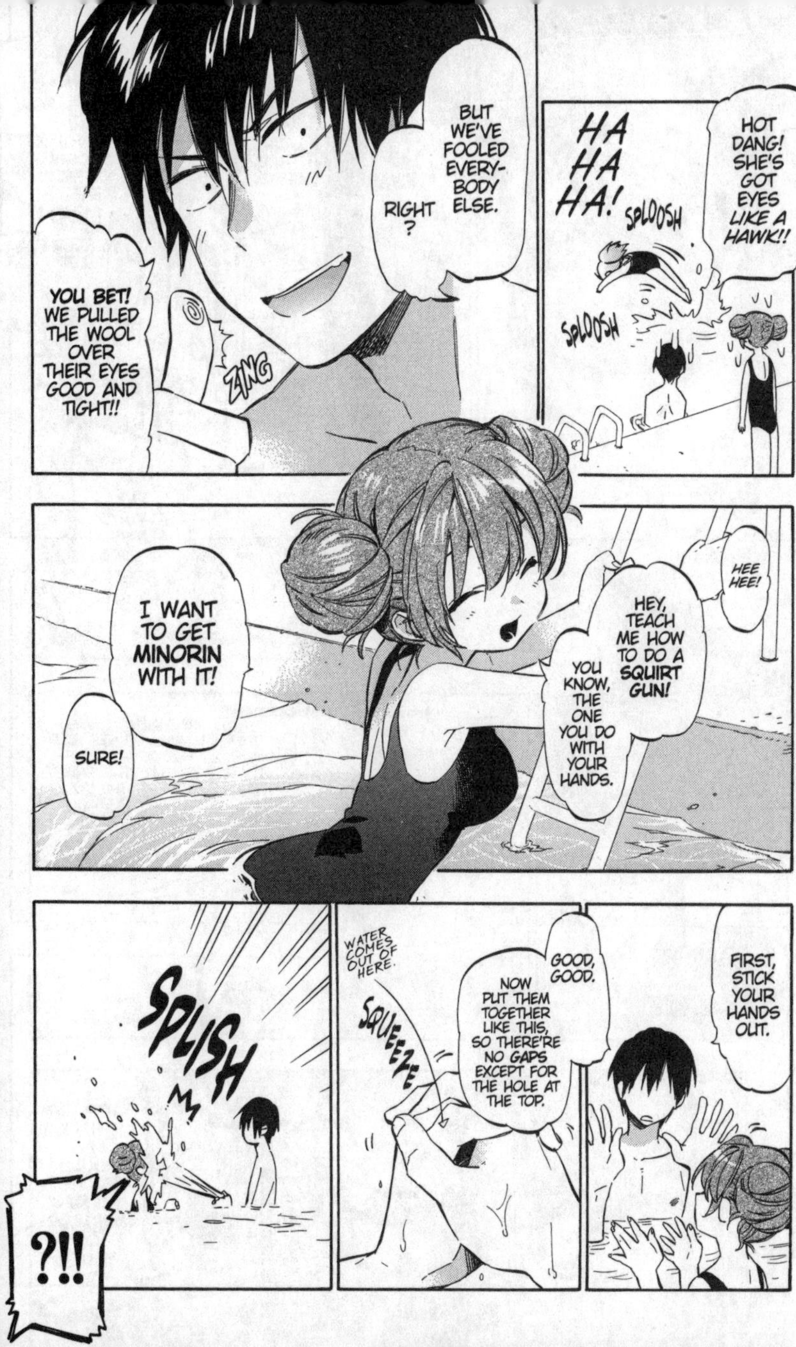
HOT DANG! SHE'S GOT EYES LIKE A HAWK!!
HA HA HA!
SPLOOSH
SPLOOSH
BUT WE'VE FOOLED EVERY-BODY ELSE.
RIGHT?
YOU BET! WE PULLED THE WOOL OVER THEIR EYES GOOD AND TIGHT!!
ZING
HEE HEE!
HEY, TEACH ME HOW TO DO A SQUIRT GUN!
YOU KNOW, THE ONE YOU DO WITH YOUR HANDS.
I WANT TO GET MINORIN WITH IT!
SURE!
FIRST, STICK YOUR HANDS OUT.
GOOD, GOOD.
NOW PUT THEM TOGETHER LIKE THIS, SO THERE'RE NO GAPS EXCEPT FOR THE HOLE AT THE TOP.
WATER COMES OUT OF HERE.
SQUEEEZE
SPLISH
?!!

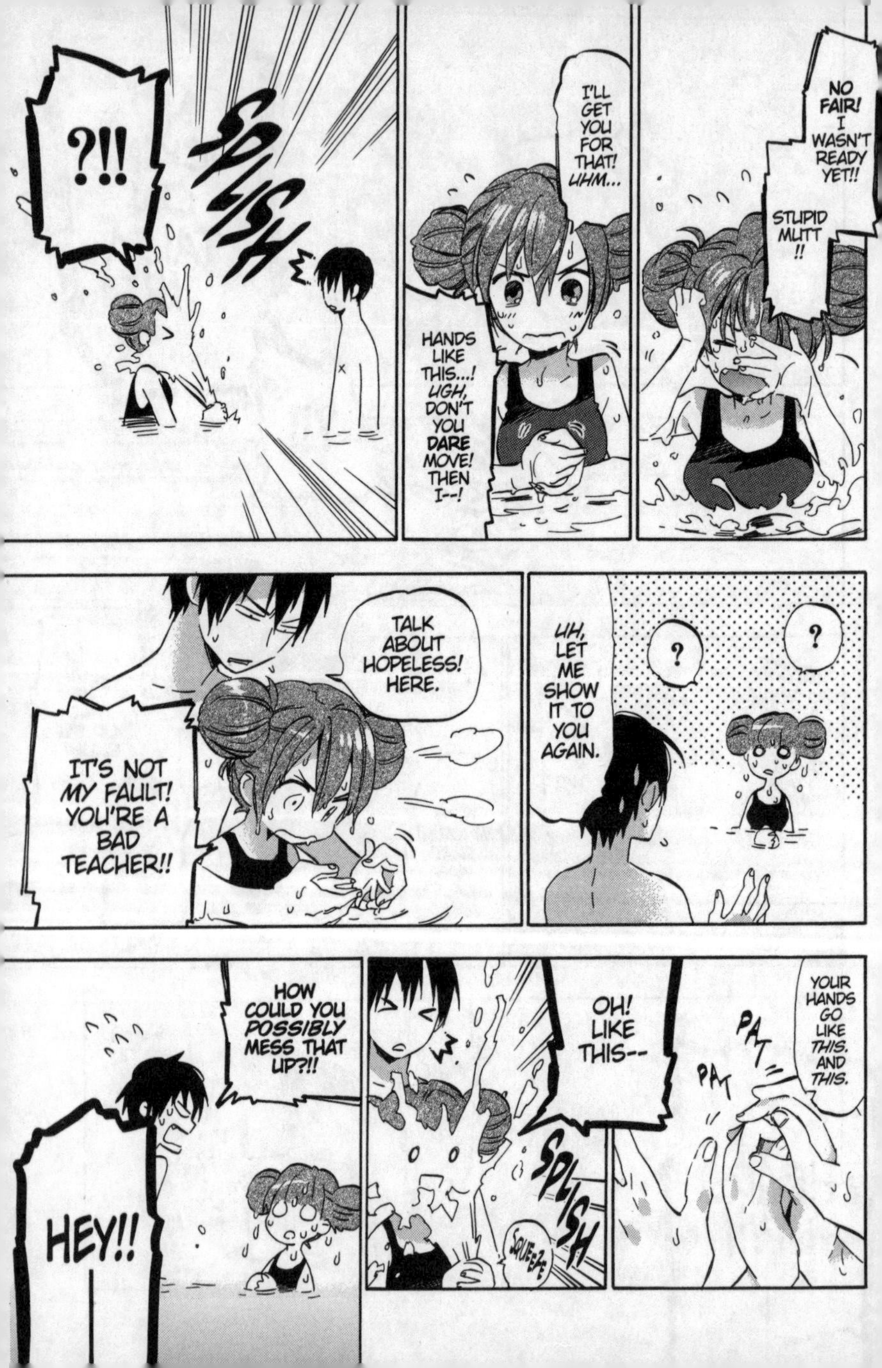
NO FAIR! I WASN'T READY YET!!
STUPID MUTT!!
I'LL GET YOU FOR THAT! UHM...
HANDS LIKE THIS...! UGH, DON'T YOU DARE MOVE! THEN I--!
SPLISH
?!!
UH, LET ME SHOW IT TO YOU AGAIN.
?
?
TALK ABOUT HOPELESS! HERE.
IT'S NOT MY FAULT! YOU'RE A BAD TEACHER!!
YOUR HANDS GO LIKE THIS. AND THIS.
PAT
PAT
OH! LIKE THIS--
SPLISH
SQUEEZE
HOW COULD YOU POSSIBLY MESS THAT UP?!!
HEY!!

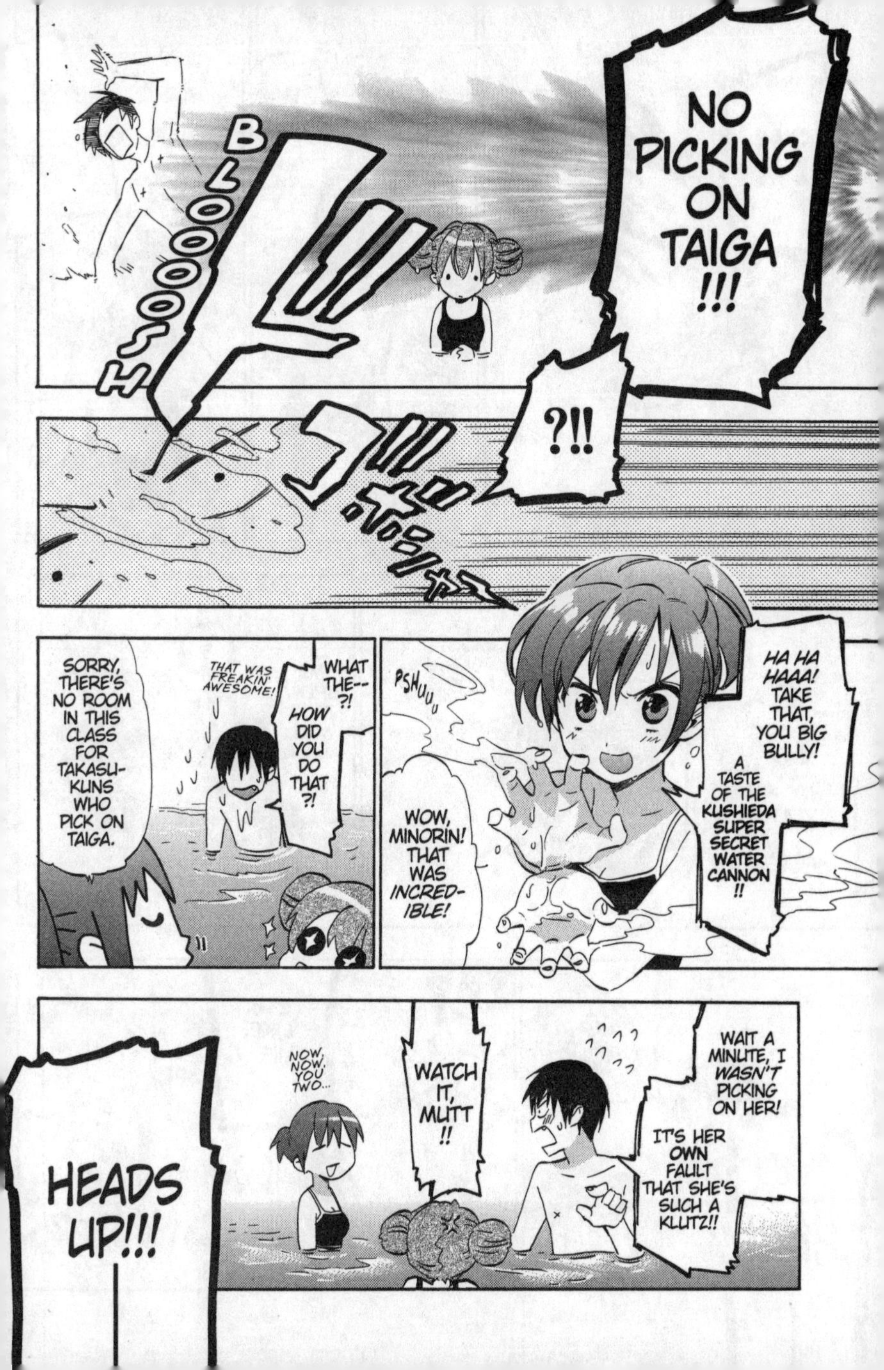
NO PICKING ON TAIGA!!!
BLOOOOOSH
?!!
HA HA HAAA! TAKE THAT, YOU BIG BULLY!
A TASTE OF THE KUSHIEDA SUPER SECRET WATER CANNON!!
PSHUUU
WOW, MINORIN! THAT WAS INCREDIBLE!
WHAT THE--?!
HOW DID YOU DO THAT?!
THAT WAS FREAKIN' AWESOME!
SORRY, THERE'S NO ROOM IN THIS CLASS FOR TAKASU-KUNS WHO PICK ON TAIGA.
WAIT A MINUTE, I WASN'T PICKING ON HER!
IT'S HER OWN FAULT THAT SHE'S SUCH A KLUTZ!!
WATCH IT, MUTT!!
NOW, NOW, YOU TWO...
HEADS UP!!!

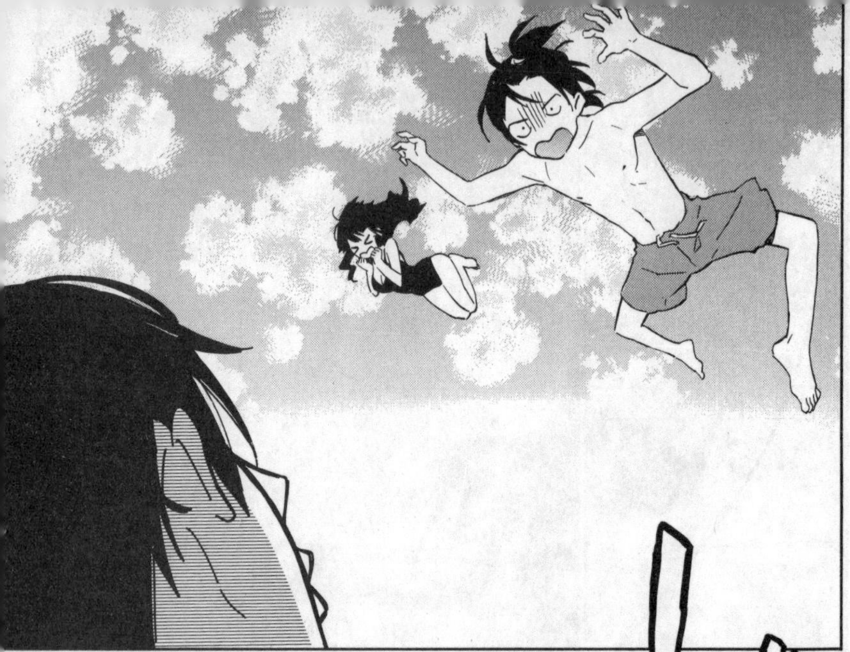

Dangerous. Do not try this at home. Seriously. Don't.

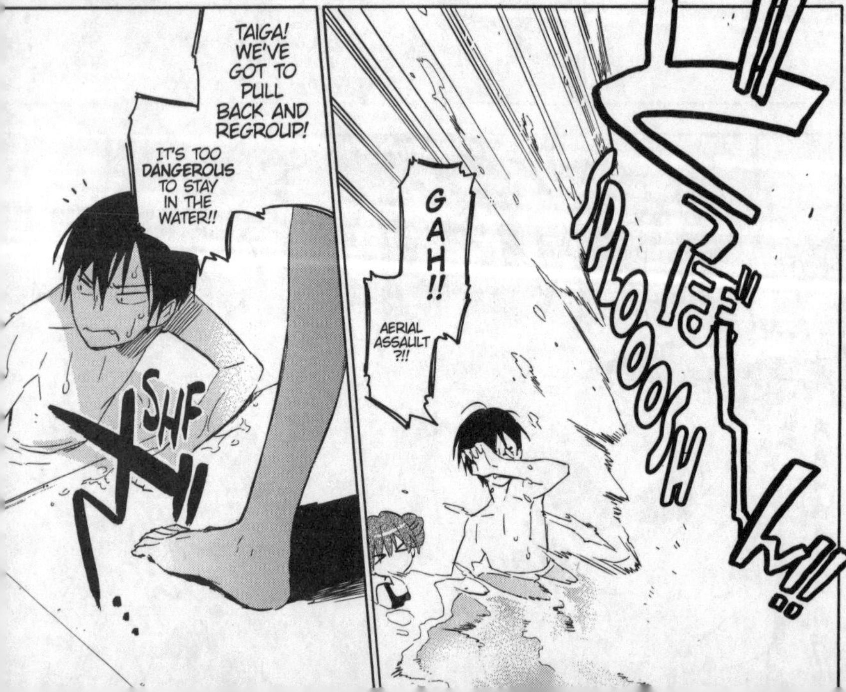
SPLOOOOSH
GAH!!
AERIAL ASSAULT ?!!
TAIGA! WE'VE GOT TO PULL BACK AND REGROUP!
IT'S TOO DANGEROUS TO STAY IN THE WATER!!
SHF

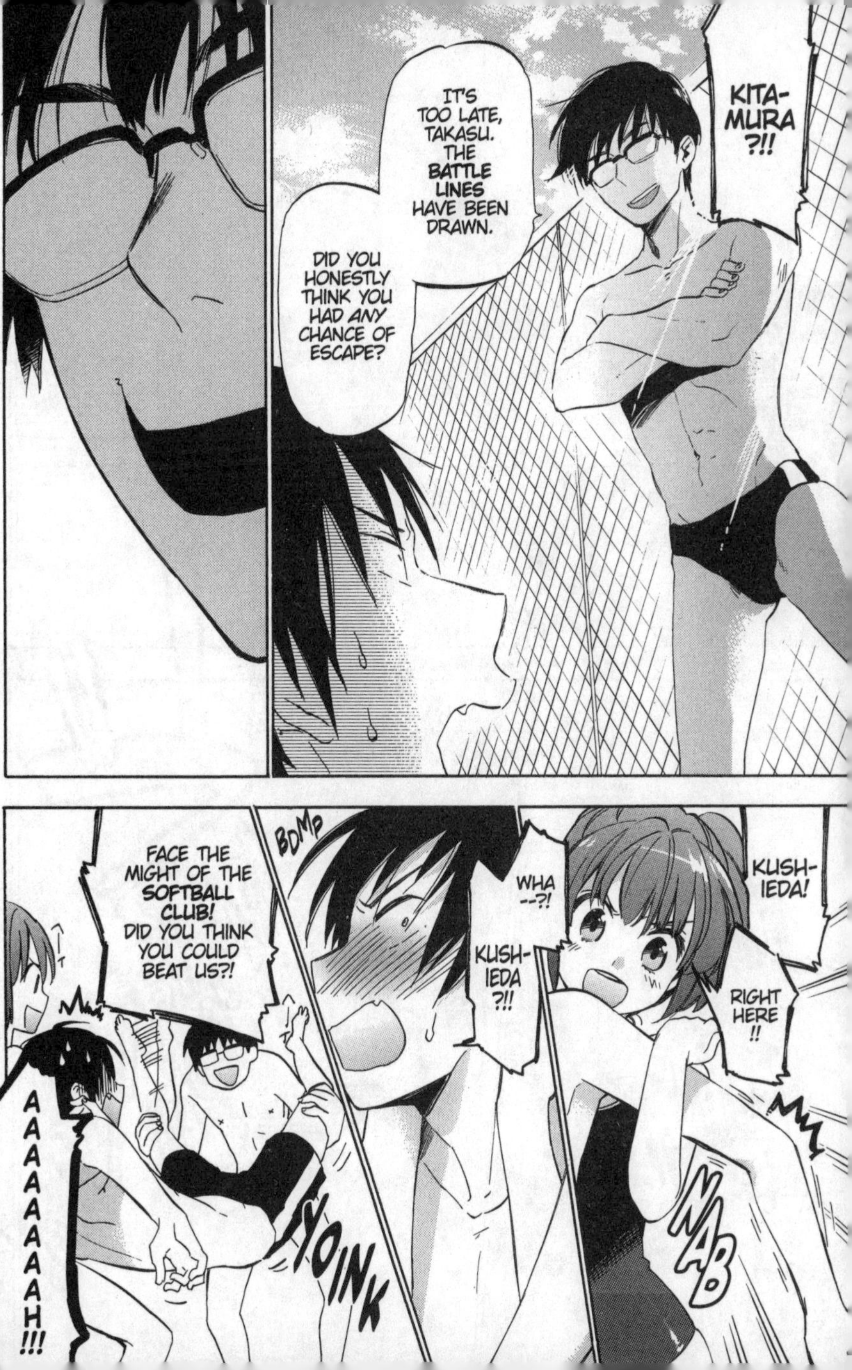
KITA-MURA?!!
IT'S TOO LATE, TAKASU. THE BATTLE LINES HAVE BEEN DRAWN.
DID YOU HONESTLY THINK YOU HAD ANY CHANCE OF ESCAPE?
KUSH-IEDA!
BDMP
WHA--?!
KUSH-IEDA?!!
RIGHT HERE!!
NAB
YOINK
FACE THE MIGHT OF THE SOFTBALL CLUB! DID YOU THINK YOU COULD BEAT US?!
AAAAAAAAAAAH!!!

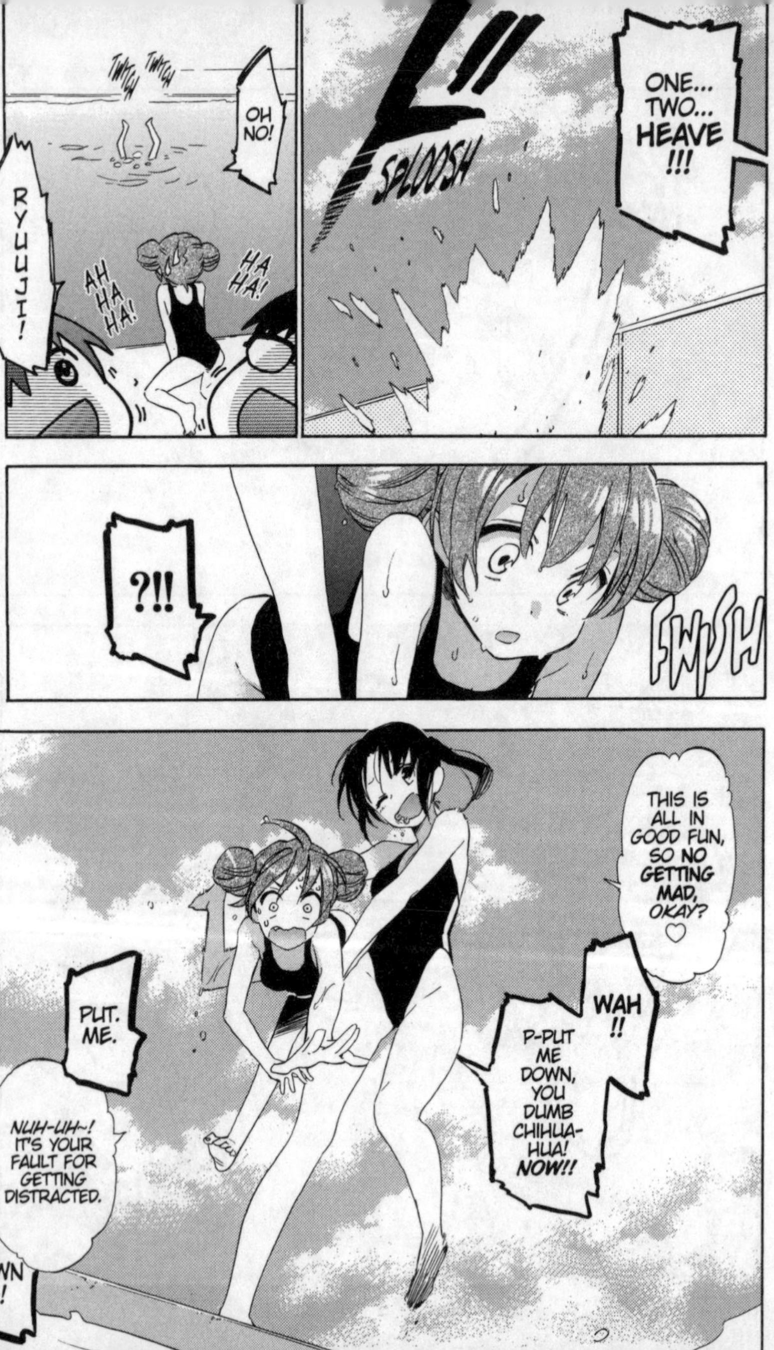
ONE... TWO... HEAVE!!!
SPLOOSH
OH NO!
TWITCH TWITCH
HA HA!
AH HA HA!
RYUUJI!
FWISH
?!!
THIS IS ALL IN GOOD FUN, SO NO GETTING MAD, OKAY? ♡
WAH!!
P-PUT ME DOWN, YOU DUMB CHIHUAHUA! NOW!!
PUT. ME.
NUH-UH~! IT'S YOUR FAULT FOR GETTING DISTRACTED.
DOWN--!

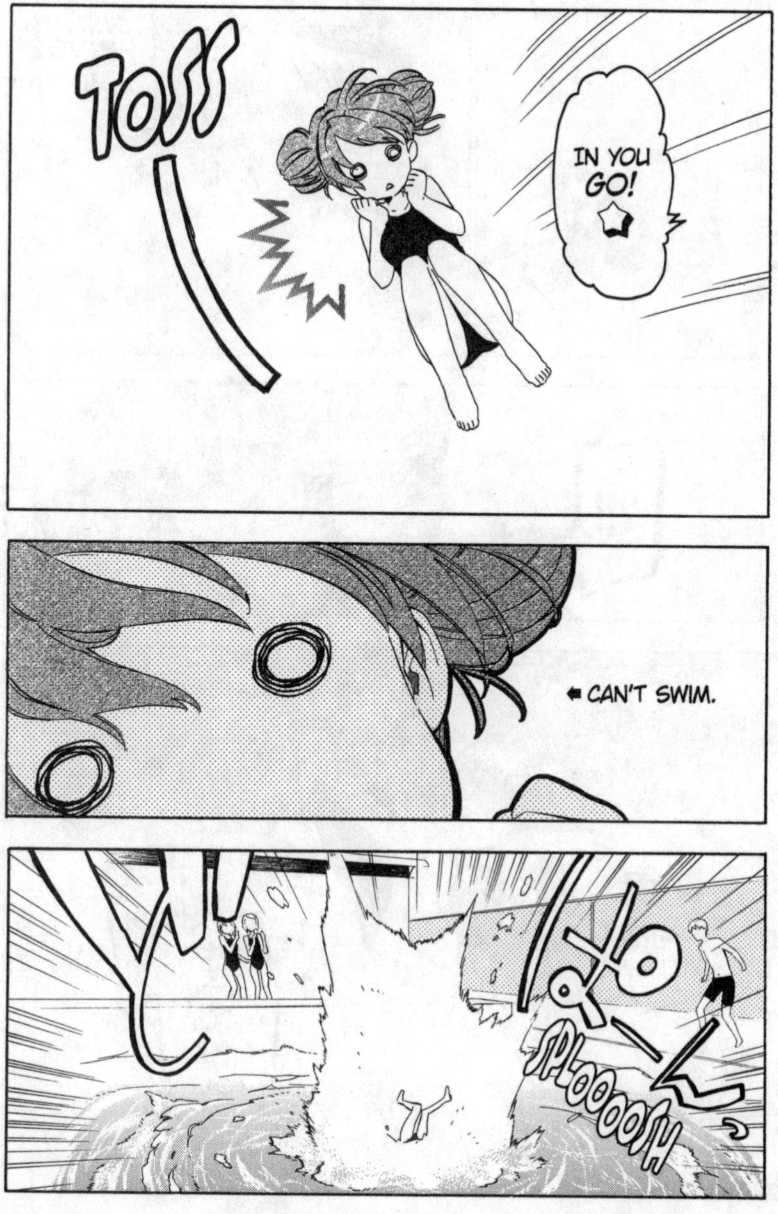
IN YOU GO!
TOSS
CAN'T SWIM.
SPLOOOOSH

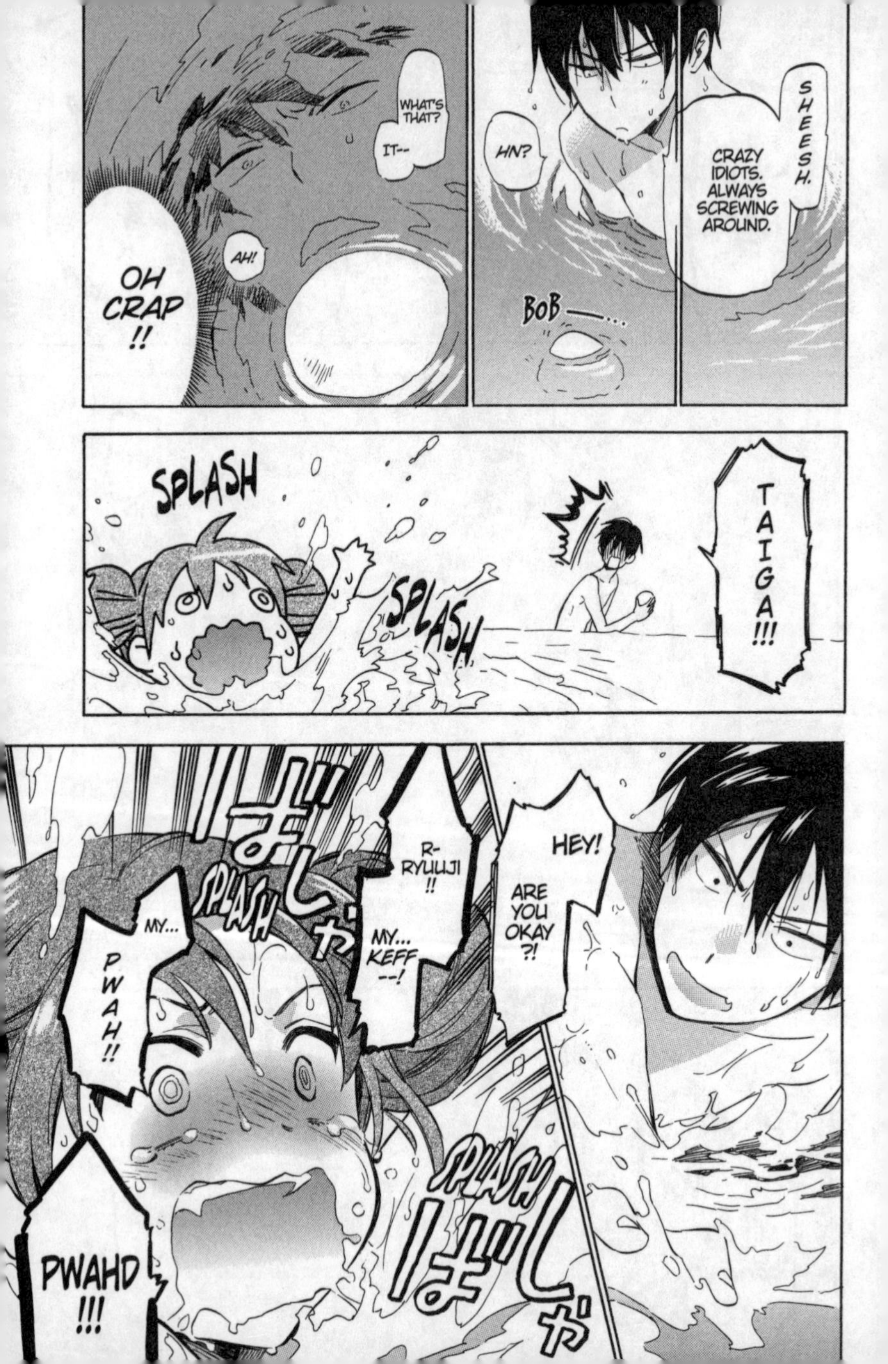
SHEESH.
CRAZY IDIOTS. ALWAYS SCREWING AROUND.
HN?
BOB——...
WHAT'S THAT?
IT--
AH!
OH CRAP!!
TAIGA!!!
SPLASH
SPLASH
HEY!
ARE YOU OKAY?!
R-RYUUJI!!
MY... KEFF--!
ばしゃ
SPLASH
MY...
PWAH!!
PWAHD!!!
ばしゃ
SPLASH

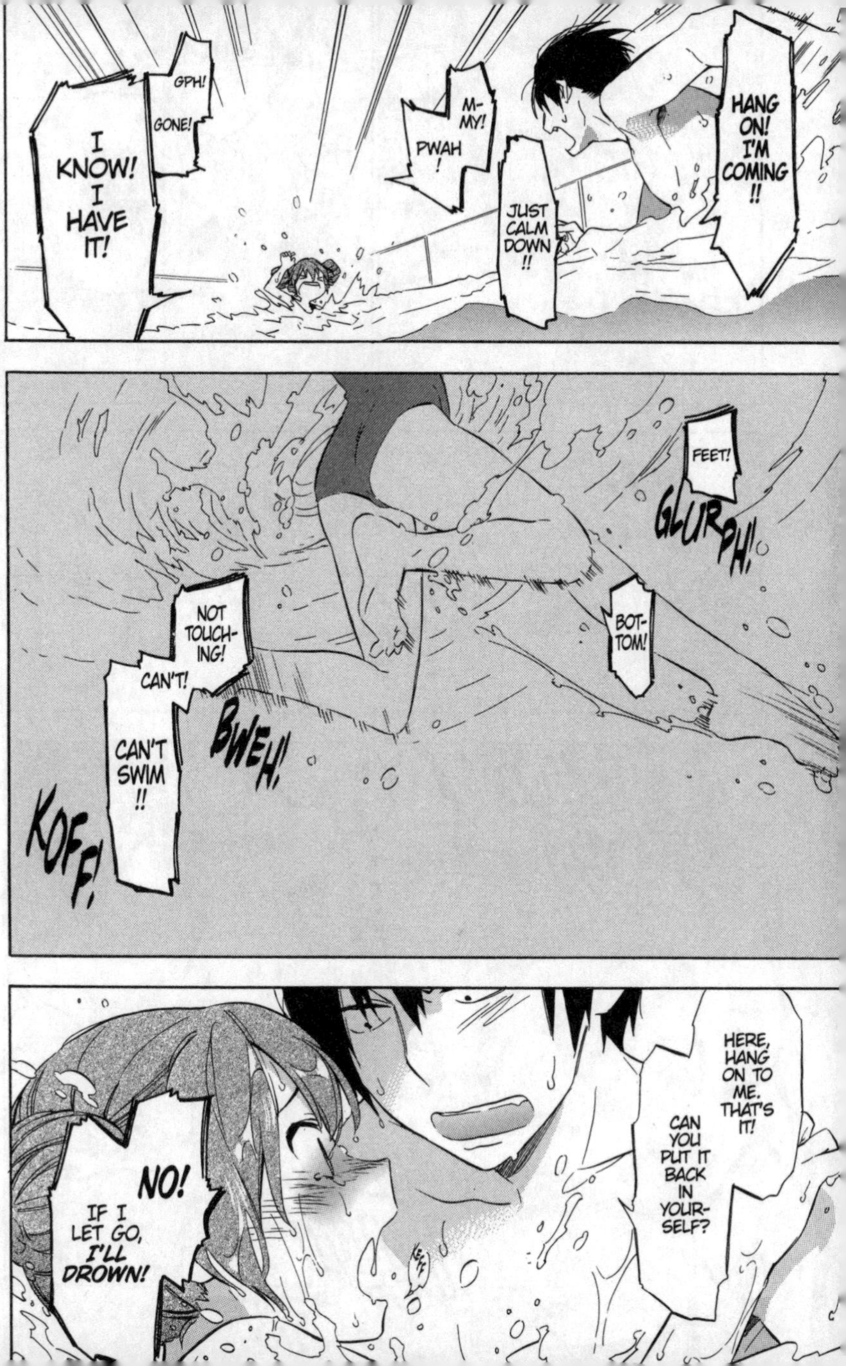
HANG ON! I'M COMING!!
JUST CALM DOWN!!
M-MY!
PWAH!
GPH!
GONE!
I KNOW! I HAVE IT!
FEET!
GLURPH!
BOT-TOM!
NOT TOUCH-ING!
CAN'T!
BWEH!
CAN'T SWIM!!
KOFF!
HERE, HANG ON TO ME. THAT'S IT!
CAN YOU PUT IT BACK IN YOURSELF?
NO!
IF I LET GO, I'LL DROWN!

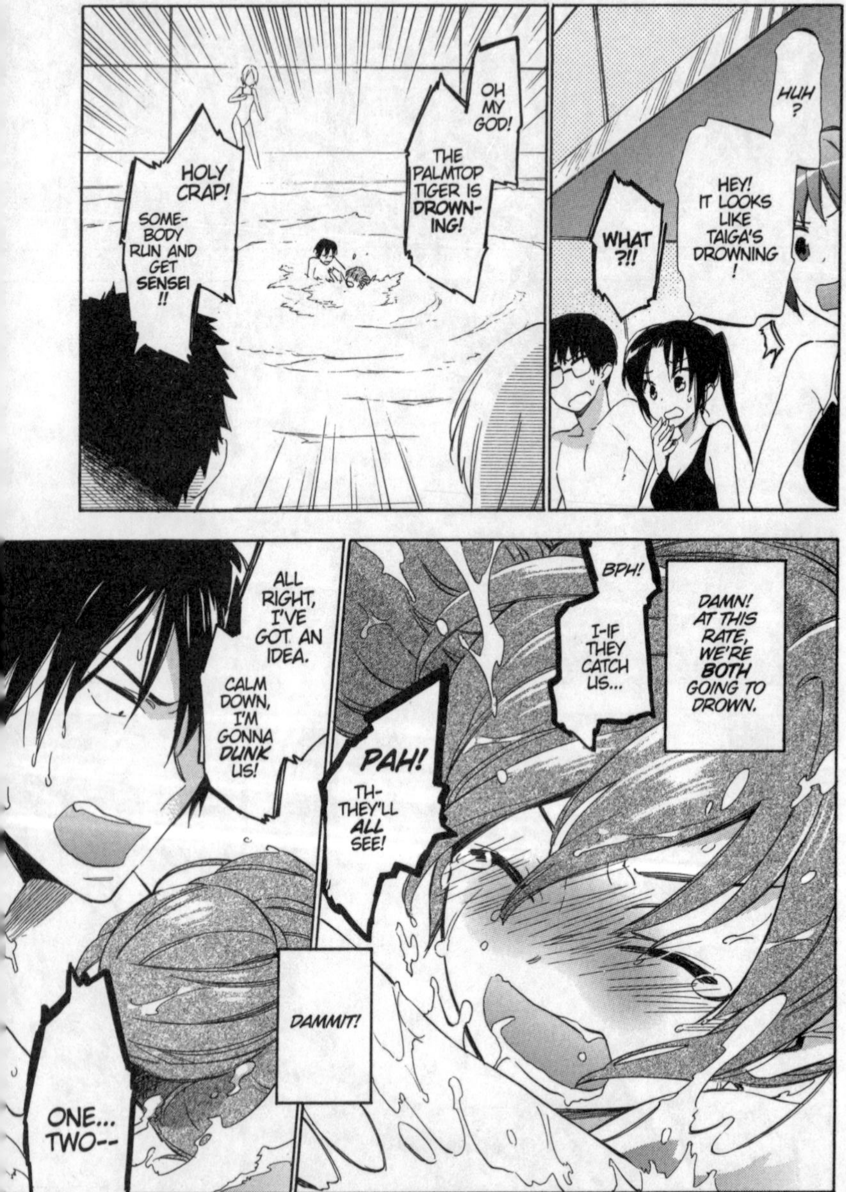
HUH?
HEY! IT LOOKS LIKE TAIGA'S DROWNING!
WHAT?!!
OH MY GOD!
THE PALMTOP TIGER IS DROWNING!
HOLY CRAP!
SOMEBODY RUN AND GET SENSEI!!
DAMN! AT THIS RATE, WE'RE BOTH GOING TO DROWN.
BPH!
I-IF THEY CATCH US...
PAH!
TH-THEY'LL ALL SEE!
DAMMIT!
ALL RIGHT, I'VE GOT AN IDEA.
CALM DOWN, I'M GONNA DUNK US!
ONE... TWO--

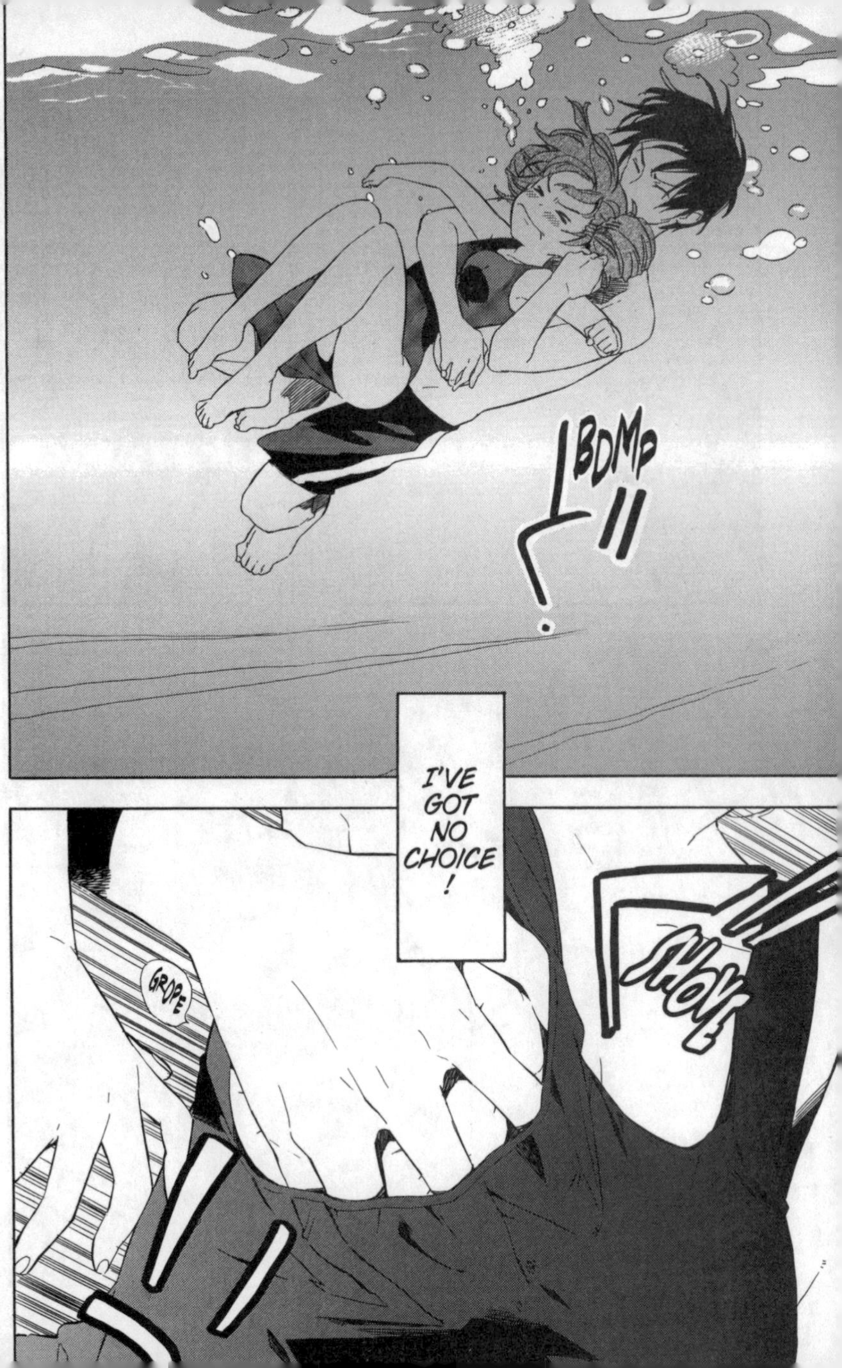
BDMP
I'VE GOT NO CHOICE!
GROPE

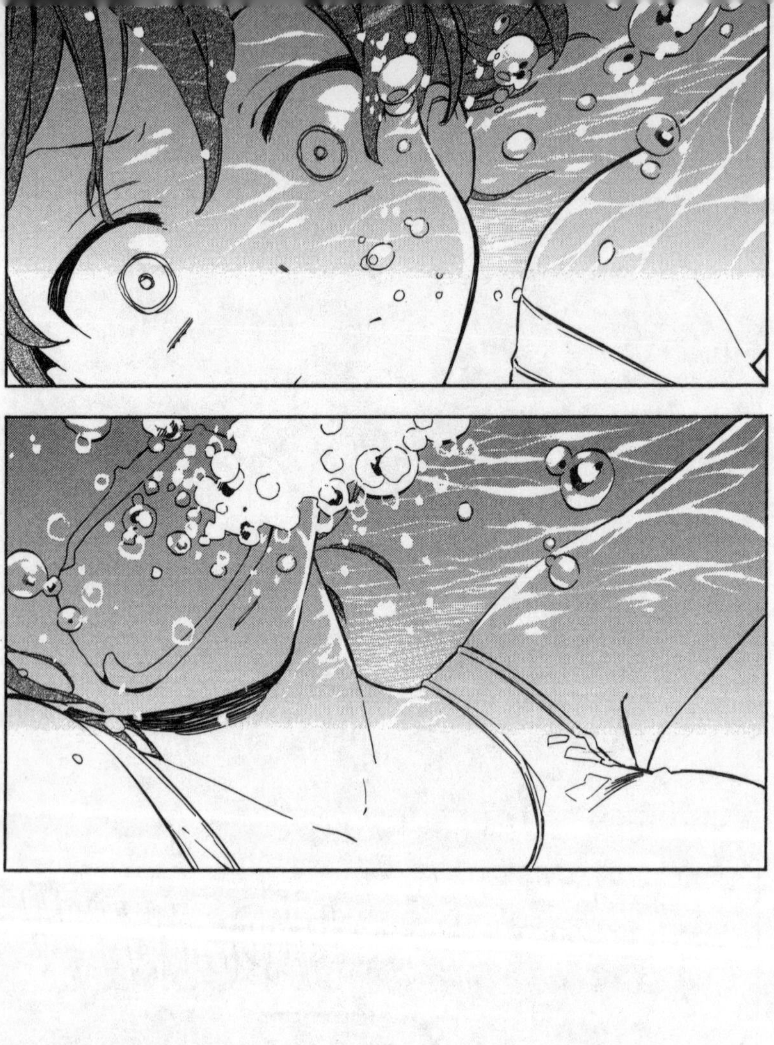

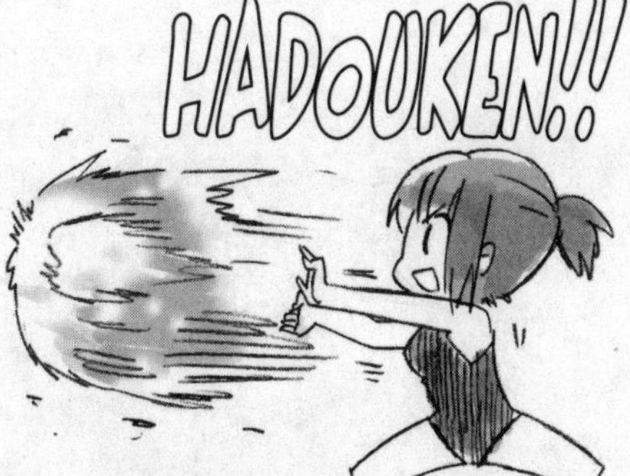
HADOUKEN!!

Chapter 29
ROUND 2, FIGHT!!

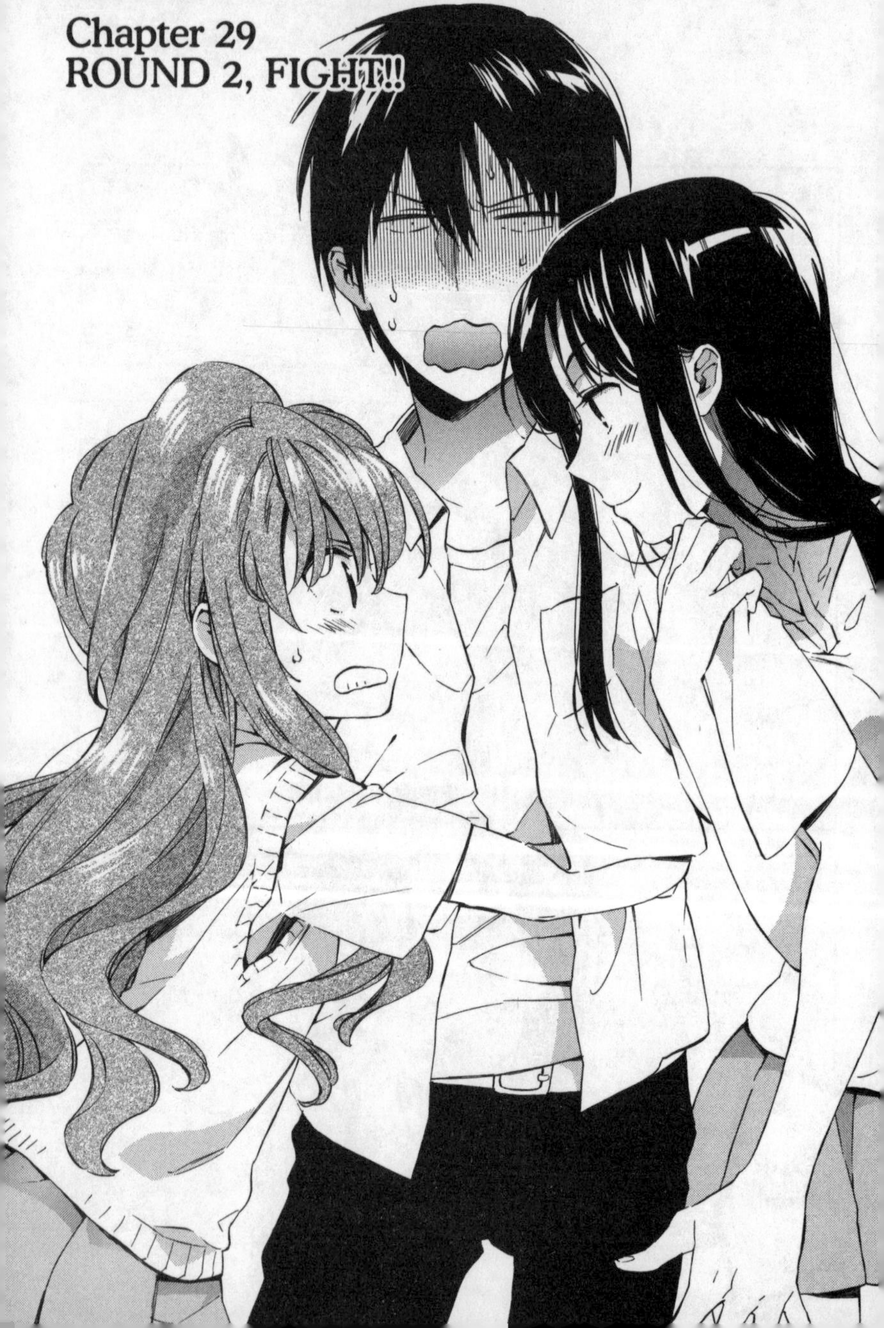

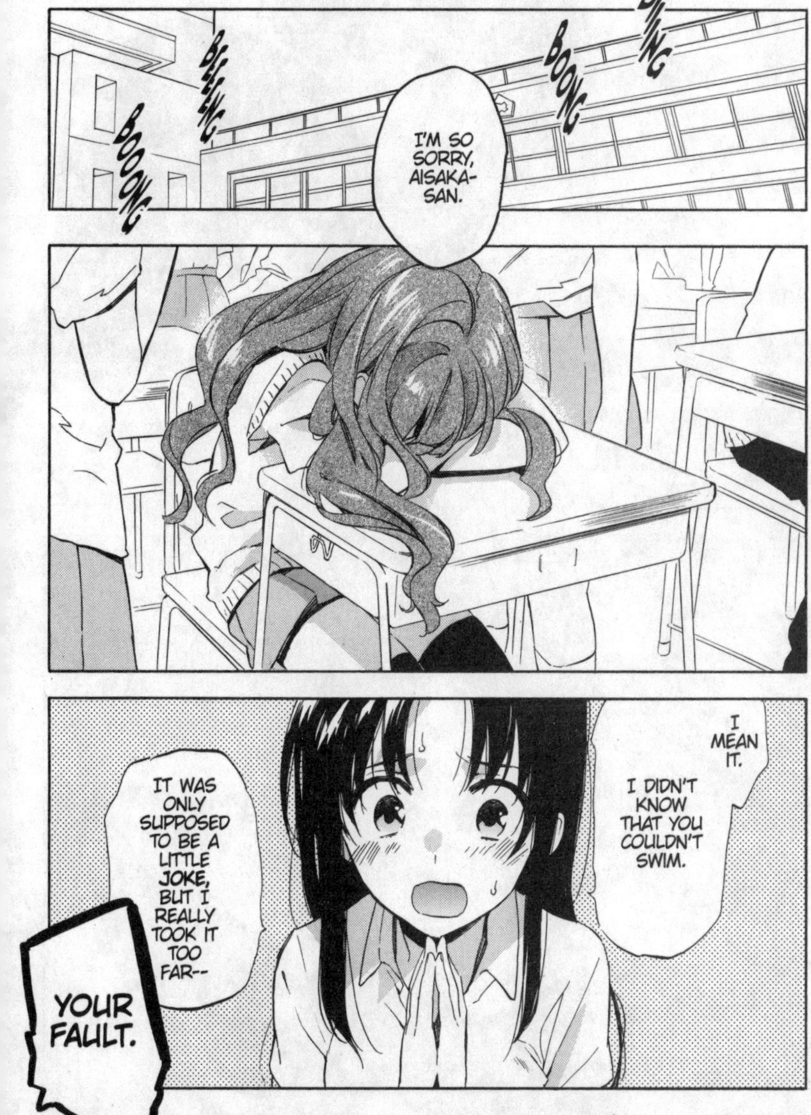
BIING BOONG
I'M SO SORRY, AISAKA-SAN.
BIEENG BOOONG
I MEAN IT.
I DIDN'T KNOW THAT YOU COULDN'T SWIM.
IT WAS ONLY SUPPOSED TO BE A LITTLE JOKE, BUT I REALLY TOOK IT TOO FAR--
YOUR FAULT.

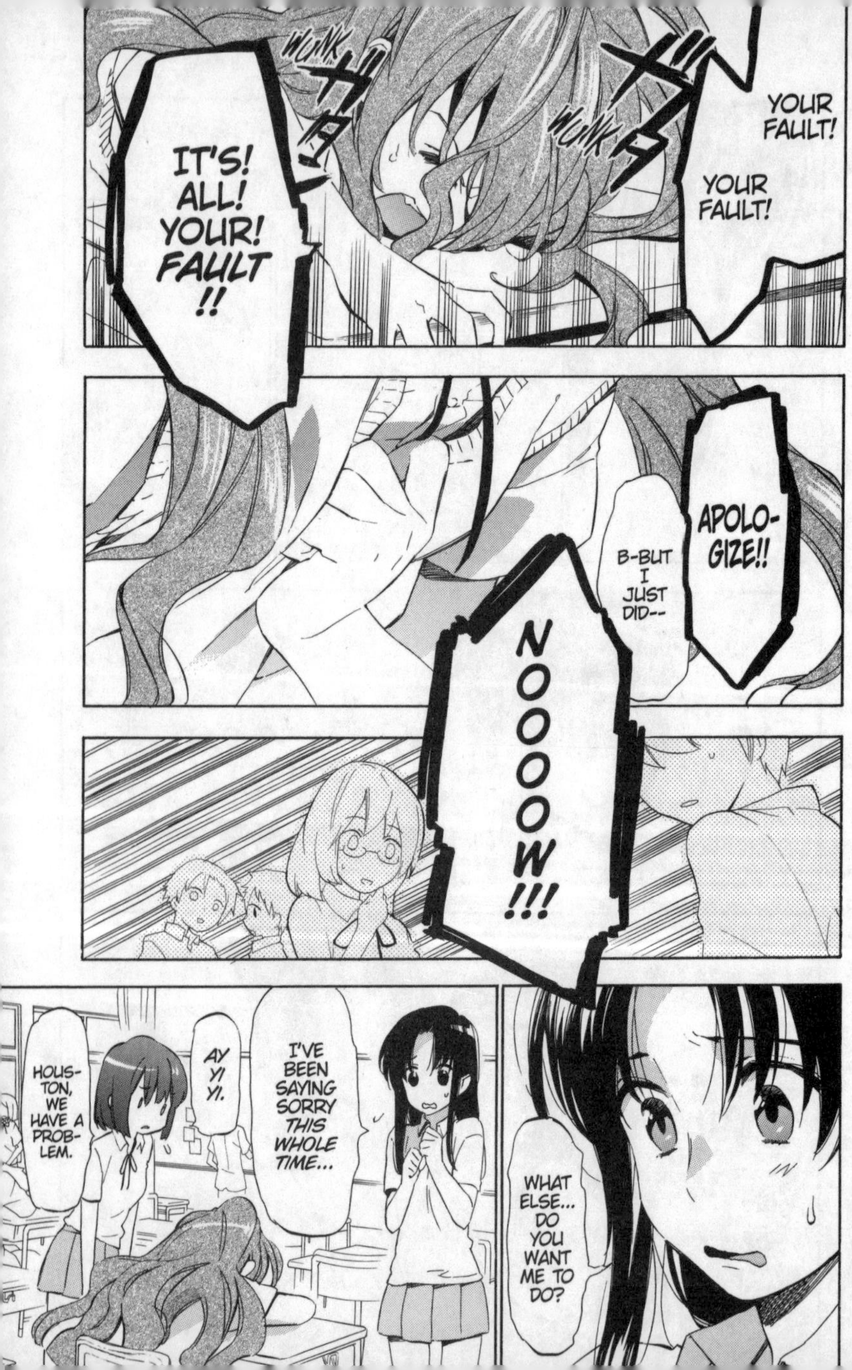
YOUR FAULT!
YOUR FAULT!
WUNK
WUNK
IT'S! ALL! YOUR! FAULT!!
APOLO-GIZE!!
B-BUT I JUST DID--
NOOOOOW!!!
WHAT ELSE... DO YOU WANT ME TO DO?
I'VE BEEN SAYING SORRY THIS WHOLE TIME...
AY YI YI.
HOUS-TON, WE HAVE A PROB-LEM.

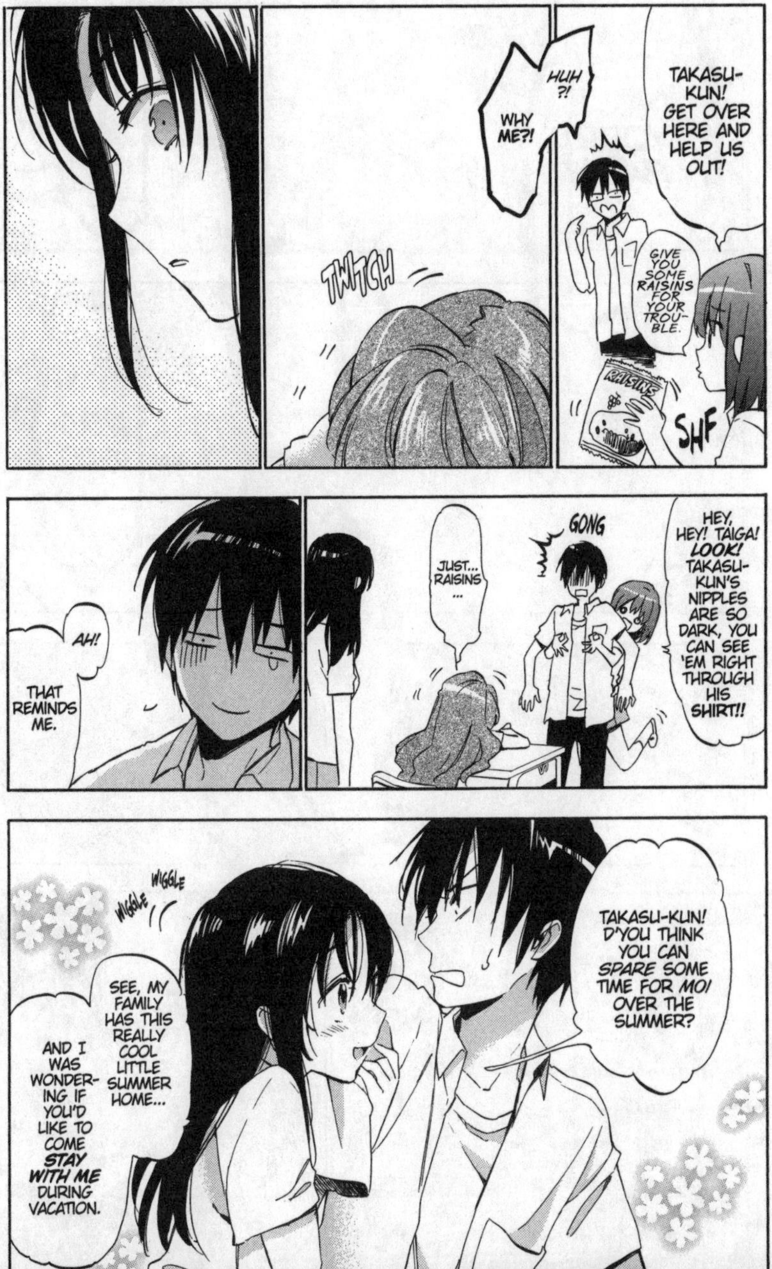
TAKASU-KUN! GET OVER HERE AND HELP US OUT!
GIVE YOU SOME RAISINS FOR YOUR TROUBLE.
RAISINS
SHF
HUH?! WHY ME?!
TWITCH
HEY, HEY! TAIGA! *LOOK!* TAKASU-KUN'S NIPPLES ARE SO DARK, YOU CAN SEE 'EM RIGHT THROUGH HIS SHIRT!!
GONG
JUST... RAISINS...
AH!
THAT REMINDS ME.
TAKASU-KUN! D'YOU THINK YOU CAN *SPARE* SOME TIME FOR *MOI* OVER THE SUMMER?
SEE, MY FAMILY HAS THIS REALLY COOL LITTLE SUMMER HOME...
AND I WAS WONDER-ING IF YOU'D LIKE TO COME **STAY WITH ME** DURING VACATION.
WIGGLE WIGGLE

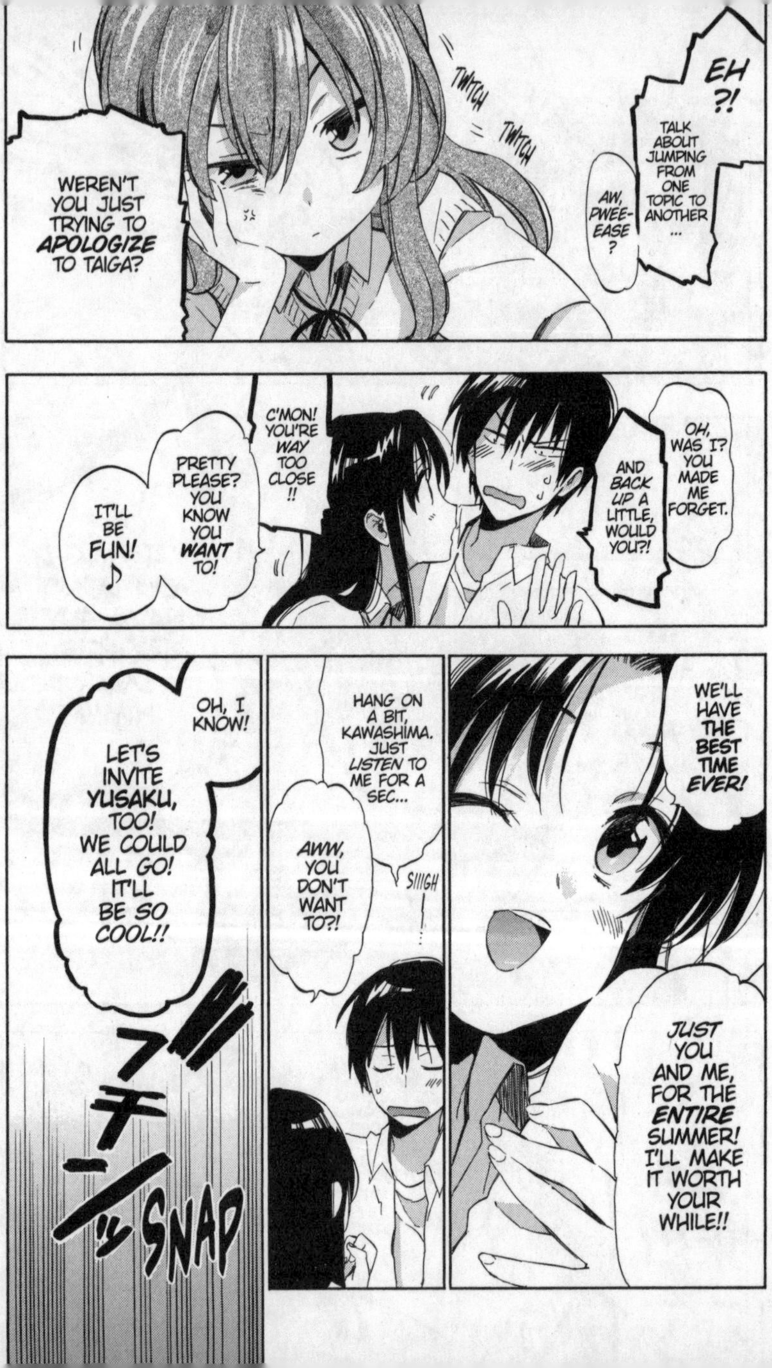
EH ?!
TALK ABOUT JUMPING FROM ONE TOPIC TO ANOTHER ...
AW, PWEE-EASE ?
TWITCH
TWITCH
WEREN'T YOU JUST TRYING TO *APOLOGIZE* TO TAIGA?
OH, WAS I? YOU MADE ME FORGET.
AND *BACK UP* A LITTLE, WOULD YOU?!
C'MON! YOU'RE *WAY* TOO CLOSE !!
PRETTY PLEASE? YOU KNOW YOU *WANT* TO!
IT'LL BE FUN! ♪
WE'LL HAVE THE BEST TIME *EVER!*
JUST YOU AND ME, FOR THE *ENTIRE* SUMMER! I'LL MAKE IT WORTH YOUR WHILE!!
HANG ON A BIT, KAWASHIMA. JUST *LISTEN* TO ME FOR A SEC...
AWW, YOU DON'T WANT TO?!
SIIIGH ...
OH, I KNOW!
LET'S INVITE YUSAKU, TOO! WE COULD ALL GO! IT'LL BE SO *COOL!!*
SNAP

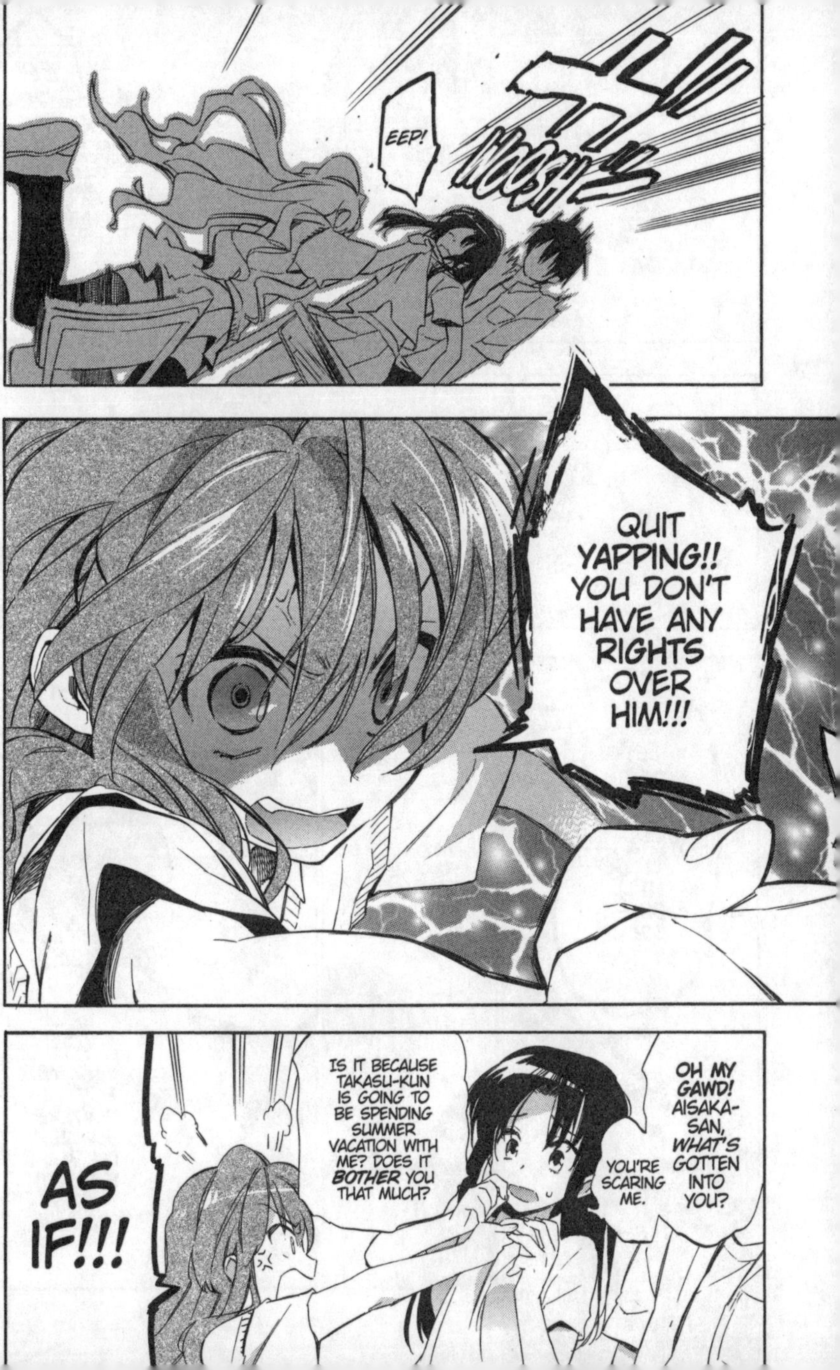
EEP!
WOOSH!
QUIT YAPPING!! YOU DON'T HAVE ANY RIGHTS OVER HIM!!!
OH MY GAWD! AISAKA-SAN, *WHAT'S* GOTTEN INTO YOU?
YOU'RE SCARING ME.
IS IT BECAUSE TAKASU-KUN IS GOING TO BE SPENDING SUMMER VACATION WITH ME? DOES IT ***BOTHER*** YOU THAT MUCH?
AS IF!!!

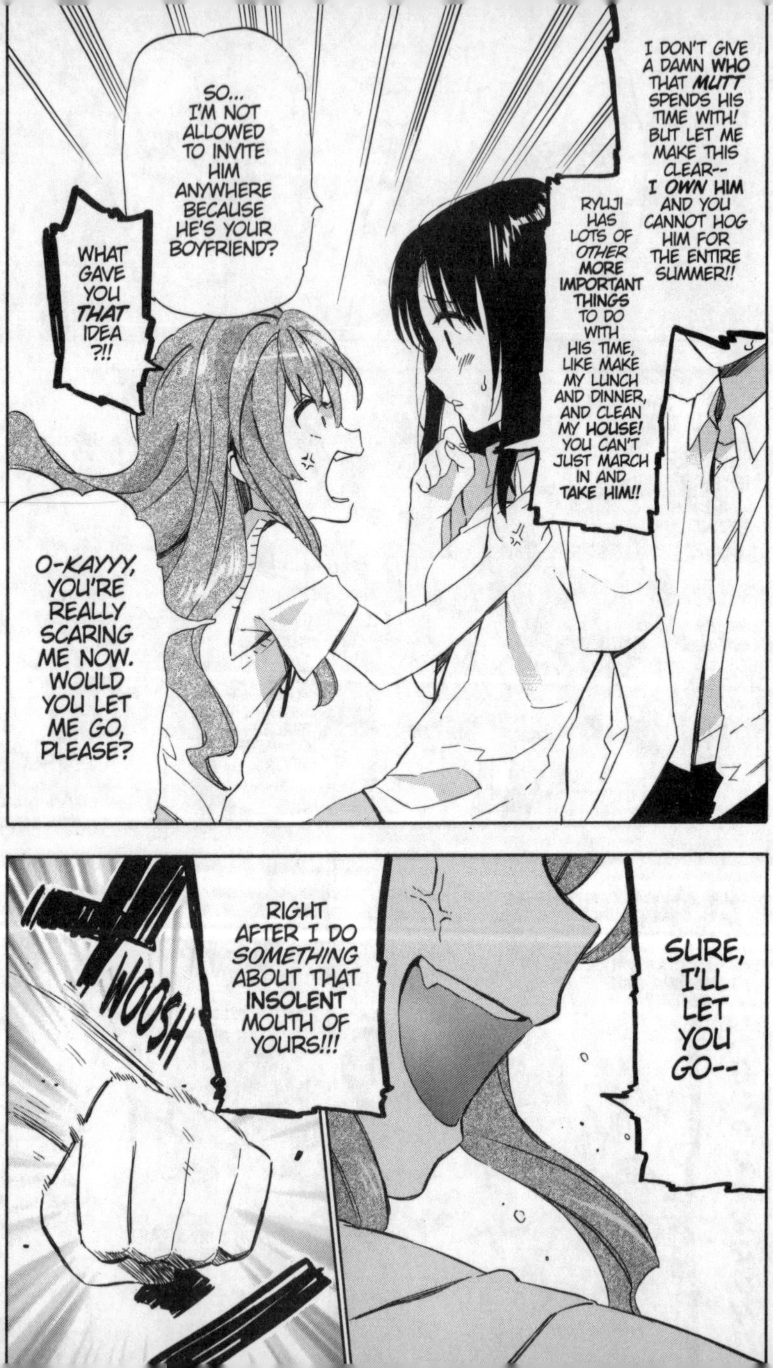
I DON'T GIVE A DAMN WHO THAT MUTT SPENDS HIS TIME WITH! BUT LET ME MAKE THIS CLEAR-- I OWN HIM AND YOU CANNOT HOG HIM FOR THE ENTIRE SUMMER!!
RYUJI HAS LOTS OF OTHER MORE IMPORTANT THINGS TO DO WITH HIS TIME, LIKE MAKE MY LUNCH AND DINNER, AND CLEAN MY HOUSE! YOU CAN'T JUST MARCH IN AND TAKE HIM!!
SO... I'M NOT ALLOWED TO INVITE HIM ANYWHERE BECAUSE HE'S YOUR BOYFRIEND?
WHAT GAVE YOU THAT IDEA?!!
O-KAYYY, YOU'RE REALLY SCARING ME NOW. WOULD YOU LET ME GO, PLEASE?
SURE, I'LL LET YOU GO--
RIGHT AFTER I DO SOMETHING ABOUT THAT INSOLENT MOUTH OF YOURS!!!
WOOSH

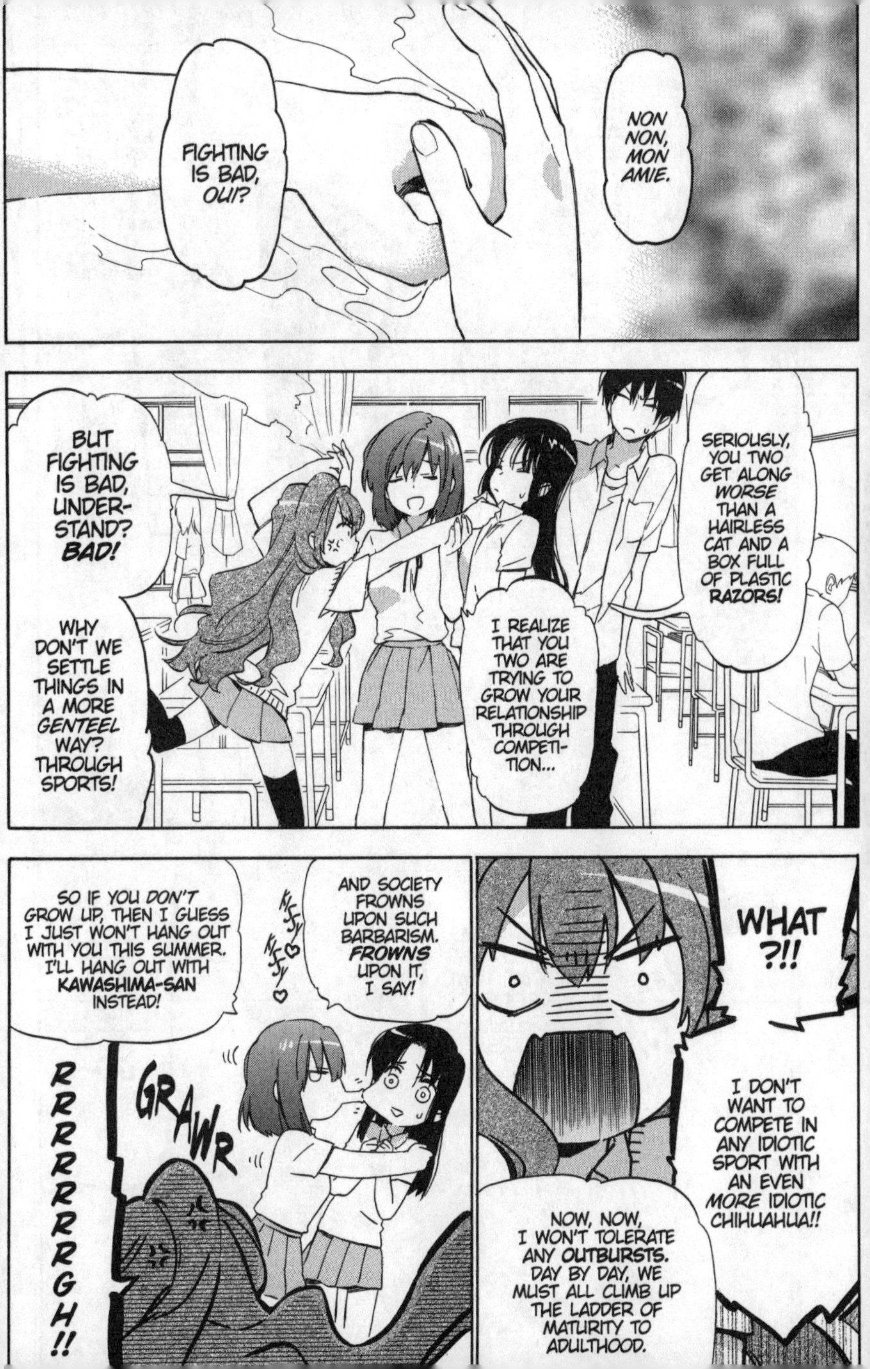
NON NON, MON AMIE.
FIGHTING IS BAD, OUI?
SERIOUSLY, YOU TWO GET ALONG WORSE THAN A HAIRLESS CAT AND A BOX FULL OF PLASTIC RAZORS!
I REALIZE THAT YOU TWO ARE TRYING TO GROW YOUR RELATIONSHIP THROUGH COMPETITION...
BUT FIGHTING IS BAD, UNDERSTAND? BAD!
WHY DON'T WE SETTLE THINGS IN A MORE GENTEEL WAY? THROUGH SPORTS!
WHAT?!!
I DON'T WANT TO COMPETE IN ANY IDIOTIC SPORT WITH AN EVEN MORE IDIOTIC CHIHUAHUA!!
NOW, NOW, I WON'T TOLERATE ANY OUTBURSTS. DAY BY DAY, WE MUST ALL CLIMB UP THE LADDER OF MATURITY TO ADULTHOOD.
AND SOCIETY FROWNS UPON SUCH BARBARISM. FROWNS UPON IT, I SAY!
KISSY KISSY
SO IF YOU DON'T GROW UP, THEN I GUESS I JUST WON'T HANG OUT WITH YOU THIS SUMMER. I'LL HANG OUT WITH KAWASHIMA-SAN INSTEAD!
GRAWR
RRRRRRRGH!!

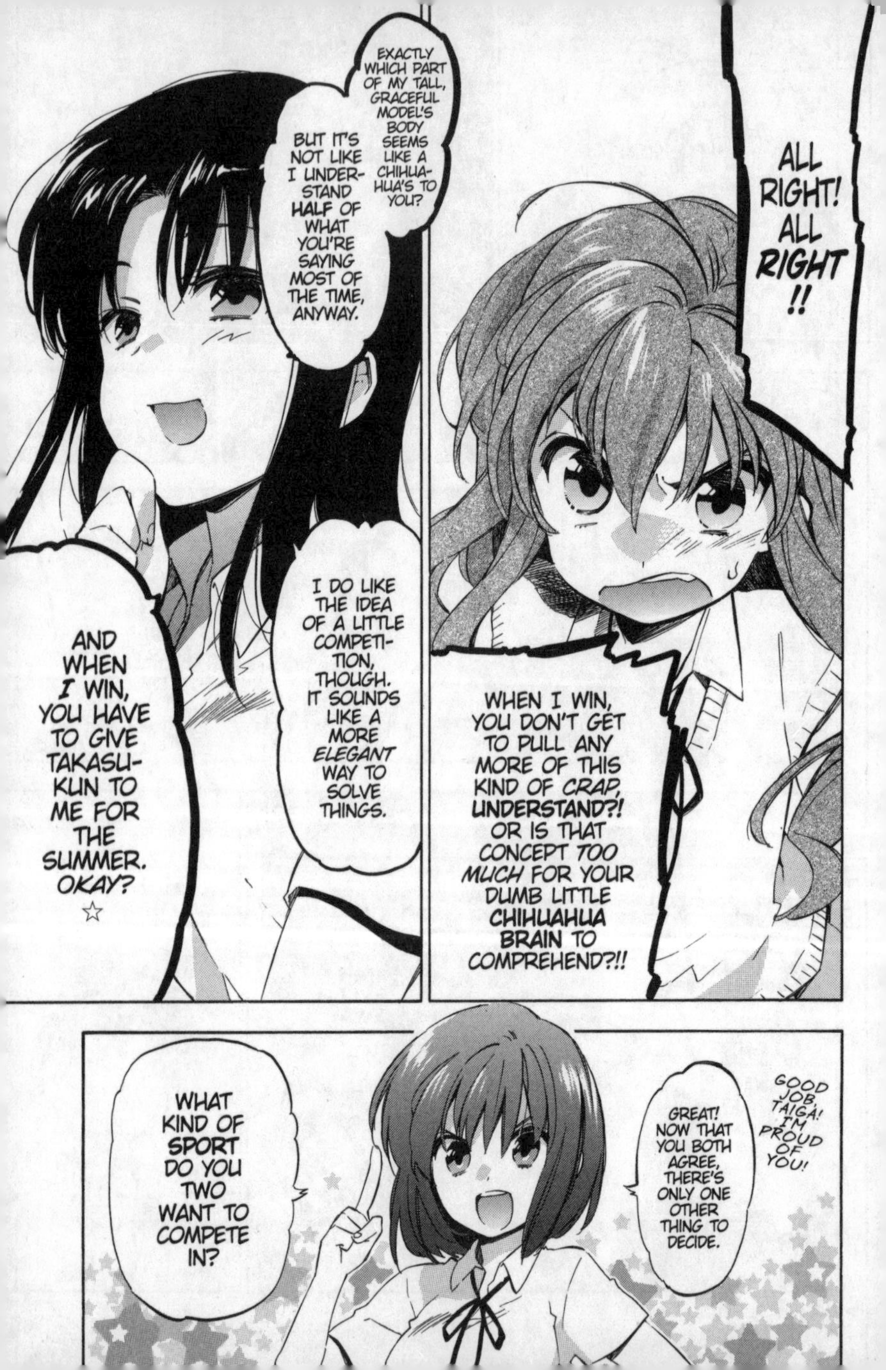
ALL RIGHT! ALL RIGHT!!
WHEN I WIN, YOU DON'T GET TO PULL ANY MORE OF THIS KIND OF CRAP, UNDERSTAND?! OR IS THAT CONCEPT TOO MUCH FOR YOUR DUMB LITTLE CHIHUAHUA BRAIN TO COMPREHEND?!!
EXACTLY WHICH PART OF MY TALL, GRACEFUL MODEL'S BODY SEEMS LIKE A CHIHUAHUA'S TO YOU?
BUT IT'S NOT LIKE I UNDERSTAND HALF OF WHAT YOU'RE SAYING MOST OF THE TIME, ANYWAY.
I DO LIKE THE IDEA OF A LITTLE COMPETITION, THOUGH. IT SOUNDS LIKE A MORE ELEGANT WAY TO SOLVE THINGS.
AND WHEN I WIN, YOU HAVE TO GIVE TAKASU-KUN TO ME FOR THE SUMMER. OKAY? ☆
GOOD JOB, TAIGA! I'M PROUD OF YOU!
GREAT! NOW THAT YOU BOTH AGREE, THERE'S ONLY ONE OTHER THING TO DECIDE.
WHAT KIND OF SPORT DO YOU TWO WANT TO COMPETE IN?

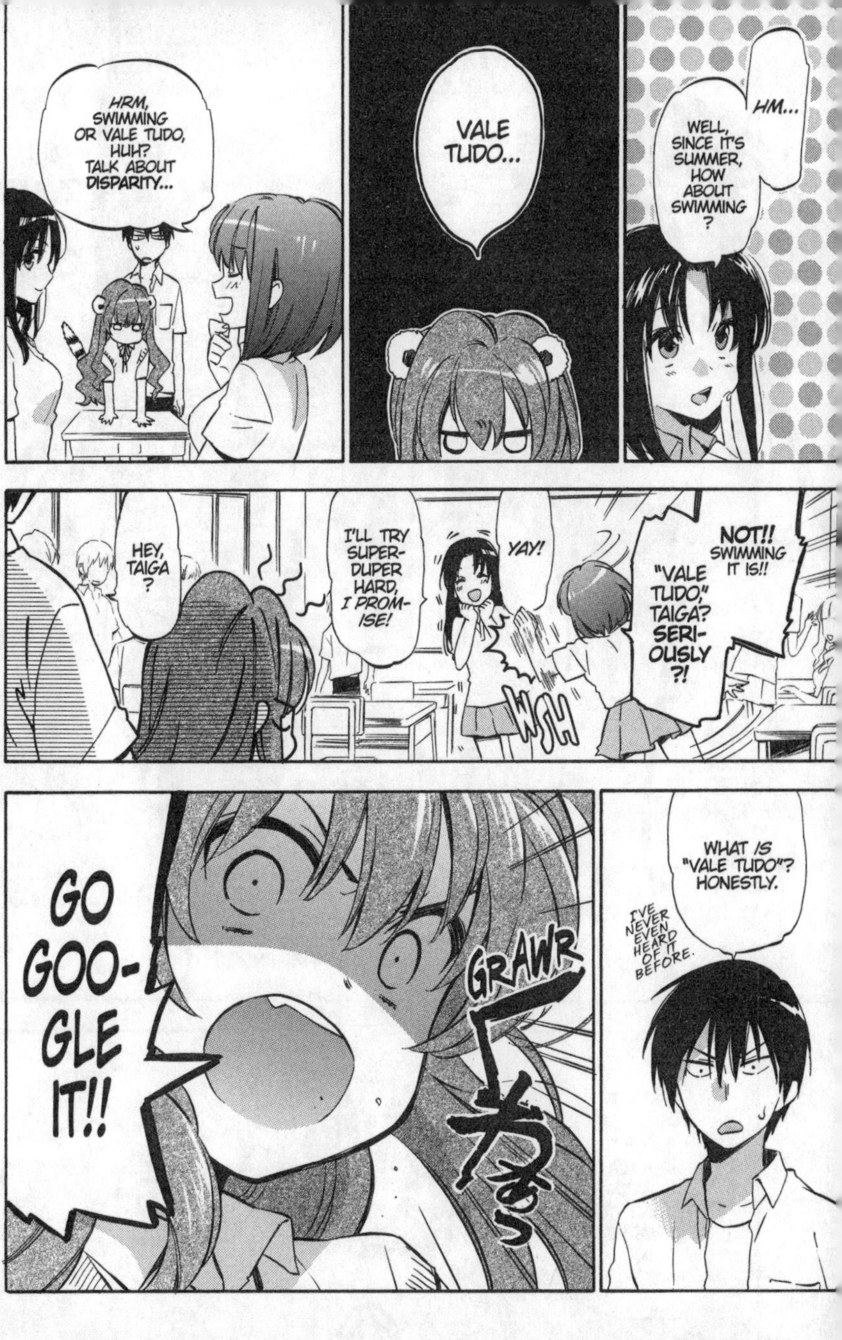

HM...
WELL, SINCE IT'S SUMMER, HOW ABOUT SWIMMING?
VALE TUDO...
HRM, SWIMMING OR VALE TUDO, HUH? TALK ABOUT DISPARITY...
"VALE TUDO," TAIGA? SERIOUSLY?!
NOT!! SWIMMING IT IS!!
WSH
YAY!
I'LL TRY SUPER-DUPER HARD, I PROMISE!
HEY, TAIGA?
WHAT IS "VALE TUDO"? HONESTLY.
I'VE NEVER EVEN HEARD OF IT BEFORE.
GRAWR
GO GOO-GLE IT!!

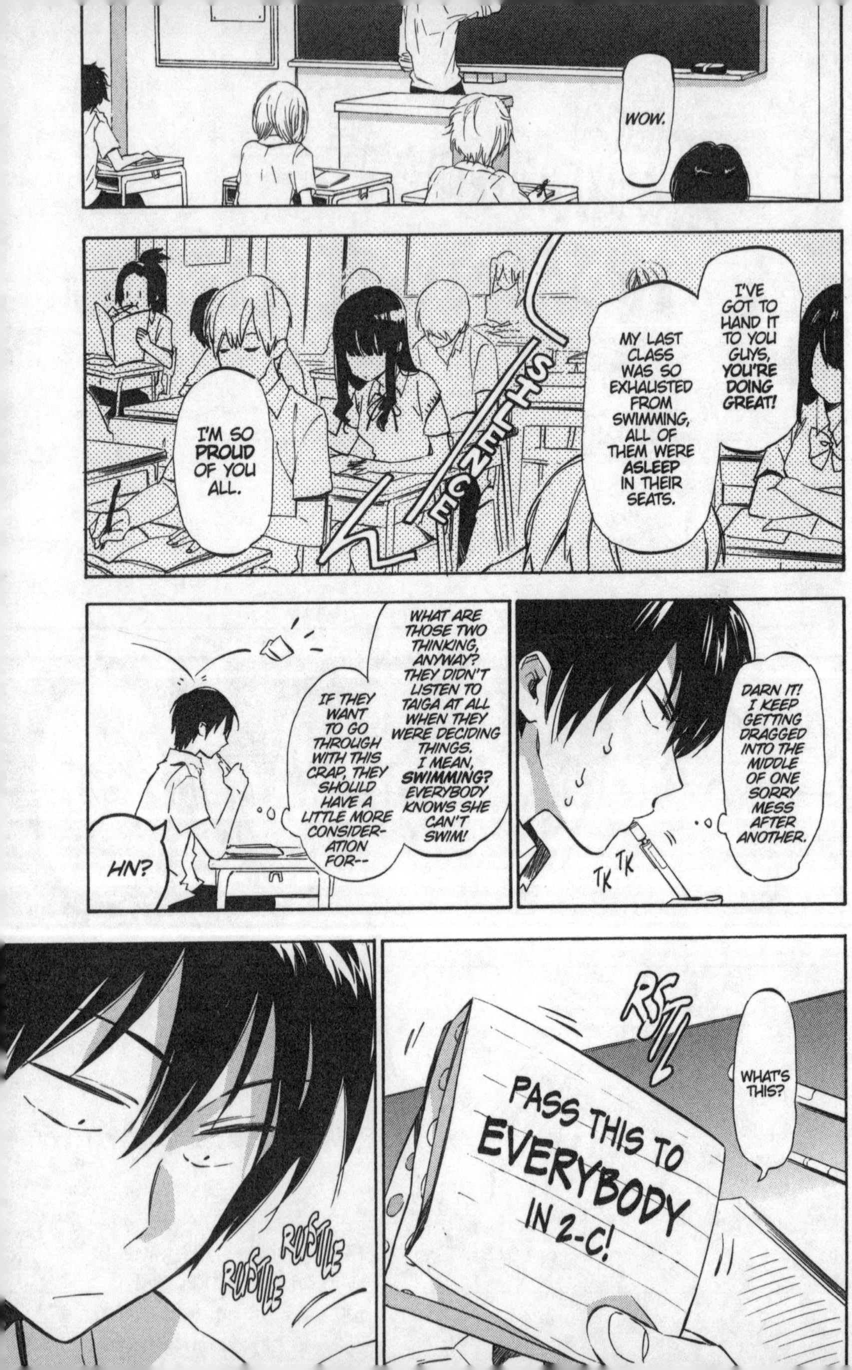
WOW.
I'VE GOT TO HAND IT TO YOU GUYS, YOU'RE DOING GREAT!
MY LAST CLASS WAS SO EXHAUSTED FROM SWIMMING, ALL OF THEM WERE ASLEEP IN THEIR SEATS.
SILENCE
I'M SO PROUD OF YOU ALL.
DARN IT! I KEEP GETTING DRAGGED INTO THE MIDDLE OF ONE SORRY MESS AFTER ANOTHER.
TK TK
WHAT ARE THOSE TWO THINKING, ANYWAY? THEY DIDN'T LISTEN TO TAIGA AT ALL WHEN THEY WERE DECIDING THINGS. I MEAN, SWIMMING? EVERYBODY KNOWS SHE CAN'T SWIM!
IF THEY WANT TO GO THROUGH WITH THIS CRAP, THEY SHOULD HAVE A LITTLE MORE CONSIDER-ATION FOR--
HN?
WHAT'S THIS?
PASS THIS TO EVERYBODY IN 2-C!
RUSTLE
RUSTLE

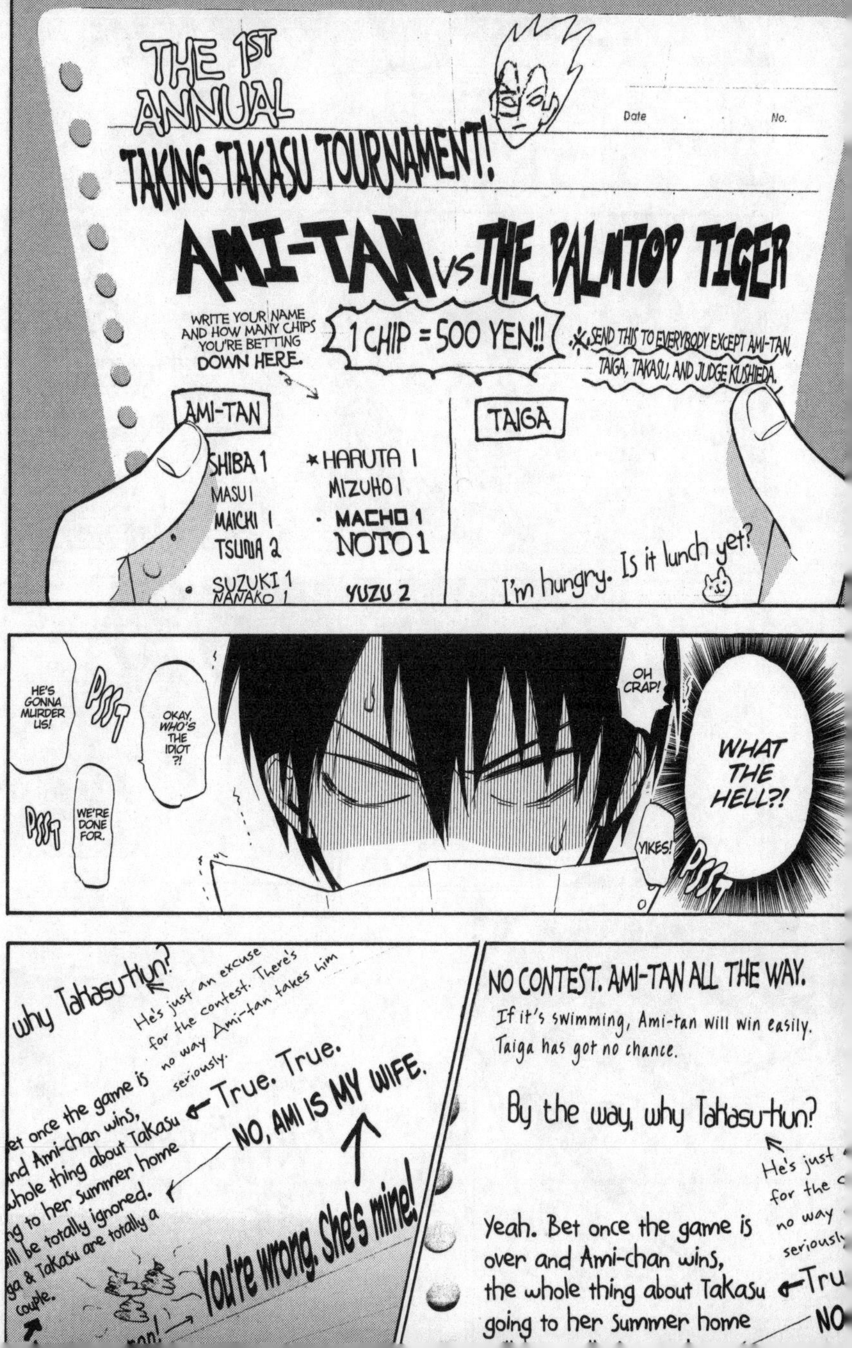
THE 1ST ANNUAL
Date
No.
TAKING TAKASU TOURNAMENT!
AMI-TAN VS THE PALMTOP TIGER
WRITE YOUR NAME AND HOW MANY CHIPS YOU'RE BETTING DOWN HERE.
1 CHIP = 500 YEN!!
※SEND THIS TO EVERYBODY EXCEPT AMI-TAN, TAIGA, TAKASU, AND JUDGE KUSHIEDA.
AMI-TAN
SHIBA 1
MASU 1
MAICHI 1
TSUMA 2
SUZUKI 1
★HARUTA 1
MIZUHO 1
MACHO 1
NOTO 1
YUZU 2
TAIGA
I'm hungry. Is it lunch yet?
WHAT THE HELL?!
OH CRAP!
YIKES!
PSST
OKAY, WHO'S THE IDIOT ?!
PSST
HE'S GONNA MURDER US!
WE'RE DONE FOR.
PSST
NO CONTEST. AMI-TAN ALL THE WAY.
If it's swimming, Ami-tan will win easily. Taiga has got no chance.
By the way, why Takasu-kun?
Yeah. Bet once the game is over and Ami-chan wins, the whole thing about Takasu going to her summer home
why Takasu-kun?
He's just an excuse for the contest. There's no way Ami-tan takes him seriously.
True. True.
NO, AMI IS MY WIFE.
You're wrong. She's mine!

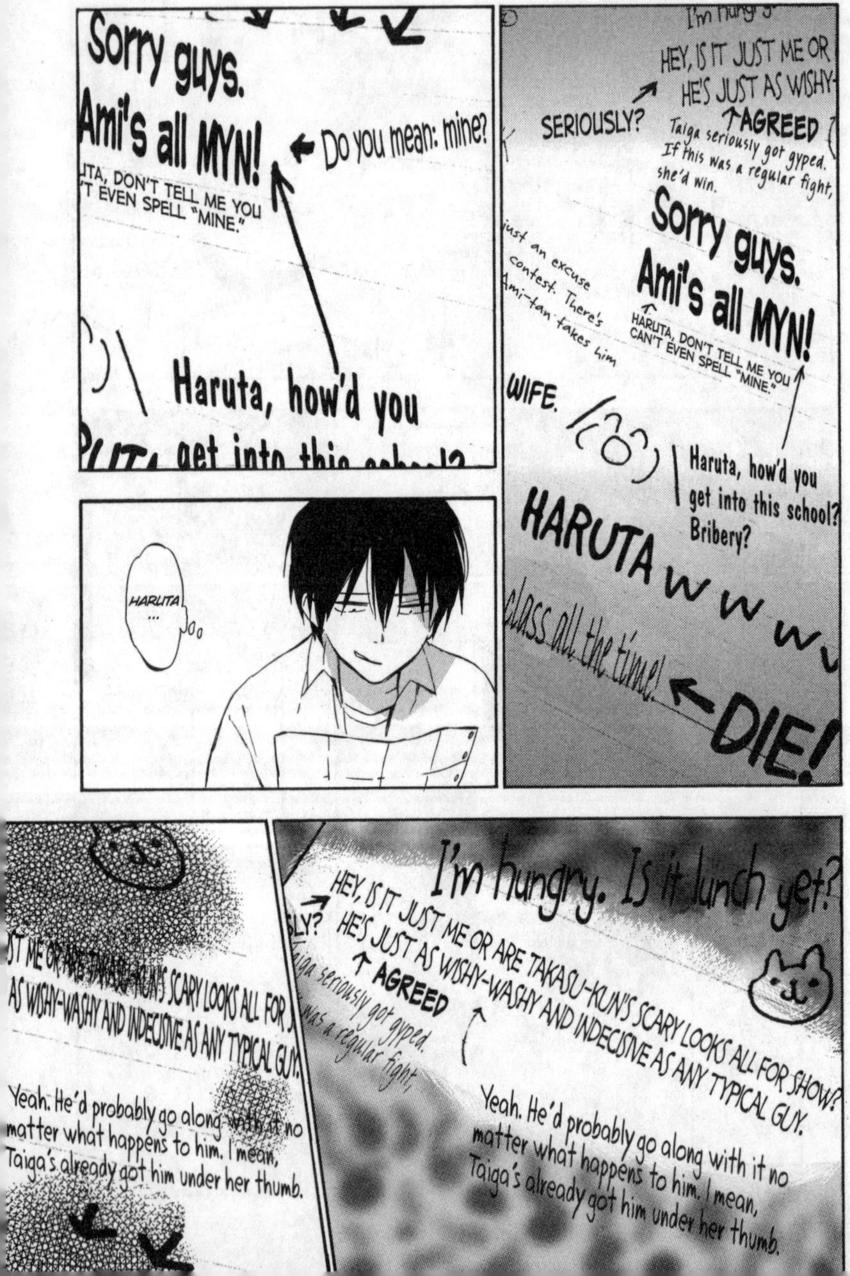
HEY, IS IT JUST ME OR
HE'S JUST AS WISHY-
SERIOUSLY?
AGREED
Taiga seriously got gyped. If this was a regular fight, she'd win.
Sorry guys. Ami's all MYN!
HARUTA, DON'T TELL ME YOU CAN'T EVEN SPELL "MINE."
just an excuse
contest. There's
Ami-tan takes him
WIFE.
Haruta, how'd you get into this school? Bribery?
HARUTA w w w w
class all the time!
DIE!
Sorry guys. Ami's all MYN!
Do you mean: mine?
UTA, DON'T TELL ME YOU
'T EVEN SPELL "MINE."
Haruta, how'd you
HARUTA ...
I'm hungry. Is it lunch yet?
HEY, IS IT JUST ME OR ARE TAKASU-KUN'S SCARY LOOKS ALL FOR SHOW? HE'S JUST AS WISHY-WASHY AND INDECISIVE AS ANY TYPICAL GUY.
AGREED
Taiga seriously got gyped.
was a regular fight,
Yeah. He'd probably go along with it no matter what happens to him. I mean, Taiga's already got him under her thumb.
ST ME OR ARE TAKASU-KUN'S SCARY LOOKS ALL FOR
AS WISHY-WASHY AND INDECISIVE AS ANY TYPICAL GUY.
Yeah. He'd probably go along with it no matter what happens to him. I mean, Taiga's already got him under her thumb.

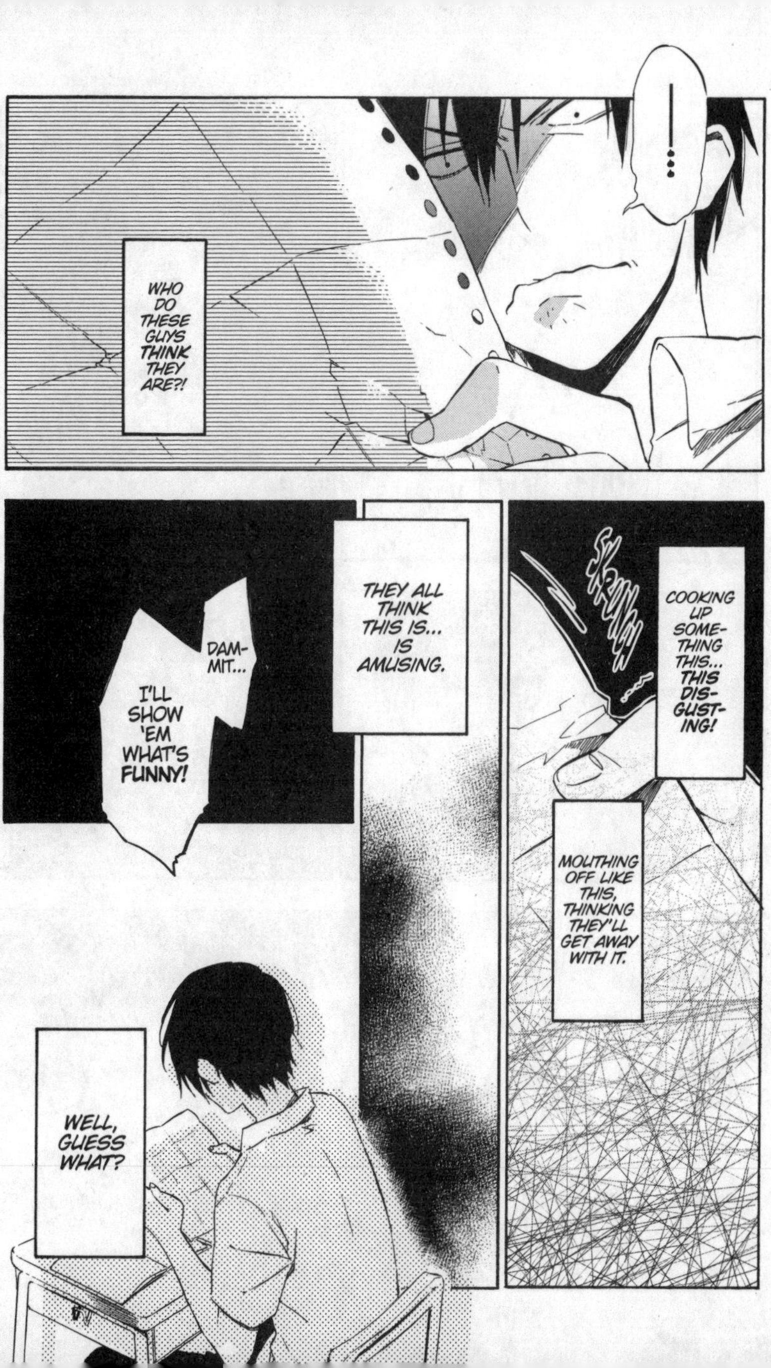
!...
WHO DO THESE GUYS THINK THEY ARE?!
COOKING UP SOMETHING THIS... THIS DISGUSTING!
MOUTHING OFF LIKE THIS, THINKING THEY'LL GET AWAY WITH IT.
THEY ALL THINK THIS IS... IS AMUSING.
DAMMIT...
I'LL SHOW 'EM WHAT'S FUNNY!
WELL, GUESS WHAT?

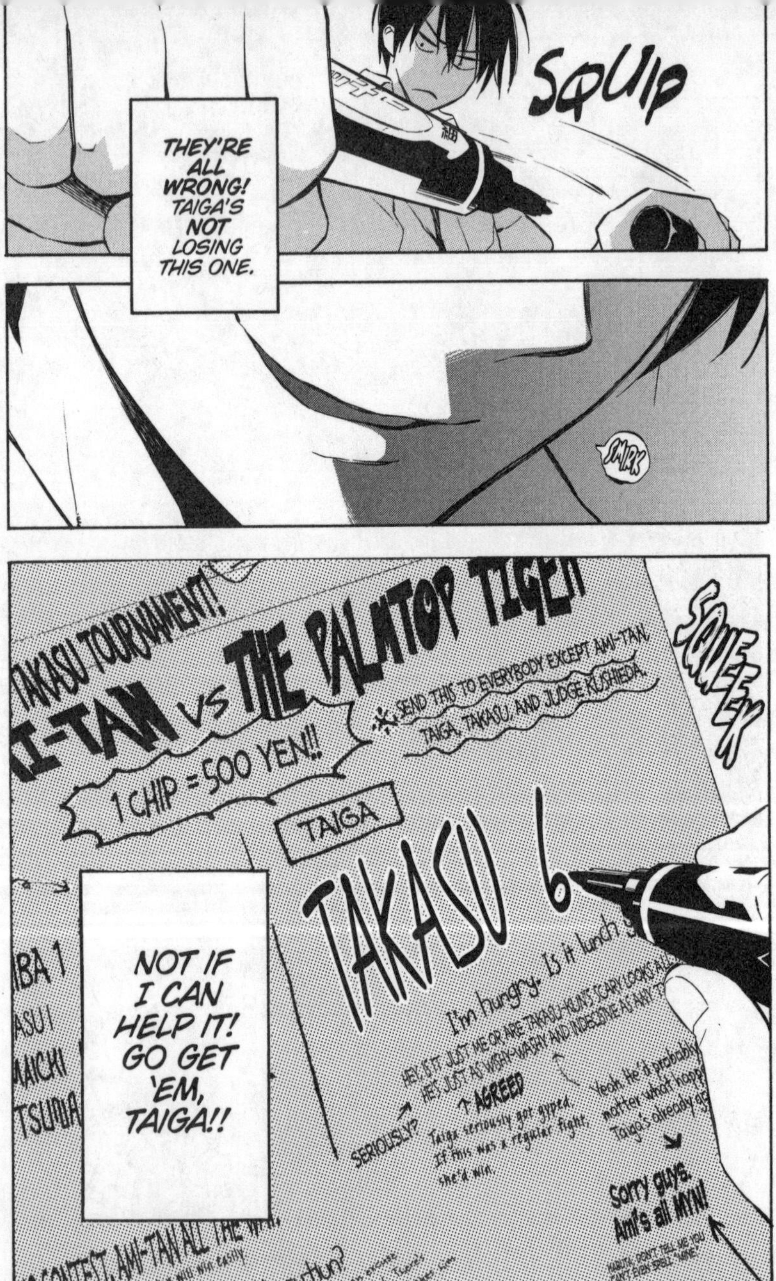
SQUIP
THEY'RE ALL WRONG! TAIGA'S NOT LOSING THIS ONE.
SMIRK
SQUEEEK
TAKASU TOURNAMENT!
THE PALMTOP TIGER
※ SEND THIS TO EVERYBODY EXCEPT AMI-TAN, TAIGA, TAKASU, AND JUDGE KUSHIEDA.
1 CHIP = 500 YEN!!
TAIGA
TAKASU 6
AGREED
SERIOUSLY?
Taiga seriously got gyped. If this was a regular fight, she'd win.
Sorry guys. Ami's all MYN!
HARUTA, DON'T TELL ME YOU CAN'T EVEN SPELL "MINE."
NOT IF I CAN HELP IT! GO GET 'EM, TAIGA!!

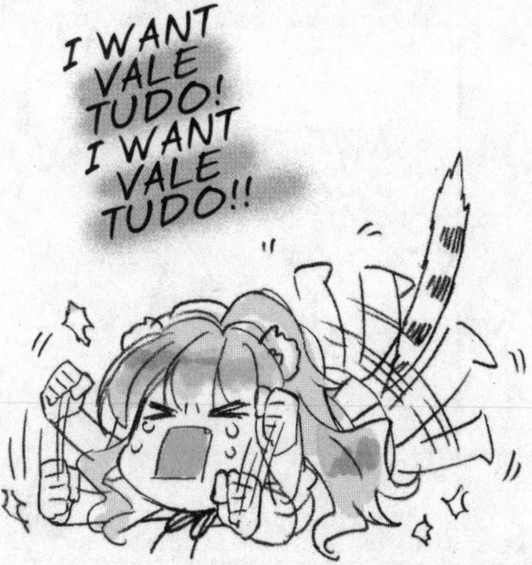
I WANT VALE TUDO! I WANT VALE TUDO!!

Chapter 30 THE DOG'S MASK

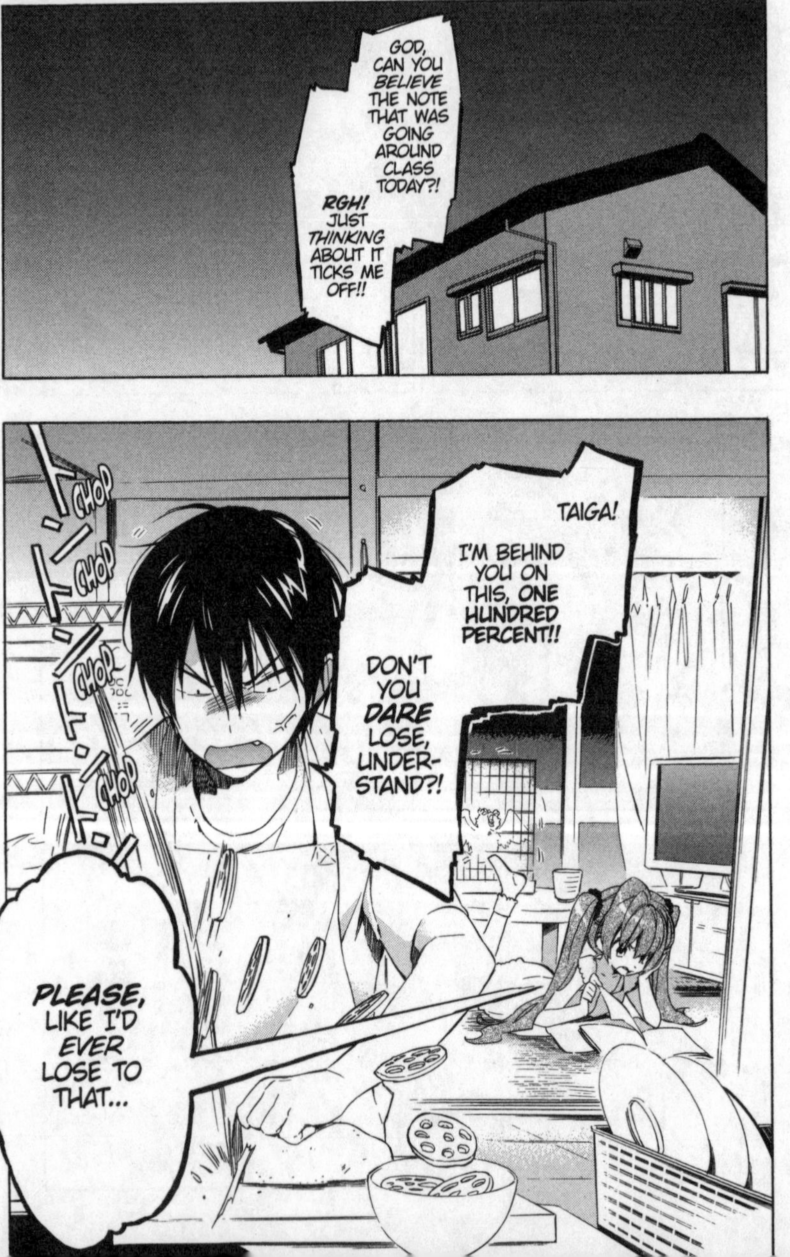
GOD, CAN YOU BELIEVE THE NOTE THAT WAS GOING AROUND CLASS TODAY?!
RGH! JUST THINKING ABOUT IT TICKS ME OFF!!
TAIGA!
I'M BEHIND YOU ON THIS, ONE HUNDRED PERCENT!!
DON'T YOU DARE LOSE, UNDER-STAND?!
CHOP
CHOP
CHOP
CHOP
PLEASE, LIKE I'D EVER LOSE TO THAT...

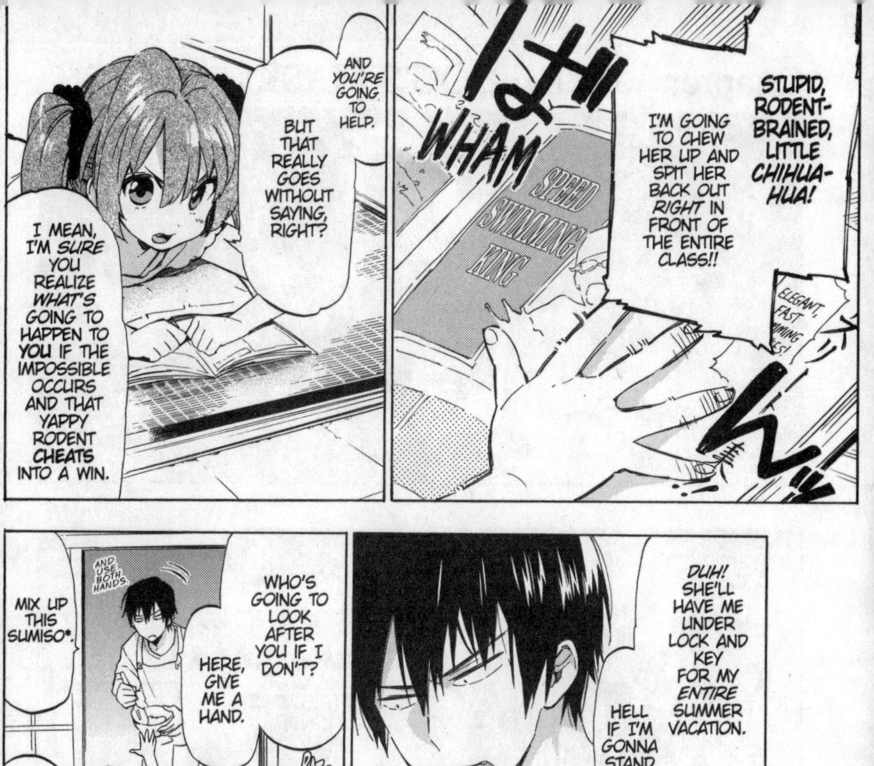
WHAM
STUPID, RODENT-BRAINED, LITTLE CHIHUAHUA!
I'M GOING TO CHEW HER UP AND SPIT HER BACK OUT RIGHT IN FRONT OF THE ENTIRE CLASS!!
SPEED SWIMMING KING
AND YOU'RE GOING TO HELP.
BUT THAT REALLY GOES WITHOUT SAYING, RIGHT?
I MEAN, I'M SURE YOU REALIZE WHAT'S GOING TO HAPPEN TO YOU IF THE IMPOSSIBLE OCCURS AND THAT YAPPY RODENT CHEATS INTO A WIN.
DUH! SHE'LL HAVE ME UNDER LOCK AND KEY FOR MY ENTIRE SUMMER VACATION.
HELL IF I'M GONNA STAND FOR THAT!
WHO'S GOING TO LOOK AFTER YOU IF I DON'T?
AND USE BOTH HANDS.
HERE, GIVE ME A HAND.
MIX UP THIS SUMISO*.
RATTLE RATTLE
WHAT WILL IT BE MIXED WITH?

*Sumiso is a type of dressing primarily made of miso paste mixed with vinegar.

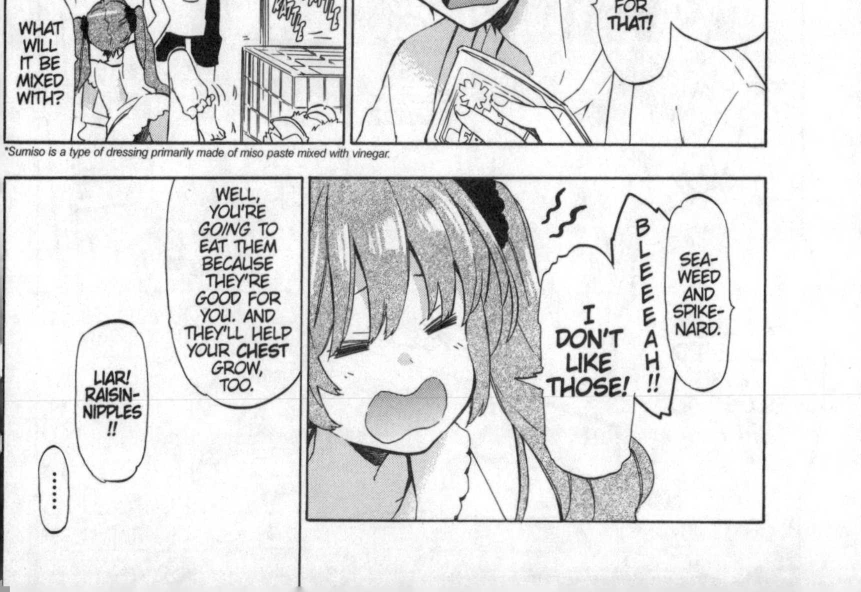
SEA-WEED AND SPIKE-NARD.
BLEEEAH!!
I DON'T LIKE THOSE!
WELL, YOU'RE GOING TO EAT THEM BECAUSE THEY'RE GOOD FOR YOU. AND THEY'LL HELP YOUR CHEST GROW, TOO.
LIAR! RAISIN-NIPPLES!!
……

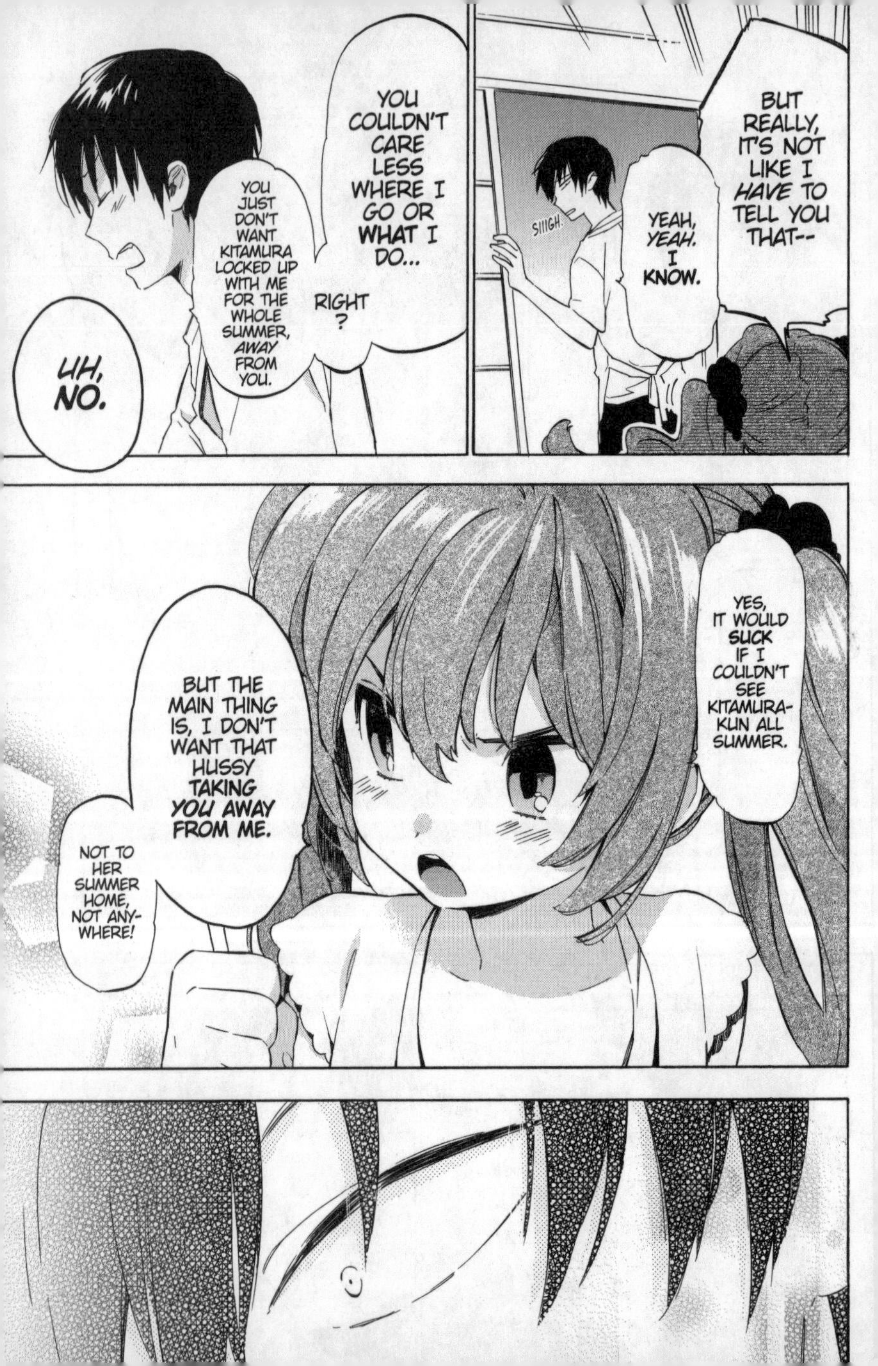
BUT REALLY, IT'S NOT LIKE I *HAVE* TO TELL YOU THAT--
YEAH, YEAH. I KNOW.
SIIIGH.
YOU COULDN'T CARE LESS WHERE I GO OR WHAT I DO...
RIGHT?
YOU JUST DON'T WANT KITAMURA LOCKED UP WITH ME FOR THE WHOLE SUMMER, *AWAY* FROM YOU.
UH, NO.
YES, IT WOULD **SUCK** IF I COULDN'T SEE KITAMURA-KUN ALL SUMMER.
BUT THE MAIN THING IS, I DON'T WANT THAT HUSSY **TAKING *YOU* AWAY FROM ME.**
NOT TO HER SUMMER HOME, NOT ANYWHERE!

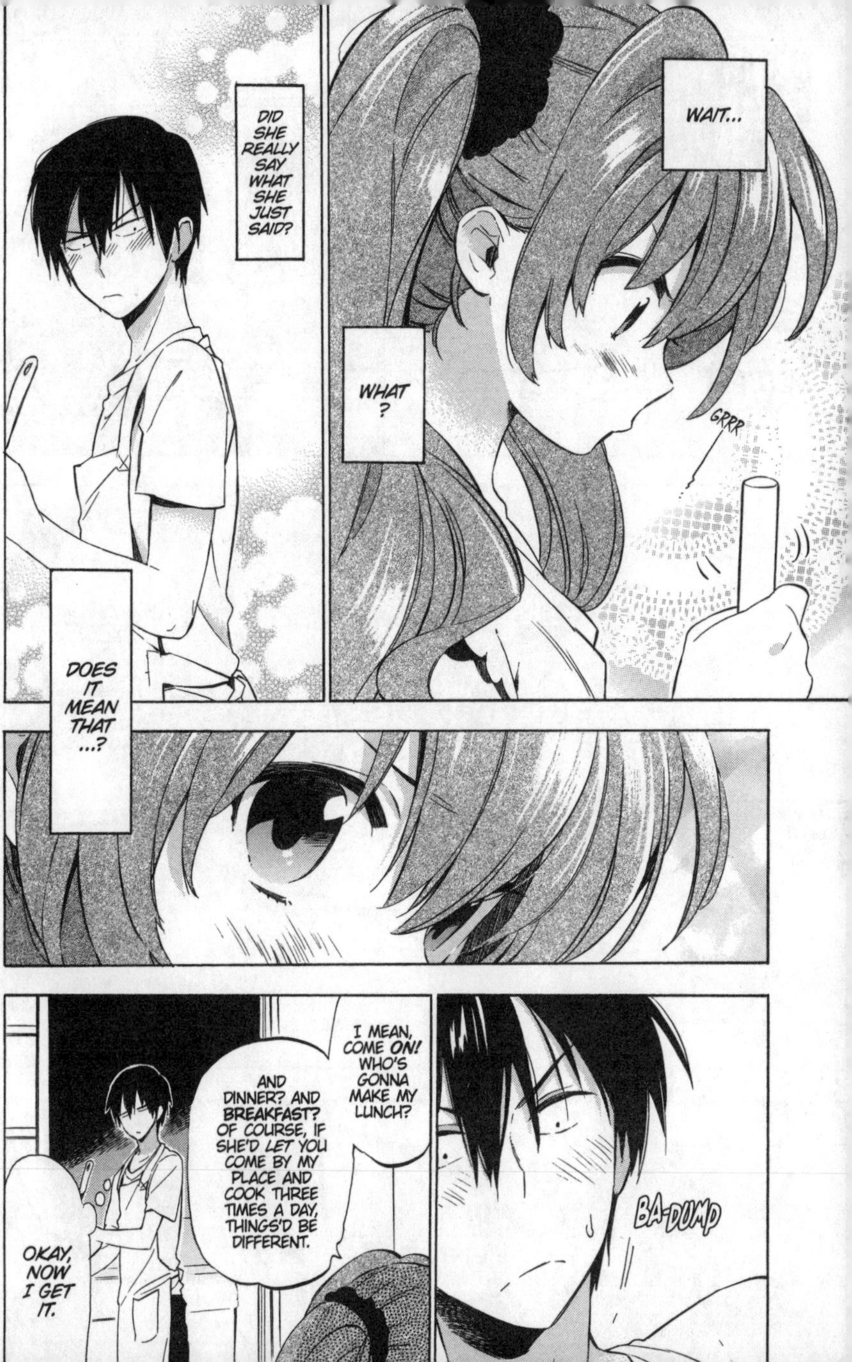
WAIT...
WHAT ?
GRRR
DID SHE REALLY SAY WHAT SHE JUST SAID?
DOES IT MEAN THAT ...?
BA-DUMP
I MEAN, COME **ON**! WHO'S GONNA MAKE MY LUNCH?
AND DINNER? AND **BREAKFAST**? OF COURSE, IF SHE'D *LET* YOU COME BY MY PLACE AND COOK THREE TIMES A DAY, THINGS'D BE DIFFERENT.
OKAY, NOW I GET IT.

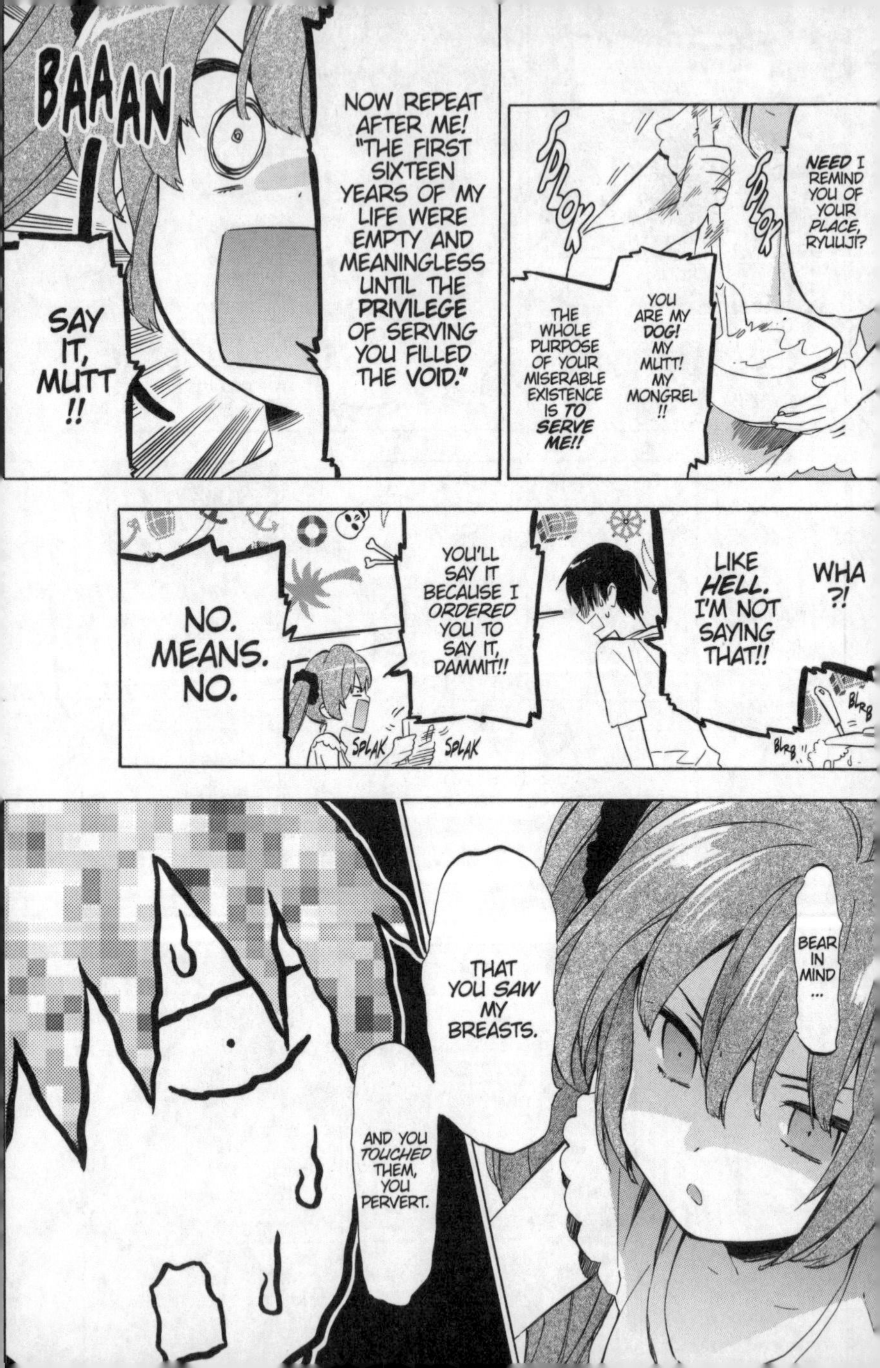
NEED I REMIND YOU OF YOUR PLACE, RYUUJI?
PLOK
PLOK
YOU ARE MY DOG! MY MUTT! MY MONGREL!!
THE WHOLE PURPOSE OF YOUR MISERABLE EXISTENCE IS TO SERVE ME!!
NOW REPEAT AFTER ME! "THE FIRST SIXTEEN YEARS OF MY LIFE WERE EMPTY AND MEANINGLESS UNTIL THE PRIVILEGE OF SERVING YOU FILLED THE VOID."
BAAAN
SAY IT, MUTT!!
WHA?!
LIKE HELL. I'M NOT SAYING THAT!!
BLRB
BLRB
YOU'LL SAY IT BECAUSE I ORDERED YOU TO SAY IT, DAMMIT!!
SPLAK
SPLAK
NO. MEANS. NO.
BEAR IN MIND...
THAT YOU SAW MY BREASTS.
AND YOU TOUCHED THEM, YOU PERVERT.

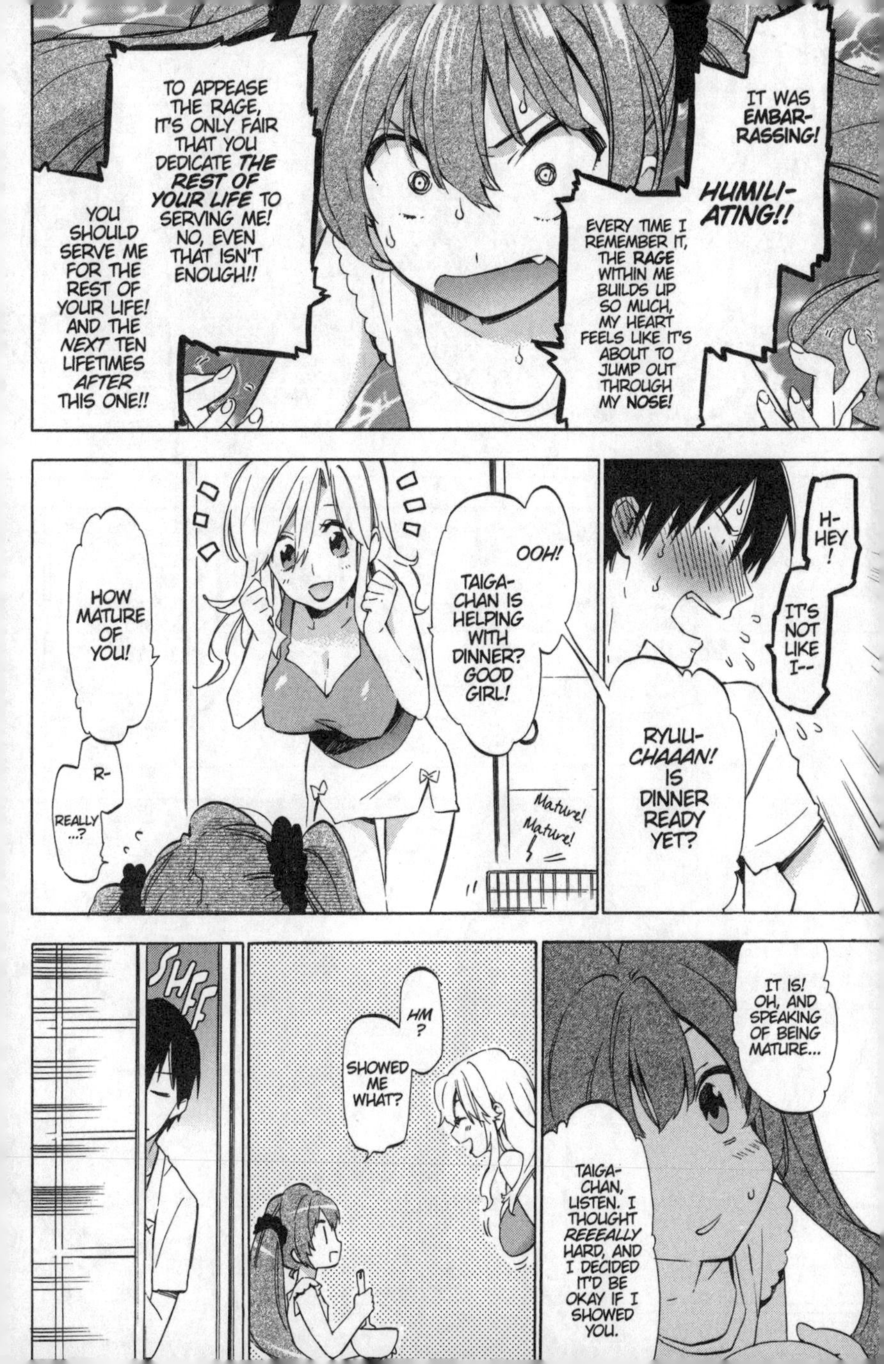
IT WAS EMBARRASSING!
HUMILIATING!!
EVERY TIME I REMEMBER IT, THE RAGE WITHIN ME BUILDS UP SO MUCH, MY HEART FEELS LIKE IT'S ABOUT TO JUMP OUT THROUGH MY NOSE!
TO APPEASE THE RAGE, IT'S ONLY FAIR THAT YOU DEDICATE THE REST OF YOUR LIFE TO SERVING ME! NO, EVEN THAT ISN'T ENOUGH!!
YOU SHOULD SERVE ME FOR THE REST OF YOUR LIFE! AND THE NEXT TEN LIFETIMES AFTER THIS ONE!!
H-HEY!
IT'S NOT LIKE I--
RYUU-CHAAAN! IS DINNER READY YET?
OOH!
TAIGA-CHAN IS HELPING WITH DINNER? GOOD GIRL!
Mature! Mature!
HOW MATURE OF YOU!
R-REALLY ...?
IT IS! OH, AND SPEAKING OF BEING MATURE...
TAIGA-CHAN, LISTEN. I THOUGHT REEEALLY HARD, AND I DECIDED IT'D BE OKAY IF I SHOWED YOU.
HM?
SHOWED ME WHAT?
SHFF

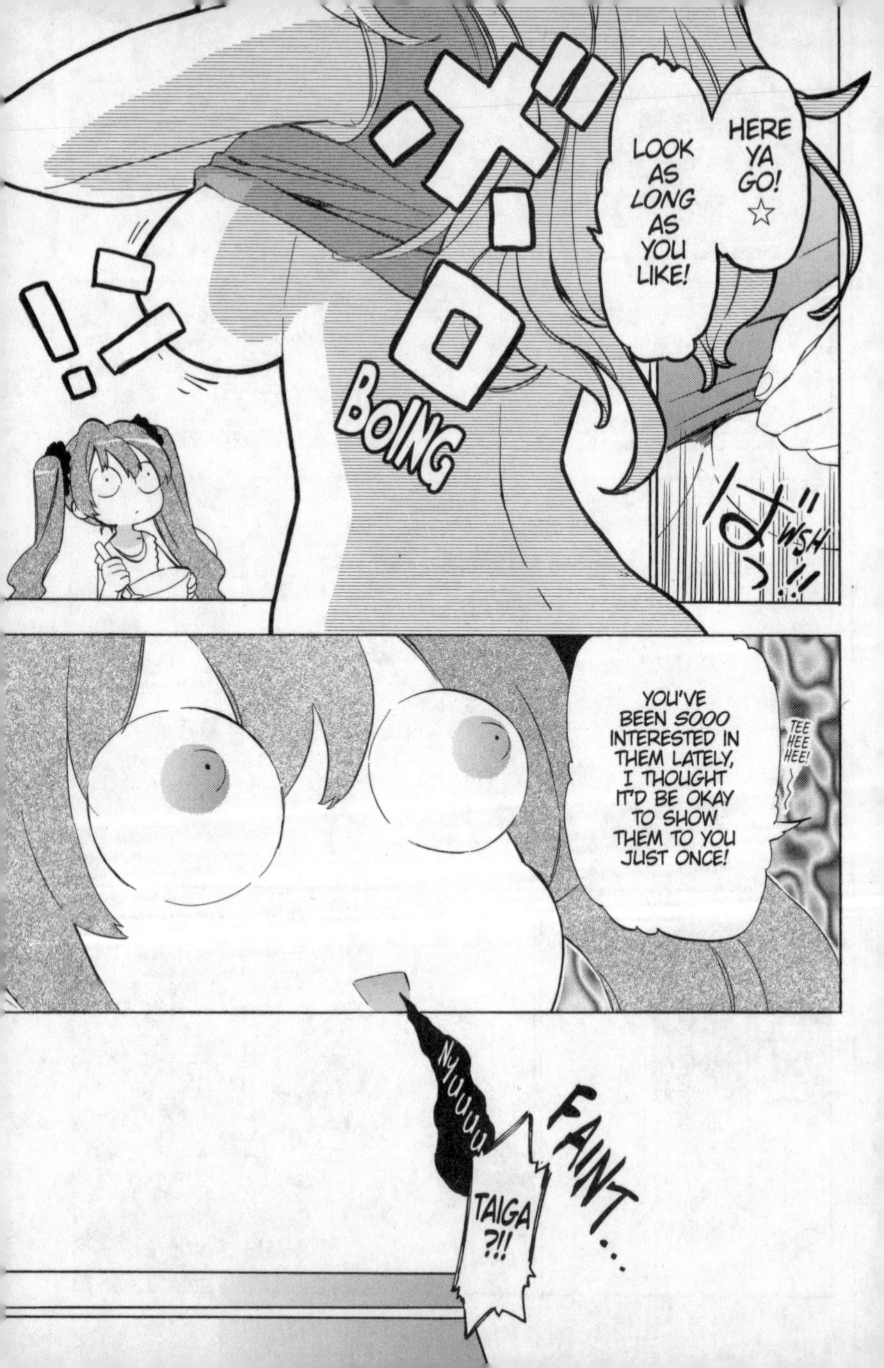
HERE YA GO! ☆
LOOK AS LONG AS YOU LIKE!
BOING
WSH
TEE HEE HEE!
YOU'VE BEEN SOOO INTERESTED IN THEM LATELY, I THOUGHT IT'D BE OKAY TO SHOW THEM TO YOU JUST ONCE!
FAINT...
TAIGA?!!
NYUUUU

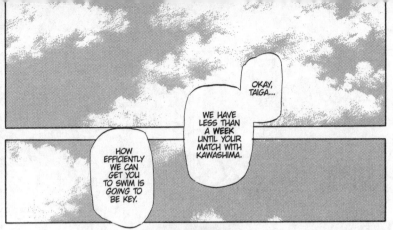

OKAY, TAIGA...

WE HAVE LESS THAN A WEEK UNTIL YOUR MATCH WITH KAWASHIMA.

HOW EFFICIENTLY WE CAN GET YOU TO SWIM IS GOING TO BE KEY.

SO LET'S KEEP IT EASY AT FIRST, OKAY?

WE'LL START BY PRACTICING YOUR PUSH OFF THE WALL.

RYUUJI.

YEAH?

AND...?

OF COURSE.

IF I'M GOING TO PUSH OFF THE WALL, THAT MEANS I'M GOING TO HAVE TO LET GO OF IT FIRST, RIGHT?

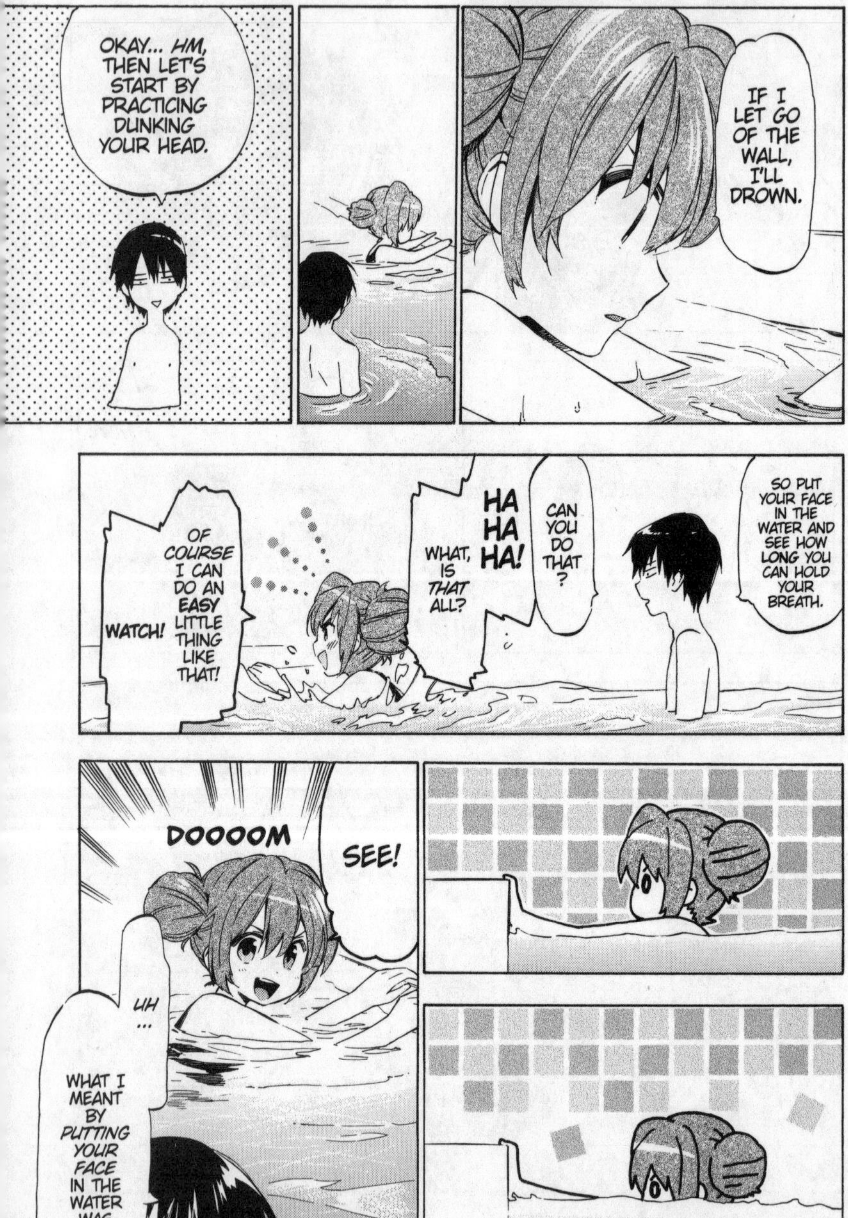
IF I LET GO OF THE WALL, I'LL DROWN.
OKAY... HM, THEN LET'S START BY PRACTICING DUNKING YOUR HEAD.
SO PUT YOUR FACE IN THE WATER AND SEE HOW LONG YOU CAN HOLD YOUR BREATH.
CAN YOU DO THAT?
HA HA HA!
WHAT, IS THAT ALL?
OF COURSE I CAN DO AN EASY LITTLE THING LIKE THAT!
WATCH!
DOOOOM
SEE!
UH ...
WHAT I MEANT BY PUTTING YOUR FACE IN THE WATER WAS THIS...

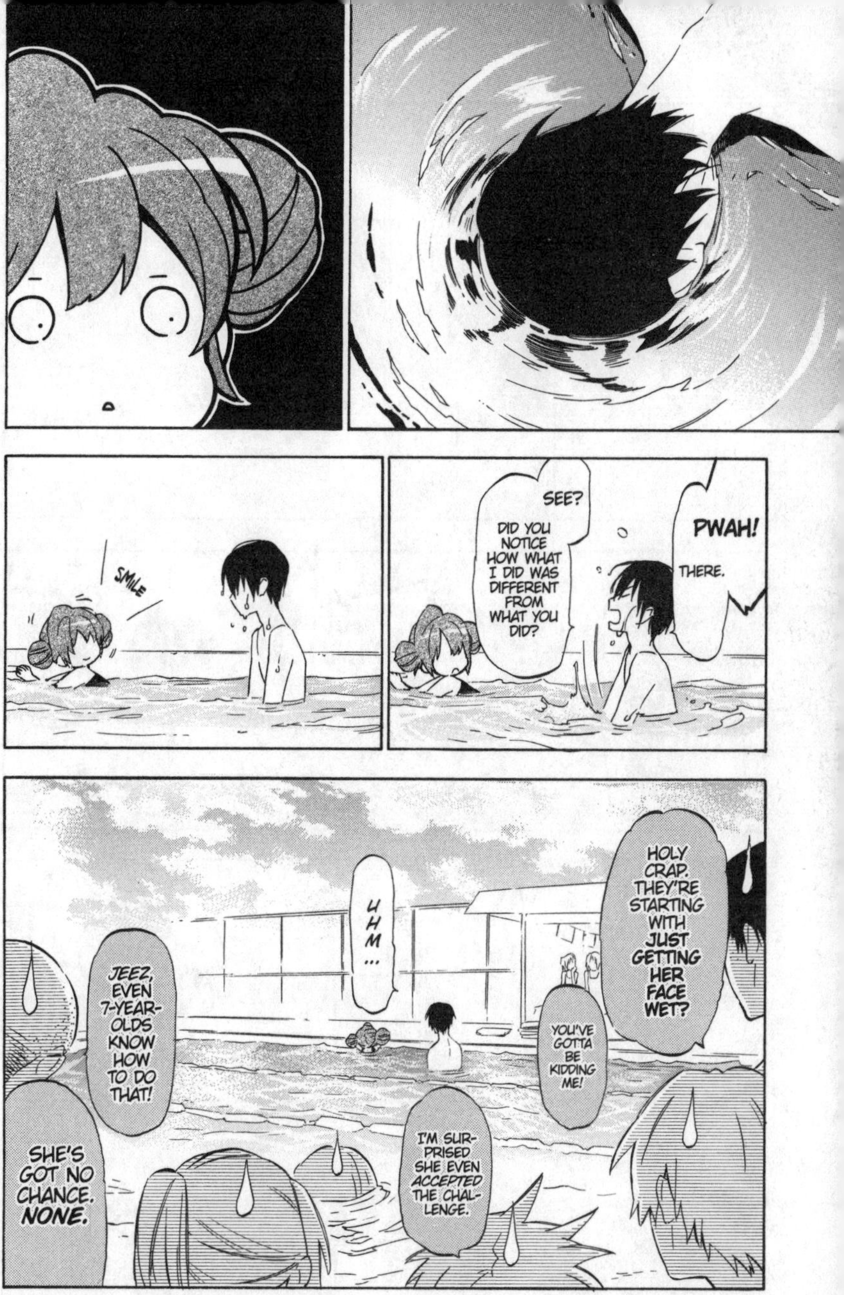
PWAH!
THERE.
SEE?
DID YOU NOTICE HOW WHAT I DID WAS DIFFERENT FROM WHAT YOU DID?
SMILE
HOLY CRAP. THEY'RE STARTING WITH **JUST GETTING HER FACE WET?**
YOU'VE GOTTA BE KIDDING ME!
UHM...
JEEZ, EVEN 7-YEAR-OLDS KNOW HOW TO DO THAT!
I'M SURPRISED SHE EVEN *ACCEPTED* THE CHALLENGE.
SHE'S GOT NO CHANCE. ***NONE.***

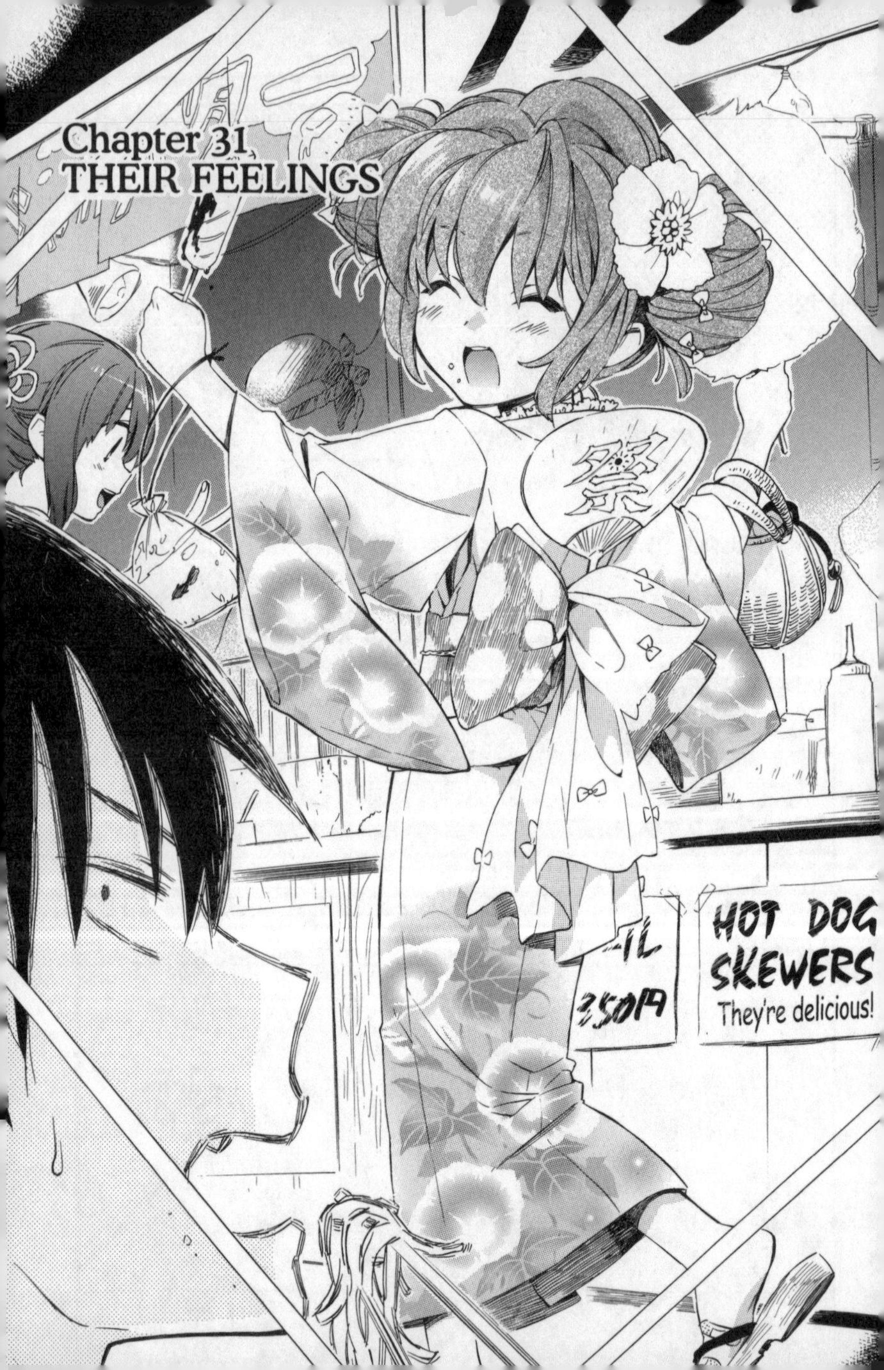
Chapter 31
THEIR FEELINGS
HOT DOG SKEWERS
They're delicious!

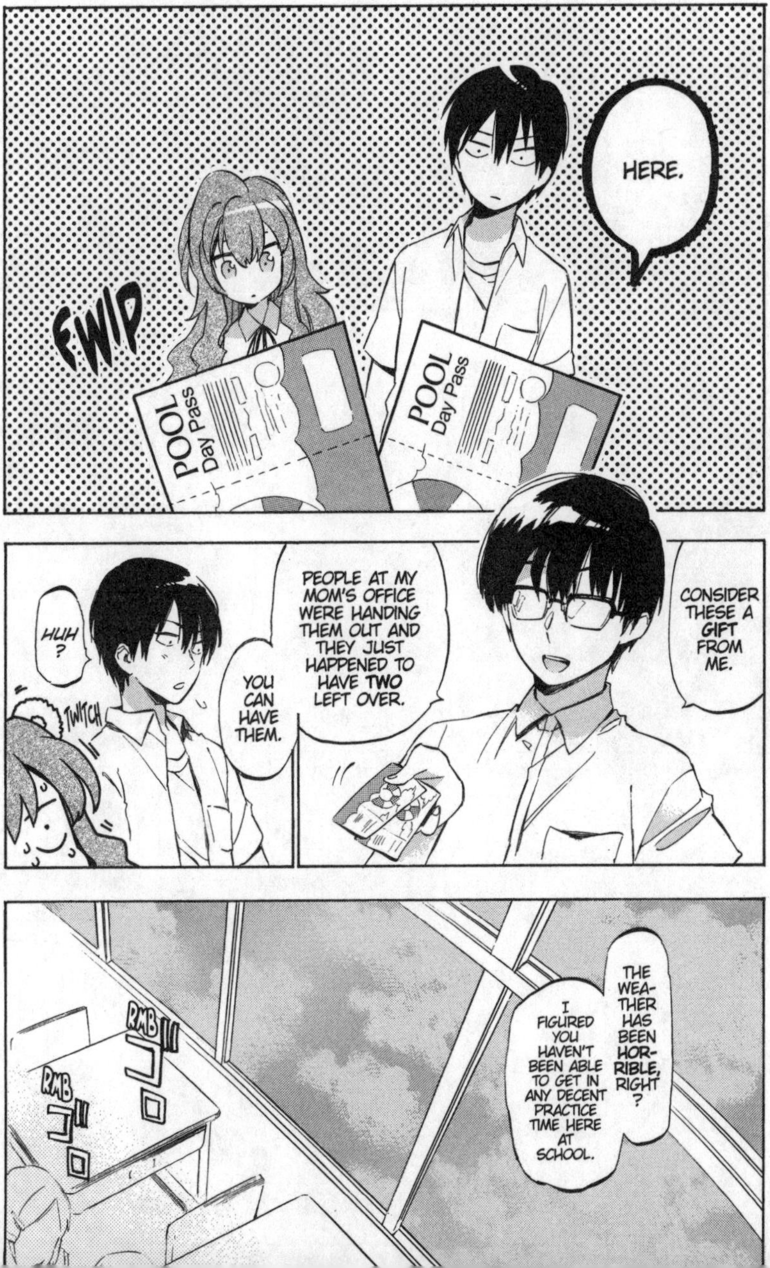
HERE.
POOL Day Pass
POOL Day Pass
FWIP
CONSIDER THESE A GIFT FROM ME.
PEOPLE AT MY MOM'S OFFICE WERE HANDING THEM OUT AND THEY JUST HAPPENED TO HAVE TWO LEFT OVER.
YOU CAN HAVE THEM.
HUH?
TWITCH
THE WEATHER HAS BEEN HORRIBLE, RIGHT?
I FIGURED YOU HAVEN'T BEEN ABLE TO GET IN ANY DECENT PRACTICE TIME HERE AT SCHOOL.
RMB
ゴロ
RMB
ゴロ

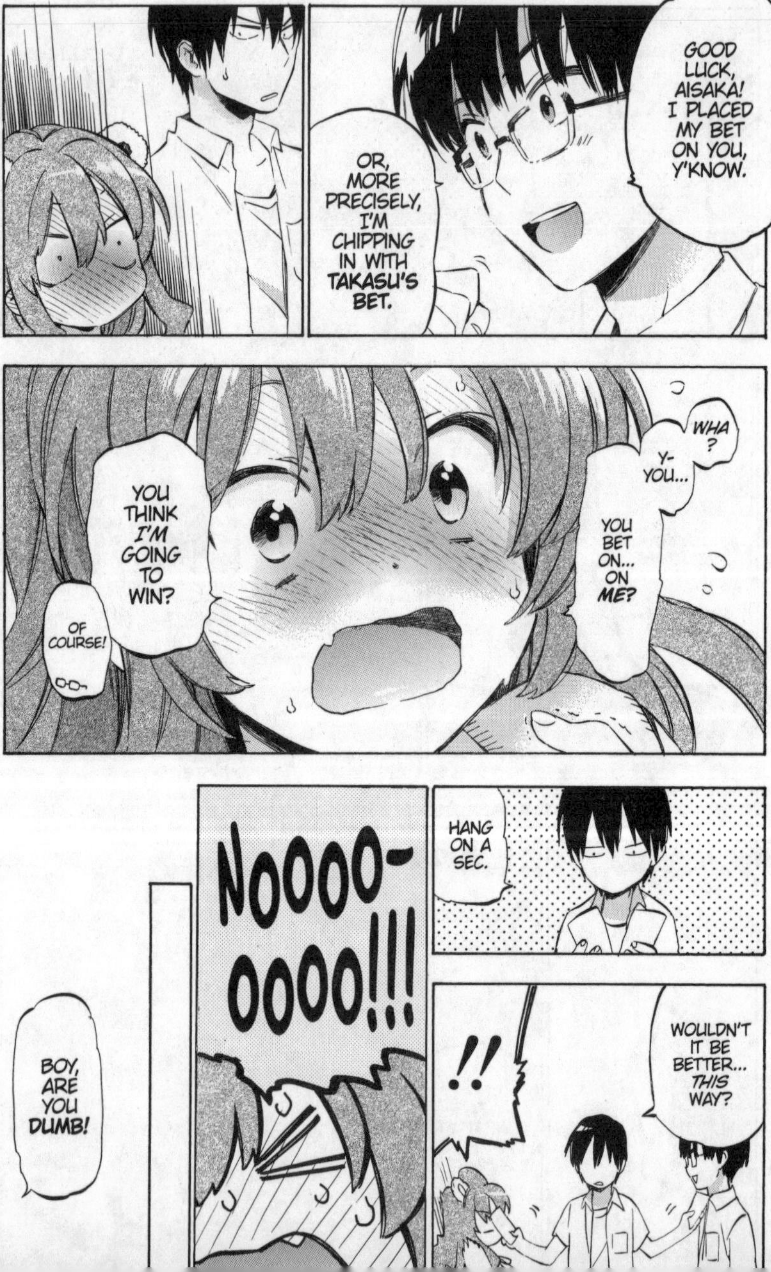
GOOD LUCK, AISAKA! I PLACED MY BET ON YOU, Y'KNOW.
OR, MORE PRECISELY, I'M CHIPPING IN WITH TAKASU'S BET.
WHA?
Y-YOU...
YOU BET ON... ON *ME?*
YOU THINK *I'M* GOING TO WIN?
OF COURSE!
HANG ON A SEC.
WOULDN'T IT BE BETTER... *THIS* WAY?
!!
NOOOO-OOOO!!!
BOY, ARE YOU **DUMB!**

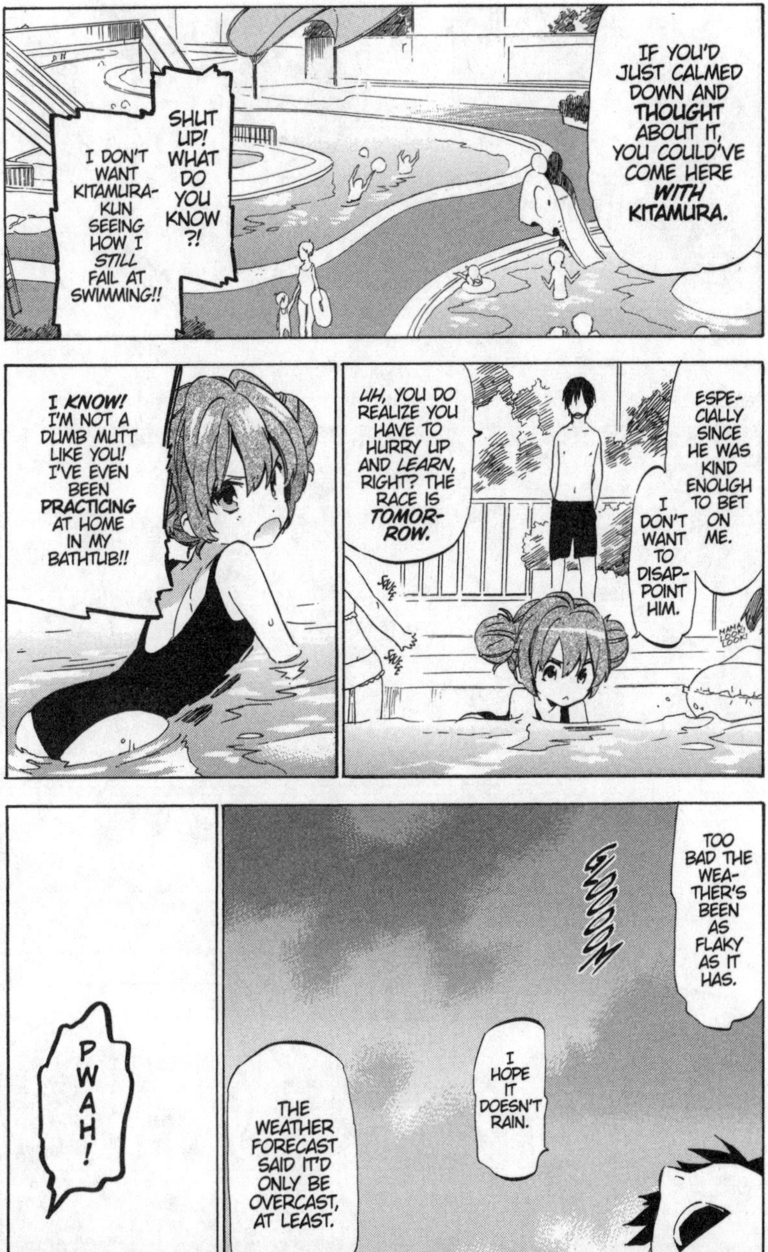
IF YOU'D JUST CALMED DOWN AND THOUGHT ABOUT IT, YOU COULD'VE COME HERE WITH KITAMURA.
SHUT UP! WHAT DO YOU KNOW ?!
I DON'T WANT KITAMURA-KUN SEEING HOW I STILL FAIL AT SWIMMING!!
ESPE-CIALLY SINCE HE WAS KIND ENOUGH TO BET ON ME.
I DON'T WANT TO DISAP-POINT HIM.
MAMA, LOOK! LOOK!
UH, YOU DO REALIZE YOU HAVE TO HURRY UP AND LEARN, RIGHT? THE RACE IS TOMOR-ROW.
I KNOW! I'M NOT A DUMB MUTT LIKE YOU! I'VE EVEN BEEN PRACTICING AT HOME IN MY BATHTUB!!
TOO BAD THE WEA-THER'S BEEN AS FLAKY AS IT HAS.
I HOPE IT DOESN'T RAIN.
THE WEATHER FORECAST SAID IT'D ONLY BE OVERCAST, AT LEAST.
PWAH!

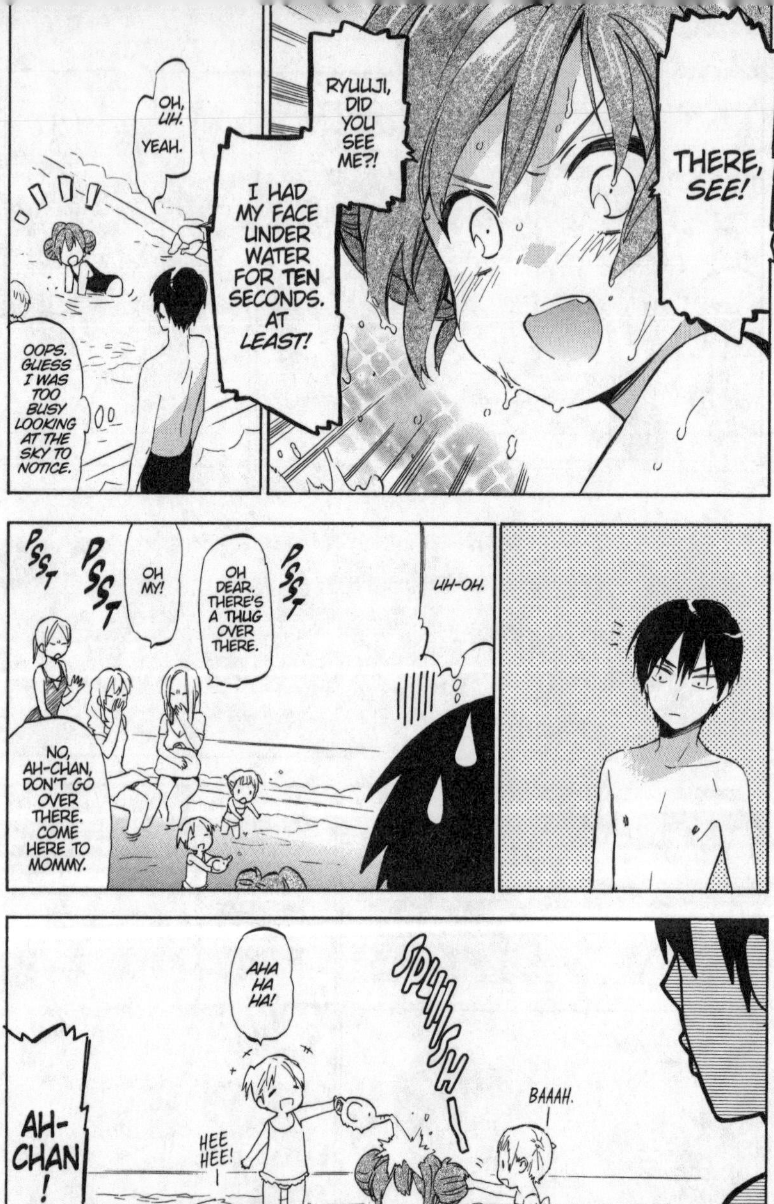
THERE, SEE!
RYUUJI, DID YOU SEE ME?!
I HAD MY FACE UNDER WATER FOR TEN SECONDS. AT LEAST!
OH, UH. YEAH.
OOPS. GUESS I WAS TOO BUSY LOOKING AT THE SKY TO NOTICE.
UH-OH.
PSST
OH DEAR. THERE'S A THUG OVER THERE.
OH MY!
PSST
PSST
NO, AH-CHAN, DON'T GO OVER THERE. COME HERE TO MOMMY.
SPLISH
AHA HA HA!
BAAAH.
HEE HEE!
AH-CHAN!

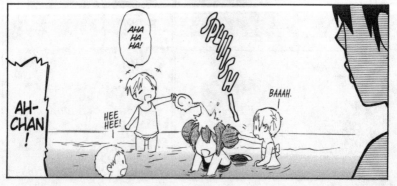

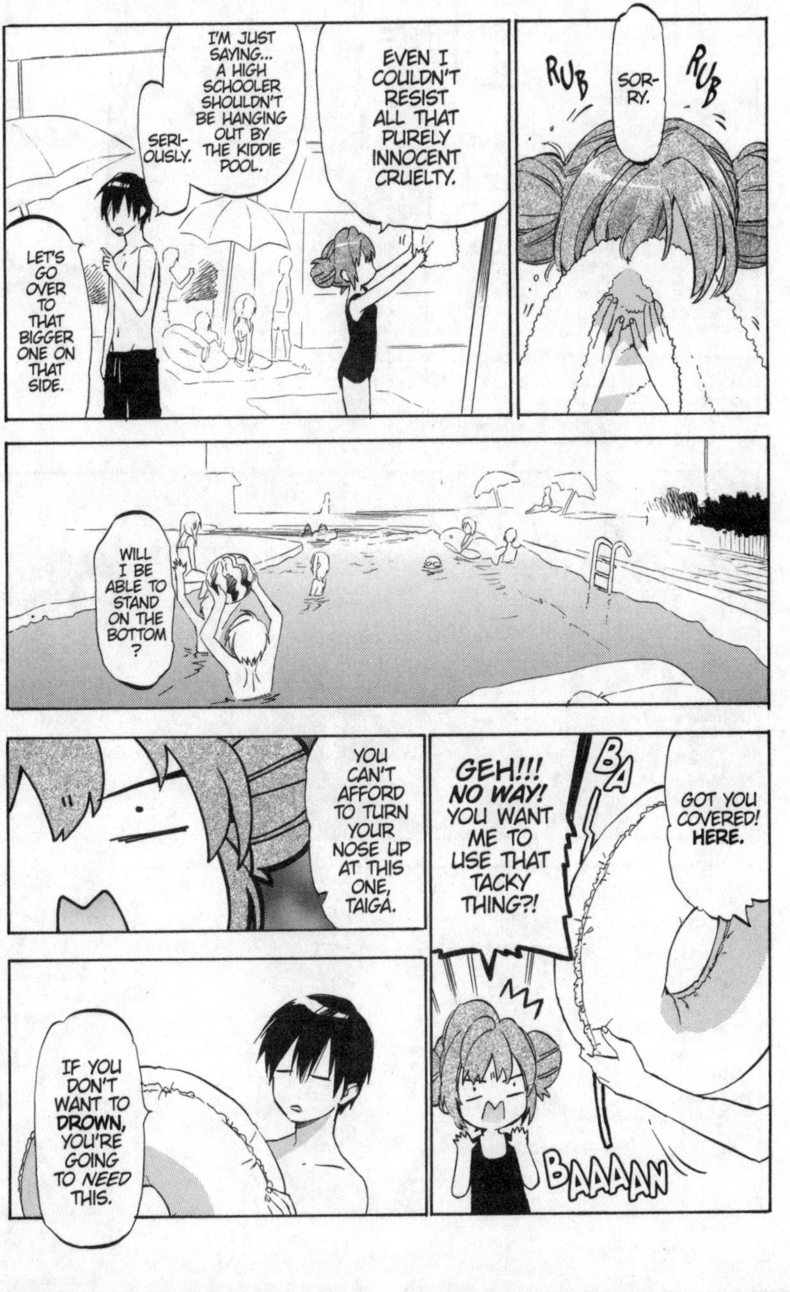
RUB
SORRY.
RUB
EVEN I COULDN'T RESIST ALL THAT PURELY INNOCENT CRUELTY.
I'M JUST SAYING... A HIGH SCHOOLER SHOULDN'T BE HANGING OUT BY THE KIDDIE POOL.
SERIOUSLY.
LET'S GO OVER TO THAT BIGGER ONE ON THAT SIDE.
WILL I BE ABLE TO STAND ON THE BOTTOM?
BA
GOT YOU COVERED! HERE.
GEH!!! NO WAY! YOU WANT ME TO USE THAT TACKY THING?!
BAAAAN
YOU CAN'T AFFORD TO TURN YOUR NOSE UP AT THIS ONE, TAIGA.
IF YOU DON'T WANT TO DROWN, YOU'RE GOING TO NEED THIS.

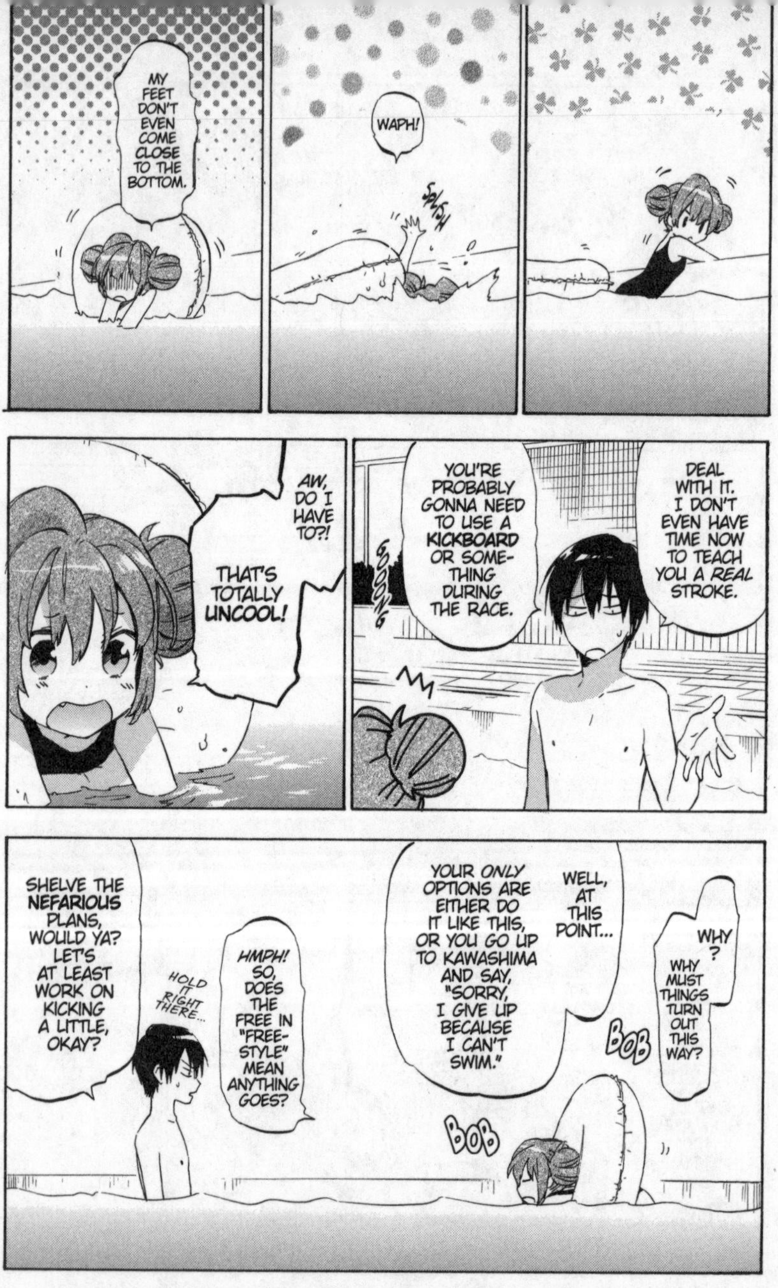
WAPH!
SPLISH
MY FEET DON'T EVEN COME CLOSE TO THE BOTTOM.
DEAL WITH IT. I DON'T EVEN HAVE TIME NOW TO TEACH YOU A *REAL* STROKE.
YOU'RE PROBABLY GONNA NEED TO USE A **KICKBOARD** OR SOMETHING DURING THE RACE.
AW, DO I HAVE TO?!
THAT'S TOTALLY **UNCOOL!**
WHY? WHY MUST THINGS TURN OUT THIS WAY?
BOB
WELL, AT THIS POINT...
YOUR *ONLY* OPTIONS ARE EITHER DO IT LIKE THIS, OR YOU GO UP TO KAWASHIMA AND SAY, "SORRY, I GIVE UP BECAUSE I CAN'T SWIM."
BOB
HMPH! SO, DOES THE FREE IN "FREE-STYLE" MEAN ANYTHING GOES?
HOLD IT RIGHT THERE...
SHELVE THE **NEFARIOUS** PLANS, WOULD YA? LET'S AT LEAST WORK ON KICKING A LITTLE, OKAY?

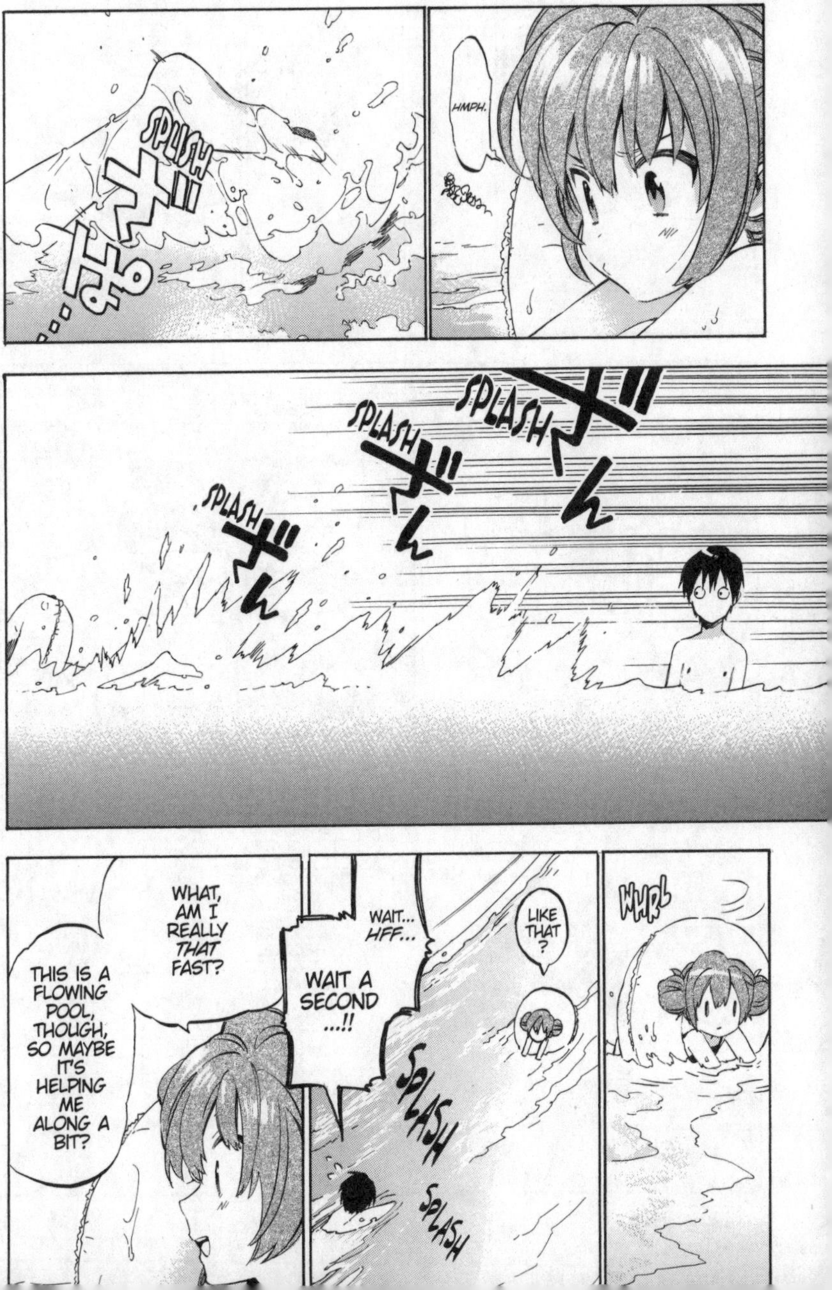
HMPH.
SPLISH
SPLASH
SPLASH
SPLASH
WHRL
LIKE THAT?
WAIT... HFF...
WAIT A SECOND ...!!
SPLASH
SPLASH
WHAT, AM I REALLY THAT FAST?
THIS IS A FLOWING POOL, THOUGH, SO MAYBE IT'S HELPING ME ALONG A BIT?

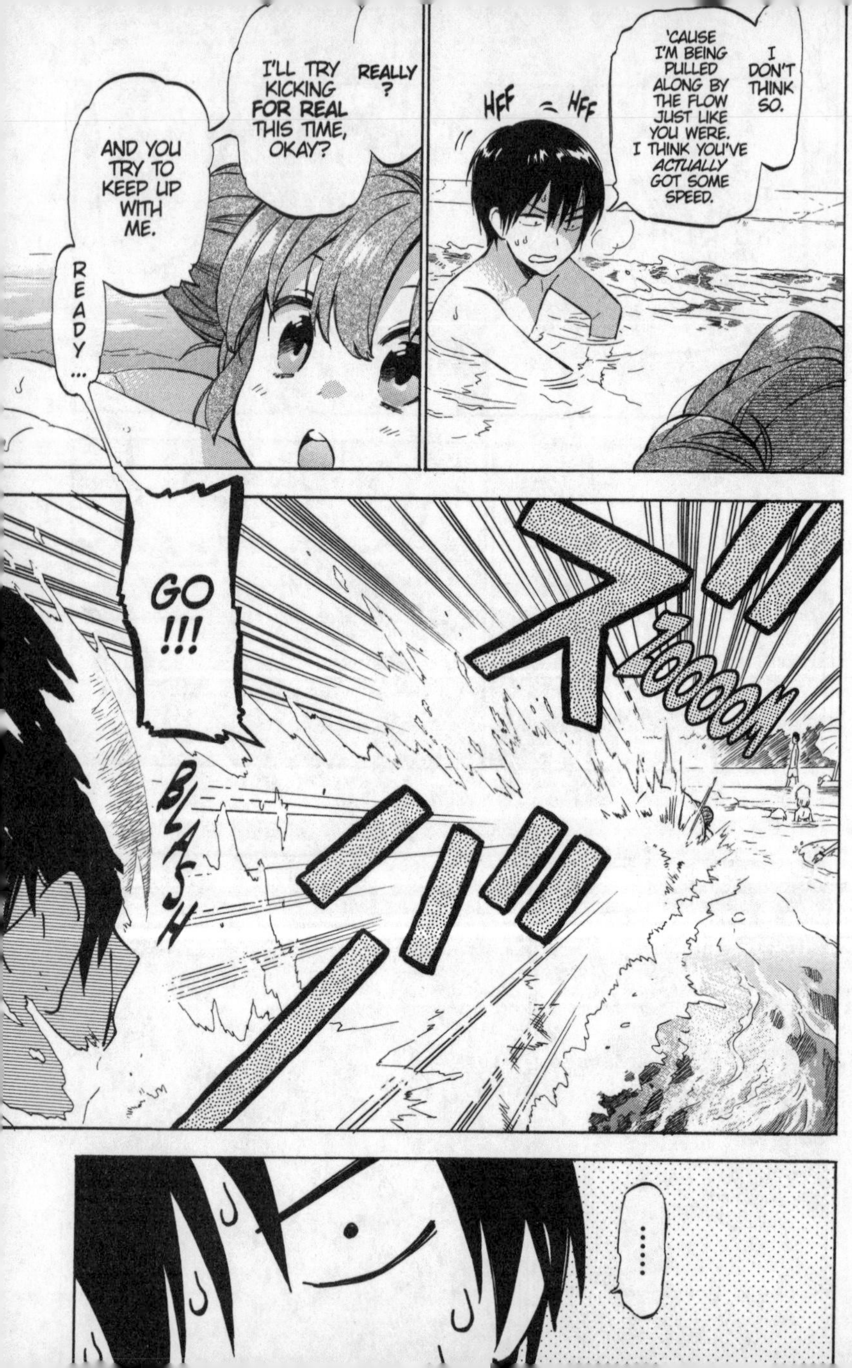
HFF HFF
I DON'T THINK SO.
'CAUSE I'M BEING PULLED ALONG BY THE FLOW JUST LIKE YOU WERE. I THINK YOU'VE *ACTUALLY* GOT SOME SPEED.
REALLY?
I'LL TRY KICKING FOR REAL THIS TIME, OKAY?
AND YOU TRY TO KEEP UP WITH ME.
READY...
GO!!!
ZOOOOM
BLASH
......

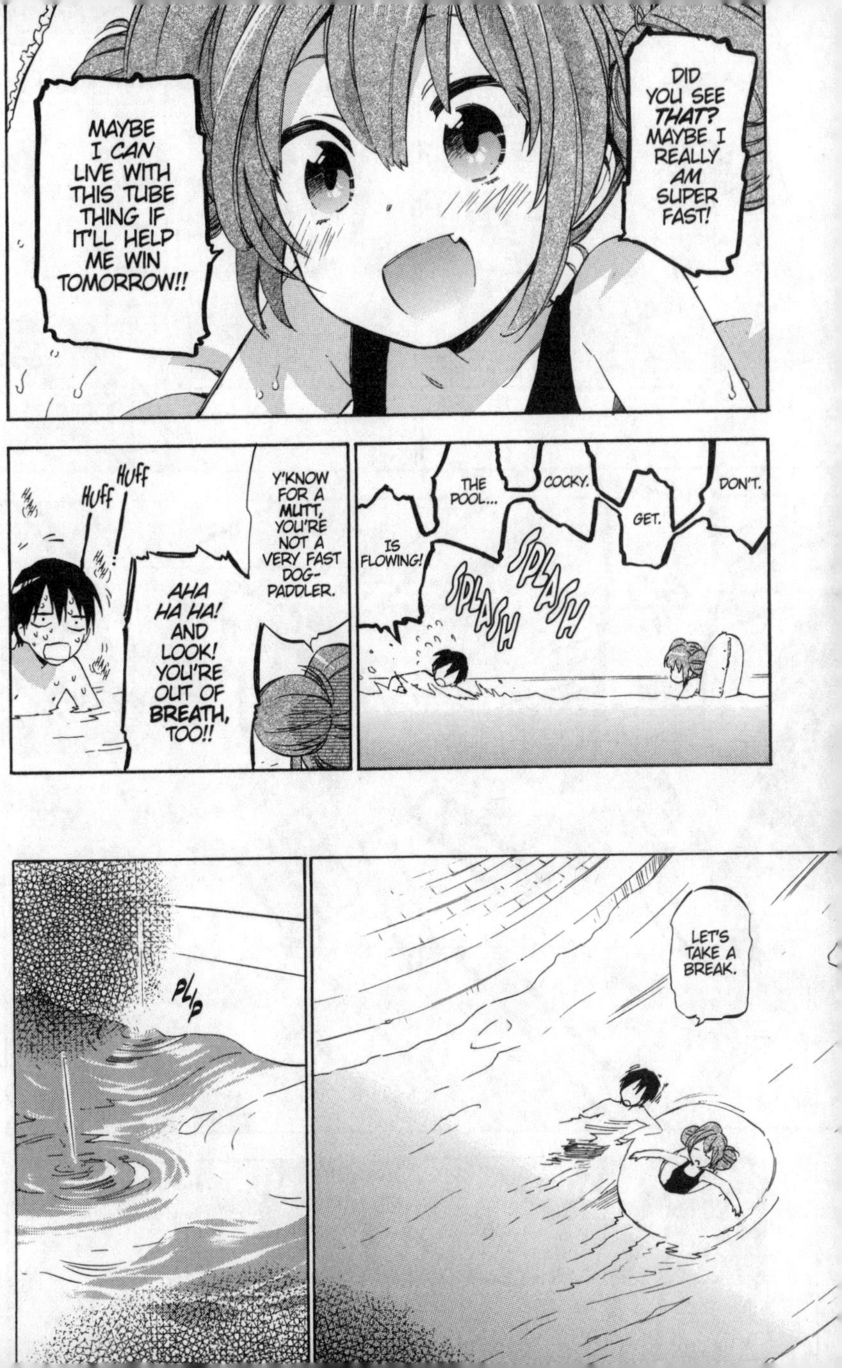
DID YOU SEE THAT? MAYBE I REALLY AM SUPER FAST!
MAYBE I CAN LIVE WITH THIS TUBE THING IF IT'LL HELP ME WIN TOMORROW!!
DON'T.
GET.
COCKY.
THE POOL...
IS FLOWING!
SPLASH
SPLASH
Y'KNOW FOR A MUTT, YOU'RE NOT A VERY FAST DOG-PADDLER.
AHA HA HA! AND LOOK! YOU'RE OUT OF BREATH, TOO!!
HUFF
HUFF
LET'S TAKE A BREAK.
PLIP

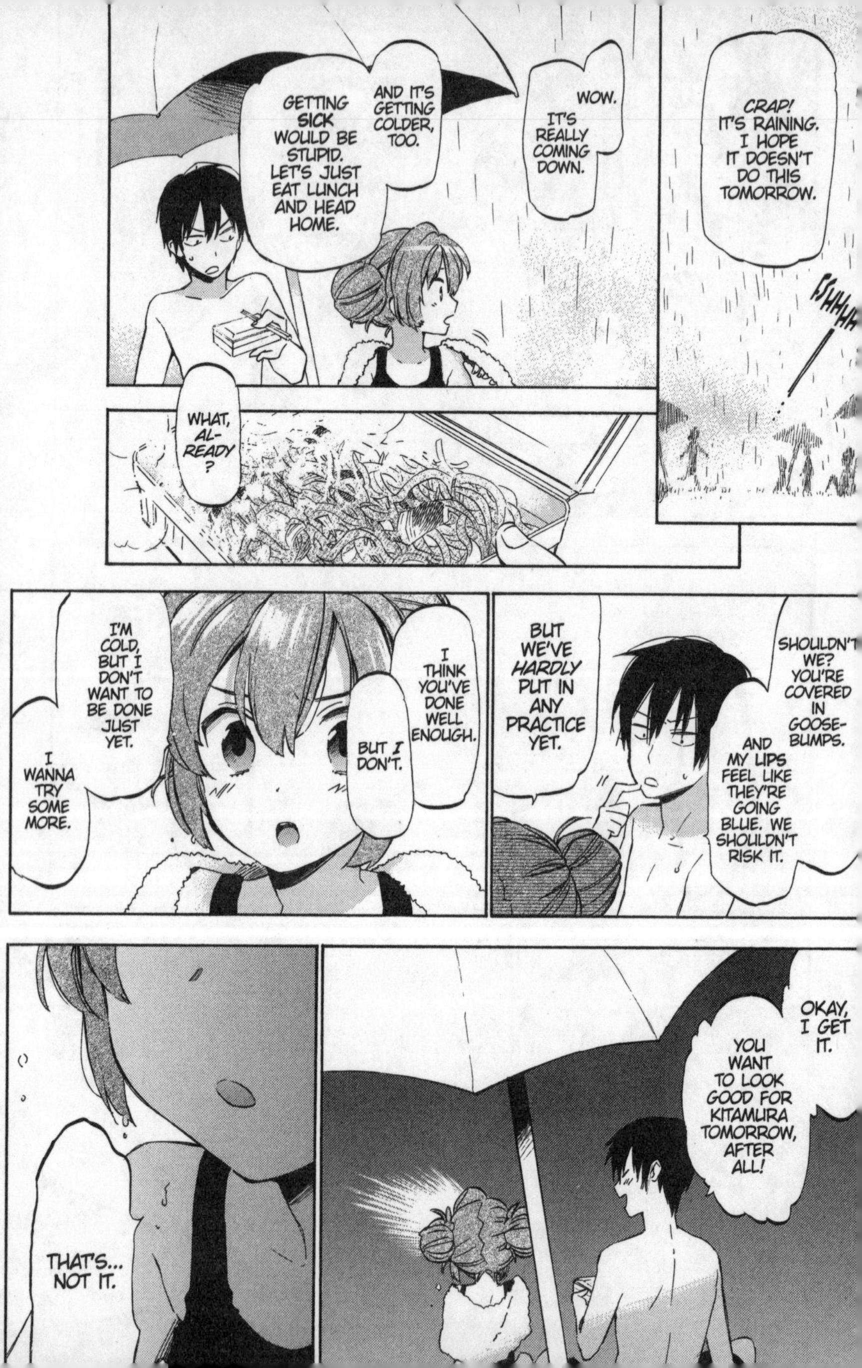

CRAP! IT'S RAINING. I HOPE IT DOESN'T DO THIS TOMORROW.
WOW. IT'S REALLY COMING DOWN.
AND IT'S GETTING COLDER, TOO.
GETTING **SICK** WOULD BE STUPID. LET'S JUST EAT LUNCH AND HEAD HOME.
WHAT, AL-*READY*?
SHOULDN'T WE? YOU'RE COVERED IN GOOSE-BUMPS.
AND MY LIPS FEEL LIKE THEY'RE GOING BLUE. WE SHOULDN'T RISK IT.
BUT WE'VE *HARDLY* PUT IN ANY PRACTICE YET.
I THINK YOU'VE DONE WELL ENOUGH.
BUT *I* DON'T.
I'M COLD, BUT I DON'T WANT TO BE DONE JUST YET.
I WANNA TRY SOME MORE.
OKAY, I GET IT.
YOU WANT TO LOOK GOOD FOR KITAMURA TOMORROW, AFTER ALL!
THAT'S... NOT IT.

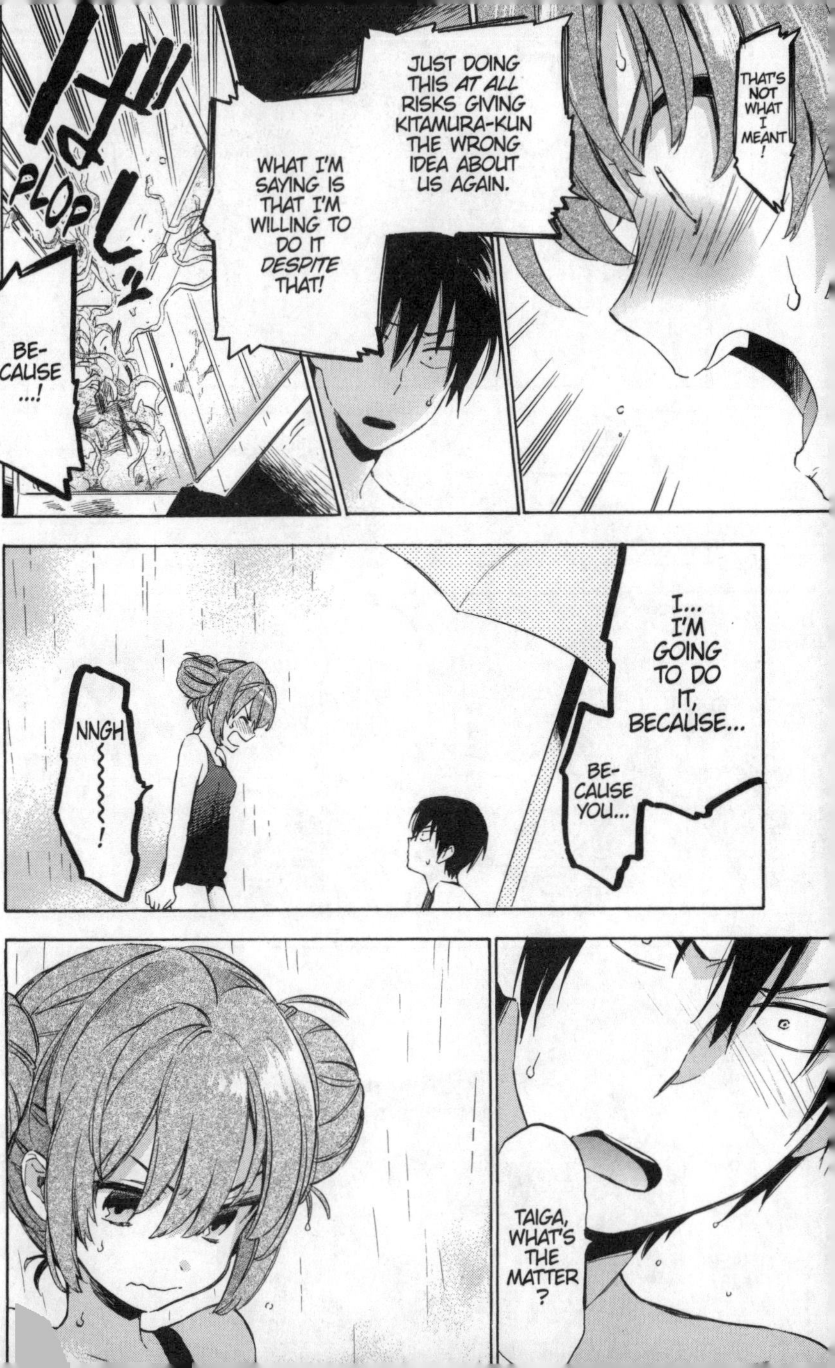
THAT'S NOT WHAT I MEANT!
JUST DOING THIS AT ALL RISKS GIVING KITAMURA-KUN THE WRONG IDEA ABOUT US AGAIN.
WHAT I'M SAYING IS THAT I'M WILLING TO DO IT DESPITE THAT!
PLOP
BE-CAUSE...!
I... I'M GOING TO DO IT, BECAUSE...
BE-CAUSE YOU...
NNGH~!
TAIGA, WHAT'S THE MATTER?

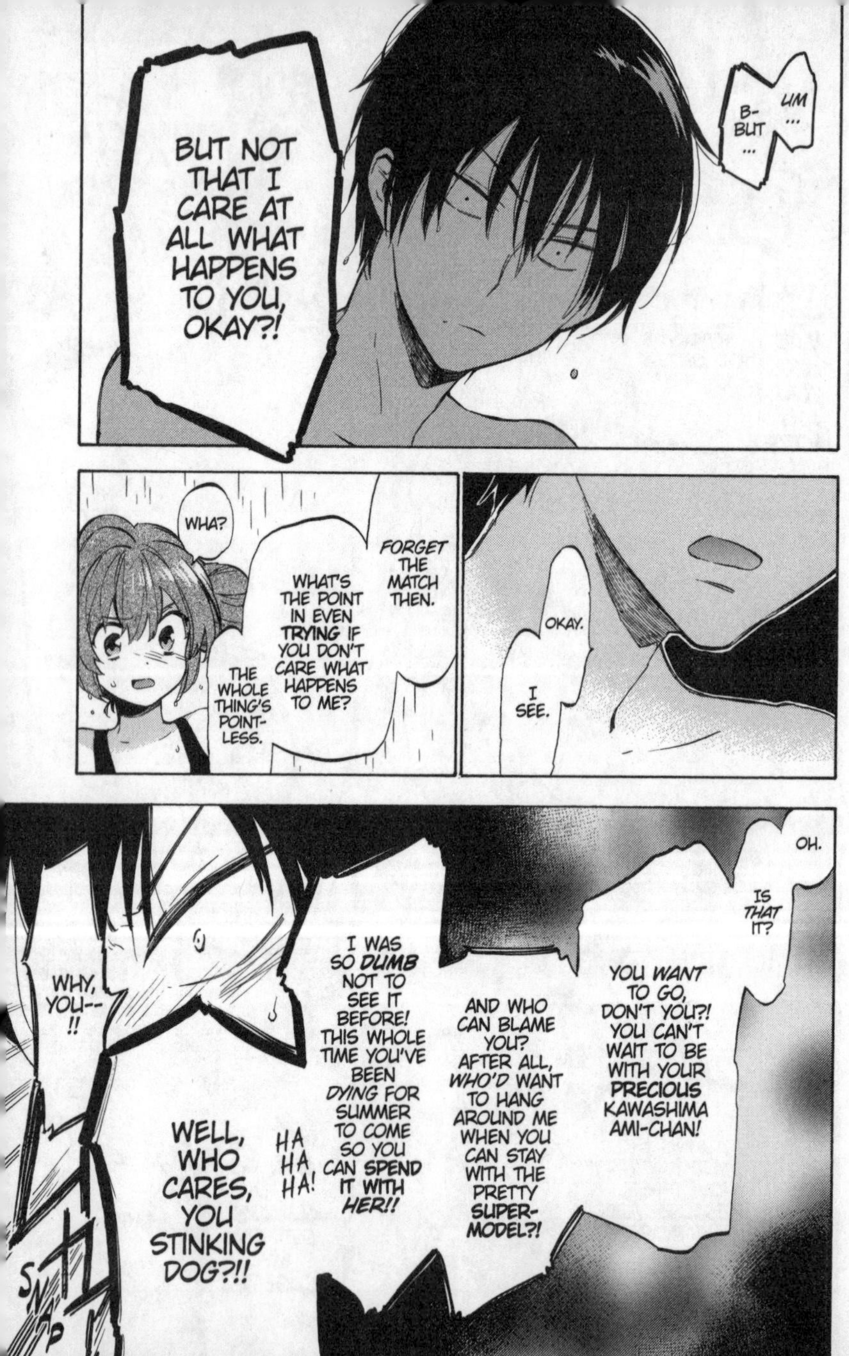

UM...
B-BUT...
BUT NOT THAT I CARE AT ALL WHAT HAPPENS TO YOU, OKAY?!
OKAY.
I SEE.
FORGET THE MATCH THEN.
WHAT'S THE POINT IN EVEN TRYING IF YOU DON'T CARE WHAT HAPPENS TO ME?
THE WHOLE THING'S POINTLESS.
WHA?
OH.
IS THAT IT?
YOU WANT TO GO, DON'T YOU?! YOU CAN'T WAIT TO BE WITH YOUR PRECIOUS KAWASHIMA AMI-CHAN!
AND WHO CAN BLAME YOU? AFTER ALL, WHO'D WANT TO HANG AROUND ME WHEN YOU CAN STAY WITH THE PRETTY SUPER-MODEL?!
I WAS SO DUMB NOT TO SEE IT BEFORE! THIS WHOLE TIME YOU'VE BEEN DYING FOR SUMMER TO COME SO YOU CAN SPEND IT WITH HER!!
HA HA HA!
WHY, YOU--!!
WELL, WHO CARES, YOU STINKING DOG?!!
SNAP

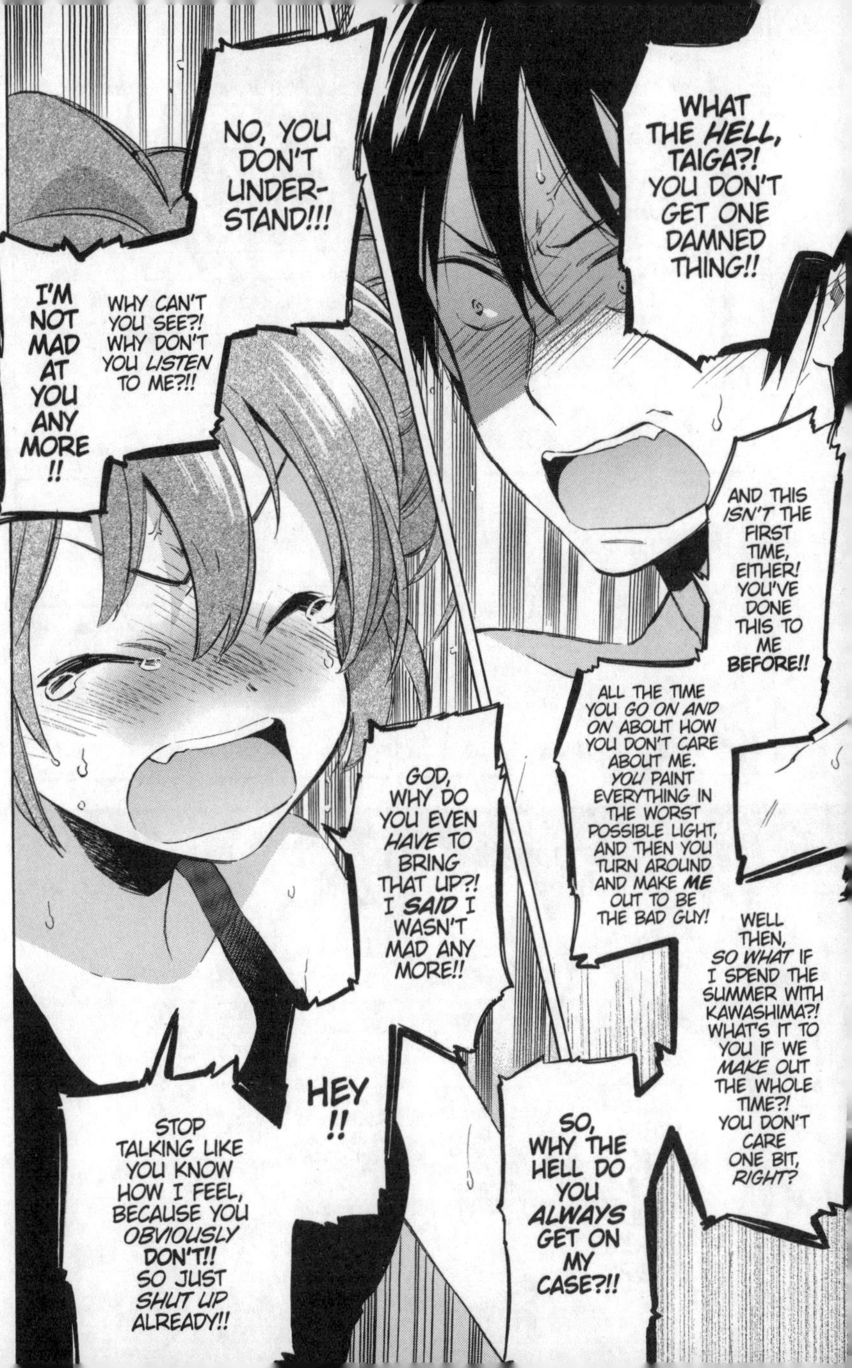
WHAT THE HELL, TAIGA?! YOU DON'T GET ONE DAMNED THING!!
NO, YOU DON'T UNDER-STAND!!!
WHY CAN'T YOU SEE?! WHY DON'T YOU LISTEN TO ME?!!
I'M NOT MAD AT YOU ANY MORE!!
AND THIS ISN'T THE FIRST TIME, EITHER! YOU'VE DONE THIS TO ME BEFORE!!
ALL THE TIME YOU GO ON AND ON ABOUT HOW YOU DON'T CARE ABOUT ME. YOU PAINT EVERYTHING IN THE WORST POSSIBLE LIGHT, AND THEN YOU TURN AROUND AND MAKE ME OUT TO BE THE BAD GUY!
GOD, WHY DO YOU EVEN HAVE TO BRING THAT UP?! I SAID I WASN'T MAD ANY MORE!!
WELL THEN, SO WHAT IF I SPEND THE SUMMER WITH KAWASHIMA?! WHAT'S IT TO YOU IF WE MAKE OUT THE WHOLE TIME?! YOU DON'T CARE ONE BIT, RIGHT?
SO, WHY THE HELL DO YOU ALWAYS GET ON MY CASE?!!
HEY!!
STOP TALKING LIKE YOU KNOW HOW I FEEL, BECAUSE YOU OBVIOUSLY DON'T!! SO JUST SHUT UP ALREADY!!

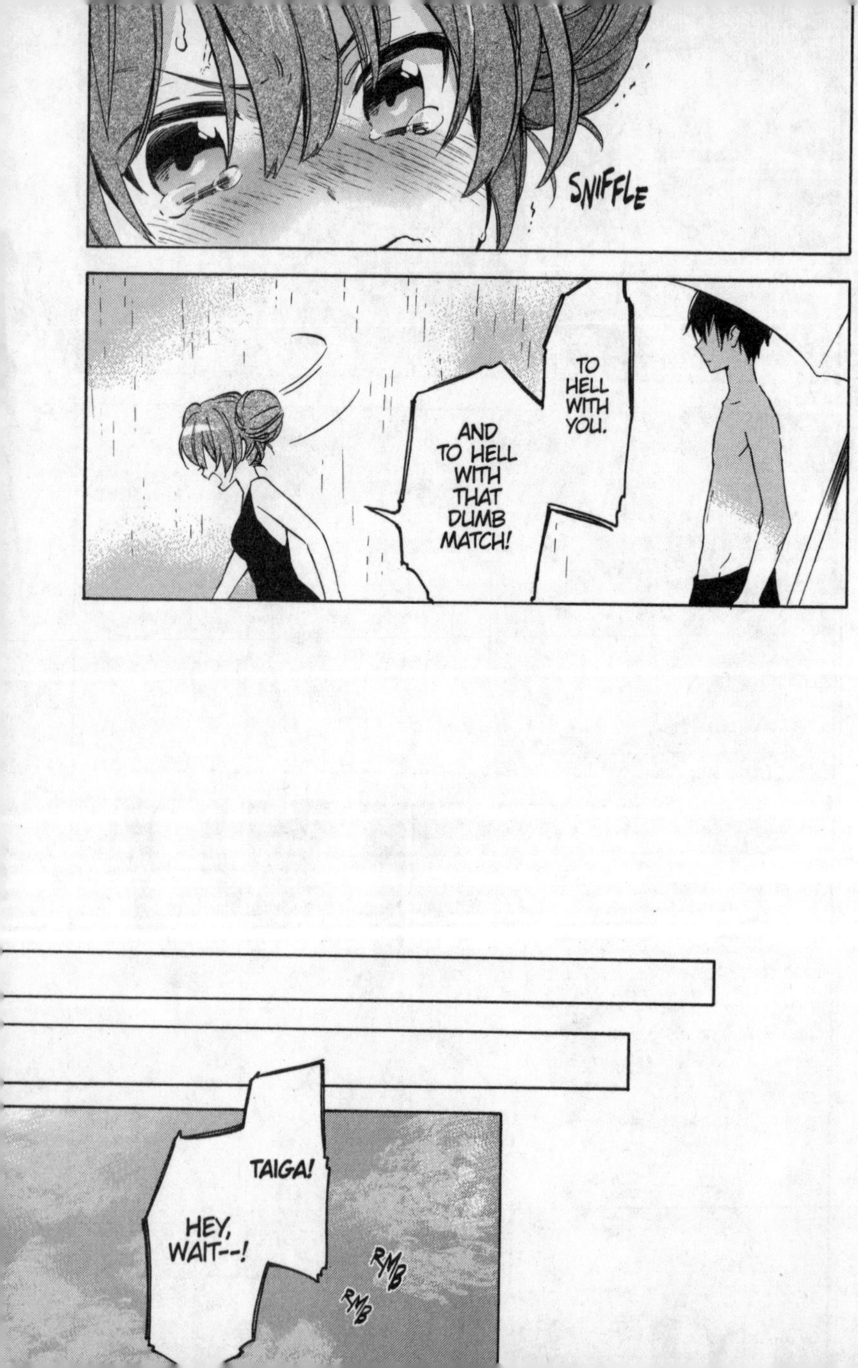
SNIFFLE
TO HELL WITH YOU.
AND TO HELL WITH THAT DUMB MATCH!
TAIGA!
HEY, WAIT--!
RMB
RMB

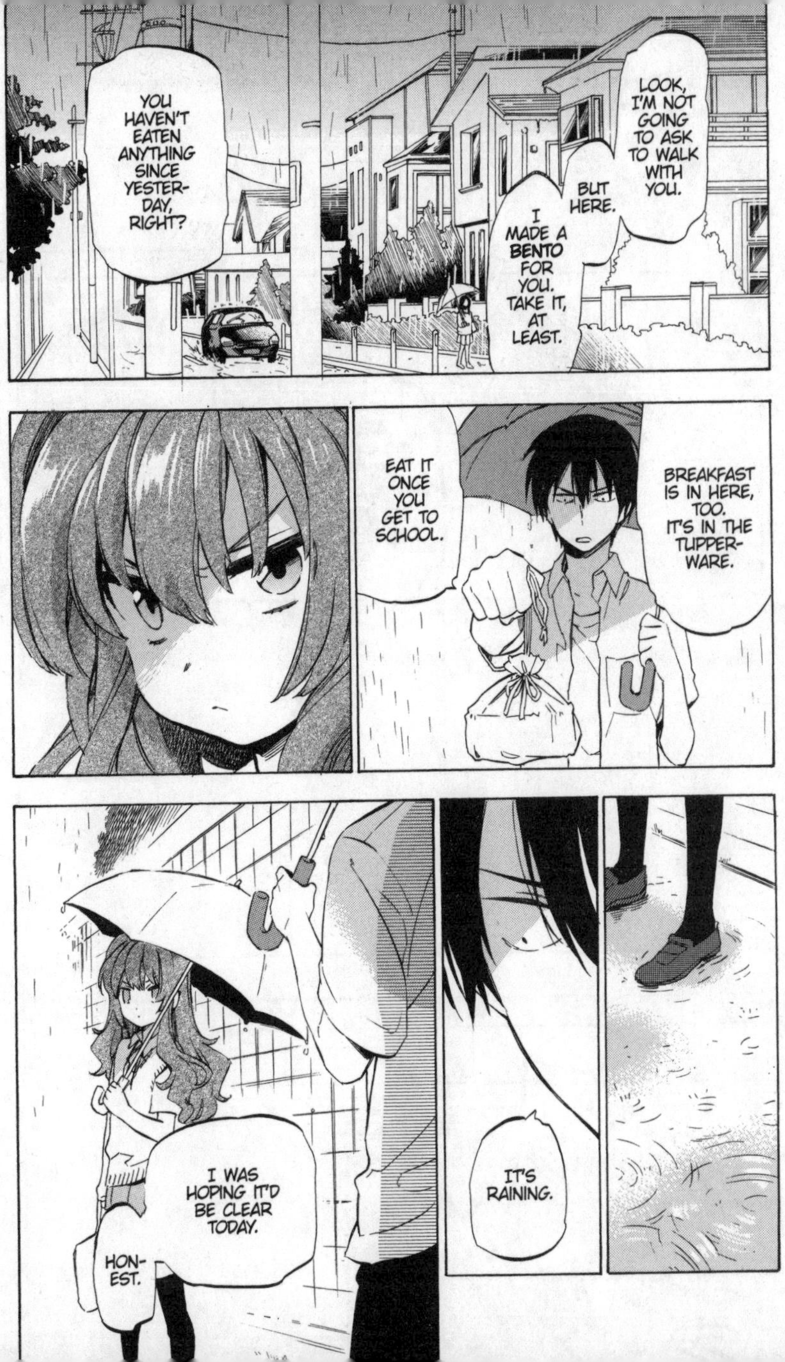
LOOK, I'M NOT GOING TO ASK TO WALK WITH YOU.
BUT HERE.
I MADE A BENTO FOR YOU. TAKE IT, AT LEAST.
YOU HAVEN'T EATEN ANYTHING SINCE YESTERDAY, RIGHT?
BREAKFAST IS IN HERE, TOO. IT'S IN THE TUPPERWARE.
EAT IT ONCE YOU GET TO SCHOOL.
IT'S RAINING.
I WAS HOPING IT'D BE CLEAR TODAY.
HONEST.

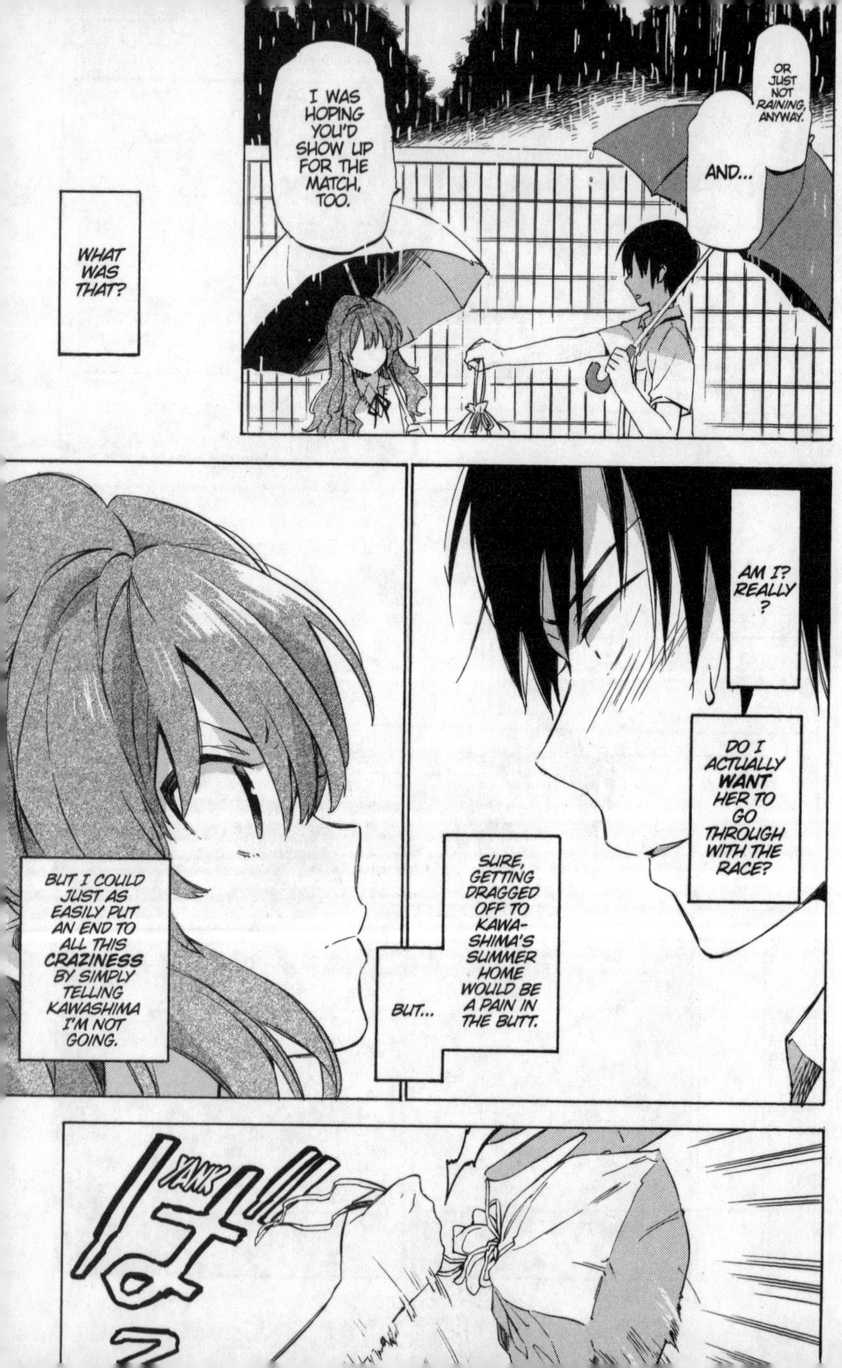
OR JUST NOT RAINING, ANYWAY.
AND...
I WAS HOPING YOU'D SHOW UP FOR THE MATCH, TOO.
WHAT WAS THAT?
AM I? REALLY?
DO I ACTUALLY WANT HER TO GO THROUGH WITH THE RACE?
SURE, GETTING DRAGGED OFF TO KAWA-SHIMA'S SUMMER HOME WOULD BE A PAIN IN THE BUTT.
BUT...
BUT I COULD JUST AS EASILY PUT AN END TO ALL THIS CRAZINESS BY SIMPLY TELLING KAWASHIMA I'M NOT GOING.
YANK

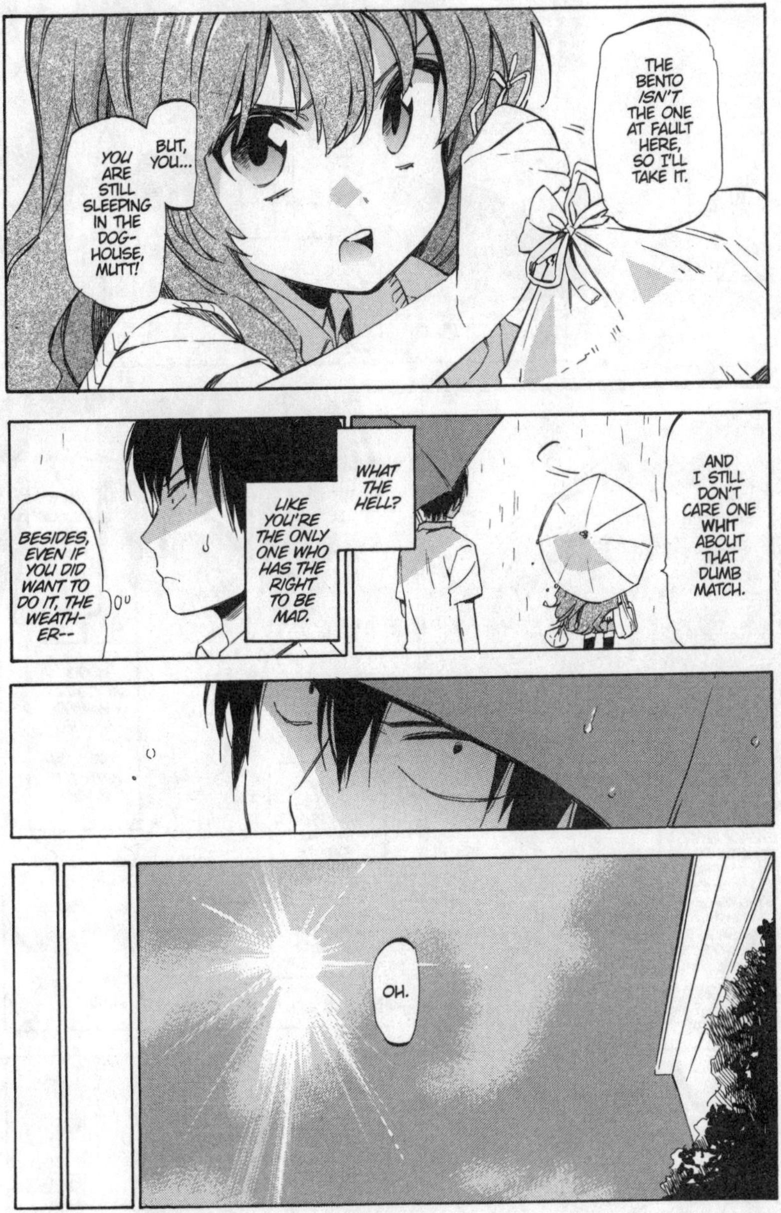
THE BENTO *ISN'T* THE ONE AT FAULT HERE, SO I'LL TAKE IT.
BUT, YOU... *YOU* ARE STILL SLEEPING IN THE DOG-HOUSE, MUTT!
AND I STILL DON'T CARE ONE WHIT ABOUT THAT DUMB MATCH.
WHAT THE HELL?
LIKE YOU'RE THE ONLY ONE WHO HAS THE RIGHT TO BE MAD.
BESIDES, EVEN IF YOU DID WANT TO DO IT, THE WEATHER--
OH.

To ra do ra !

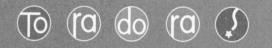

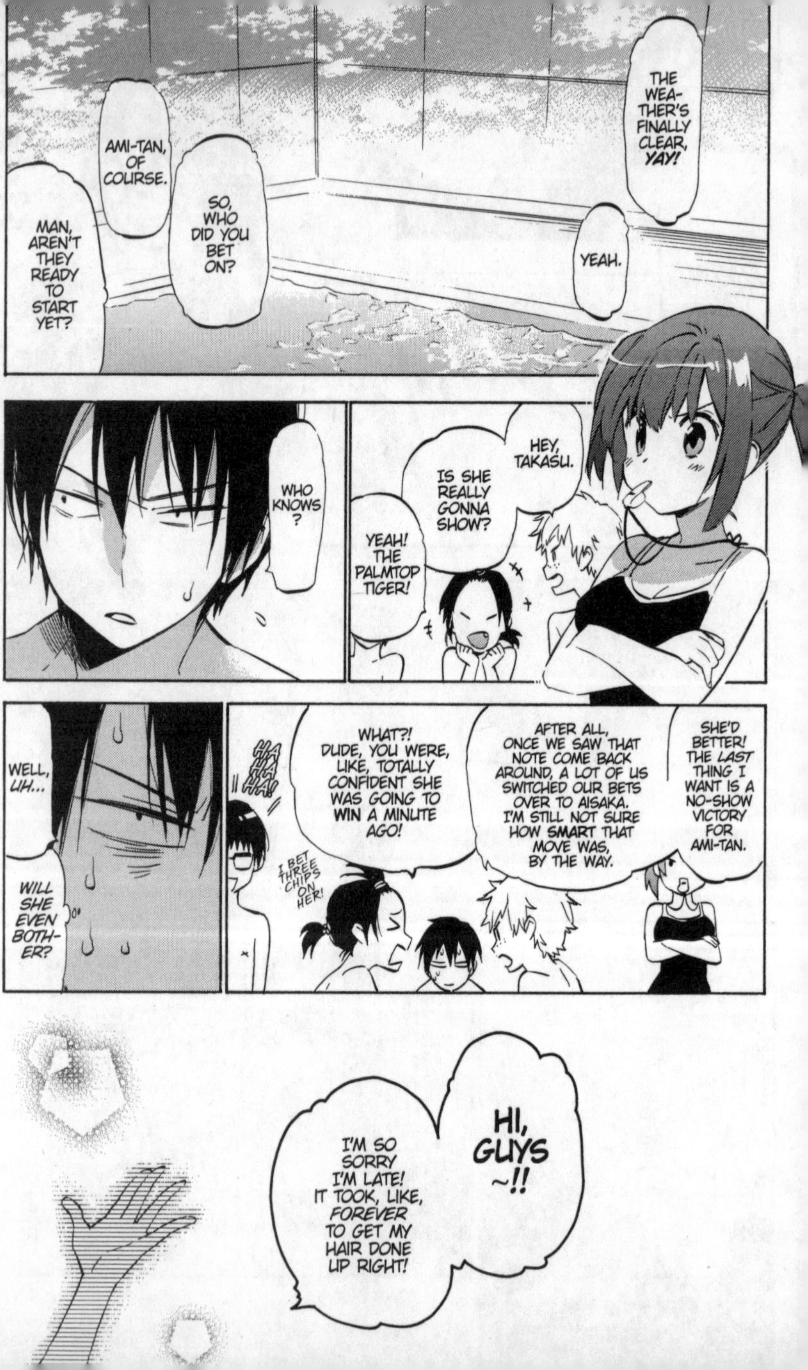
THE WEATHER'S FINALLY CLEAR, YAY!
YEAH.
SO, WHO DID YOU BET ON?
AMI-TAN, OF COURSE.
MAN, AREN'T THEY READY TO START YET?
HEY, TAKASU.
IS SHE REALLY GONNA SHOW?
YEAH! THE PALMTOP TIGER!
WHO KNOWS?
SHE'D BETTER! THE *LAST* THING I WANT IS A NO-SHOW VICTORY FOR AMI-TAN.
AFTER ALL, ONCE WE SAW THAT NOTE COME BACK AROUND, A LOT OF US SWITCHED OUR BETS OVER TO AISAKA. I'M STILL NOT SURE HOW **SMART** THAT MOVE WAS, BY THE WAY.
WHAT?! DUDE, YOU WERE, LIKE, TOTALLY CONFIDENT SHE WAS GOING TO **WIN** A MINUTE AGO!
I BET THREE CHIPS ON HER!
HA HA HA HA!
WELL, *UH...*
WILL SHE EVEN BOTHER?
HI, GUYS ~!!
I'M SO SORRY I'M LATE! IT TOOK, LIKE, *FOREVER* TO GET MY HAIR DONE UP RIGHT!

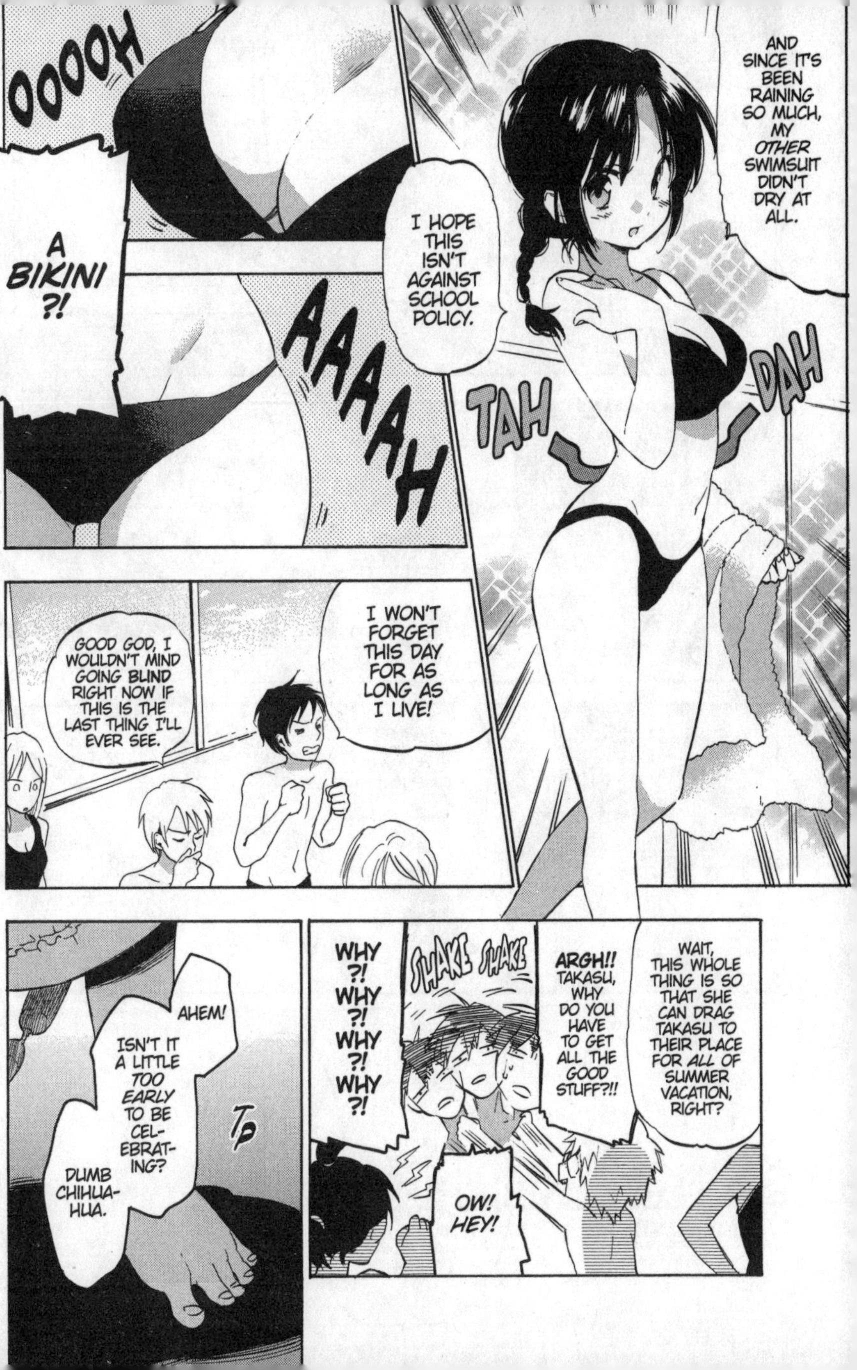
AND SINCE IT'S BEEN RAINING SO MUCH, MY *OTHER* SWIMSUIT DIDN'T DRY AT ALL.
I HOPE THIS ISN'T AGAINST SCHOOL POLICY.
TAH-DAH
OOOOH
A BIKINI ?!
AAAAAH
I WON'T FORGET THIS DAY FOR AS LONG AS I LIVE!
GOOD GOD, I WOULDN'T MIND GOING BLIND RIGHT NOW IF THIS IS THE LAST THING I'LL EVER SEE.
WAIT, THIS WHOLE THING IS SO THAT SHE CAN DRAG TAKASU TO THEIR PLACE FOR *ALL* OF SUMMER VACATION, RIGHT?
ARGH!! TAKASU, WHY DO YOU HAVE TO GET ALL THE GOOD STUFF?!!
SHAKE SHAKE
WHY ?! WHY ?! WHY ?! WHY ?!
OW! HEY!
AHEM!
ISN'T IT A LITTLE *TOO EARLY* TO BE CEL-EBRAT-ING?
DUMB CHIHUA-HUA.

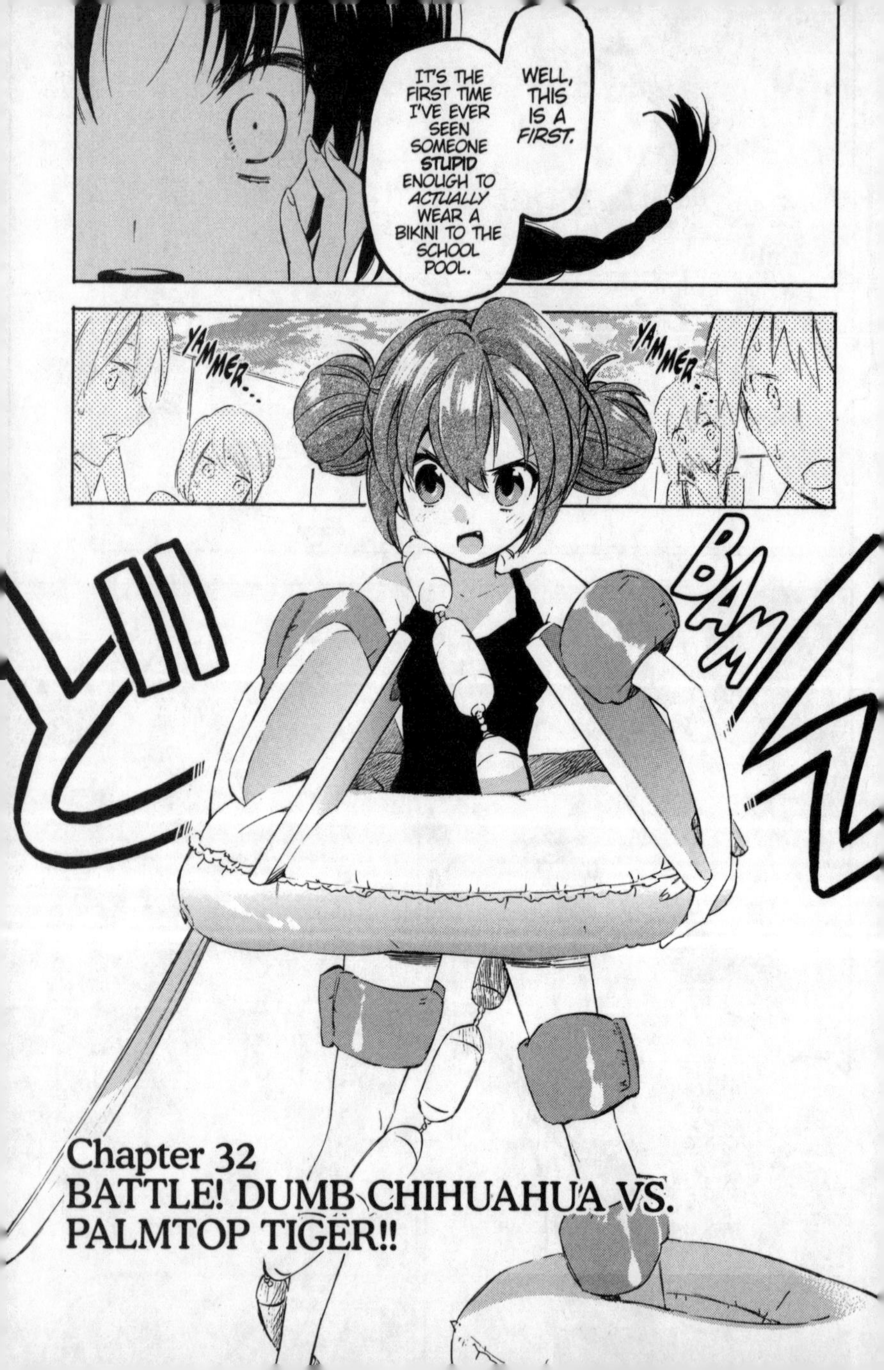
WELL, THIS IS A *FIRST.*
IT'S THE FIRST TIME I'VE EVER SEEN SOMEONE **STUPID** ENOUGH TO *ACTUALLY* WEAR A BIKINI TO THE SCHOOL POOL.
YAMMER
YAMMER...
BAM

Chapter 32
BATTLE! DUMB CHIHUAHUA VS. PALMTOP TIGER!!

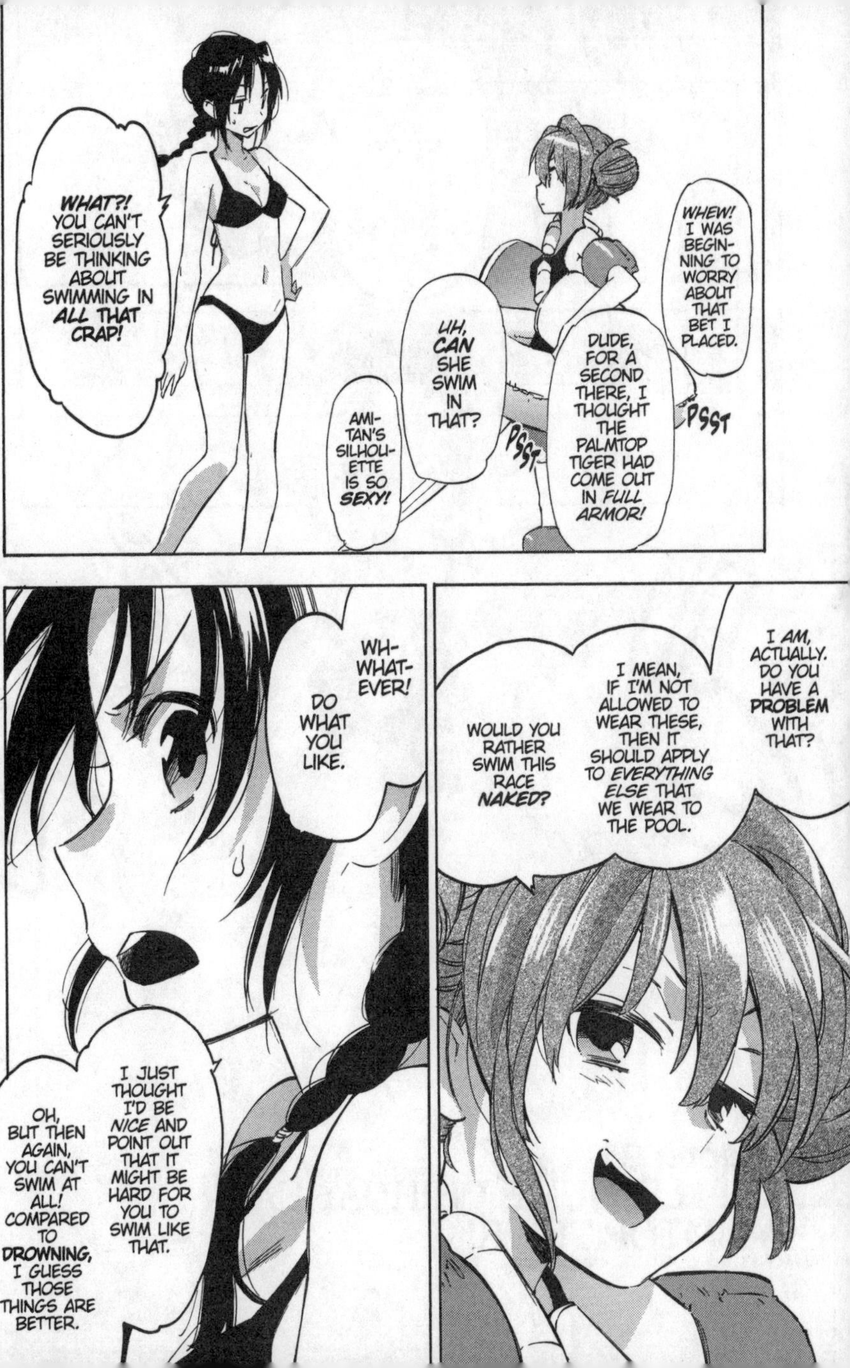
WHEW! I WAS BEGINNING TO WORRY ABOUT THAT BET I PLACED.
DUDE, FOR A SECOND THERE, I THOUGHT THE PALMTOP TIGER HAD COME OUT IN FULL ARMOR!
PSST
PSST
UH, CAN SHE SWIM IN THAT?
AMI-TAN'S SILHOUETTE IS SO SEXY!
WHAT?! YOU CAN'T SERIOUSLY BE THINKING ABOUT SWIMMING IN ALL THAT CRAP!
I AM, ACTUALLY. DO YOU HAVE A PROBLEM WITH THAT?
I MEAN, IF I'M NOT ALLOWED TO WEAR THESE, THEN IT SHOULD APPLY TO EVERYTHING ELSE THAT WE WEAR TO THE POOL.
WOULD YOU RATHER SWIM THIS RACE NAKED?
WH-WHAT-EVER! DO WHAT YOU LIKE.
I JUST THOUGHT I'D BE NICE AND POINT OUT THAT IT MIGHT BE HARD FOR YOU TO SWIM LIKE THAT.
OH, BUT THEN AGAIN, YOU CAN'T SWIM AT ALL! COMPARED TO DROWNING, I GUESS THOSE THINGS ARE BETTER.

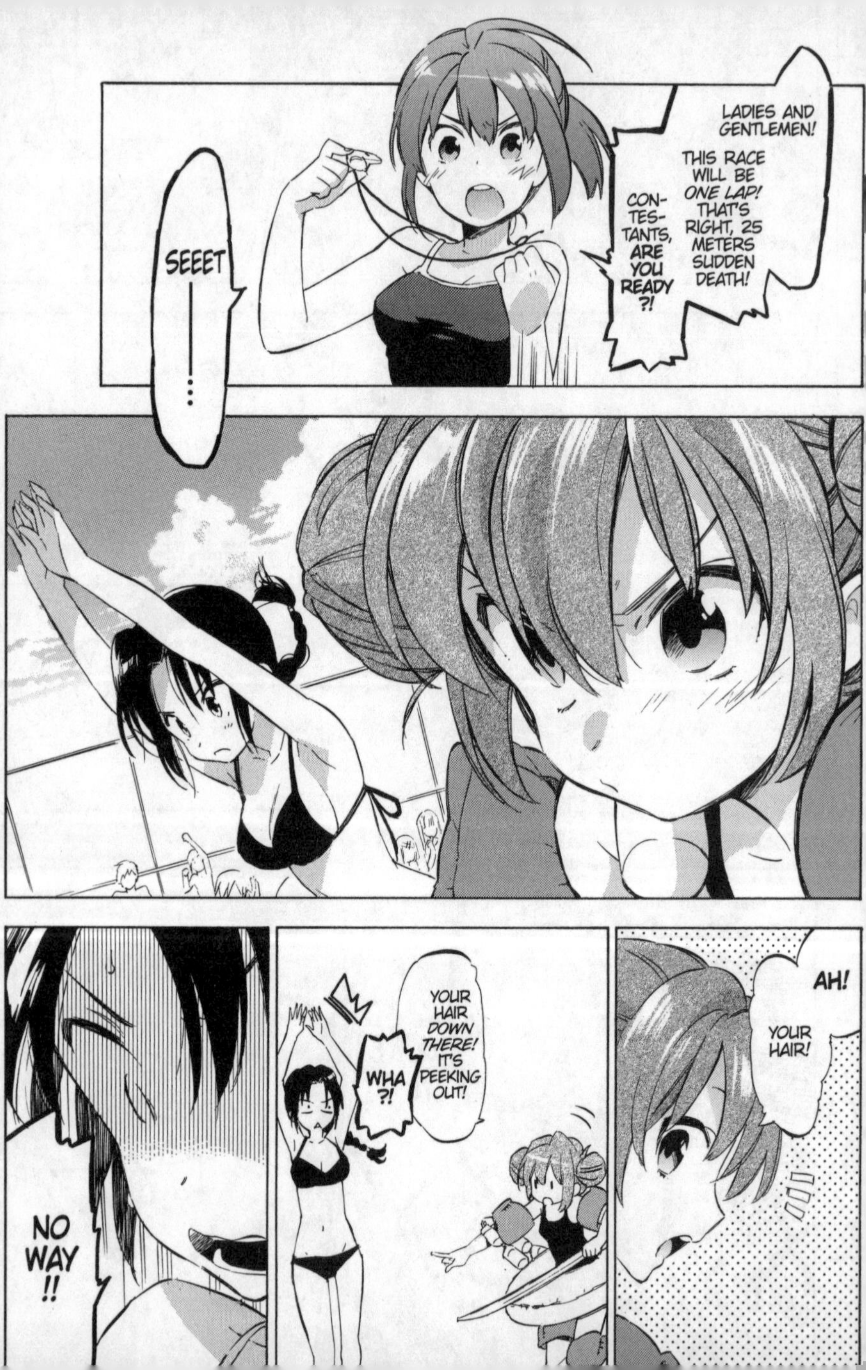
LADIES AND GENTLEMEN!
THIS RACE WILL BE *ONE LAP!* THAT'S RIGHT, 25 METERS SUDDEN DEATH!
CONTESTANTS, ARE YOU READY?!
SEEET—…
AH!
YOUR HAIR!
YOUR HAIR *DOWN THERE!* IT'S PEEKING OUT!
WHA?!
NO WAY!!

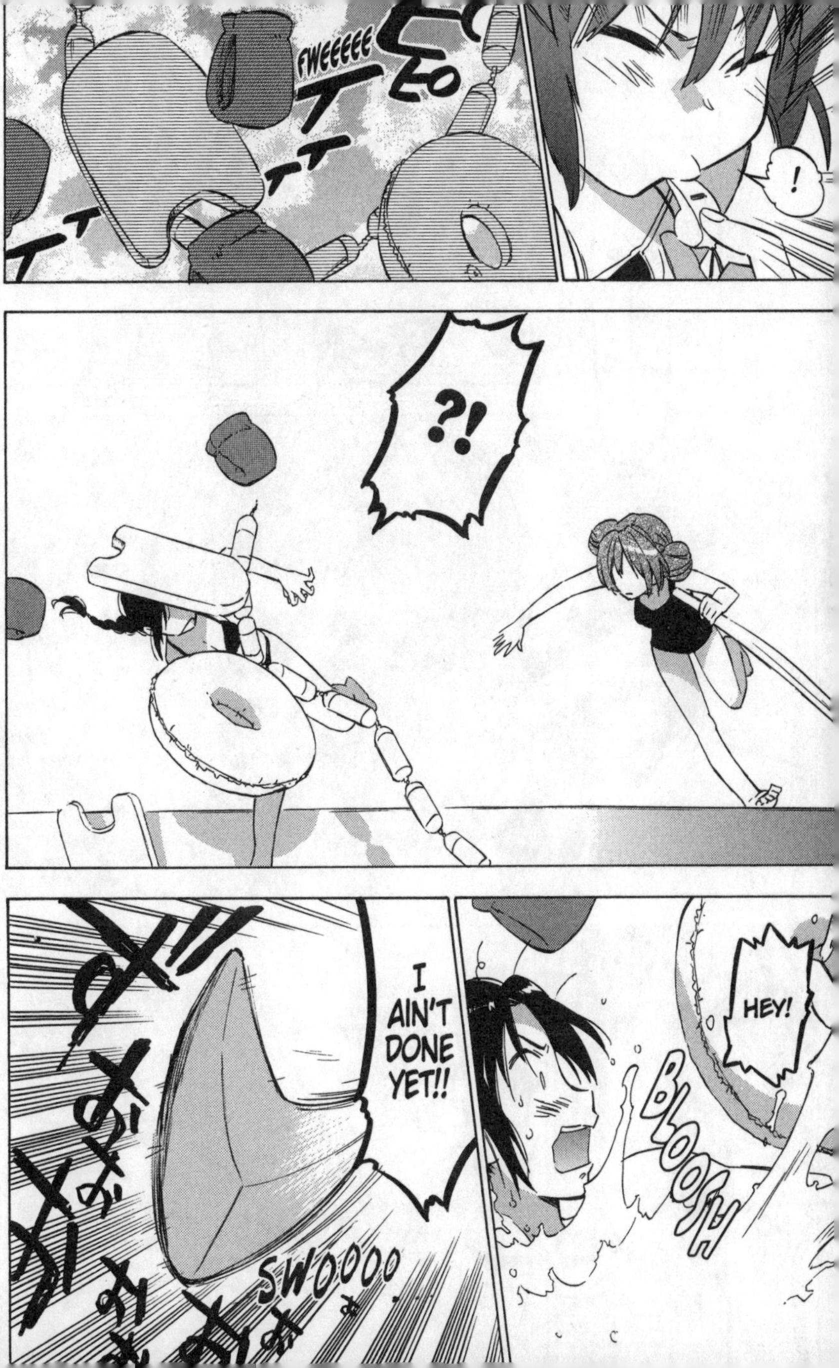
!
FWEEEEE
?!
HEY!
BLOOSH
I AIN'T DONE YET!!
SWOOOO

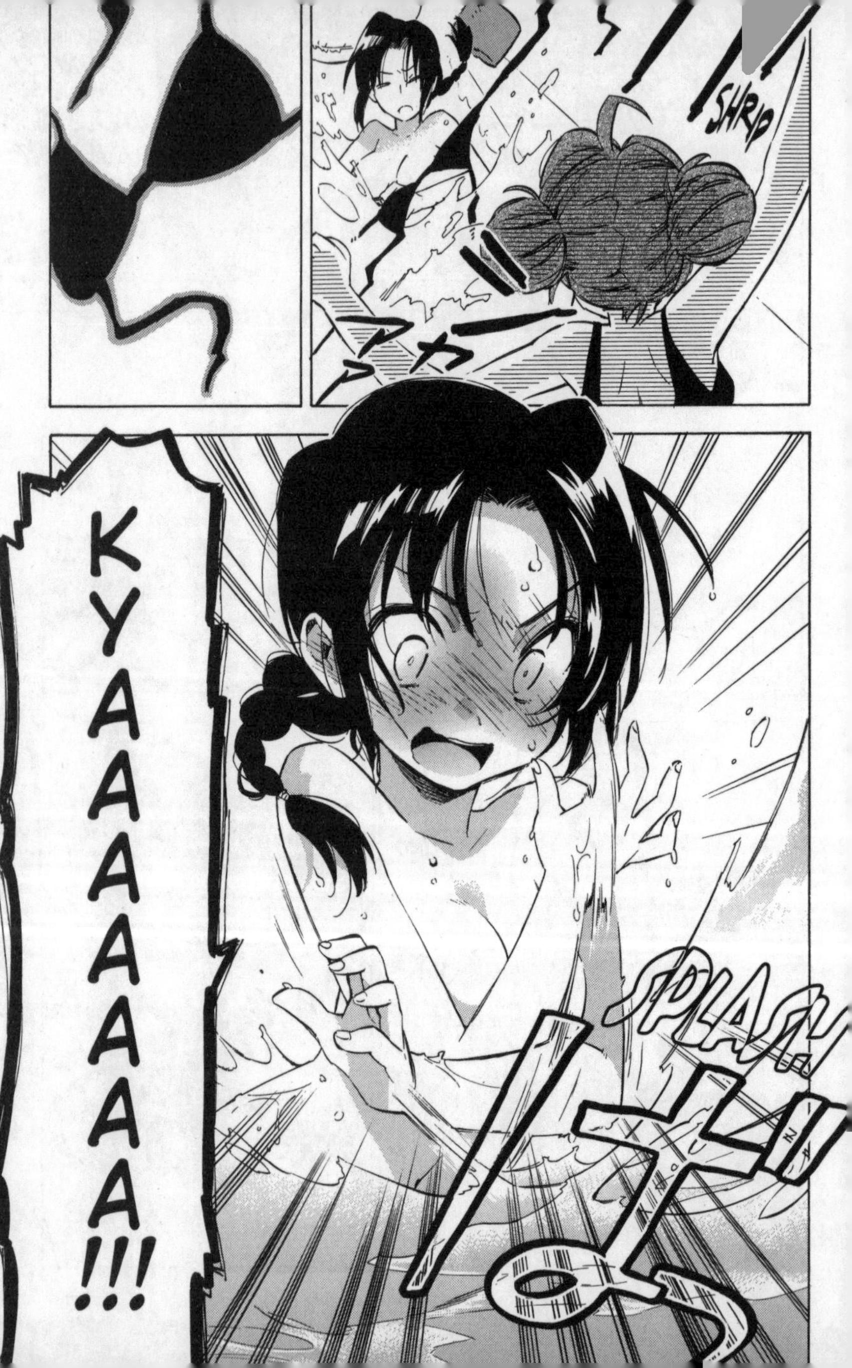
SHRIP
SPLASH
KYAAAAAAA!!!

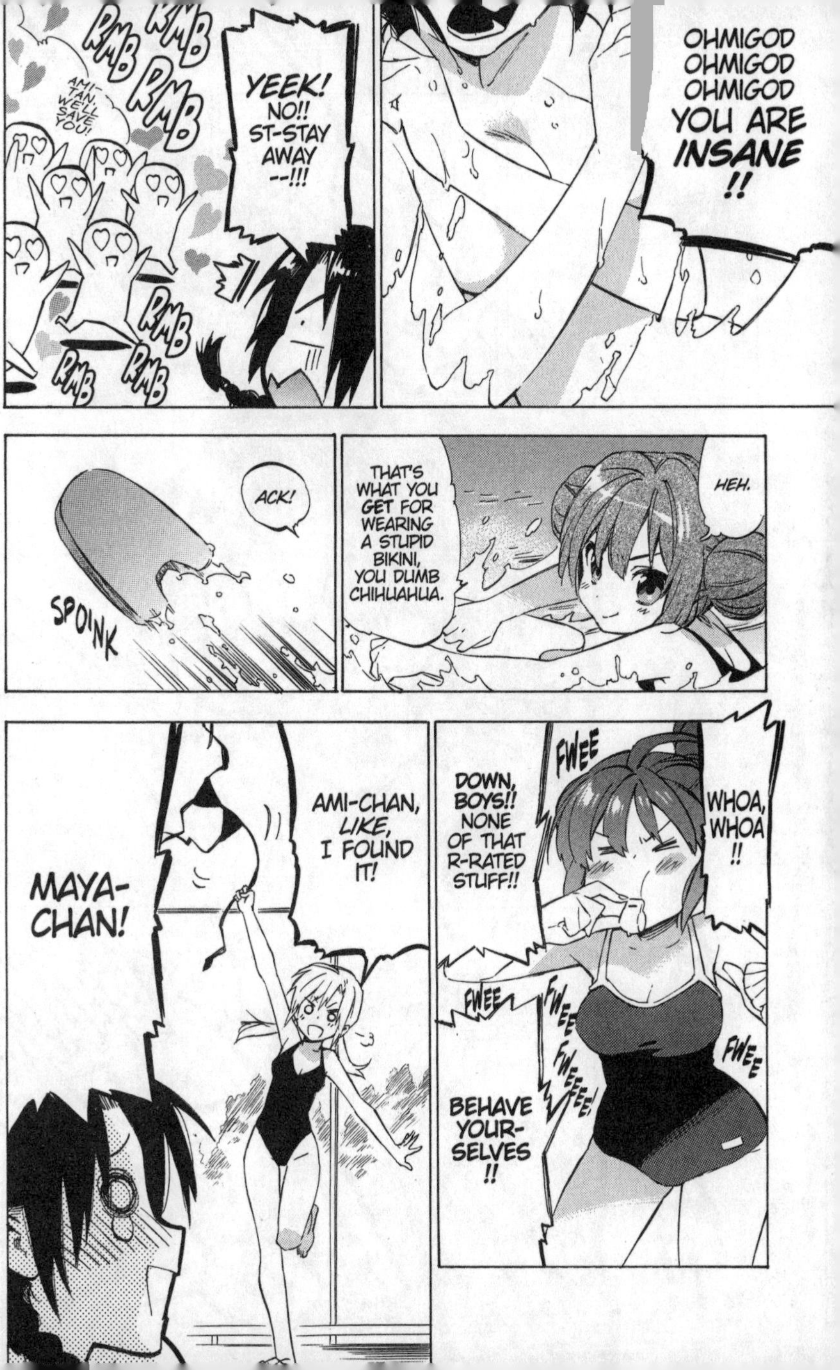
OHMIGOD OHMIGOD OHMIGOD YOU ARE INSANE !!
YEEK! NO!! ST-STAY AWAY --!!!
RMB RMB RMB RMB
AMI-TAN, WE'LL SAVE YOU!
RMB RMB RMB
HEH.
THAT'S WHAT YOU GET FOR WEARING A STUPID BIKINI, YOU DUMB CHIHUAHUA.
ACK!
SPOINK
WHOA, WHOA !!
FWEE
DOWN, BOYS!! NONE OF THAT R-RATED STUFF!!
FWEE
FWEE
FWEEEE!
BEHAVE YOUR-SELVES !!
FWEE
AMI-CHAN, LIKE, I FOUND IT!
MAYA-CHAN!

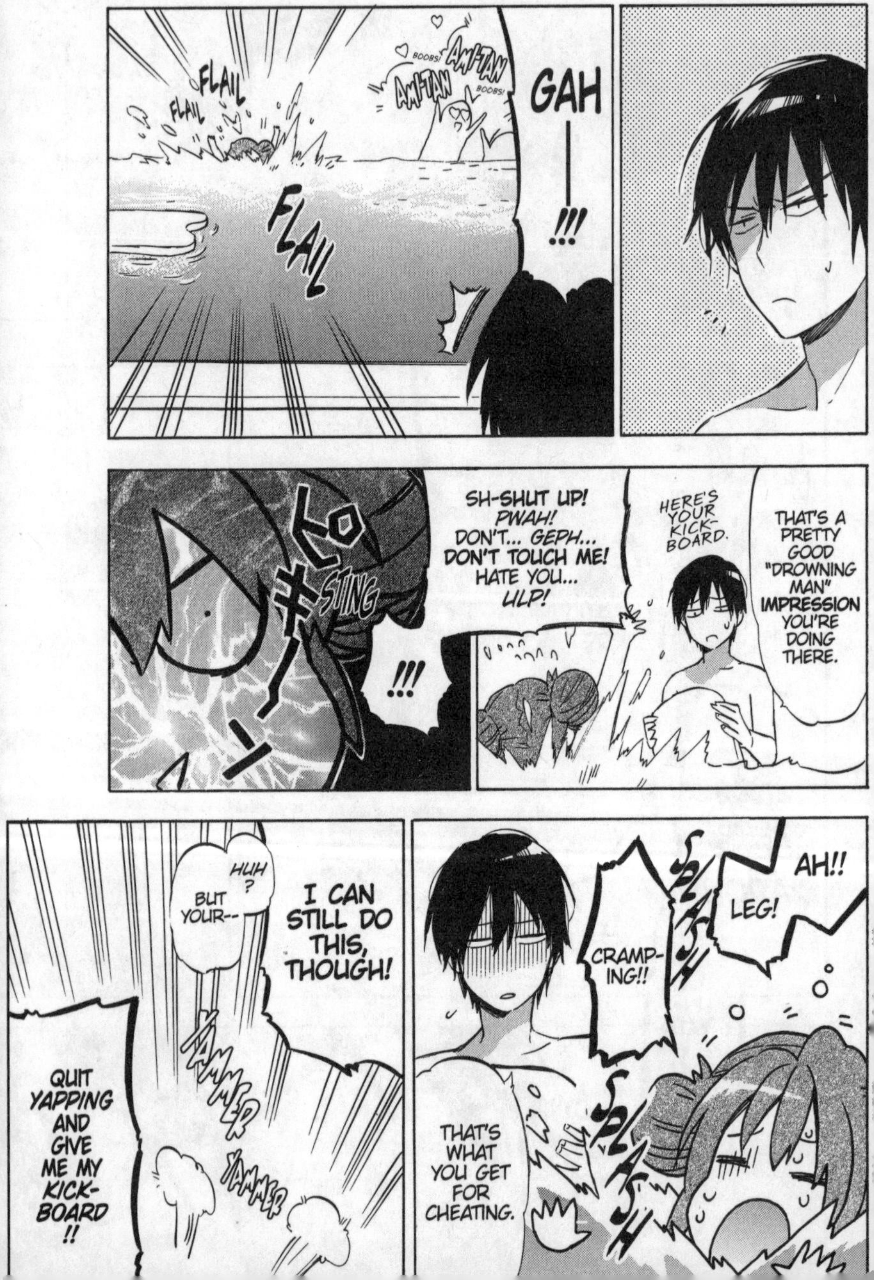
GAH—!!!
AMI-TAN BOOBS!
AMI-TAN BOOBS!
FLAIL
FLAIL
FLAIL
THAT'S A PRETTY GOOD "DROWNING MAN" IMPRESSION YOU'RE DOING THERE.
HERE'S YOUR KICK-BOARD.
SH-SHUT UP! PWAH! DON'T... GEPH... DON'T TOUCH ME! HATE YOU... ULP!
STING
!!!
AH!!
LEG!
SPLASH
CRAMPING!!
THAT'S WHAT YOU GET FOR CHEATING.
SPLASH
HUH? BUT YOUR--
I CAN STILL DO THIS, THOUGH!
YAMMER
YAMMER
QUIT YAPPING AND GIVE ME MY KICK-BOARD!!

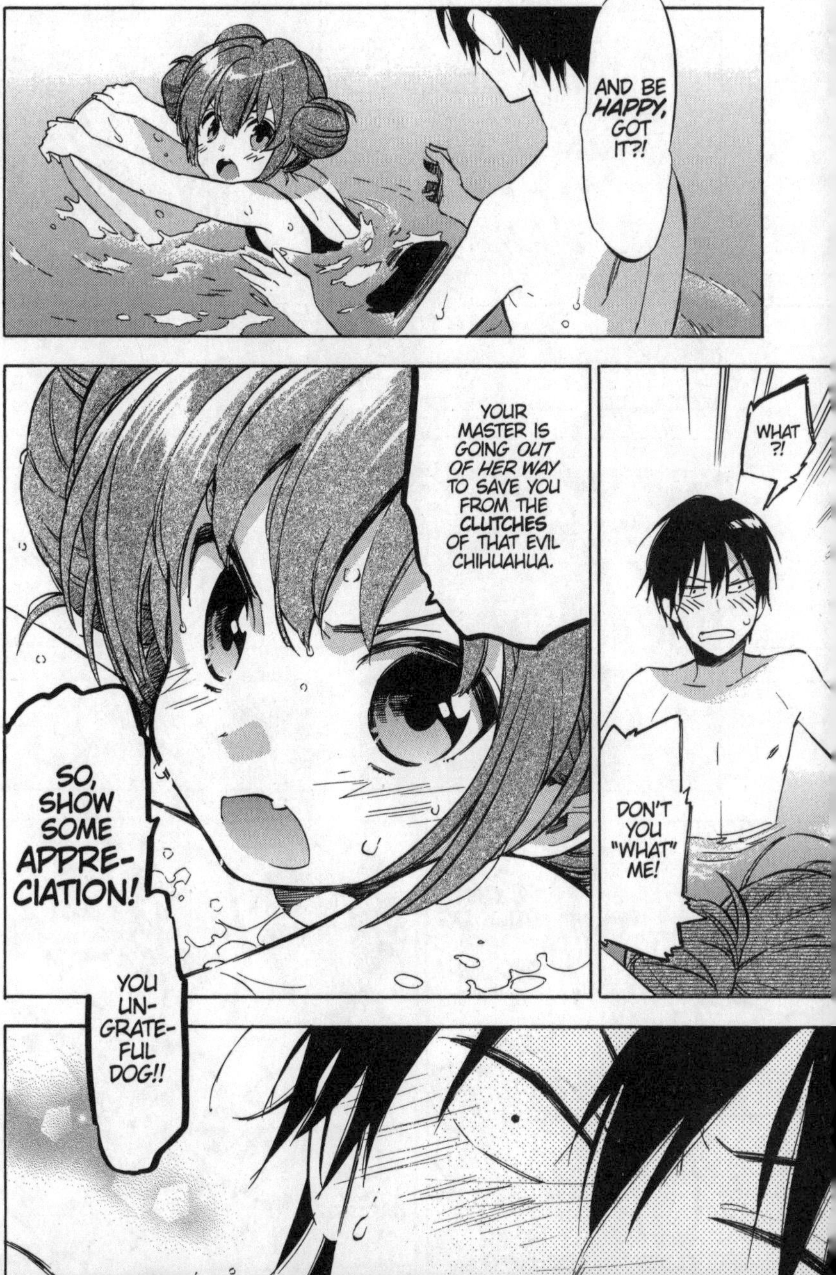
AND BE HAPPY, GOT IT?!
WHAT?!
DON'T YOU "WHAT" ME!
YOUR MASTER IS GOING OUT OF HER WAY TO SAVE YOU FROM THE CLUTCHES OF THAT EVIL CHIHUAHUA.
SO, SHOW SOME APPRECIATION!
YOU UNGRATEFUL DOG!!

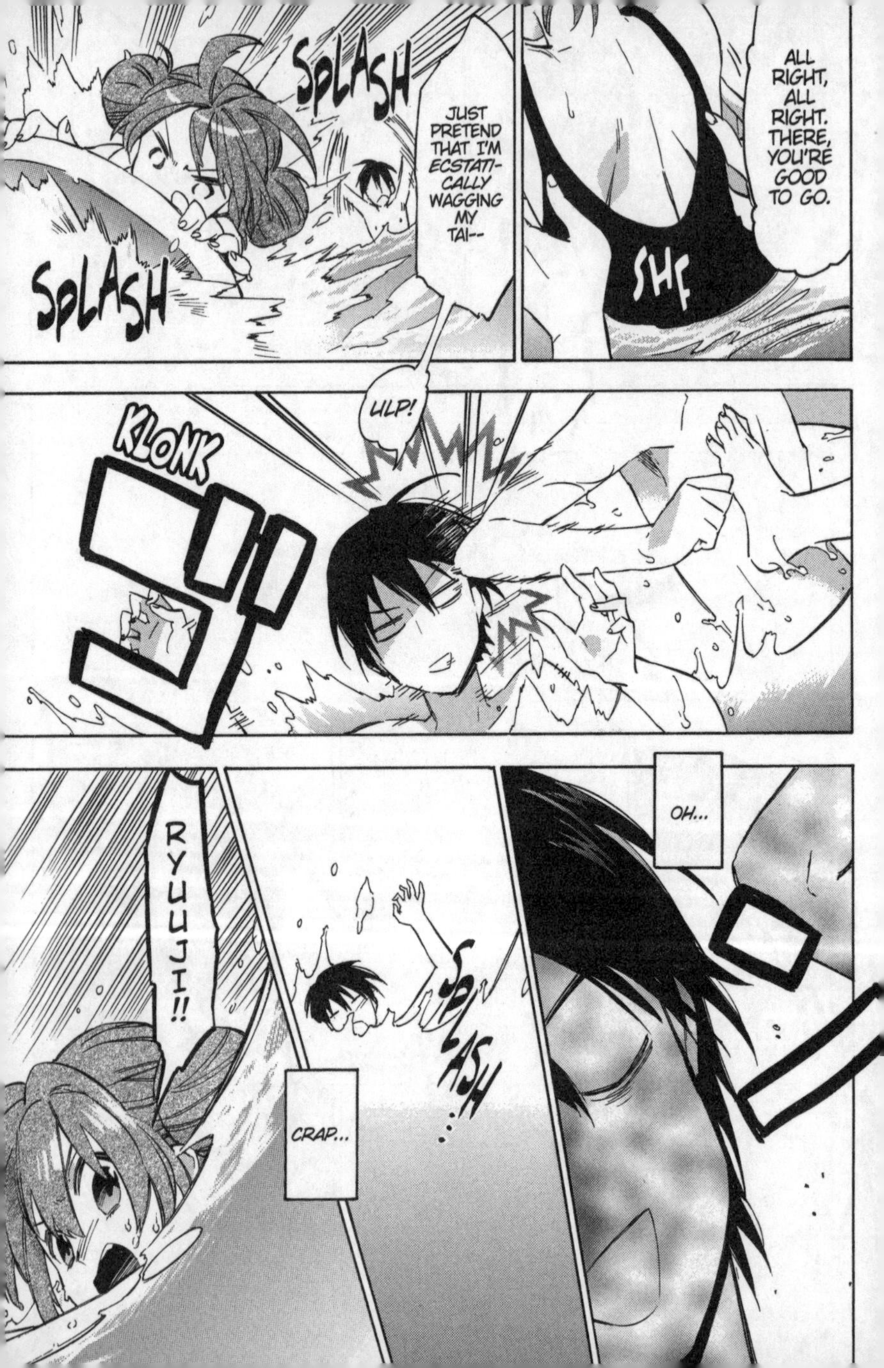
ALL RIGHT, ALL RIGHT. THERE, YOU'RE GOOD TO GO.
SHF
SPLASH
JUST PRETEND THAT I'M ECSTATICALLY WAGGING MY TAI--
SPLASH
ULP!
KLONK
OH...
SPLASH...
CRAP...
RYUUJI!!

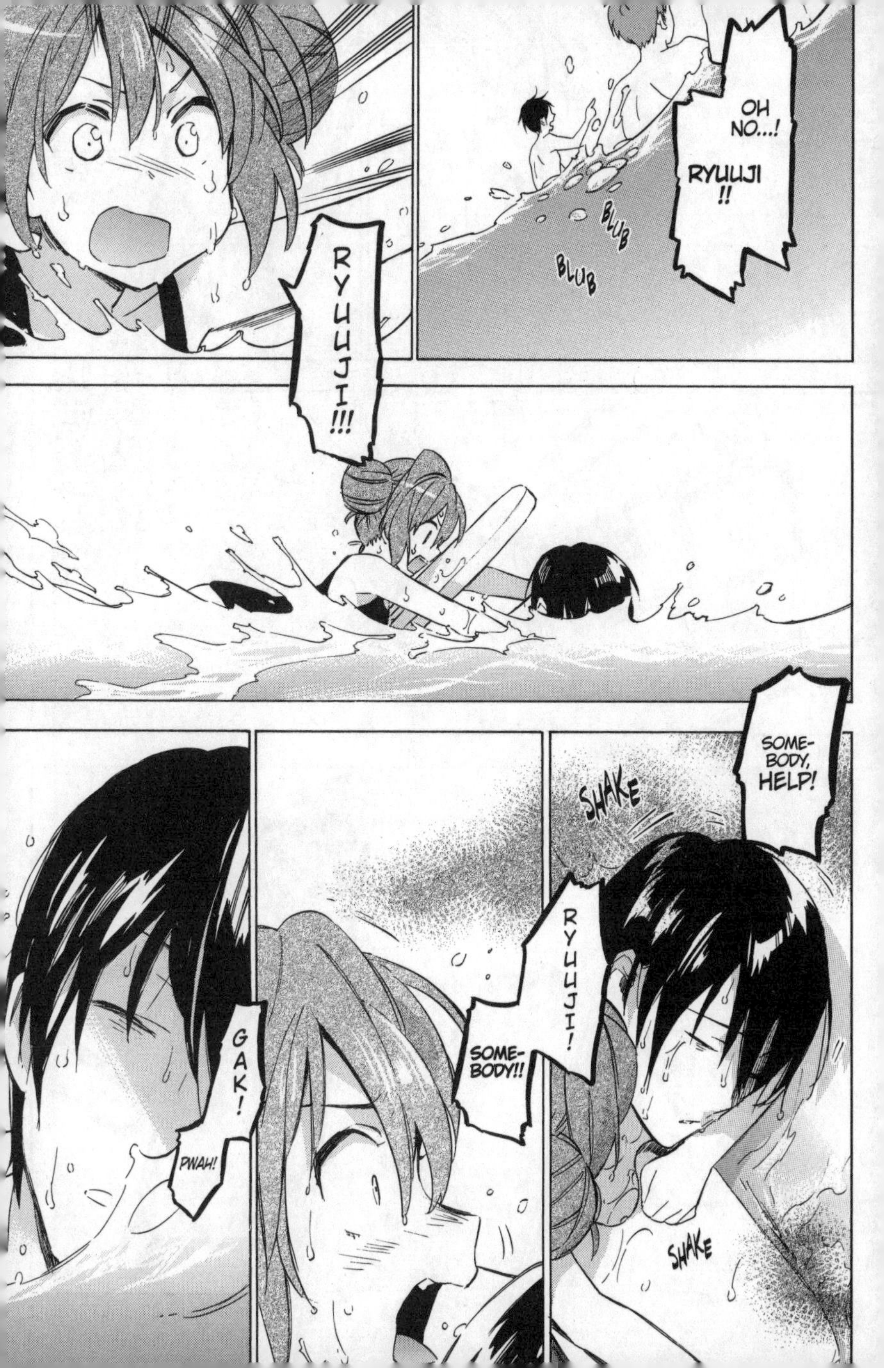
OH NO...!
RYUUJI!!
BLUB
BLUB
RYUUJI!!!
SOME-BODY, HELP!
SHAKE
RYUUJI!
SOME-BODY!!
SHAKE
GAK!
PWAH!

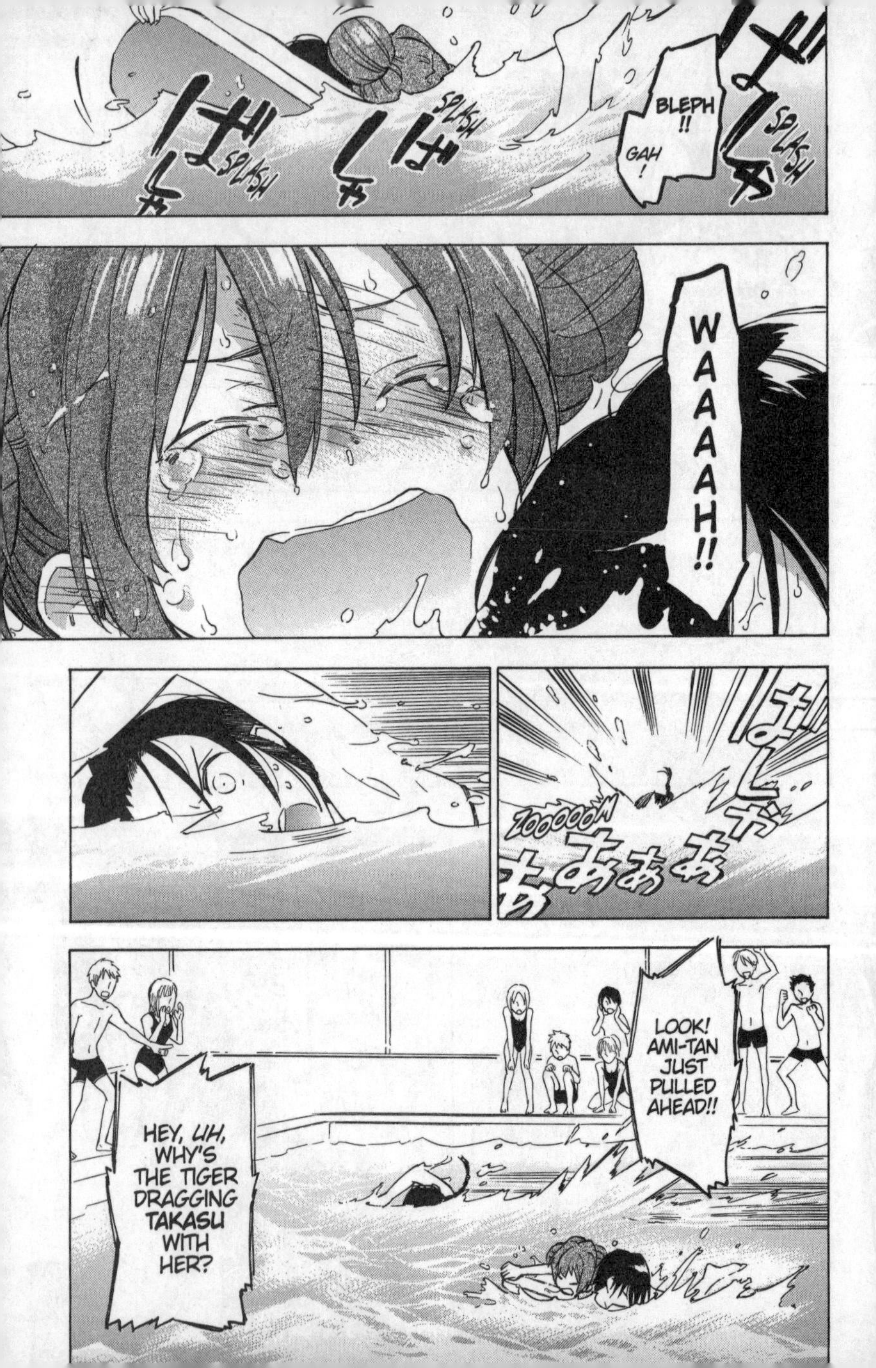

ばしゃ
SPLASH
BLEPH!!
GAH!
ばしゃ
SPLASH
ばしゃ
SPLASH
WAAAAAH!!
ばしゃあああ
ZOOOOOM
LOOK! AMI-TAN JUST PULLED AHEAD!!
HEY, UH, WHY'S THE TIGER DRAGGING TAKASU WITH HER?

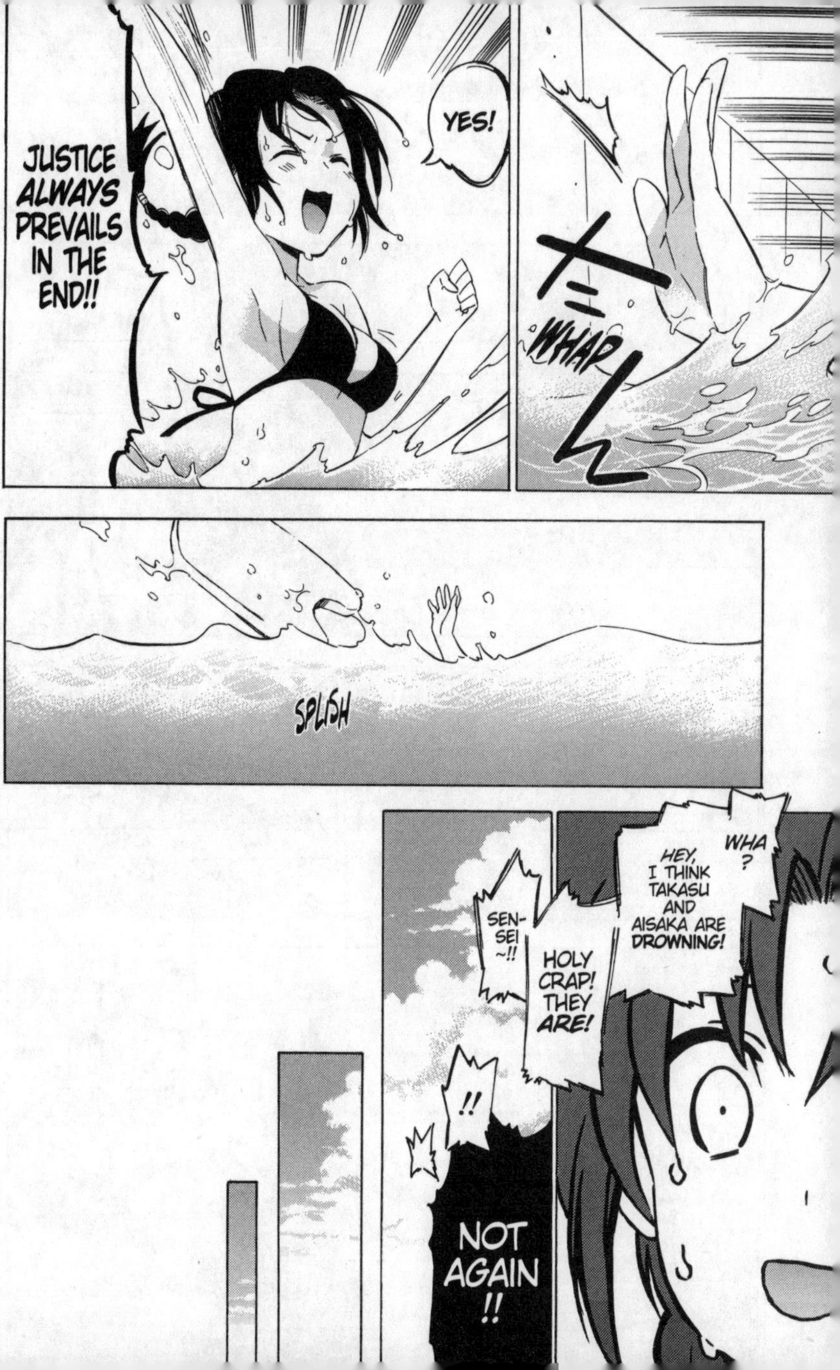
WHAP
YES!
JUSTICE ALWAYS PREVAILS IN THE END!!
SPLISH
WHA?
HEY, I THINK TAKASU AND AISAKA ARE DROWNING!
HOLY CRAP! THEY ARE!
SEN-SEI~!!
!!
NOT AGAIN!!

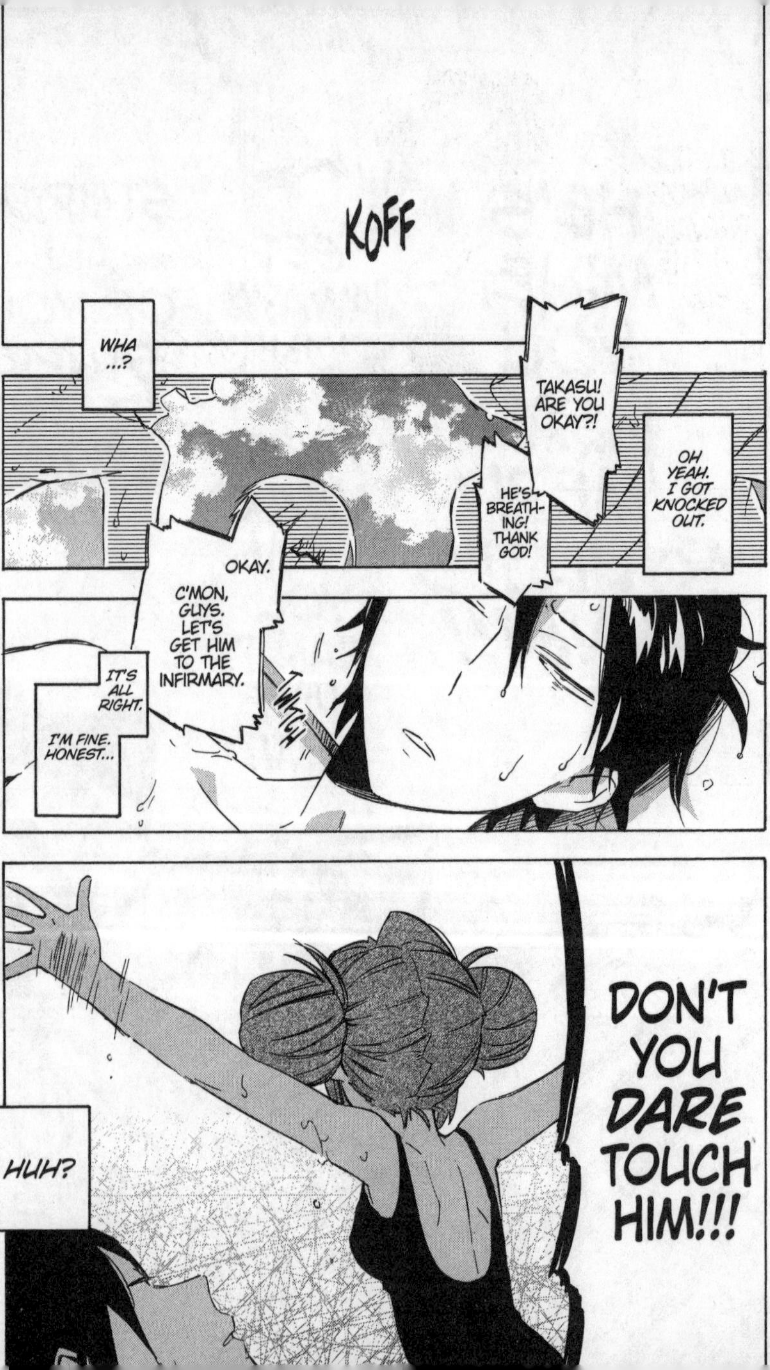
KOFF
WHA ...?
TAKASU! ARE YOU OKAY?!
OH YEAH. I GOT KNOCKED OUT.
HE'S BREATH-ING! THANK GOD!
OKAY.
C'MON, GUYS. LET'S GET HIM TO THE INFIRMARY.
TWITCH
IT'S ALL RIGHT.
I'M FINE. HONEST...
DON'T YOU DARE TOUCH HIM!!!
HUH?

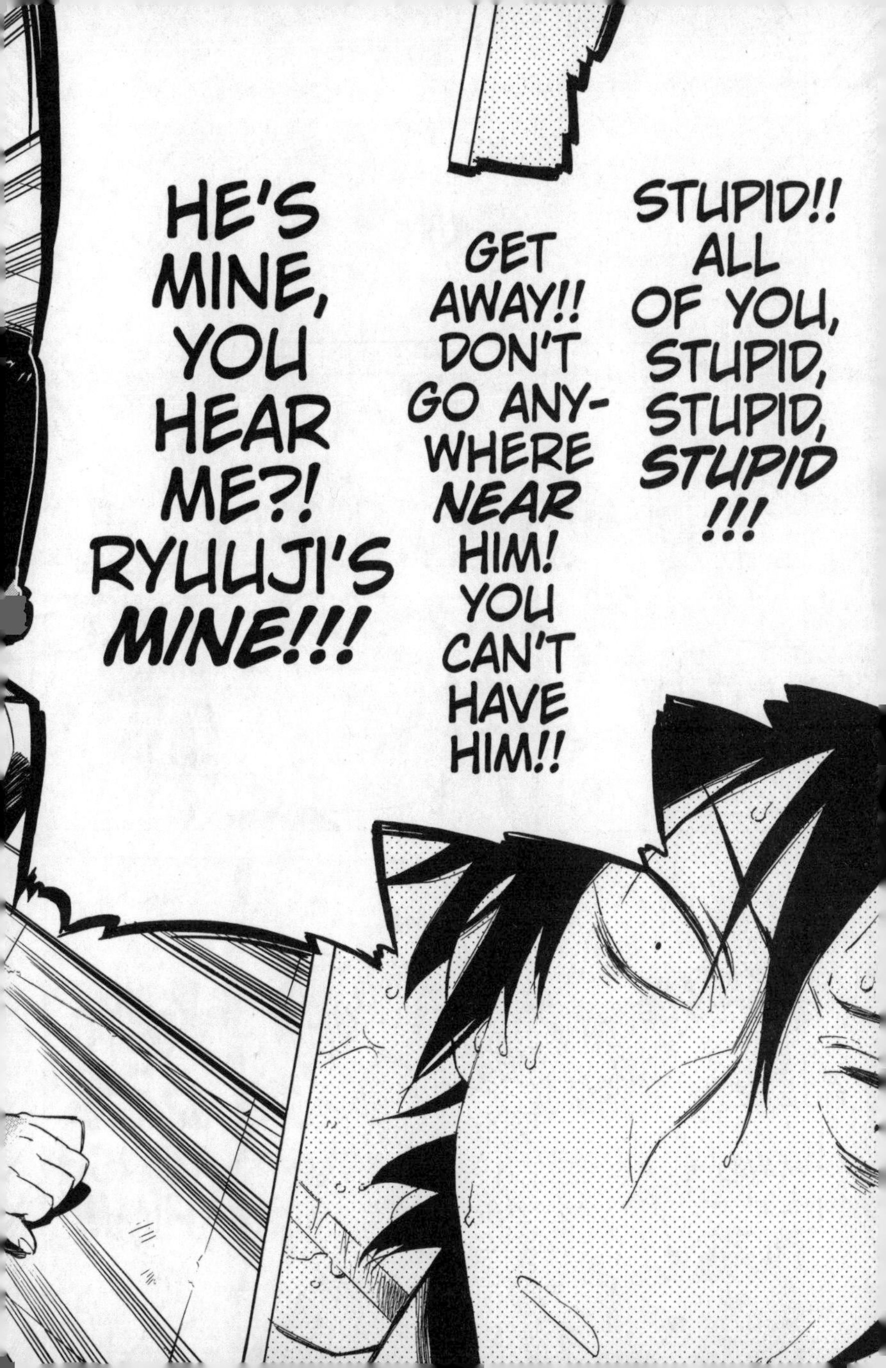
STUPID!! ALL OF YOU, STUPID, STUPID, STUPID!!!
GET AWAY!! DON'T GO ANYWHERE NEAR HIM! YOU CAN'T HAVE HIM!!
HE'S MINE, YOU HEAR ME?! RYUUJI'S MINE!!!

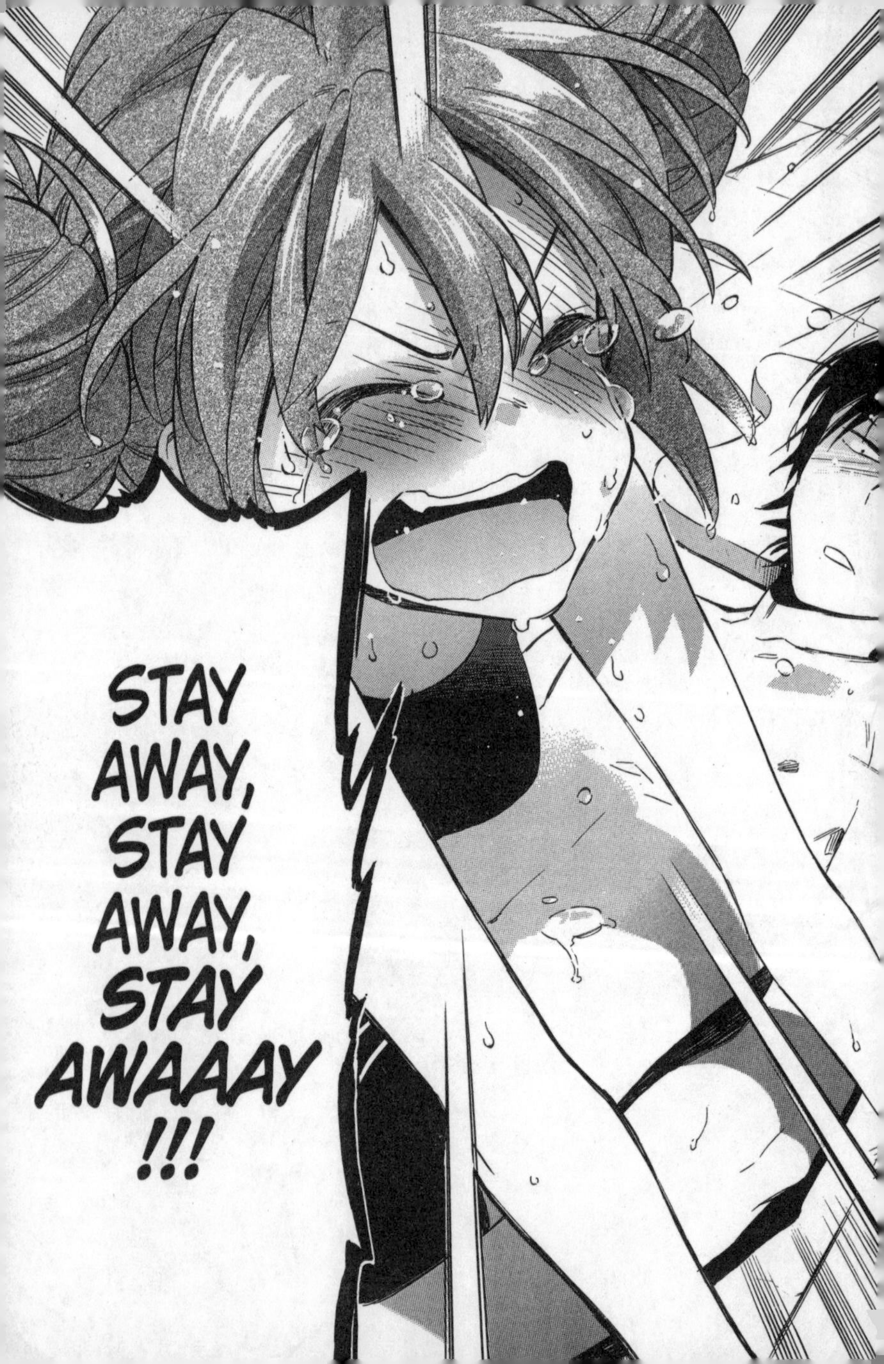
STAY AWAY, STAY AWAY, STAY AWAAAY !!!

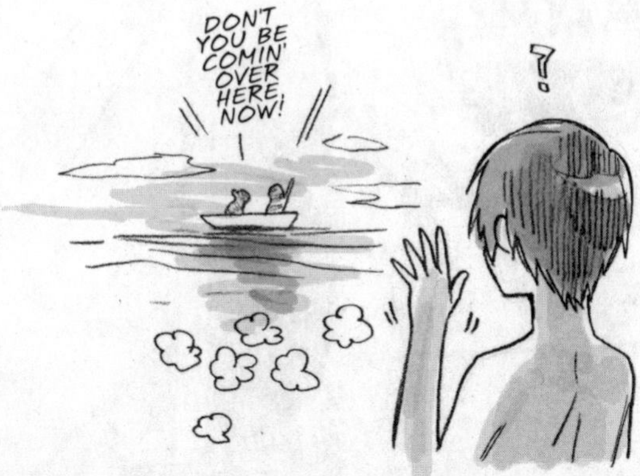
DON'T YOU BE COMIN' OVER HERE, NOW!
?

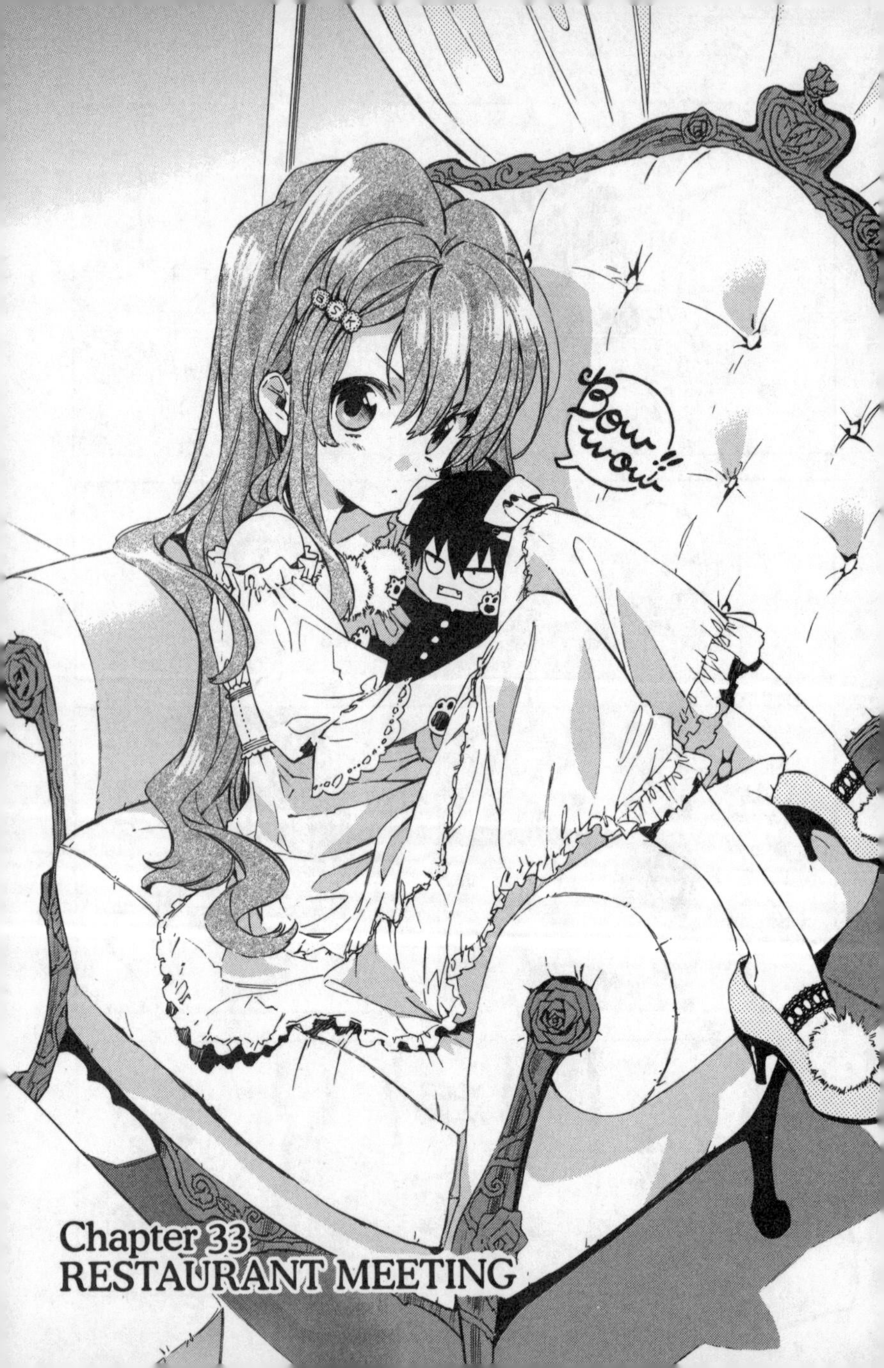
Bow wow!!

Chapter 33
RESTAURANT MEETING

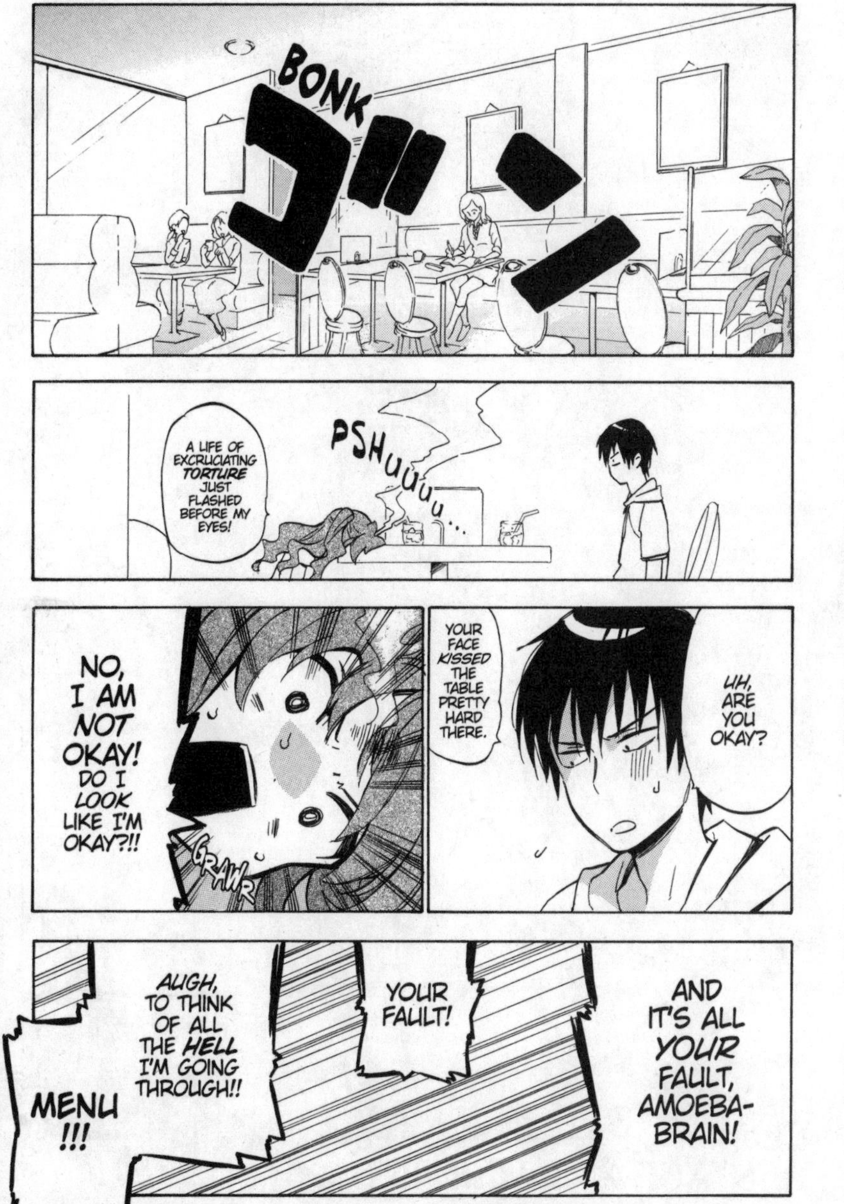
BONK
PSHUUUUU...
A LIFE OF EXCRUCIATING *TORTURE* JUST FLASHED BEFORE MY EYES!
UH, ARE YOU OKAY?
YOUR FACE *KISSED* THE TABLE PRETTY HARD THERE.
NO, I AM *NOT* OKAY! DO I *LOOK* LIKE I'M OKAY?!!
GRAWR
AND IT'S ALL *YOUR* FAULT, AMOEBA-BRAIN!
YOUR FAULT!
AUGH, TO THINK OF ALL THE *HELL* I'M GOING THROUGH!!
MENU !!!

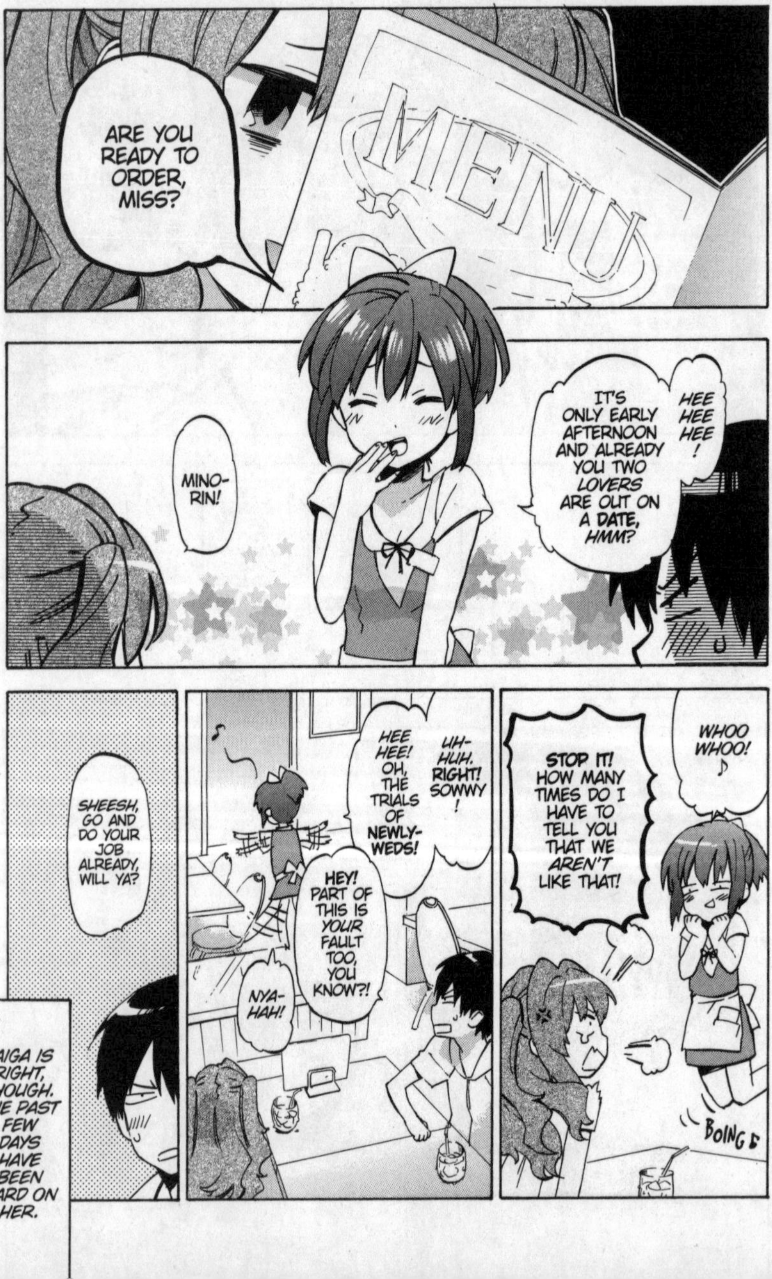
ARE YOU READY TO ORDER, MISS?
HEE HEE HEE!
IT'S ONLY EARLY AFTERNOON AND ALREADY YOU TWO *LOVERS* ARE OUT ON A DATE, *HMM?*
MINO-RIN!
WHOO WHOO! ♪
STOP IT! HOW MANY TIMES DO I HAVE TO TELL YOU THAT WE *AREN'T* LIKE THAT!
BOING
UH-HUH. RIGHT! SOWWY!
HEE HEE! OH, THE TRIALS OF NEWLY-WEDS!
HEY! PART OF THIS IS *YOUR* FAULT TOO, YOU KNOW?!
NYA-HAH!
SHEESH, GO AND DO YOUR JOB ALREADY, WILL YA?
TAIGA IS RIGHT, THOUGH. THE PAST FEW DAYS HAVE BEEN HARD ON HER.

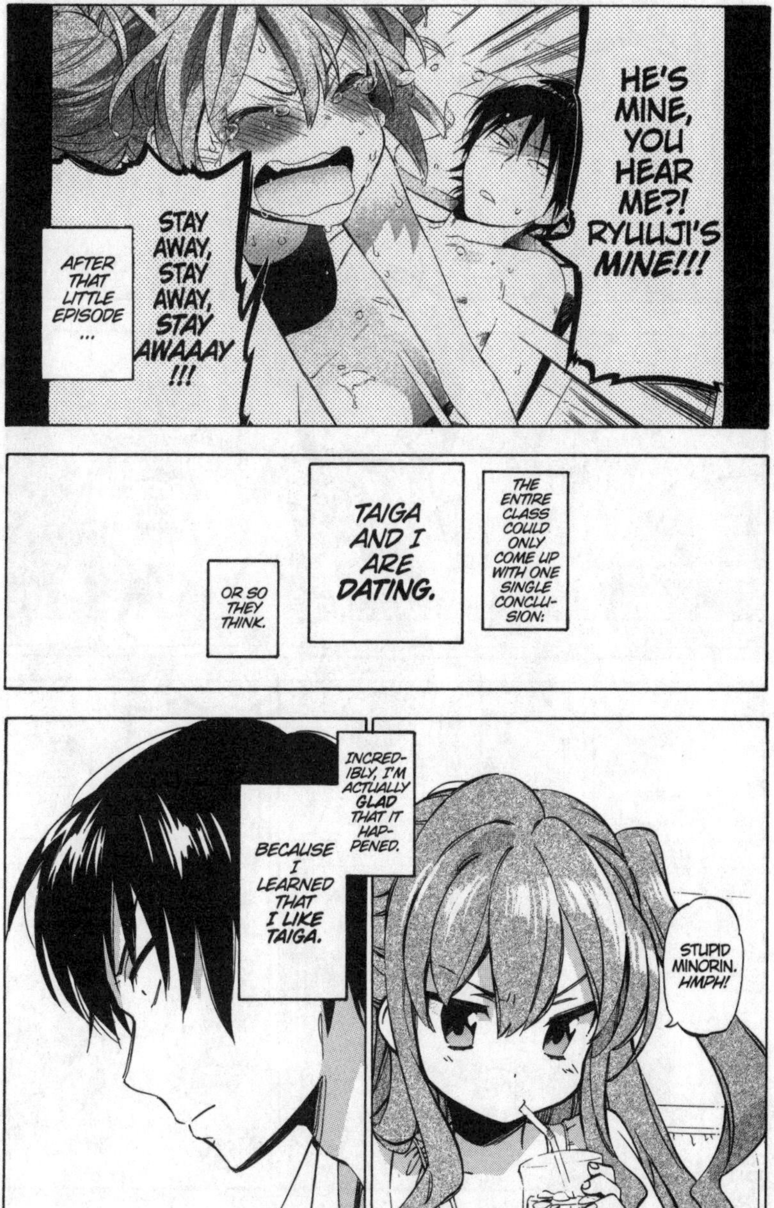
HE'S MINE, YOU HEAR ME?! RYUUJI'S MINE!!!
STAY AWAY, STAY AWAY, STAY AWAAAY!!!
AFTER THAT LITTLE EPISODE...
THE ENTIRE CLASS COULD ONLY COME UP WITH ONE SINGLE CONCLUSION:
TAIGA AND I ARE DATING.
OR SO THEY THINK.
INCREDIBLY, I'M ACTUALLY GLAD THAT IT HAPPENED.
STUPID MINORIN. HMPH!
BECAUSE I LEARNED THAT I LIKE TAIGA.

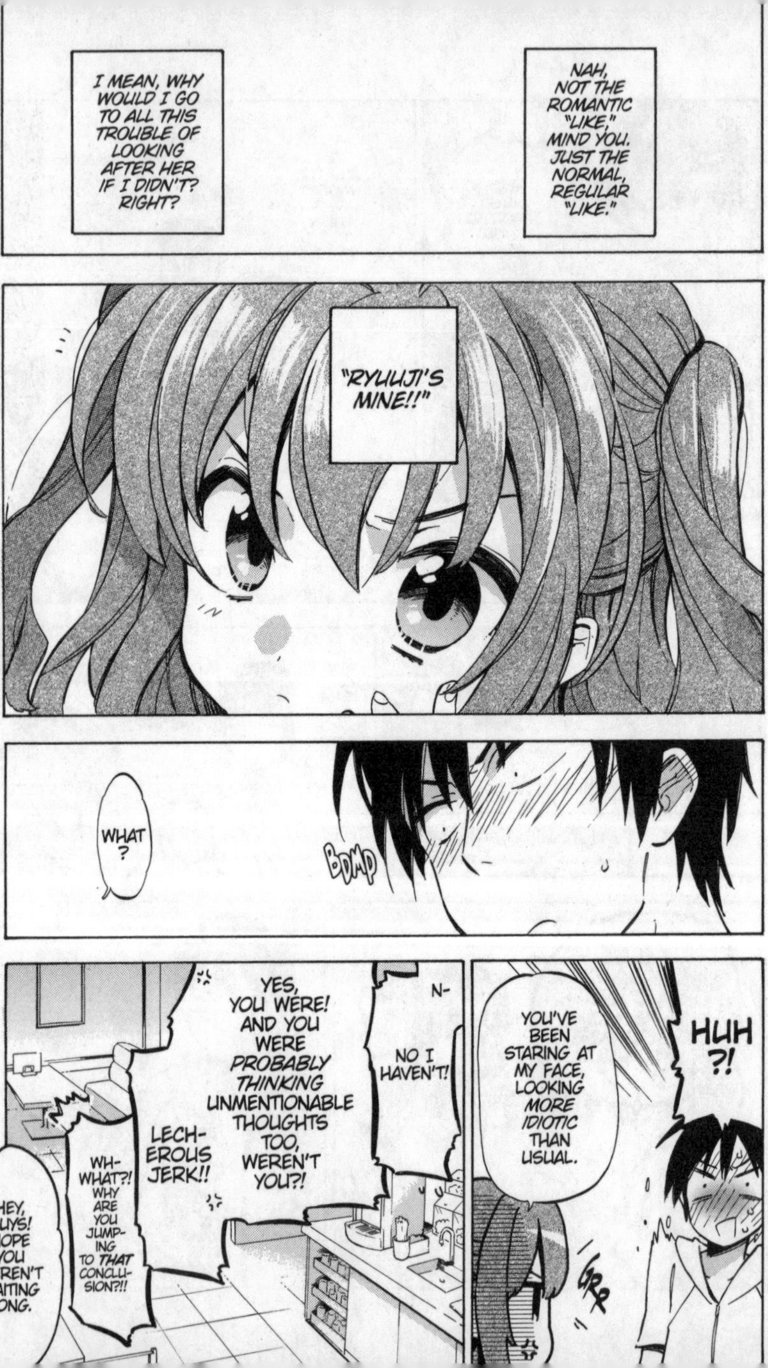
NAH, NOT THE ROMANTIC "LIKE," MIND YOU. JUST THE NORMAL, REGULAR "LIKE."
I MEAN, WHY WOULD I GO TO ALL THIS TROUBLE OF LOOKING AFTER HER IF I DIDN'T? RIGHT?
"RYUUJI'S MINE!!"
BDMP
WHAT?
HUH?!
YOU'VE BEEN STARING AT MY FACE, LOOKING MORE IDIOTIC THAN USUAL.
GRR
N- NO I HAVEN'T!
YES, YOU WERE! AND YOU WERE PROBABLY THINKING UNMENTIONABLE THOUGHTS TOO, WEREN'T YOU?!
LECH-EROUS JERK!!
WH-WHAT?! WHY ARE YOU JUMPING TO THAT CONCLUSION?!!
HEY, GUYS! HOPE YOU WEREN'T WAITING LONG.

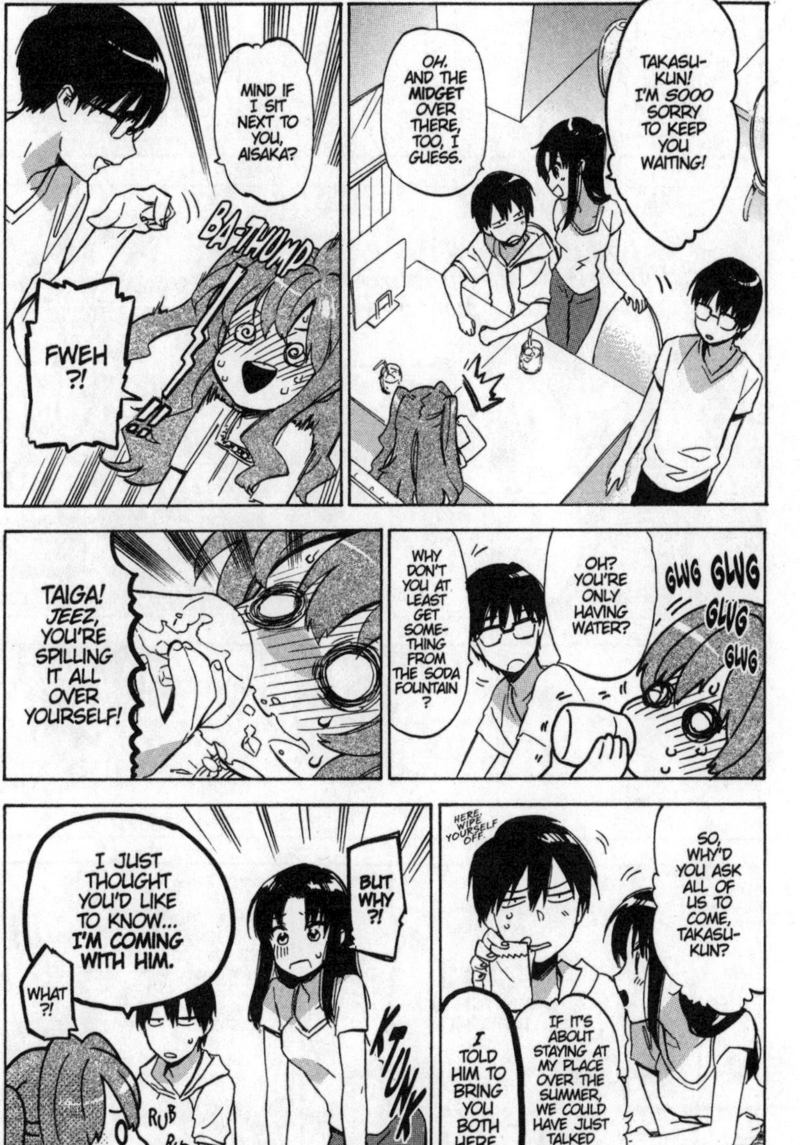
TAKASU-KUN! I'M SOOO SORRY TO KEEP YOU WAITING!
OH. AND THE MIDGET OVER THERE, TOO, I GUESS.
MIND IF I SIT NEXT TO YOU, AISAKA?
BA-THUMP
FWEH ?!
GLUG GLUG GLUG GLUG
OH? YOU'RE ONLY HAVING WATER?
WHY DON'T YOU AT LEAST GET SOMETHING FROM THE SODA FOUNTAIN ?
TAIGA! JEEZ, YOU'RE SPILLING IT ALL OVER YOURSELF!
SO, WHY'D YOU ASK ALL OF US TO COME, TAKASU-KUN?
HERE. WIPE YOURSELF OFF.
IF IT'S ABOUT STAYING AT MY PLACE OVER THE SUMMER, WE COULD HAVE JUST TALKED ABOUT IT... ALONE.
I TOLD HIM TO BRING YOU BOTH HERE.
BUT WHY ?!
KTUNK
I JUST THOUGHT YOU'D LIKE TO KNOW... I'M COMING WITH HIM.
WHAT ?!
RUB RUB

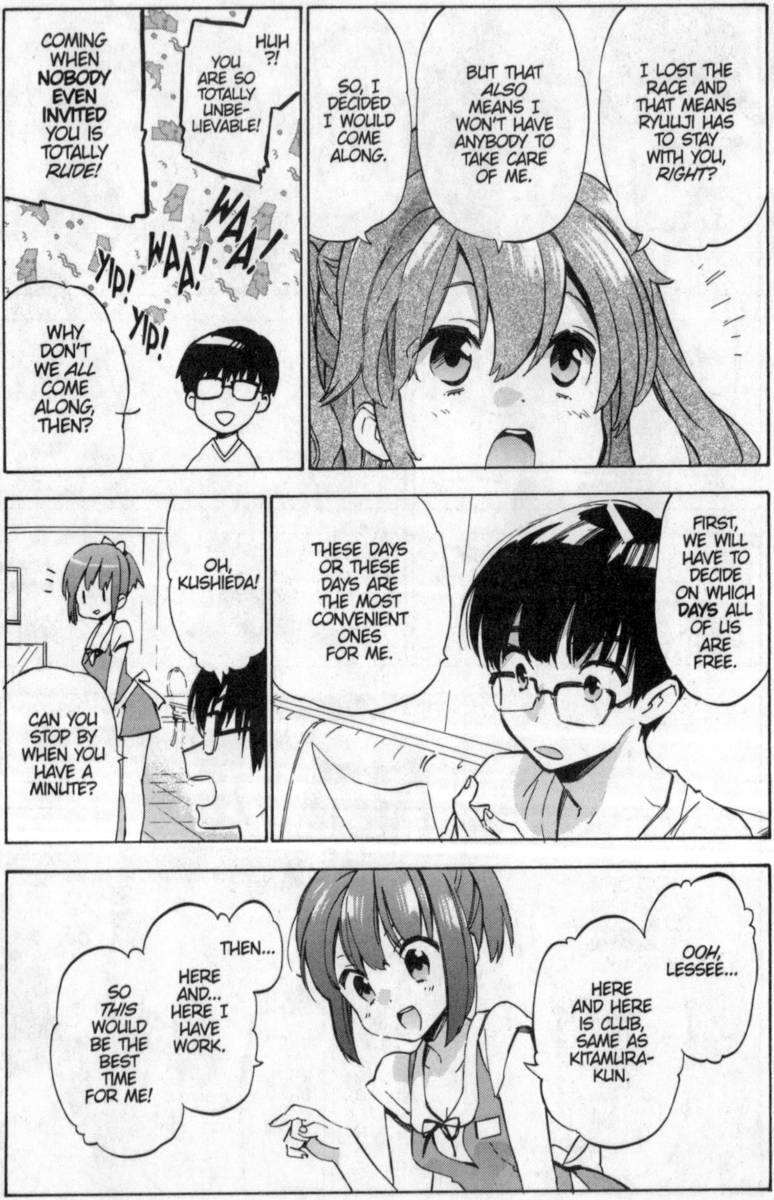
I LOST THE RACE AND THAT MEANS RYUUJI HAS TO STAY WITH YOU, *RIGHT?*
BUT THAT *ALSO* MEANS I WON'T HAVE ANYBODY TO TAKE CARE OF ME.
SO, I DECIDED I WOULD COME ALONG.
HUH ?!
YOU ARE SO TOTALLY UNBE-LIEVABLE!
COMING WHEN **NOBODY EVEN INVITED** YOU IS TOTALLY *RUDE!*
WAA!
WAA!
YIP!
YIP!
WHY DON'T WE *ALL* COME ALONG, THEN?
FIRST, WE WILL HAVE TO DECIDE ON WHICH **DAYS** ALL OF US ARE FREE.
THESE DAYS OR THESE DAYS ARE THE MOST CONVENIENT ONES FOR ME.
OH, KUSHIEDA!
CAN YOU STOP BY WHEN YOU HAVE A MINUTE?
OOH, LESSEE...
HERE AND HERE IS CLUB, SAME AS KITAMURA-KUN.
THEN...
HERE AND... HERE I HAVE WORK.
SO *THIS* WOULD BE THE BEST TIME FOR ME!

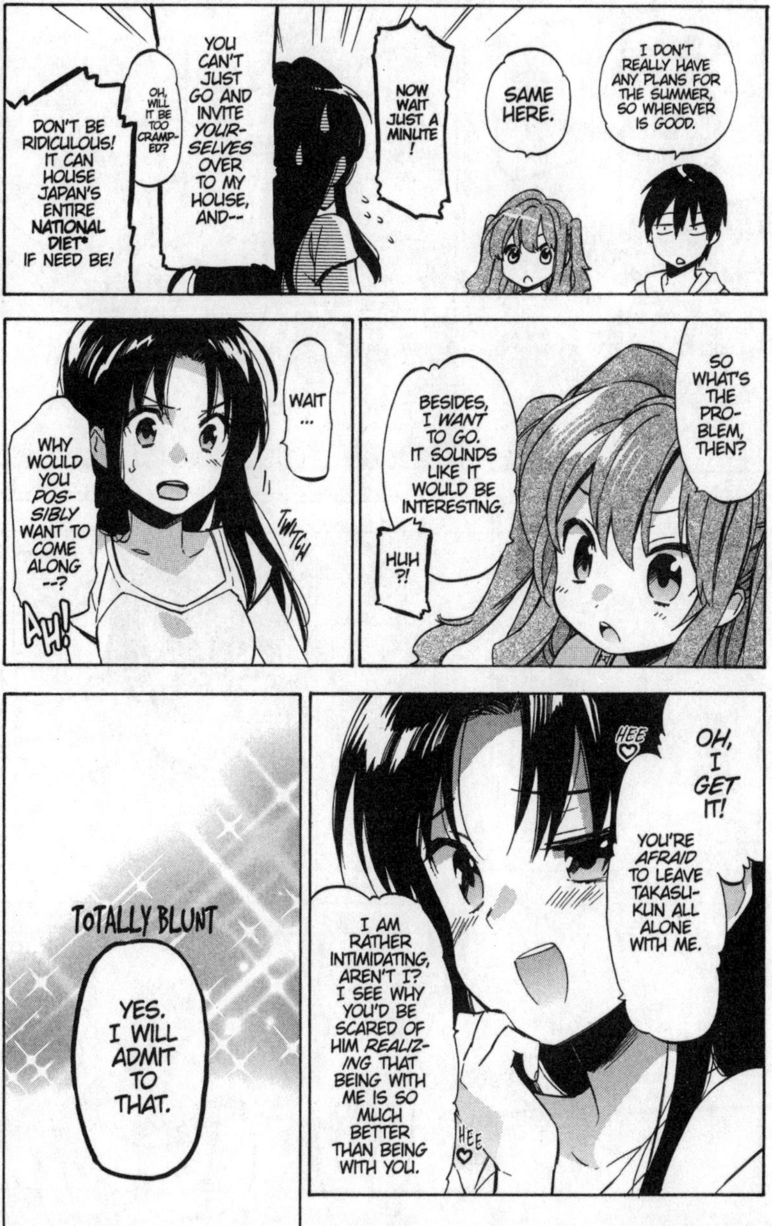
I DON'T REALLY HAVE ANY PLANS FOR THE SUMMER, SO WHENEVER IS GOOD.
SAME HERE.
NOW WAIT JUST A MINUTE!
YOU CAN'T JUST GO AND INVITE *YOURSELVES* OVER TO MY HOUSE, AND--
OH, WILL IT BE TOO CRAMPED?
DON'T BE RIDICULOUS! IT CAN HOUSE JAPAN'S ENTIRE NATIONAL DIET* IF NEED BE!
SO WHAT'S THE PROBLEM, THEN?
BESIDES, I *WANT* TO GO. IT SOUNDS LIKE IT WOULD BE INTERESTING.
HUH?!
WAIT...
TWITCH
WHY WOULD YOU *POSSIBLY* WANT TO COME ALONG--?
AH!
HEE
OH, I GET IT!
YOU'RE *AFRAID* TO LEAVE TAKASU-KUN ALL ALONE WITH ME.
I AM RATHER INTIMIDATING, AREN'T I? I SEE WHY YOU'D BE SCARED OF HIM *REALIZING* THAT BEING WITH ME IS SO MUCH BETTER THAN BEING WITH YOU.
HEE
TOTALLY BLUNT
YES. I WILL ADMIT TO THAT.

*Japan's bicameral legislature. It is composed of a lower house, called the House of Representatives, and an upper house, called the House of Councilors.

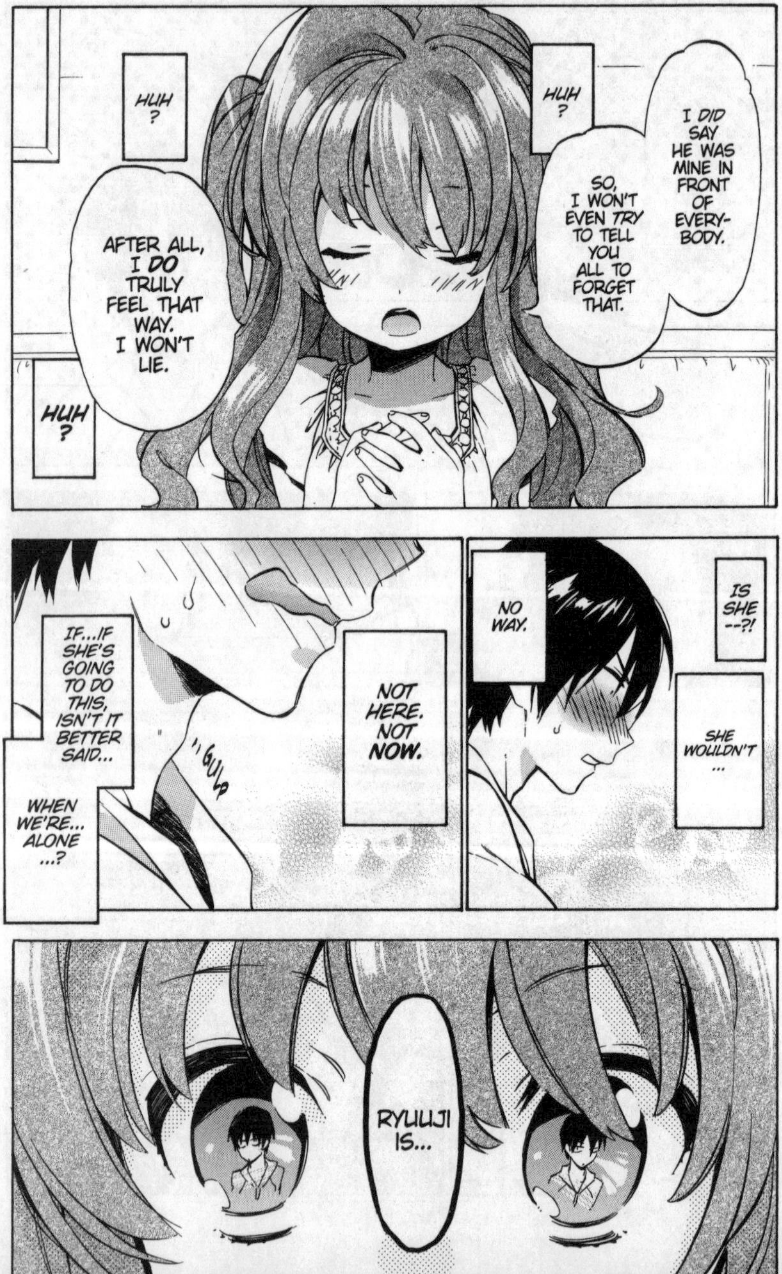
I DID SAY HE WAS MINE IN FRONT OF EVERY-BODY.
HUH?
SO, I WON'T EVEN TRY TO TELL YOU ALL TO FORGET THAT.
HUH?
AFTER ALL, I DO TRULY FEEL THAT WAY. I WON'T LIE.
HUH?
IS SHE--?!
NO WAY.
SHE WOULDN'T...
NOT HERE. NOT NOW.
IF...IF SHE'S GOING TO DO THIS, ISN'T IT BETTER SAID...
GULP
WHEN WE'RE... ALONE...?
RYUUJI IS...

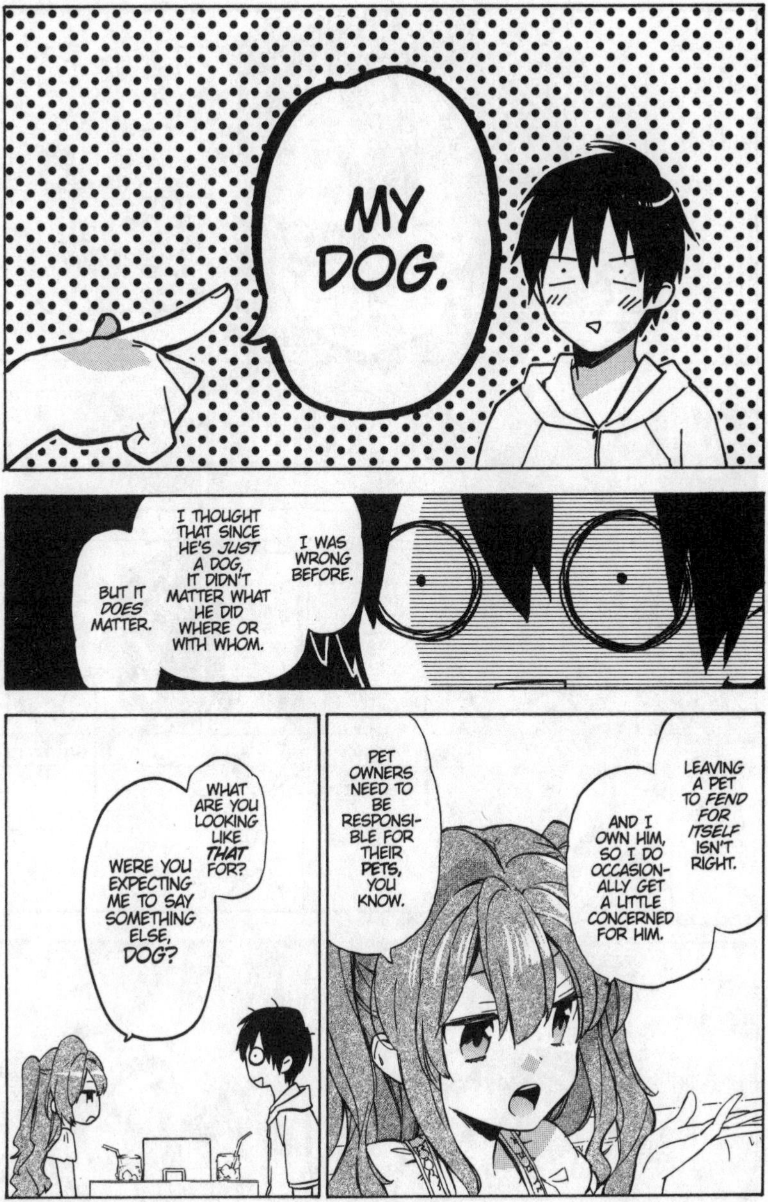
MY DOG.
I WAS WRONG BEFORE.
I THOUGHT THAT SINCE HE'S *JUST* A DOG, IT DIDN'T MATTER WHAT HE DID WHERE OR WITH WHOM.
BUT IT *DOES* MATTER.
LEAVING A PET TO *FEND FOR ITSELF* ISN'T RIGHT.
AND I OWN HIM, SO I DO OCCASIONALLY GET A LITTLE CONCERNED FOR HIM.
PET OWNERS NEED TO BE RESPONSIBLE FOR THEIR **PETS**, YOU KNOW.
WHAT ARE YOU LOOKING LIKE ***THAT*** FOR?
WERE YOU EXPECTING ME TO SAY SOMETHING ELSE, **DOG**?

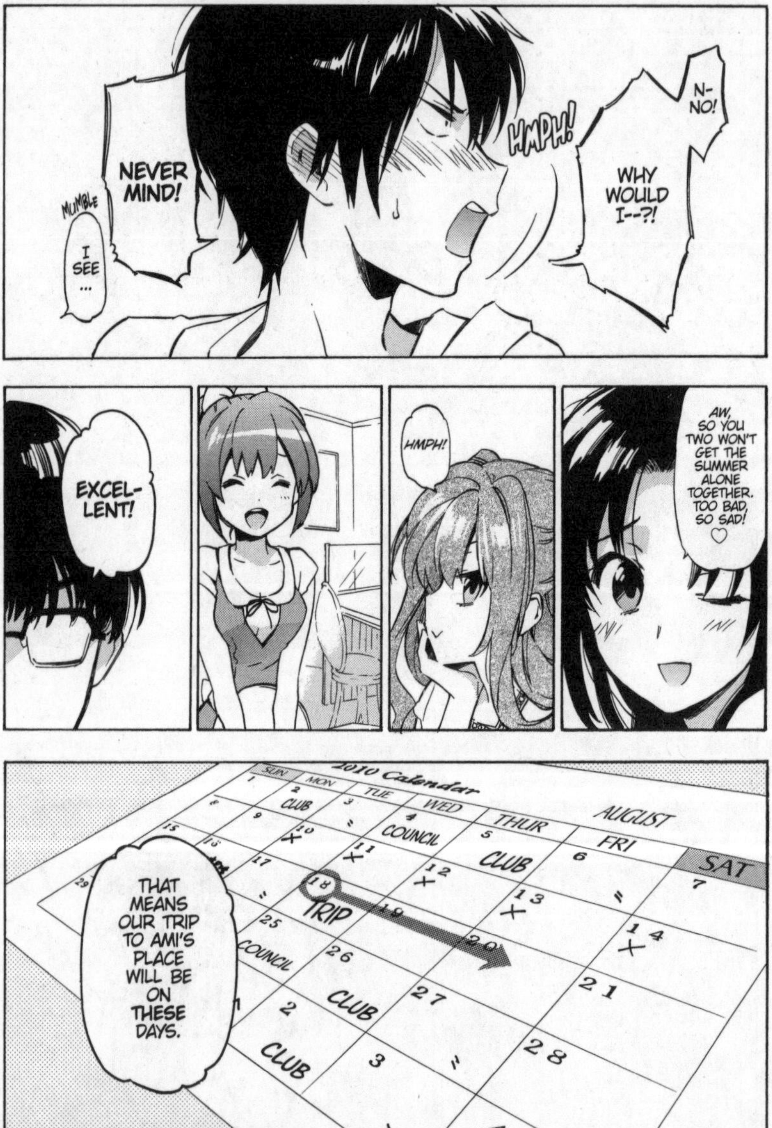
N-NO!
WHY WOULD I--?!
HMPH!
NEVER MIND!
MUMBLE
I SEE...
AW, SO YOU TWO WON'T GET THE SUMMER ALONE TOGETHER. TOO BAD, SO SAD! ♡
HMPH!
EXCEL-LENT!
2010 Calendar
AUGUST
SUN MON TUE WED THUR FRI SAT
CLUB
COUNCIL
CLUB
TRIP
COUNCIL
CLUB
CLUB
THAT MEANS OUR TRIP TO AMI'S PLACE WILL BE ON THESE DAYS.

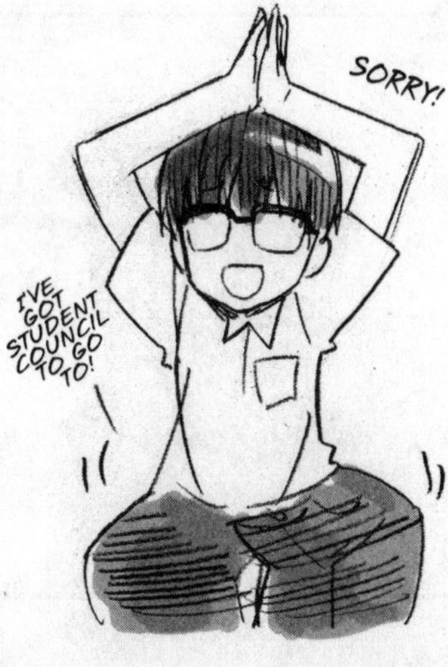
SORRY!
I'VE GOT STUDENT COUNCIL TO GO TO!

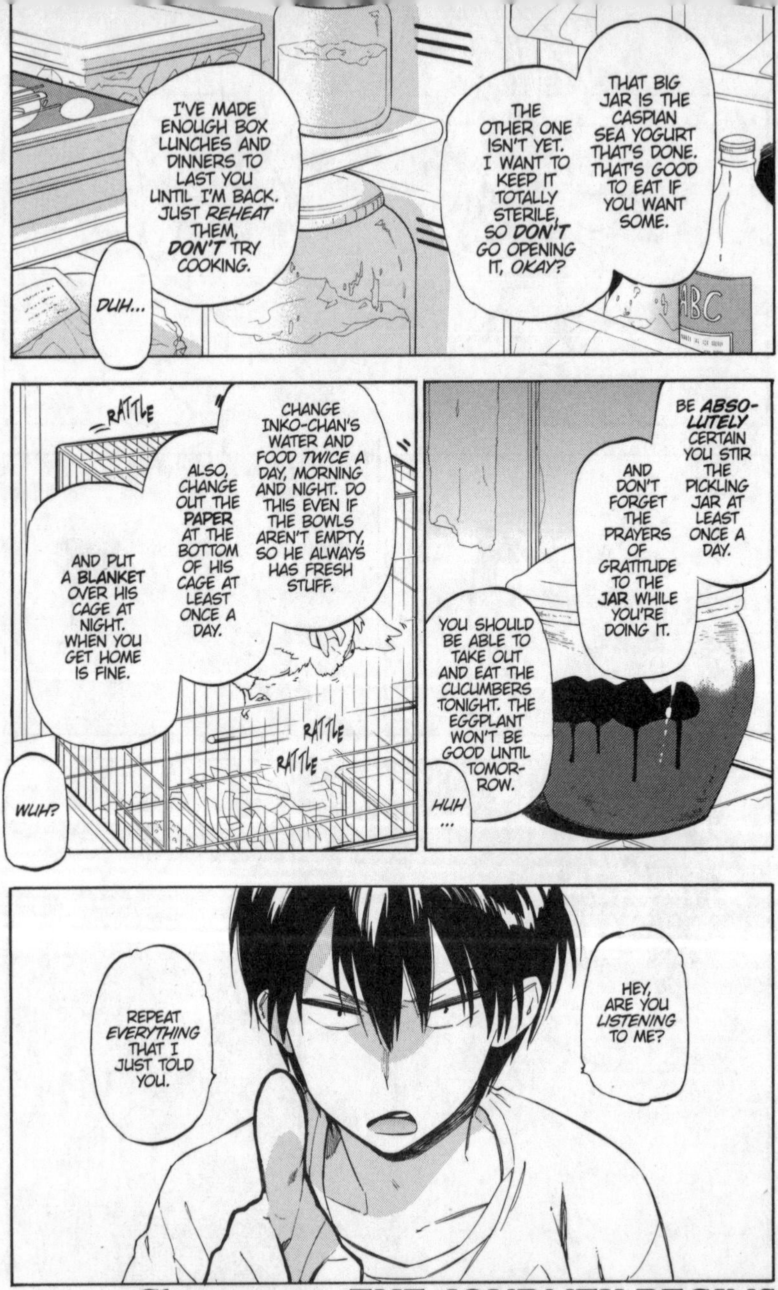
THAT BIG JAR IS THE CASPIAN SEA YOGURT THAT'S DONE. THAT'S GOOD TO EAT IF YOU WANT SOME.
THE OTHER ONE ISN'T YET. I WANT TO KEEP IT TOTALLY STERILE, SO DON'T GO OPENING IT, OKAY?
I'VE MADE ENOUGH BOX LUNCHES AND DINNERS TO LAST YOU UNTIL I'M BACK. JUST REHEAT THEM, DON'T TRY COOKING.
DUH...
BE ABSOLUTELY CERTAIN YOU STIR THE PICKLING JAR AT LEAST ONCE A DAY.
AND DON'T FORGET THE PRAYERS OF GRATITUDE TO THE JAR WHILE YOU'RE DOING IT.
YOU SHOULD BE ABLE TO TAKE OUT AND EAT THE CUCUMBERS TONIGHT. THE EGGPLANT WON'T BE GOOD UNTIL TOMOR-ROW.
HUH...
RATTLE
CHANGE INKO-CHAN'S WATER AND FOOD TWICE A DAY, MORNING AND NIGHT. DO THIS EVEN IF THE BOWLS AREN'T EMPTY, SO HE ALWAYS HAS FRESH STUFF.
ALSO, CHANGE OUT THE PAPER AT THE BOTTOM OF HIS CAGE AT LEAST ONCE A DAY.
AND PUT A BLANKET OVER HIS CAGE AT NIGHT. WHEN YOU GET HOME IS FINE.
RATTLE
RATTLE
WUH?
HEY, ARE YOU LISTENING TO ME?
REPEAT EVERYTHING THAT I JUST TOLD YOU.

Chapter 34 THE JOURNEY BEGINS

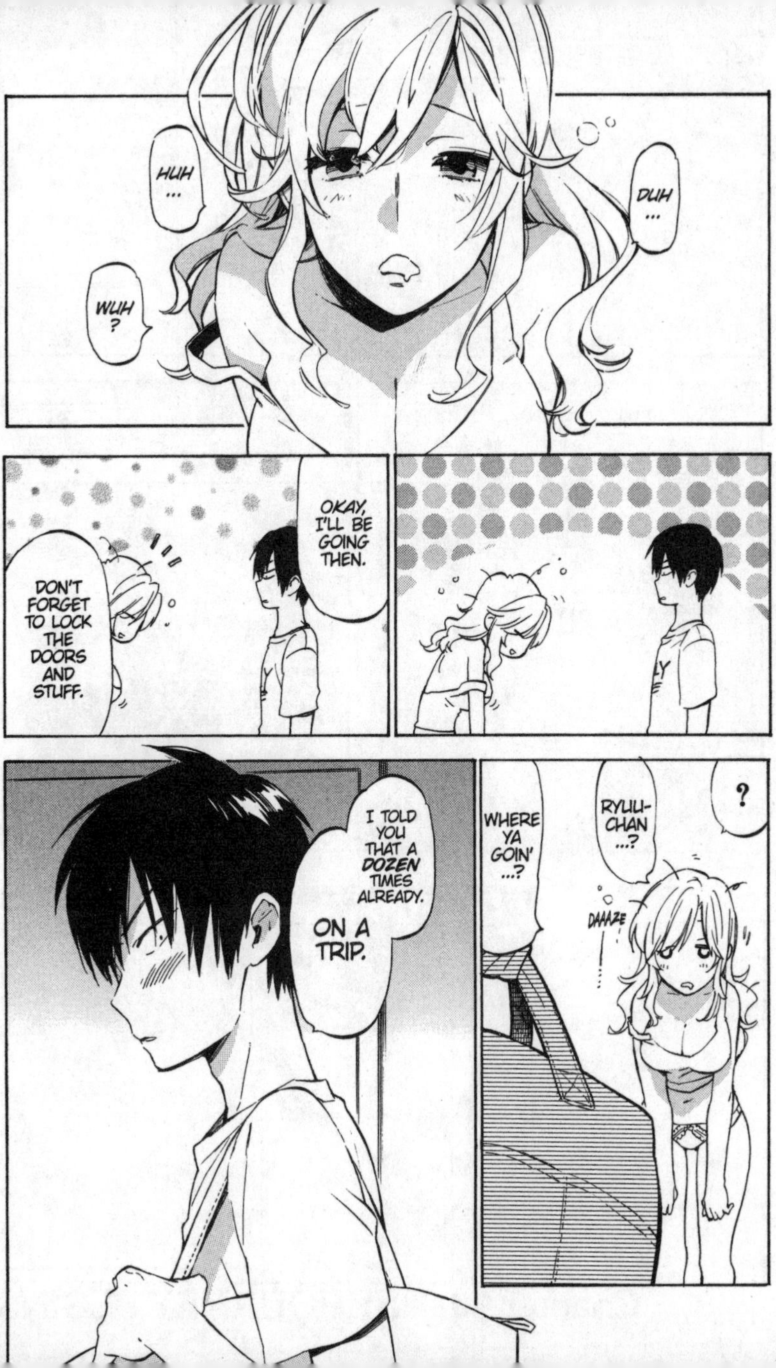
DUH ...
HUH ...
WUH ?
OKAY, I'LL BE GOING THEN.
DON'T FORGET TO LOCK THE DOORS AND STUFF.
?
RYUU-CHAN ...?
WHERE YA GOIN' ...?
DAAAZE
I TOLD YOU THAT A DOZEN TIMES ALREADY.
ON A TRIP.

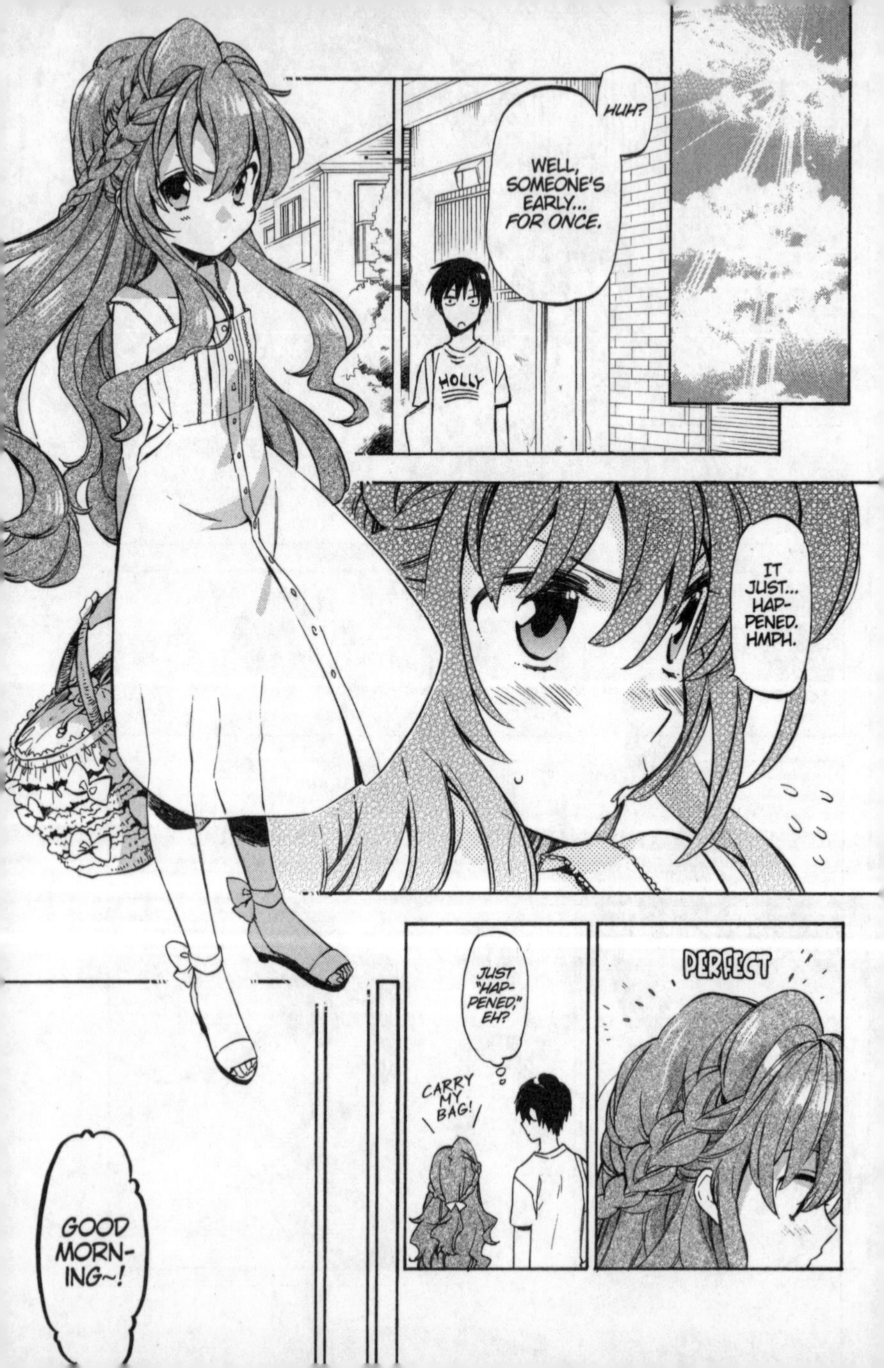
HUH?
WELL, SOMEONE'S EARLY... FOR ONCE.
HOLLY
IT JUST... HAP-PENED. HMPH.
PERFECT
JUST "HAP-PENED," EH?
CARRY MY BAG!
GOOD MORN-ING~!

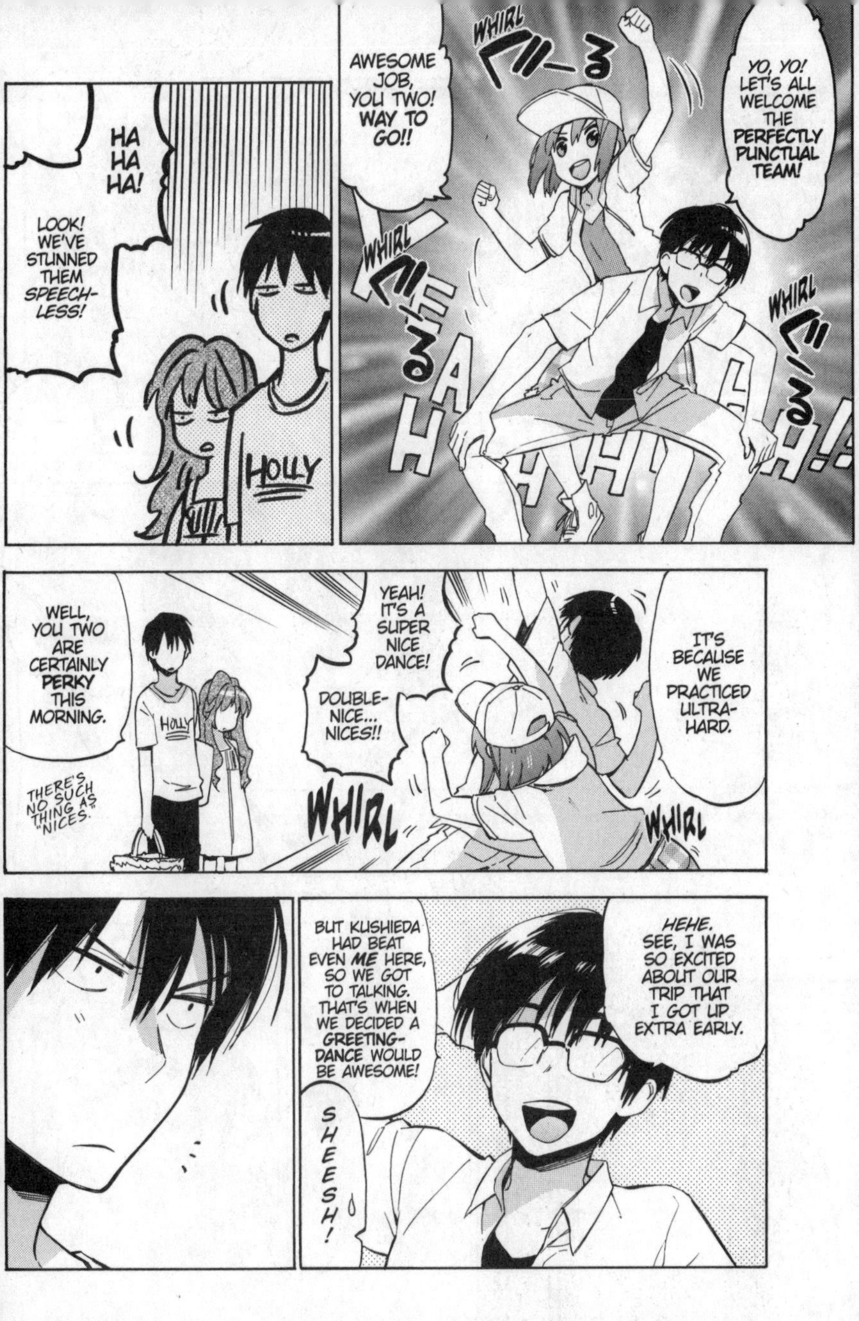
YO, YO! LET'S ALL WELCOME THE PERFECTLY PUNCTUAL TEAM!
WHIRL
AWESOME JOB, YOU TWO! WAY TO GO!!
WHIRL
WHIRL
HA HA HA!
LOOK! WE'VE STUNNED THEM SPEECHLESS!
HOLLY
IT'S BECAUSE WE PRACTICED ULTRA-HARD.
YEAH! IT'S A SUPER NICE DANCE!
DOUBLE-NICE... NICES!!
WHIRL
WHIRL
WELL, YOU TWO ARE CERTAINLY PERKY THIS MORNING.
THERE'S NO SUCH THING AS "NICES."
HOLLY
HEHE. SEE, I WAS SO EXCITED ABOUT OUR TRIP THAT I GOT UP EXTRA EARLY.
BUT KUSHIEDA HAD BEAT EVEN ME HERE, SO WE GOT TO TALKING. THAT'S WHEN WE DECIDED A GREETING-DANCE WOULD BE AWESOME!
SHEESH!

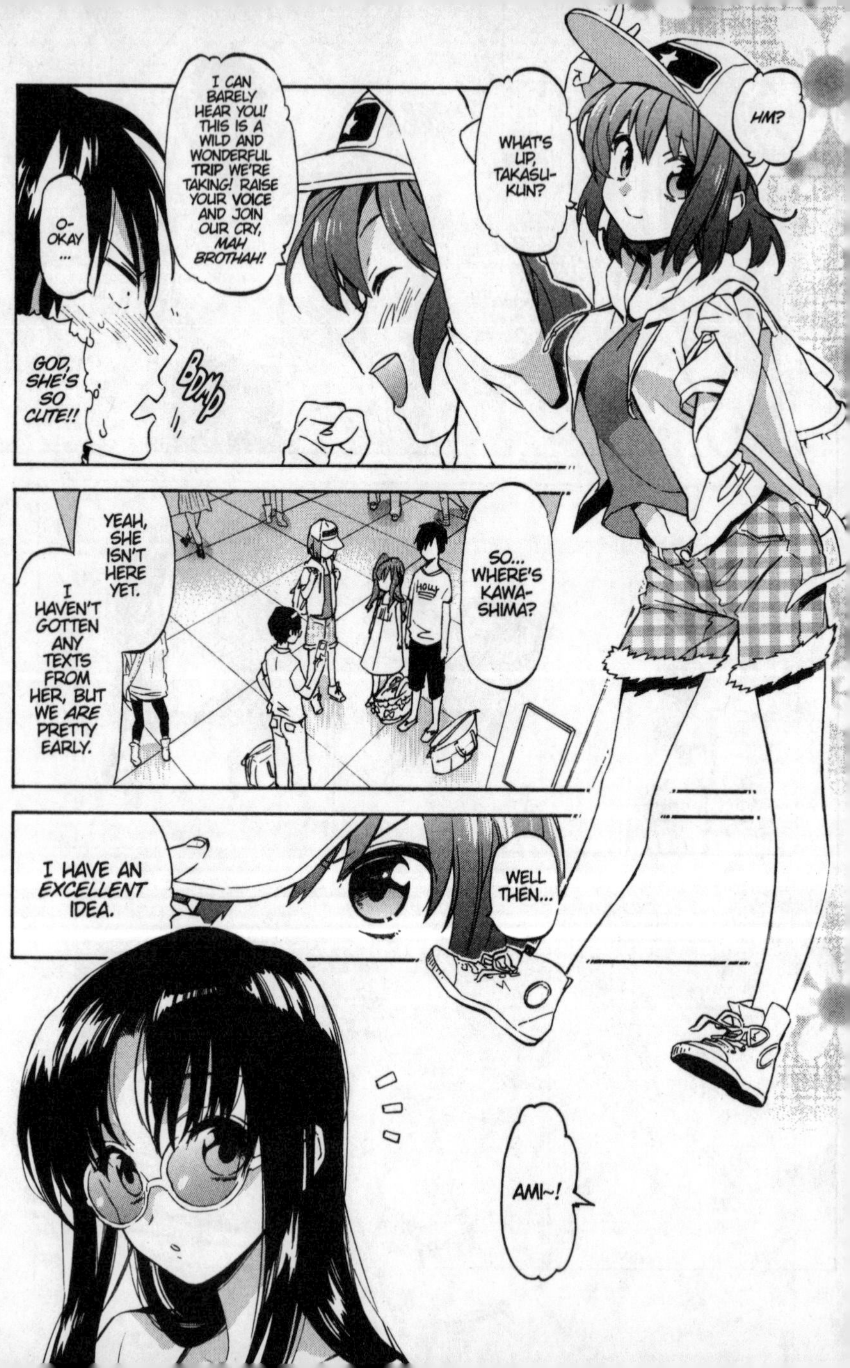
HM?
WHAT'S UP, TAKASU-KUN?
I CAN BARELY HEAR YOU! THIS IS A WILD AND WONDERFUL TRIP WE'RE TAKING! RAISE YOUR VOICE AND JOIN OUR CRY, MAH BROTHAH!
O-OKAY ...
BDMP
GOD, SHE'S SO CUTE!!
SO... WHERE'S KAWA-SHIMA?
YEAH, SHE ISN'T HERE YET.
I HAVEN'T GOTTEN ANY TEXTS FROM HER, BUT WE ARE PRETTY EARLY.
WELL THEN...
I HAVE AN EXCELLENT IDEA.
AMI~!

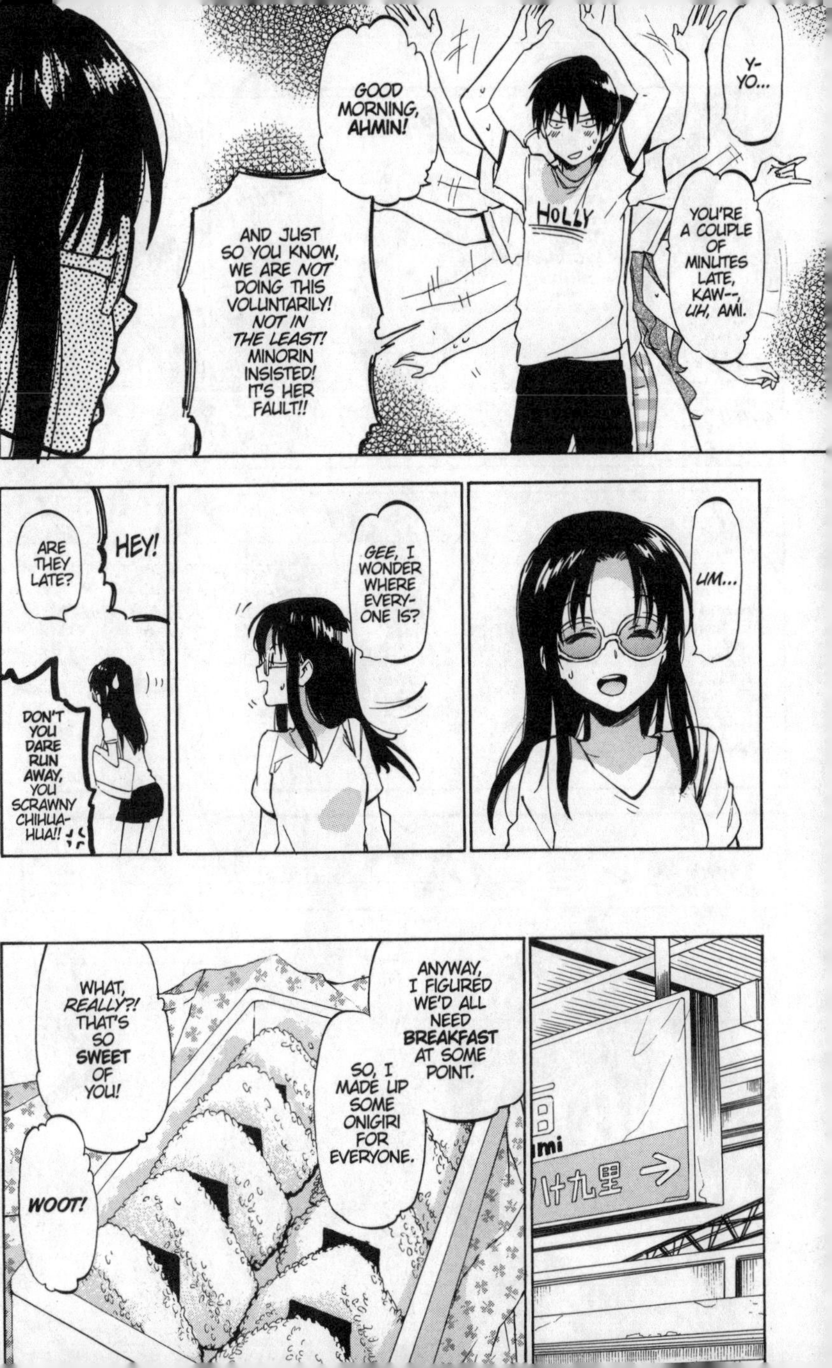
Y-YO...
YOU'RE A COUPLE OF MINUTES LATE, KAW--, UH, AMI.
GOOD MORNING, AHMIN!
HOLLY
AND JUST SO YOU KNOW, WE ARE *NOT* DOING THIS VOLUNTARILY! *NOT IN THE LEAST!* MINORIN INSISTED! IT'S HER FAULT!!
UM...
GEE, I WONDER WHERE EVERYONE IS?
ARE THEY LATE?
HEY!
DON'T YOU DARE RUN AWAY, YOU SCRAWNY CHIHUAHUA!!
ANYWAY, I FIGURED WE'D ALL NEED BREAKFAST AT SOME POINT.
SO, I MADE UP SOME ONIGIRI FOR EVERYONE.
WHAT, *REALLY?!* THAT'S SO SWEET OF YOU!
WOOT!

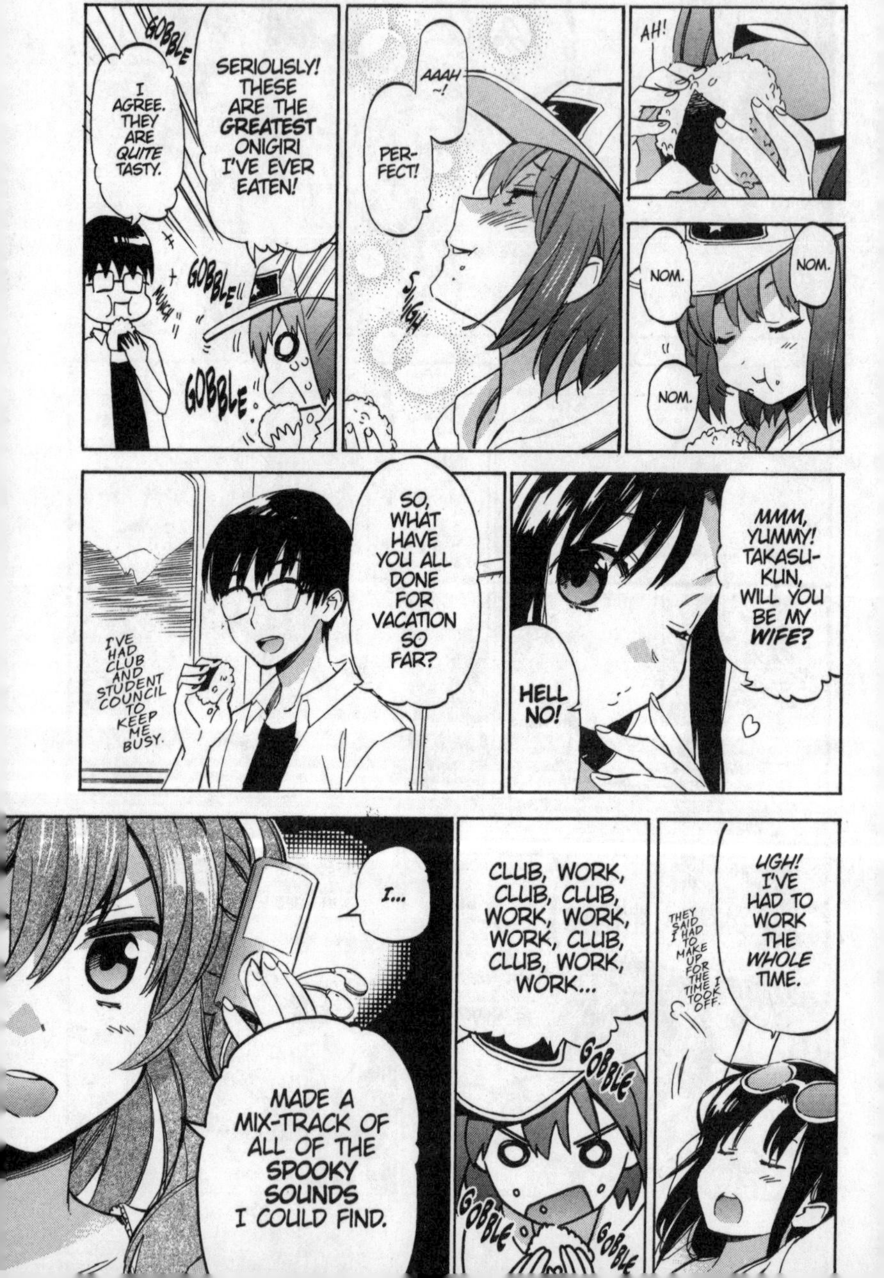
AH!
NOM.
NOM.
NOM.
AAAH~!
PERFECT!
SIGH
SERIOUSLY! THESE ARE THE GREATEST ONIGIRI I'VE EVER EATEN!
GOBBLE
I AGREE. THEY ARE QUITE TASTY.
GOBBLE
MUNCH
GOBBLE
MMM, YUMMY! TAKASU-KUN, WILL YOU BE MY WIFE?
HELL NO!
SO, WHAT HAVE YOU ALL DONE FOR VACATION SO FAR?
I'VE HAD CLUB AND STUDENT COUNCIL TO KEEP ME BUSY.
UGH! I'VE HAD TO WORK THE WHOLE TIME.
THEY SAID I HAD TO MAKE UP FOR THE TIME I TOOK OFF.
CLUB, WORK, CLUB, CLUB, WORK, WORK, WORK, CLUB, CLUB, WORK, WORK...
GOBBLE
GOBBLE
GOBBLE
I...
MADE A MIX-TRACK OF ALL OF THE SPOOKY SOUNDS I COULD FIND.

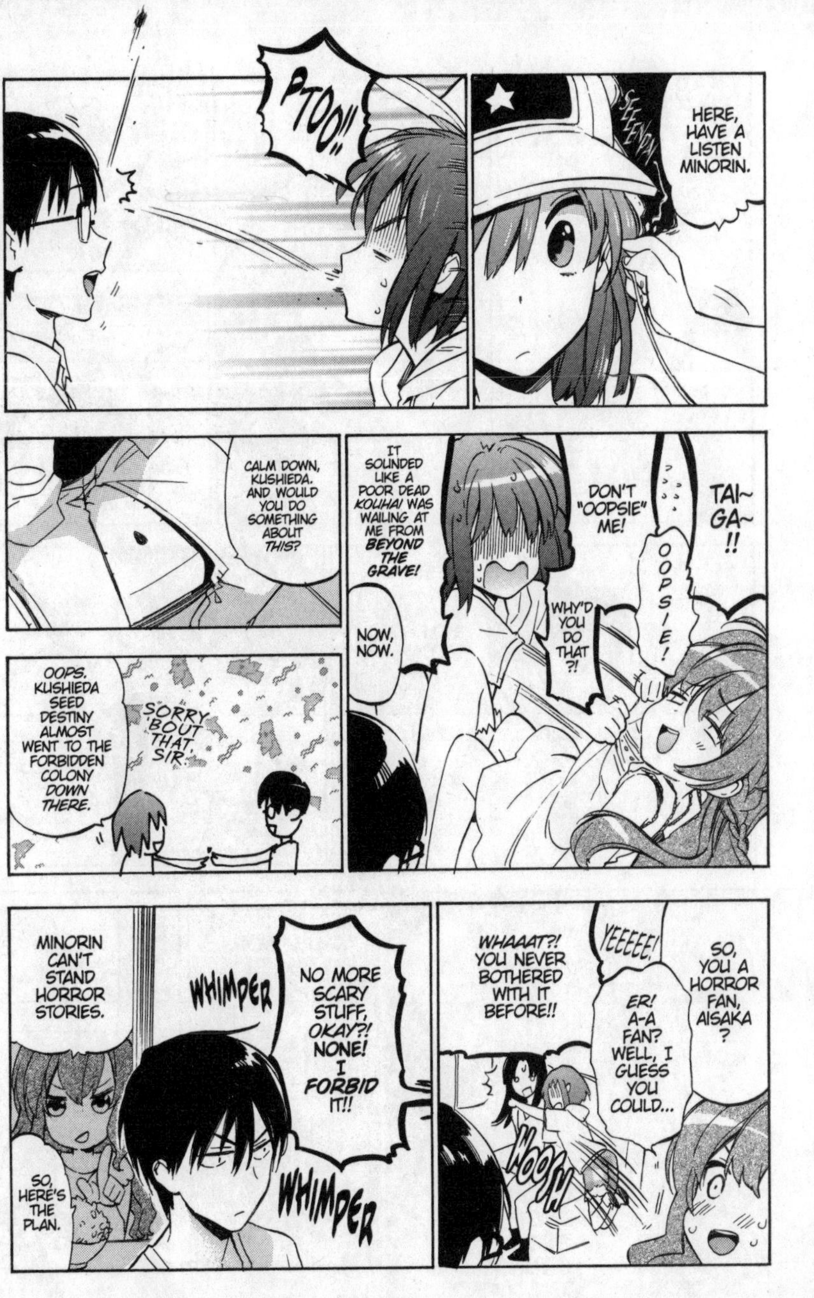
HERE, HAVE A LISTEN MINORIN.
PTOO!!
TAI~ GA~ !!
OOPSIE!
DON'T "OOPSIE" ME!
IT SOUNDED LIKE A POOR DEAD KOUHAI WAS WAILING AT ME FROM BEYOND THE GRAVE!
WHY'D YOU DO THAT ?!
NOW, NOW.
CALM DOWN, KUSHIEDA. AND WOULD YOU DO SOMETHING ABOUT THIS?
SORRY 'BOUT THAT, SIR.
OOPS. KUSHIEDA SEED DESTINY ALMOST WENT TO THE FORBIDDEN COLONY DOWN THERE.
SO, YOU A HORROR FAN, AISAKA ?
YEEEEE!
ER! A-A FAN? WELL, I GUESS YOU COULD...
WHAAAT?! YOU NEVER BOTHERED WITH IT BEFORE!!
WHOOSH
NO MORE SCARY STUFF, OKAY?! NONE! I FORBID IT!!
WHIMPER
WHIMPER
MINORIN CAN'T STAND HORROR STORIES.
SO, HERE'S THE PLAN.

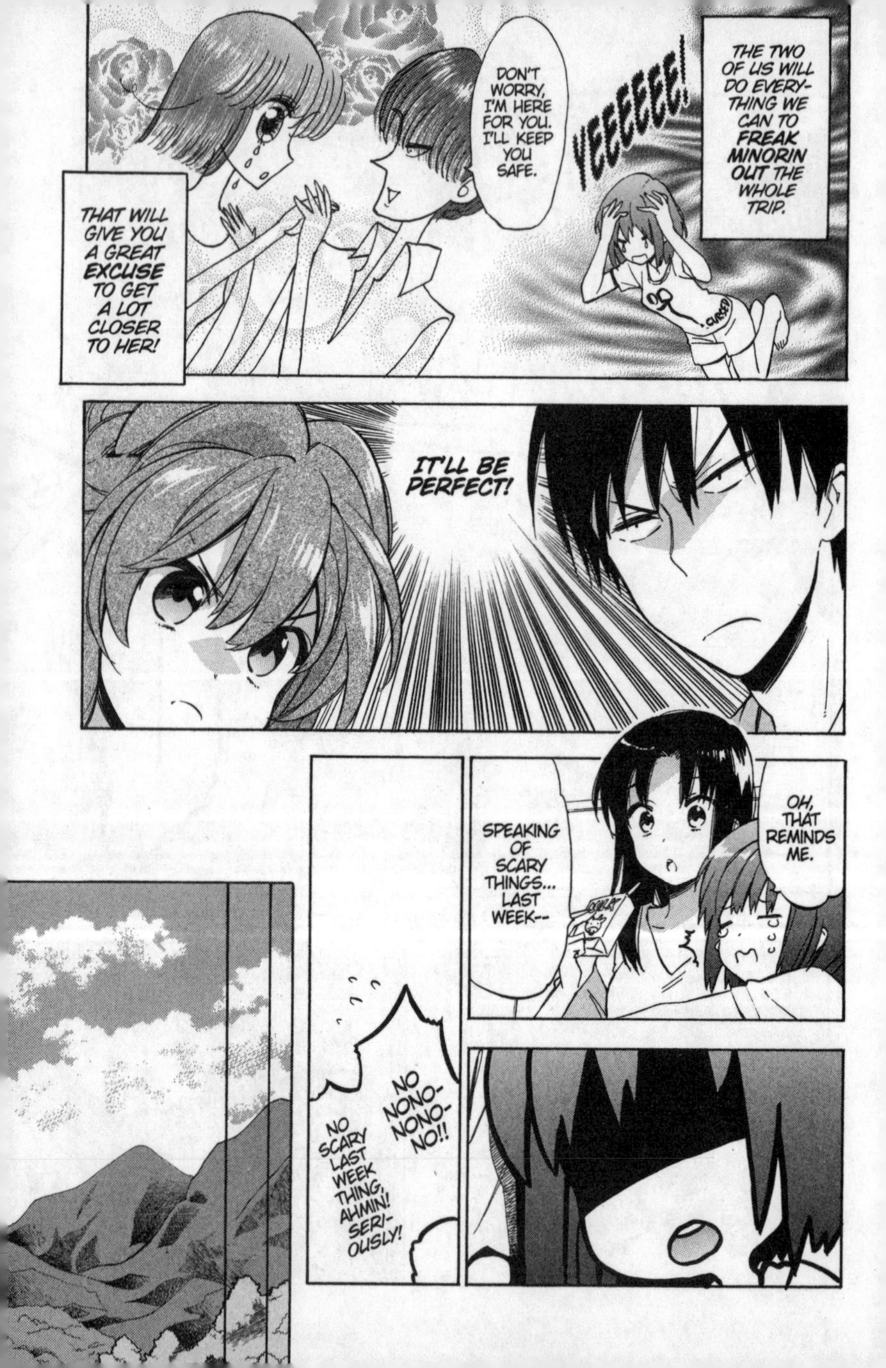
THE TWO OF US WILL DO EVERY-THING WE CAN TO FREAK MINORIN OUT THE WHOLE TRIP.
YEEEEEE!
DON'T WORRY, I'M HERE FOR YOU. I'LL KEEP YOU SAFE.
THAT WILL GIVE YOU A GREAT EXCUSE TO GET A LOT CLOSER TO HER!
IT'LL BE PERFECT!
OH, THAT REMINDS ME.
SPEAKING OF SCARY THINGS... LAST WEEK--
NO NONO-NONO-NO!!
NO SCARY LAST WEEK THING, AHMIN! SERI-OUSLY!

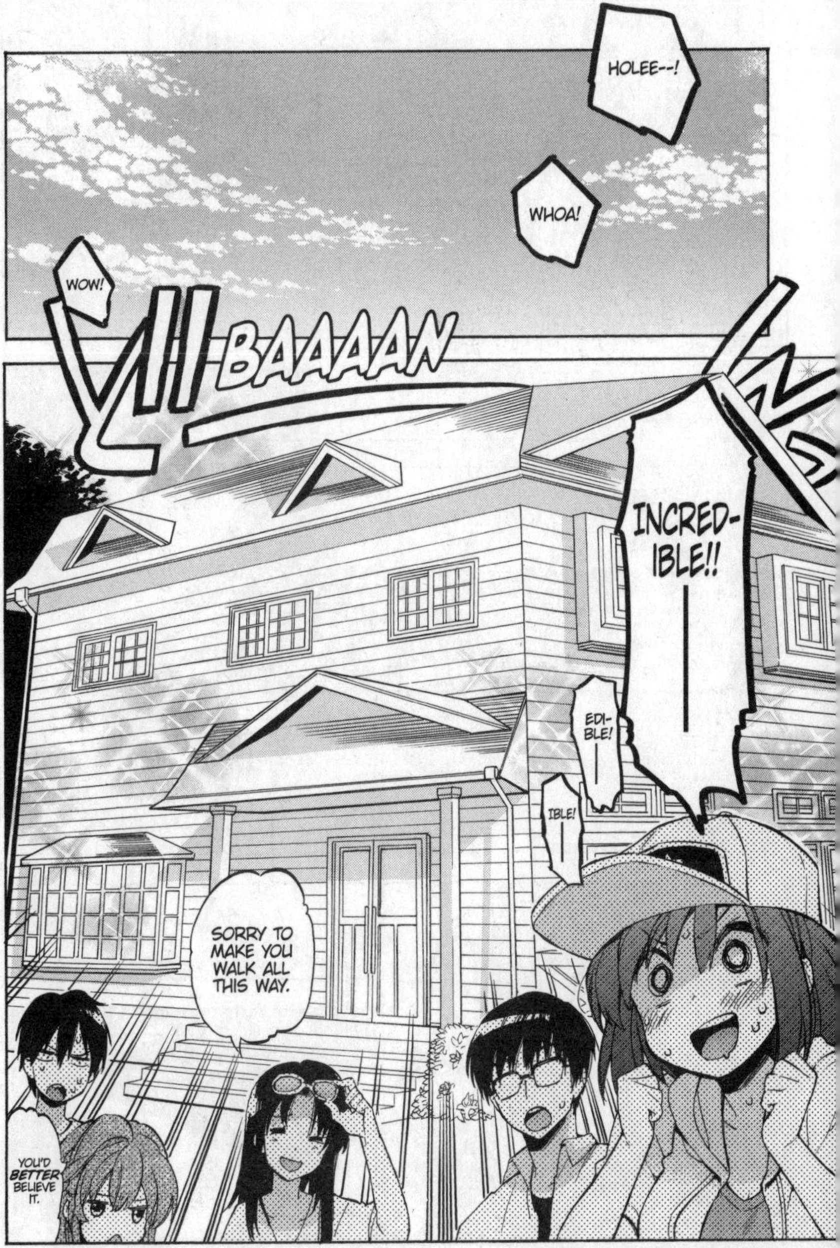
HOLEE--!
WHOA!
WOW!
BAAAAN
INCRED-IBLE!!
EDI-BLE!
IBLE!
SORRY TO MAKE YOU WALK ALL THIS WAY.
YOU'D BETTER BELIEVE IT.

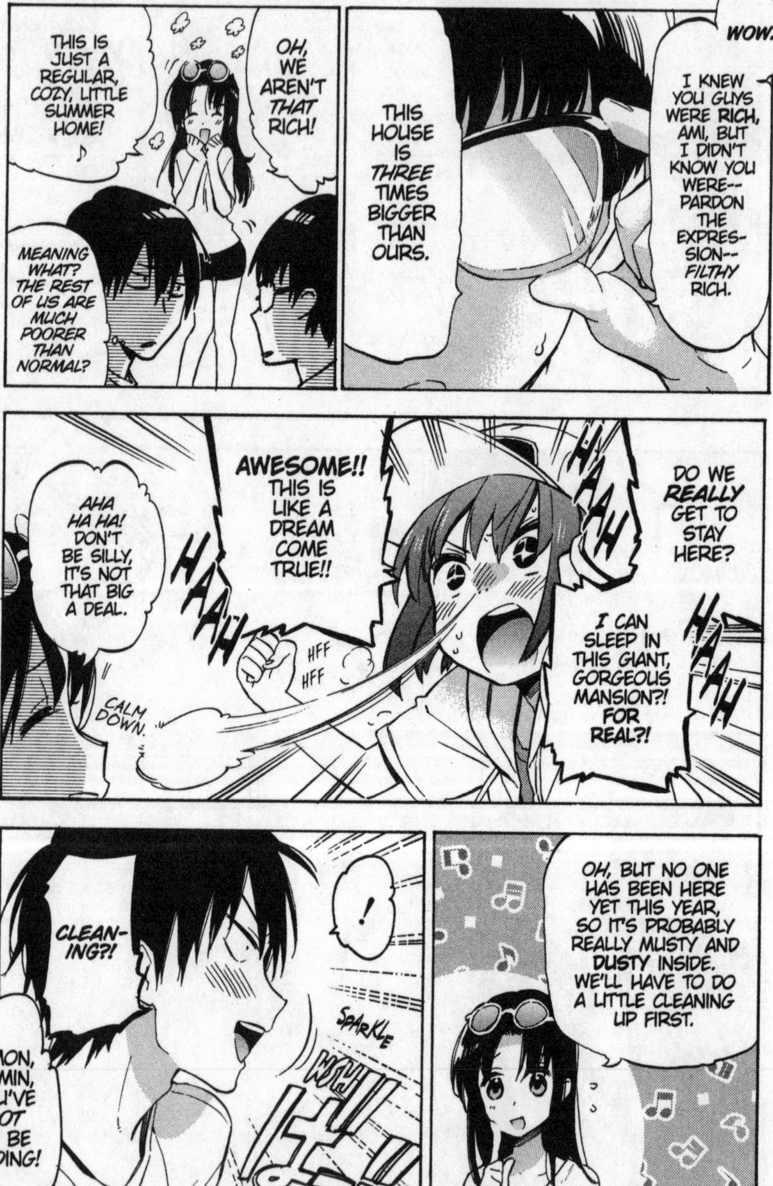
WOW.
I KNEW YOU GUYS WERE RICH, AMI, BUT I DIDN'T KNOW YOU WERE--PARDON THE EXPRESSION--FILTHY RICH.
THIS HOUSE IS THREE TIMES BIGGER THAN OURS.
OH, WE AREN'T THAT RICH!
THIS IS JUST A REGULAR, COZY, LITTLE SUMMER HOME! ♪
MEANING WHAT? THE REST OF US ARE MUCH POORER THAN NORMAL?
DO WE REALLY GET TO STAY HERE?
HAAAH
I CAN SLEEP IN THIS GIANT, GORGEOUS MANSION?! FOR REAL?!
HAAAH
AWESOME!! THIS IS LIKE A DREAM COME TRUE!!
HFF HFF
HAAAH
AHA HA HA! DON'T BE SILLY, IT'S NOT THAT BIG A DEAL.
CALM DOWN.
OH, BUT NO ONE HAS BEEN HERE YET THIS YEAR, SO IT'S PROBABLY REALLY MUSTY AND DUSTY INSIDE. WE'LL HAVE TO DO A LITTLE CLEANING UP FIRST.
!
CLEANING?!
SPARKLE
C'MON, AHMIN, YOU'VE GOT TO BE KIDDING!

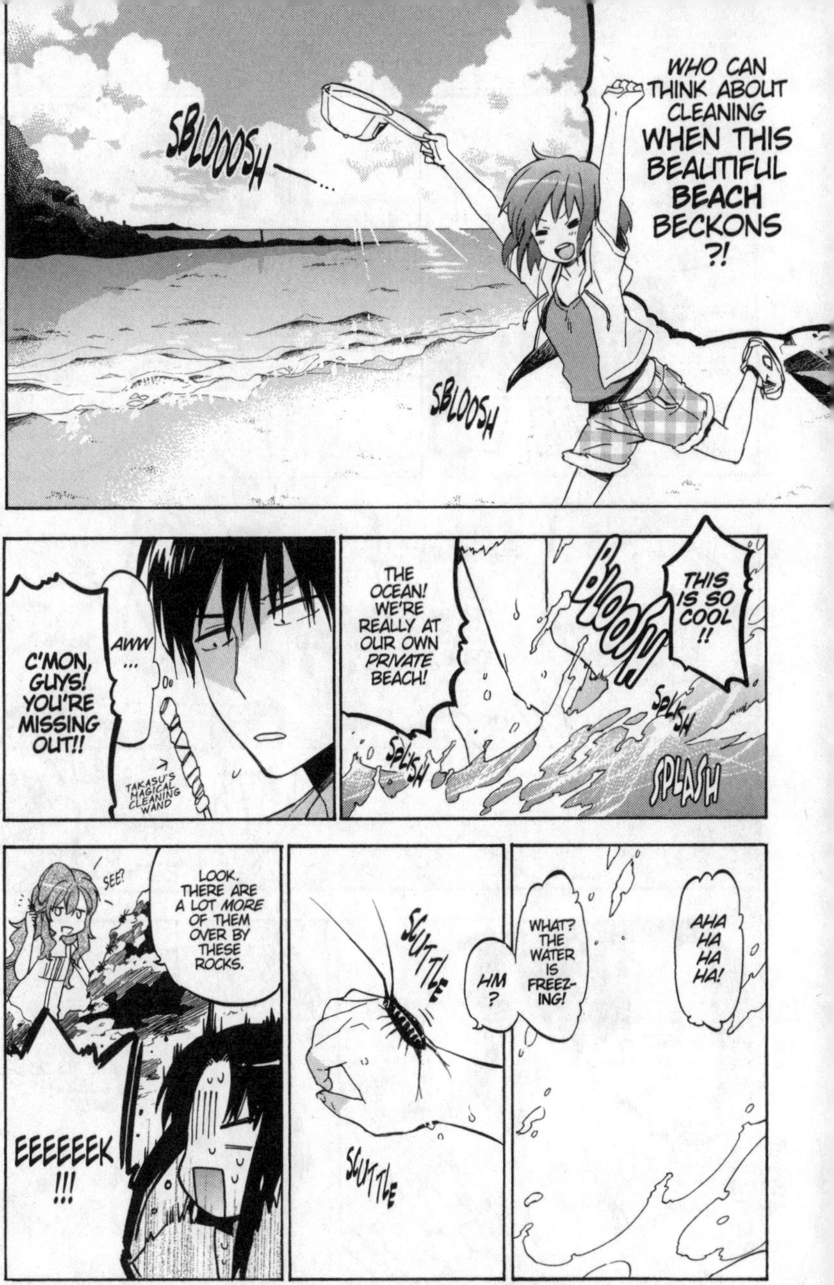
WHO CAN THINK ABOUT CLEANING WHEN THIS BEAUTIFUL BEACH BECKONS ?!
SBLOOOSH—...
SBLOOSH
THIS IS SO COOL !!
BLOOSH
THE OCEAN! WE'RE REALLY AT OUR OWN *PRIVATE* BEACH!
SPLISH
SPLISH
SPLASH
AWW ...
C'MON, GUYS! YOU'RE MISSING OUT!!
TAKASU'S MAGICAL CLEANING WAND
AHA HA HA HA!
WHAT? THE WATER IS FREEZ-ING!
HM ?
SCUTTLE
SCUTTLE
LOOK. THERE ARE A LOT *MORE* OF THEM OVER BY THESE ROCKS.
SEE?
EEEEEEK !!!

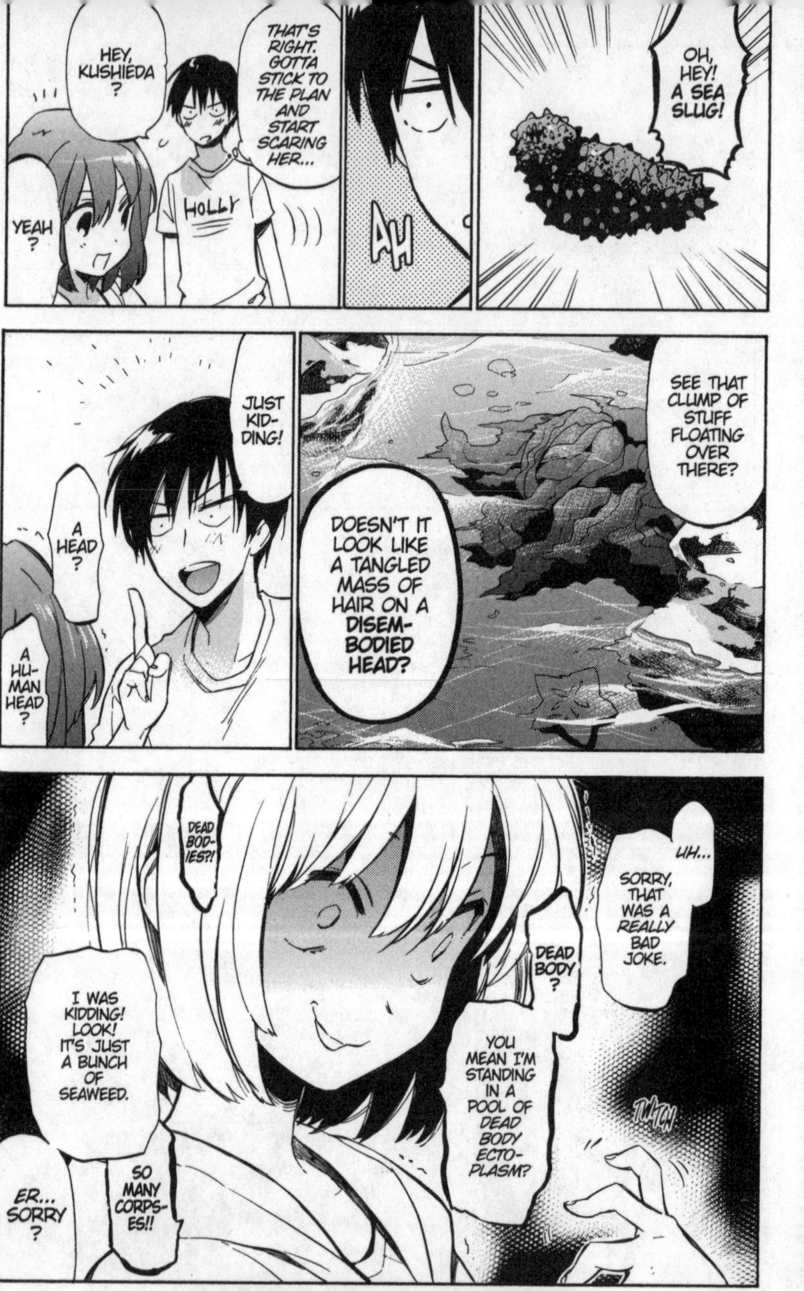
OH, HEY! A SEA SLUG!
AH
THAT'S RIGHT. GOTTA STICK TO THE PLAN AND START SCARING HER...
HEY, KUSHIEDA?
YEAH?
SEE THAT CLUMP OF STUFF FLOATING OVER THERE?
DOESN'T IT LOOK LIKE A TANGLED MASS OF HAIR ON A DISEMBODIED HEAD?
JUST KIDDING!
A HEAD?
A HUMAN HEAD?
UH... SORRY, THAT WAS A REALLY BAD JOKE.
TWITCH
DEAD BODY?
YOU MEAN I'M STANDING IN A POOL OF DEAD BODY ECTOPLASM?
DEAD BODIES?!
I WAS KIDDING! LOOK! IT'S JUST A BUNCH OF SEAWEED.
SO MANY CORPSES!!
ER... SORRY?

TO BE CONTINUED!!

sea slug

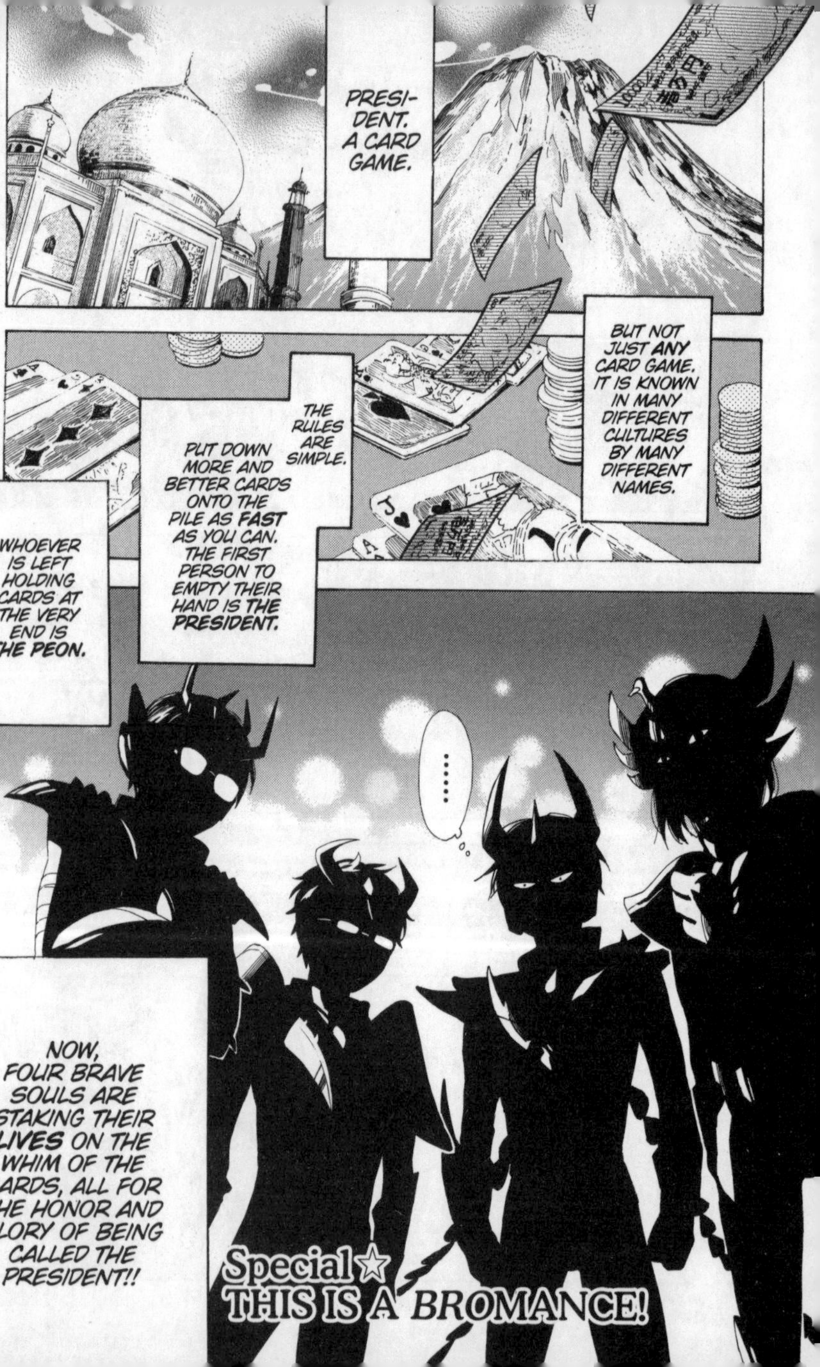
PRESI-DENT. A CARD GAME.
BUT NOT JUST ANY CARD GAME. IT IS KNOWN IN MANY DIFFERENT CULTURES BY MANY DIFFERENT NAMES.
THE RULES ARE SIMPLE.
PUT DOWN MORE AND BETTER CARDS ONTO THE PILE AS FAST AS YOU CAN. THE FIRST PERSON TO EMPTY THEIR HAND IS THE PRESIDENT.
WHOEVER IS LEFT HOLDING CARDS AT THE VERY END IS THE PEON.
......
NOW, FOUR BRAVE SOULS ARE STAKING THEIR LIVES ON THE WHIM OF THE CARDS, ALL FOR THE HONOR AND GLORY OF BEING CALLED THE PRESIDENT!!
Special☆
THIS IS A BROMANCE!

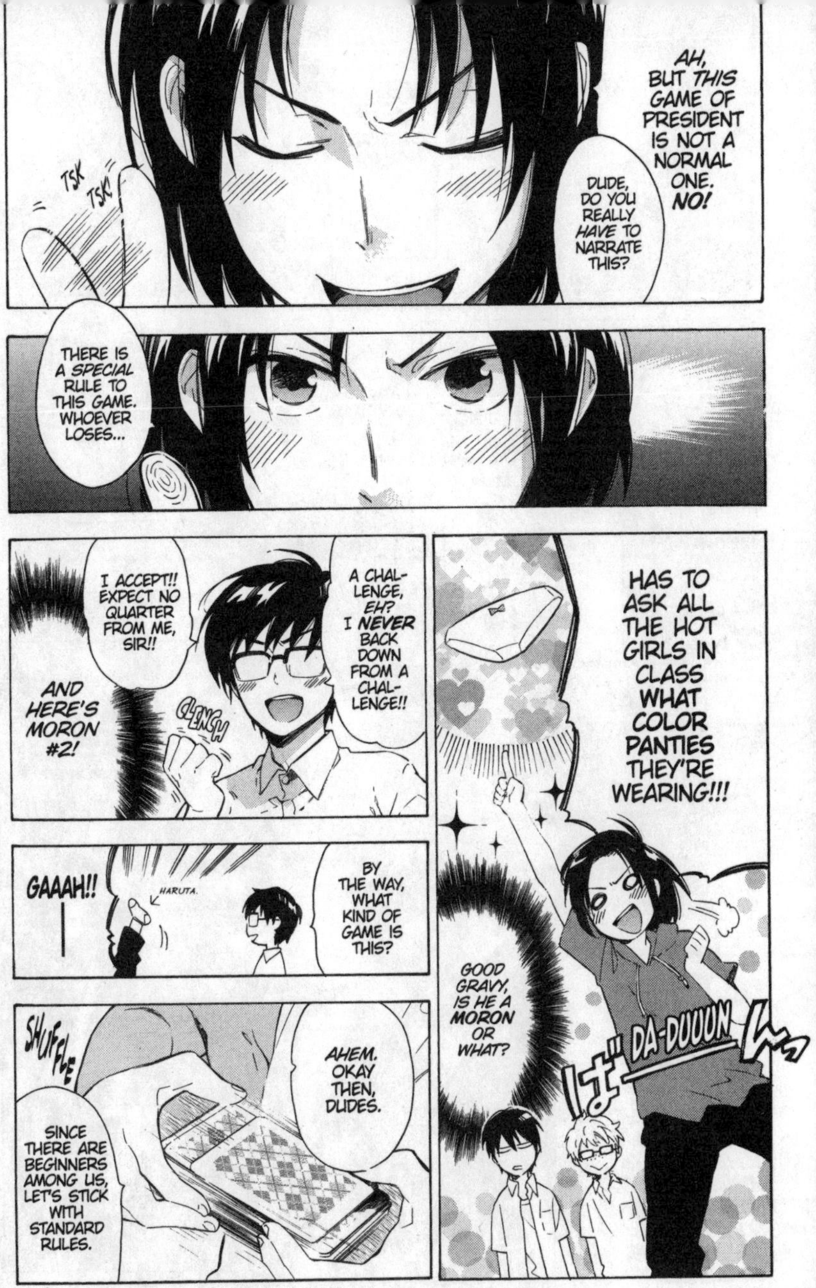
AH, BUT THIS GAME OF PRESIDENT IS NOT A NORMAL ONE. NO!
DUDE, DO YOU REALLY HAVE TO NARRATE THIS?
TSK TSK!
THERE IS A SPECIAL RULE TO THIS GAME. WHOEVER LOSES...
HAS TO ASK ALL THE HOT GIRLS IN CLASS WHAT COLOR PANTIES THEY'RE WEARING!!!
ば DA-DUUUN
GOOD GRAVY, IS HE A MORON OR WHAT?
A CHAL-LENGE, EH? I NEVER BACK DOWN FROM A CHAL-LENGE!!
CLENCH
I ACCEPT!! EXPECT NO QUARTER FROM ME, SIR!!
AND HERE'S MORON #2!
BY THE WAY, WHAT KIND OF GAME IS THIS?
HARUTA.
GAAAH!!
AHEM. OKAY THEN, DUDES.
SHUFFLE
SINCE THERE ARE BEGINNERS AMONG US, LET'S STICK WITH STANDARD RULES.

↑ THERE ARE LOTS OF REGIONAL VARIATIONS.

BY THE WAY, IN ZEKKYO'S REGION, THE 3 OF SPADES ♠ IS "HIGHEST." ←LOCAL RULE.

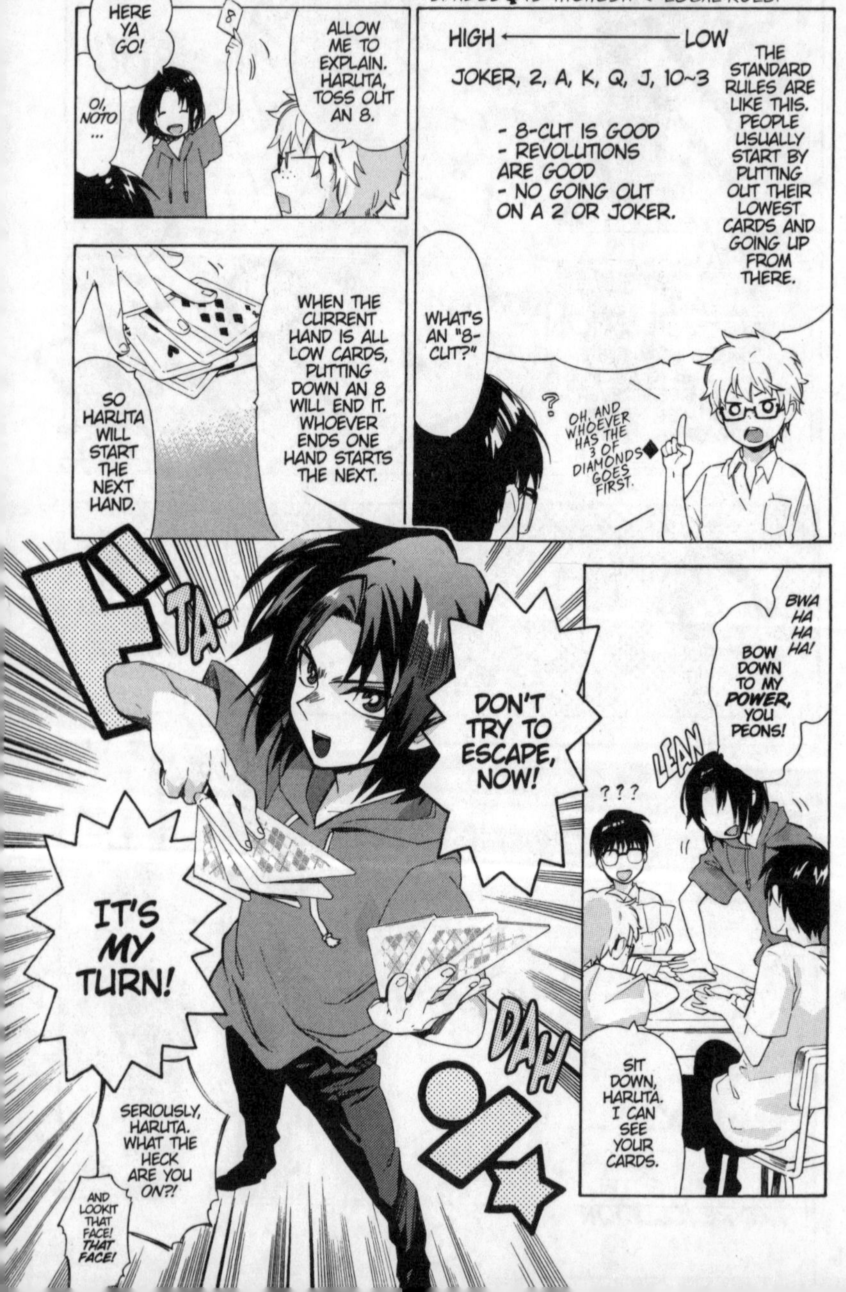
THE STANDARD RULES ARE LIKE THIS. PEOPLE USUALLY START BY PUTTING OUT THEIR LOWEST CARDS AND GOING UP FROM THERE.
HIGH ← LOW
JOKER, 2, A, K, Q, J, 10~3
- 8-CUT IS GOOD
- REVOLUTIONS ARE GOOD
- NO GOING OUT ON A 2 OR JOKER.
OH, AND WHOEVER HAS THE 3 OF DIAMONDS ♦ GOES FIRST.
?
WHAT'S AN "8-CUT?"
ALLOW ME TO EXPLAIN. HARUTA, TOSS OUT AN 8.
8
HERE YA GO!
OI, NOTO ...
WHEN THE CURRENT HAND IS ALL LOW CARDS, PUTTING DOWN AN 8 WILL END IT. WHOEVER ENDS ONE HAND STARTS THE NEXT.
SO HARUTA WILL START THE NEXT HAND.
BWA HA HA HA!
BOW DOWN TO MY POWER, YOU PEONS!
LEAN
???
SIT DOWN, HARUTA. I CAN SEE YOUR CARDS.
TA-
DON'T TRY TO ESCAPE, NOW!
IT'S MY TURN!
DAH
SERIOUSLY, HARUTA. WHAT THE HECK ARE YOU ON?!
AND LOOKIT THAT FACE! THAT FACE!

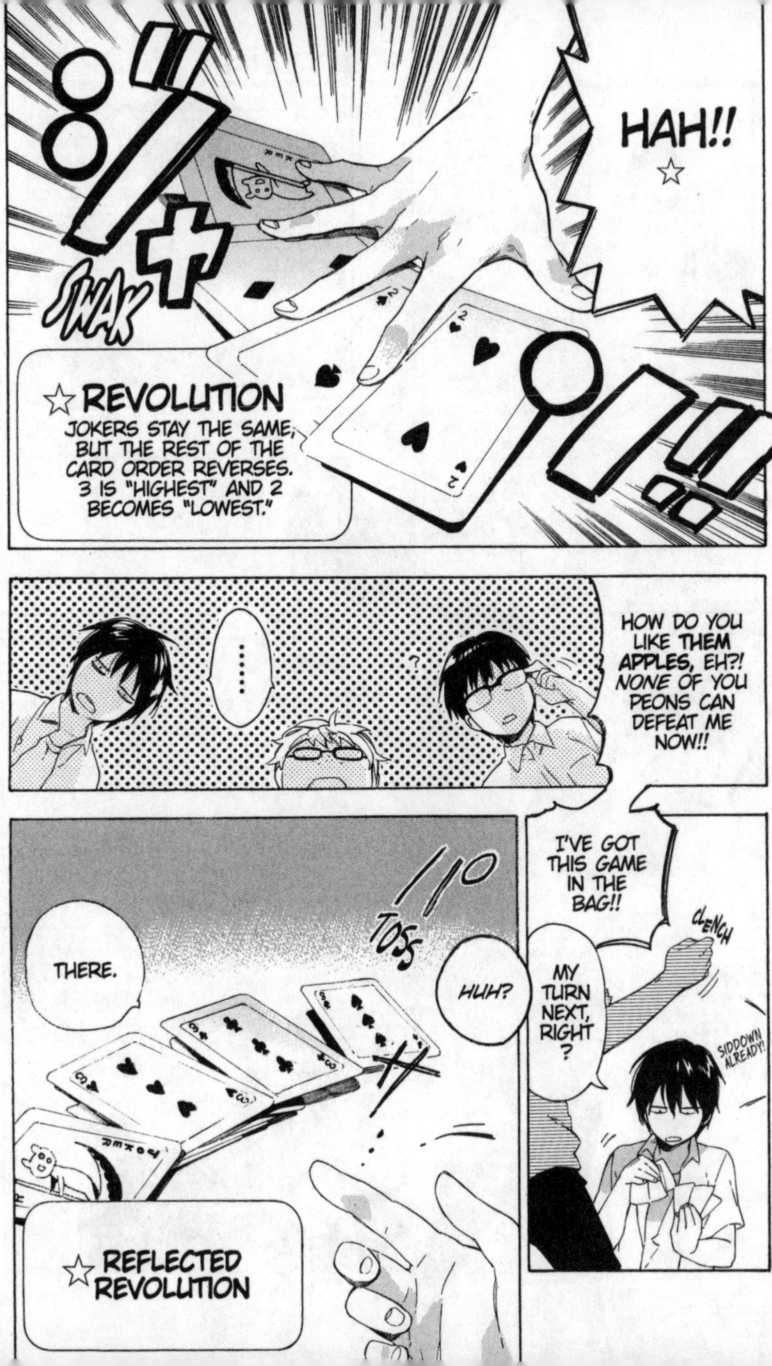
HAH!! ☆
SWAK
☆ REVOLUTION
JOKERS STAY THE SAME, BUT THE REST OF THE CARD ORDER REVERSES. 3 IS "HIGHEST" AND 2 BECOMES "LOWEST."
HOW DO YOU LIKE THEM APPLES, EH?! NONE OF YOU PEONS CAN DEFEAT ME NOW!!
......
?
I'VE GOT THIS GAME IN THE BAG!!
CLENCH
MY TURN NEXT, RIGHT?
SIDDOWN ALREADY!
HUH?
TOSS
THERE.
☆ REFLECTED REVOLUTION

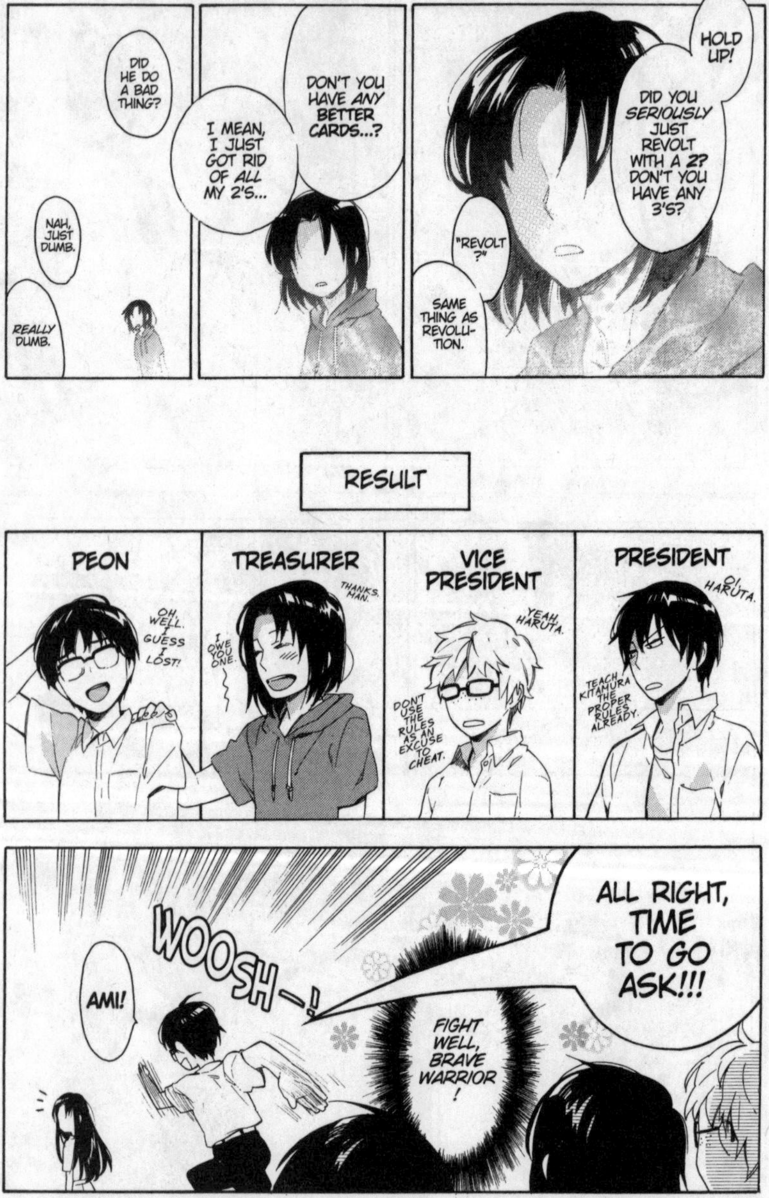
HOLD UP!
DID YOU SERIOUSLY JUST REVOLT WITH A 2? DON'T YOU HAVE ANY 3'S?
"REVOLT?"
SAME THING AS REVOLUTION.
DON'T YOU HAVE ANY BETTER CARDS...?
I MEAN, I JUST GOT RID OF ALL MY 2'S...
DID HE DO A BAD THING?
NAH, JUST DUMB.
REALLY DUMB.
RESULT
PRESIDENT
OI, HARUTA.
TEACH KITAMURA THE PROPER RULES ALREADY.
VICE PRESIDENT
YEAH, HARUTA.
DON'T USE THE RULES AS AN EXCUSE TO CHEAT.
TREASURER
THANKS, MAN.
I OWE YOU ONE.
PEON
OH, WELL. I GUESS I LOST!
ALL RIGHT, TIME TO GO ASK!!!
FIGHT WELL, BRAVE WARRIOR!
WOOSH—!
AMI!

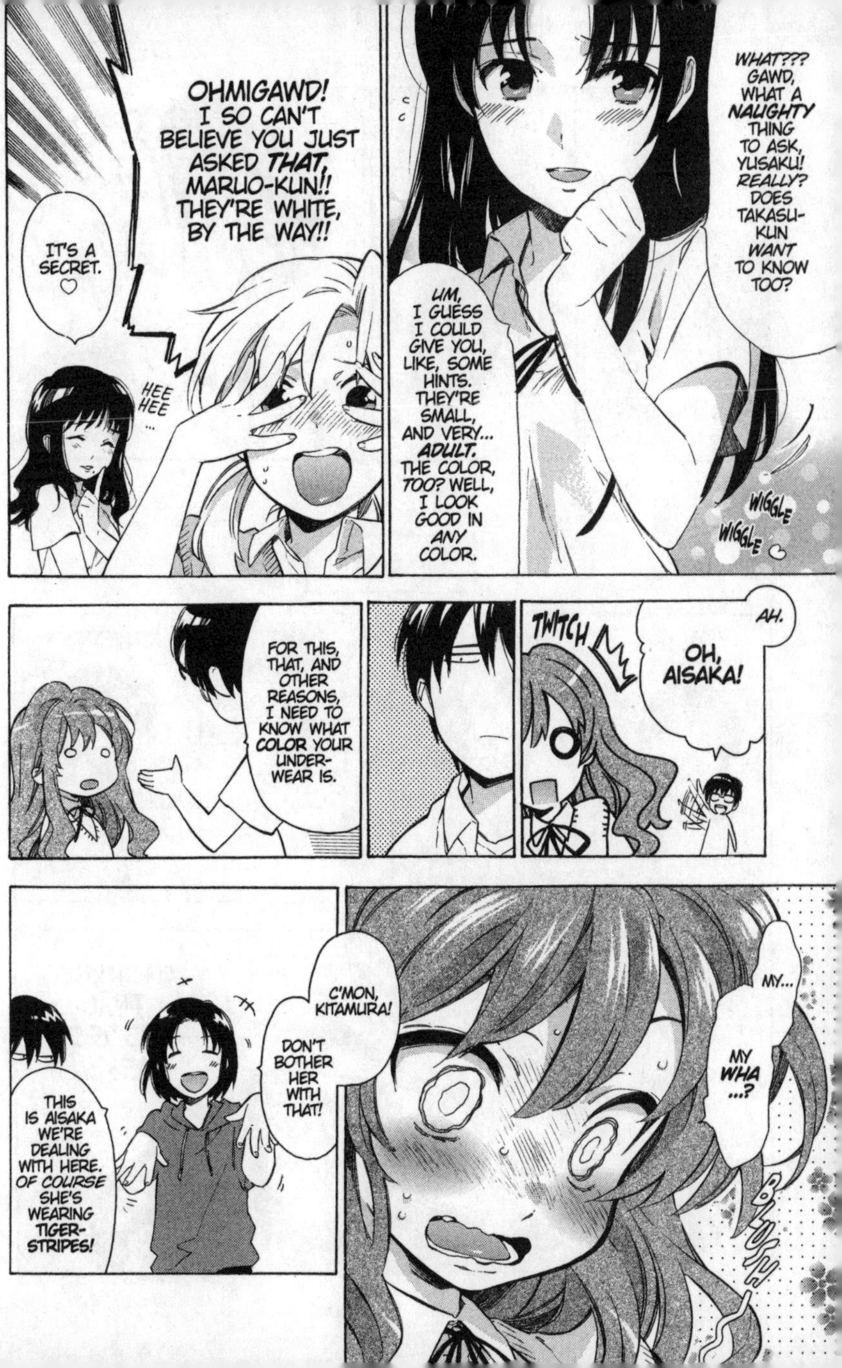
WHAT??? GAWD, WHAT A NAUGHTY THING TO ASK, YUSAKU! REALLY? DOES TAKASU-KUN WANT TO KNOW TOO?
UM, I GUESS I COULD GIVE YOU, LIKE, SOME HINTS. THEY'RE SMALL, AND VERY... ADULT. THE COLOR, TOO? WELL, I LOOK GOOD IN ANY COLOR.
WIGGLE
WIGGLE
OHMIGAWD! I SO CAN'T BELIEVE YOU JUST ASKED THAT, MARUO-KUN!! THEY'RE WHITE, BY THE WAY!!
IT'S A SECRET. ♡
HEE HEE ...
AH.
OH, AISAKA!
TWITCH
FOR THIS, THAT, AND OTHER REASONS, I NEED TO KNOW WHAT COLOR YOUR UNDERWEAR IS.
MY...
MY WHA ...?
C'MON, KITAMURA!
DON'T BOTHER HER WITH THAT!
THIS IS AISAKA WE'RE DEALING WITH HERE. OF COURSE SHE'S WEARING TIGER-STRIPES!

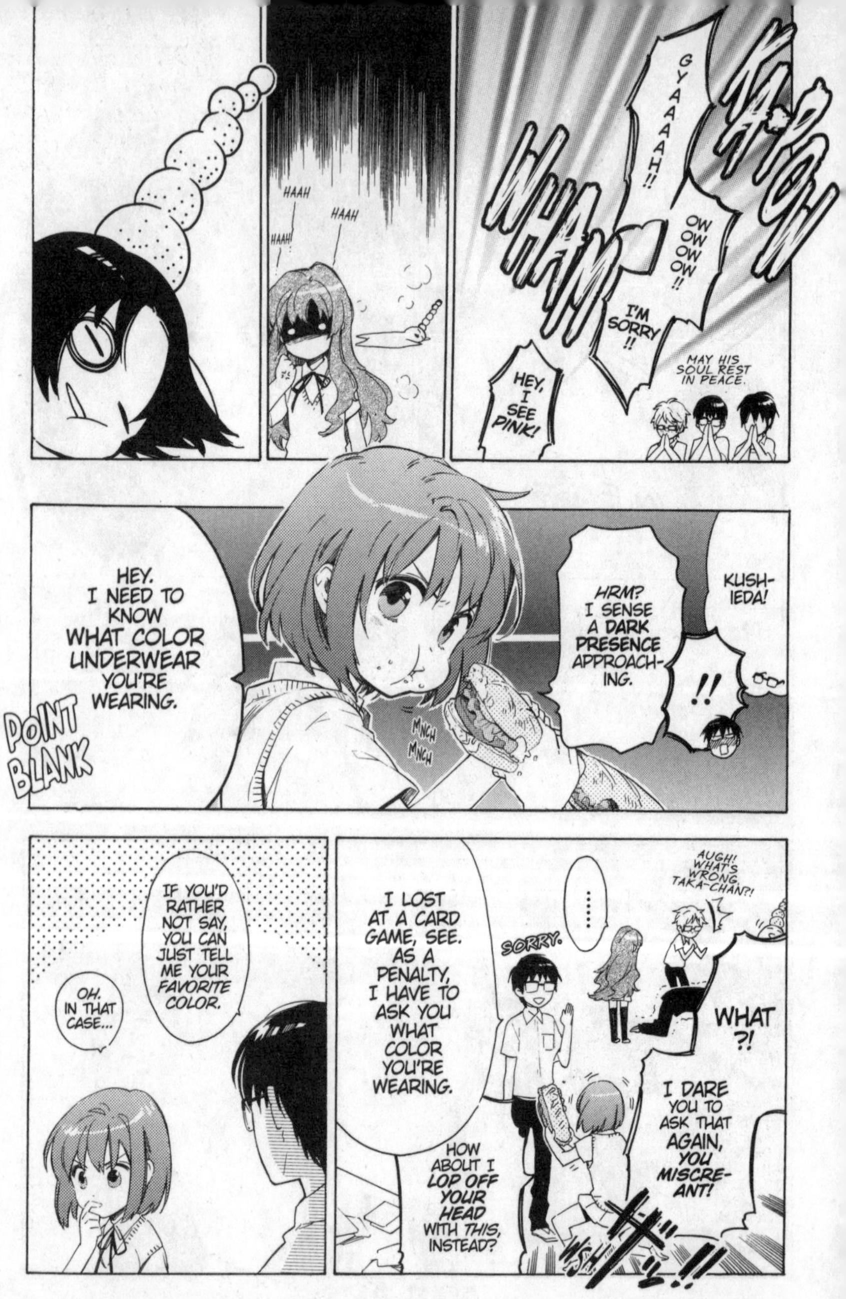
WHAM
GYAAAAAH!!
OW OW OW OW!!
I'M SORRY!!
HEY, I SEE PINK!
MAY HIS SOUL REST IN PEACE.
HAAH
HAAH
HAAH
KUSH-IEDA!
!!
HRM? I SENSE A DARK PRESENCE APPROACHING.
MNCH MNCH
HEY. I NEED TO KNOW WHAT COLOR UNDERWEAR YOU'RE WEARING.
POINT BLANK
AUGH! WHAT'S WRONG, TAKA-CHAN?!
WHAT?!
......
SORRY.
I LOST AT A CARD GAME, SEE. AS A PENALTY, I HAVE TO ASK YOU WHAT COLOR YOU'RE WEARING.
I DARE YOU TO ASK THAT AGAIN, YOU MISCREANT!
HOW ABOUT I LOP OFF YOUR HEAD WITH THIS, INSTEAD?
WSH
IF YOU'D RATHER NOT SAY, YOU CAN JUST TELL ME YOUR FAVORITE COLOR.
OH. IN THAT CASE...

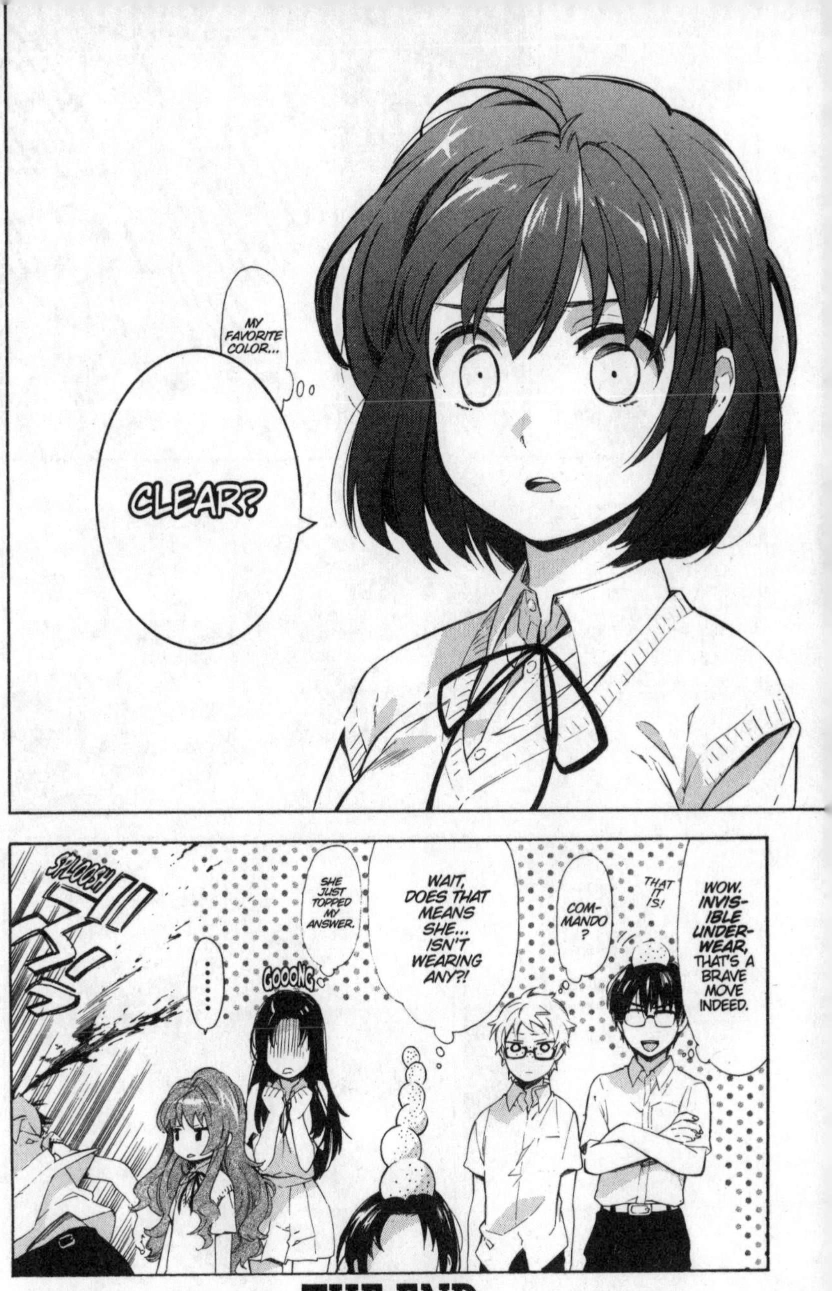
MY FAVORITE COLOR...
CLEAR?
WOW. INVISIBLE UNDERWEAR, THAT'S A BRAVE MOVE INDEED.
THAT IS!
COMMANDO?
WAIT, DOES THAT MEANS SHE... ISN'T WEARING ANY?!
SHE JUST TOPPED MY ANSWER.
GOOONG
......
SPLOOSH

THE END

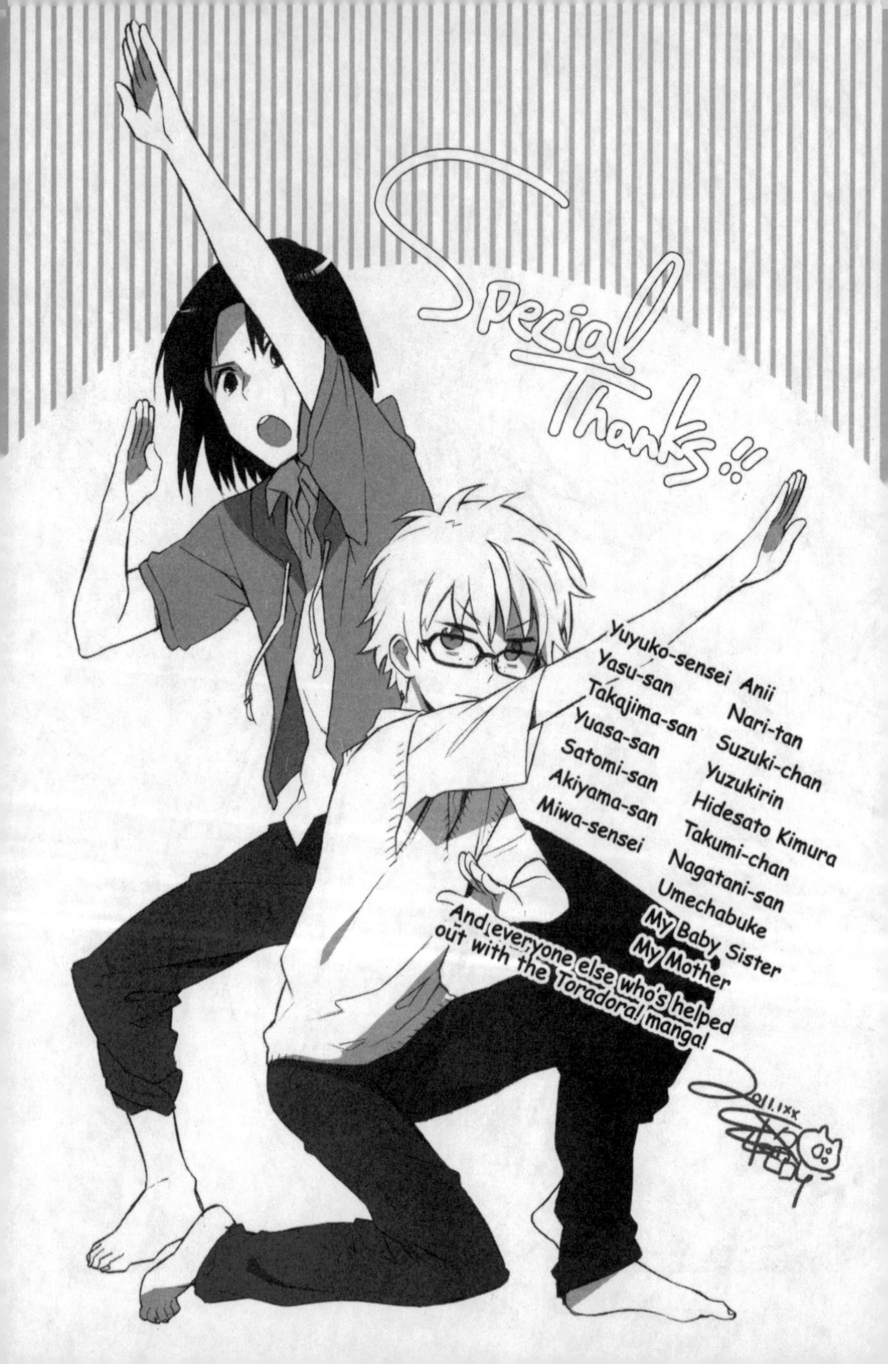
Special Thanks!!
Yuyuko-sensei Anii
Yasu-san Nari-tan
Takajima-san Suzuki-chan
Yuasa-san Yuzukirin
Satomi-san Hidesato Kimura
Akiyama-san Takumi-chan
Miwa-sensei Nagatani-san
Umechabuke
My Baby Sister
My Mother
And everyone else who's helped out with the Toradora! manga!
2011.xx

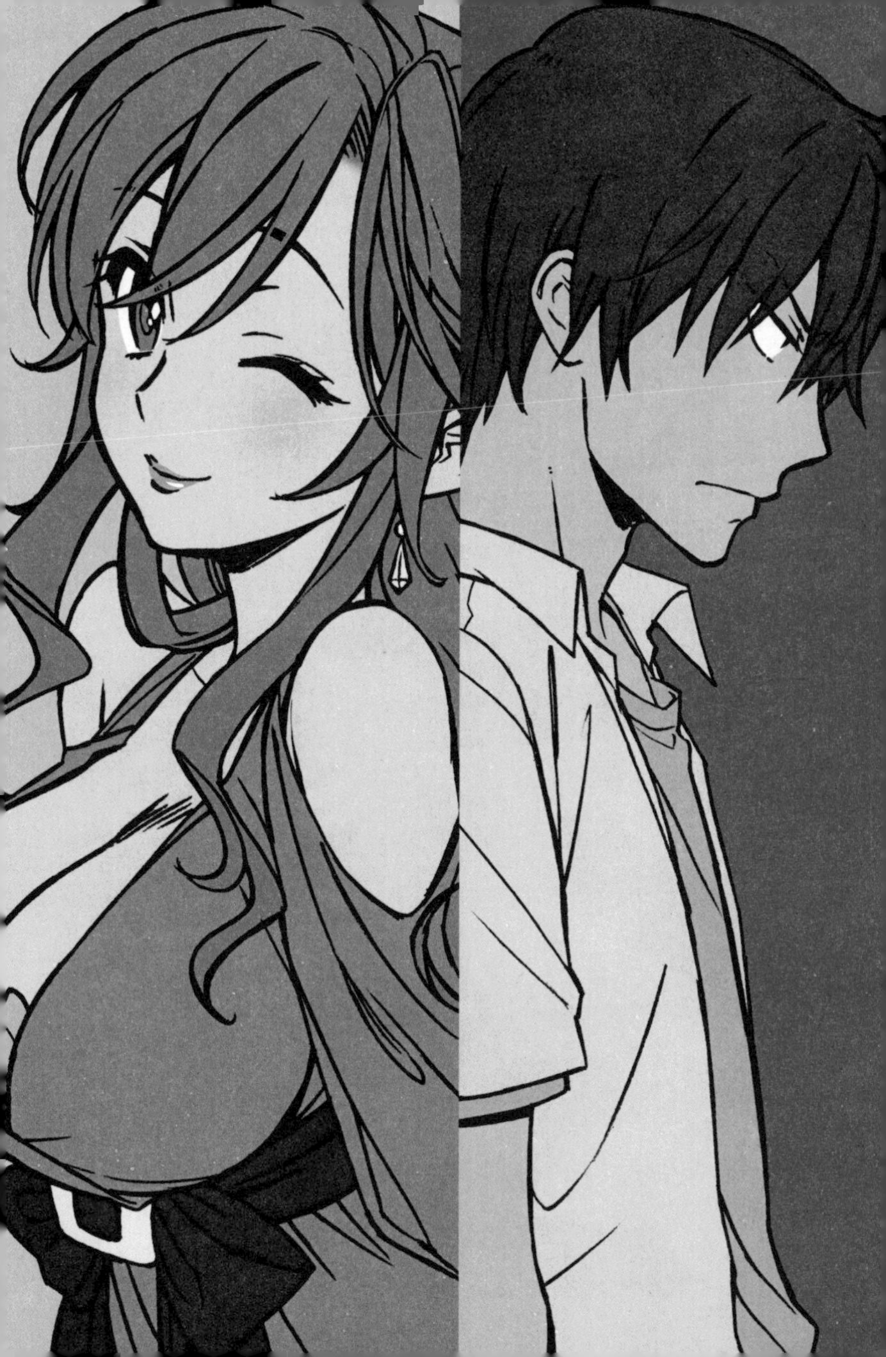

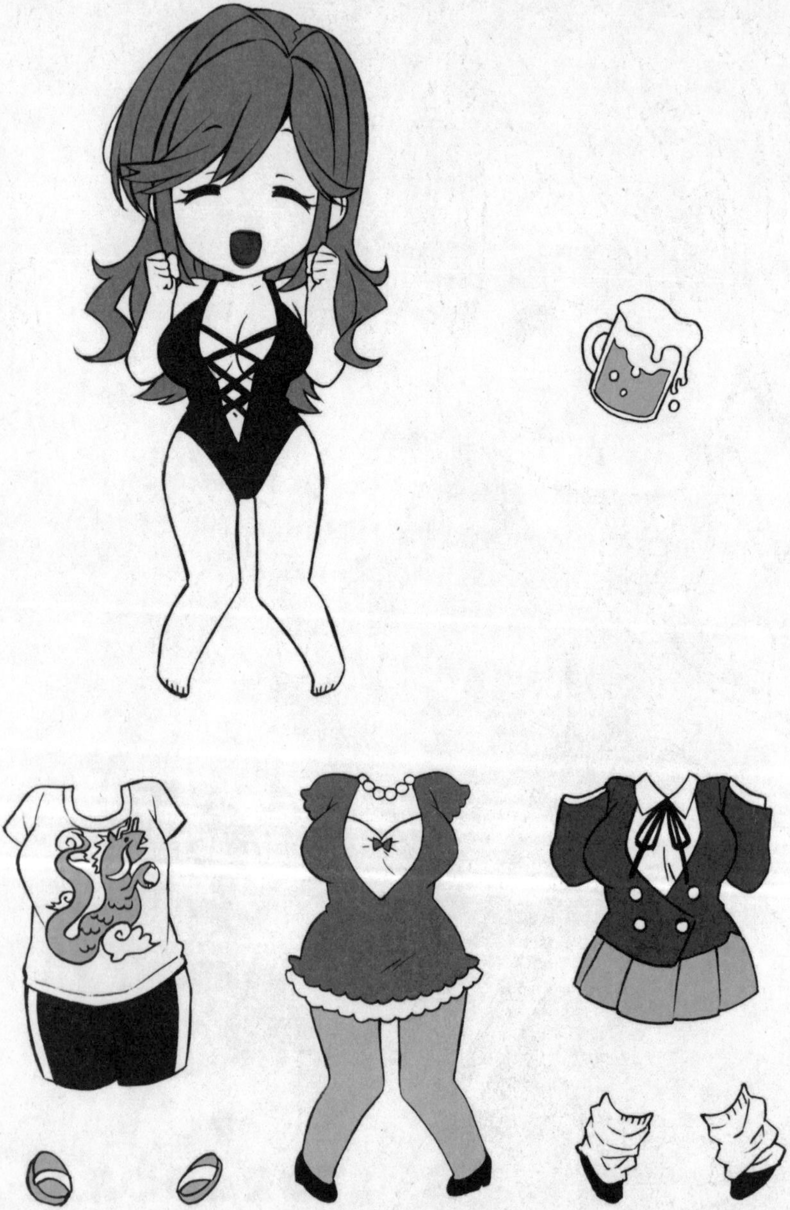

TORADORA!

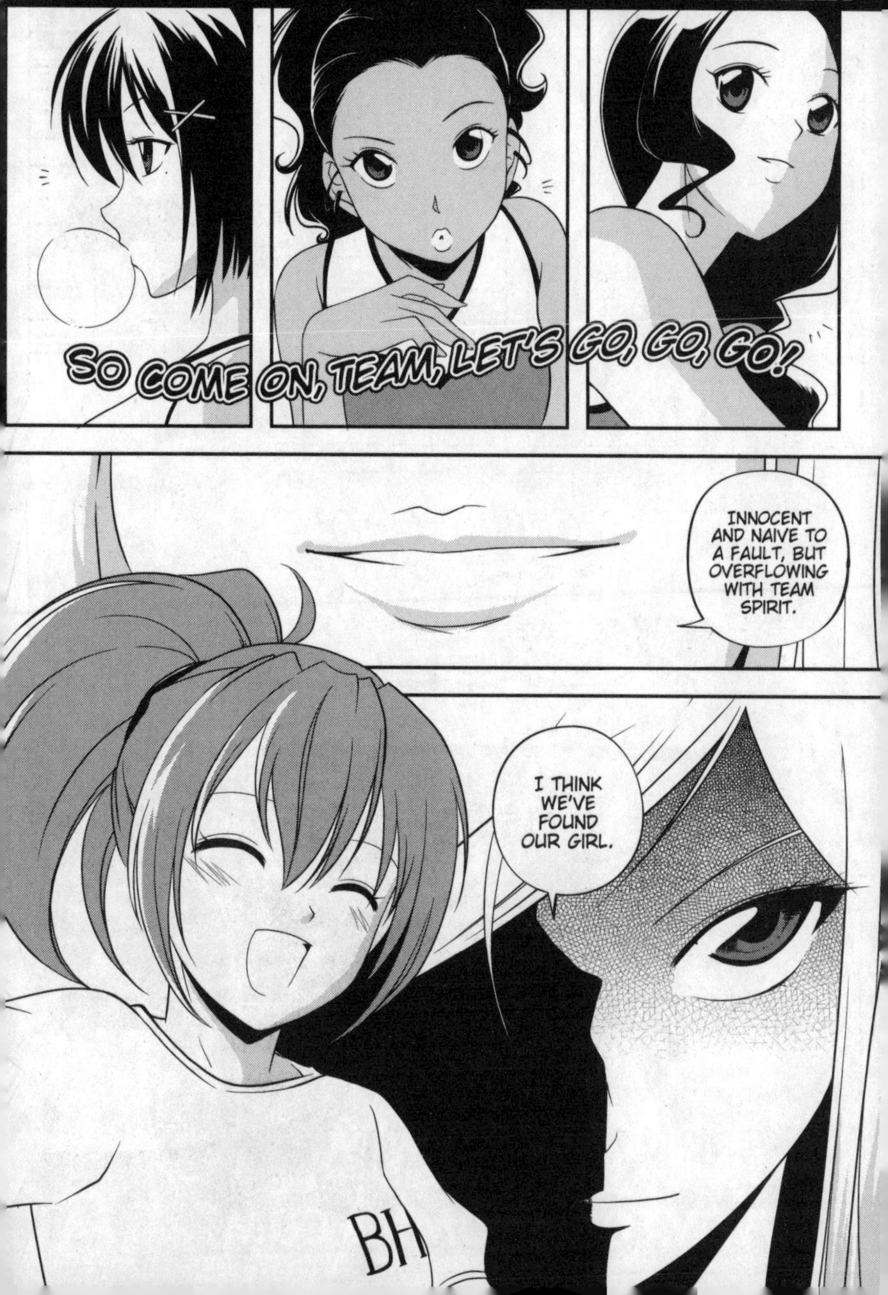
SO COME ON, TEAM, LET'S GO, GO, GO!
INNOCENT AND NAIVE TO A FAULT, BUT OVERFLOWING WITH TEAM SPIRIT.
I THINK WE'VE FOUND OUR GIRL.
BH

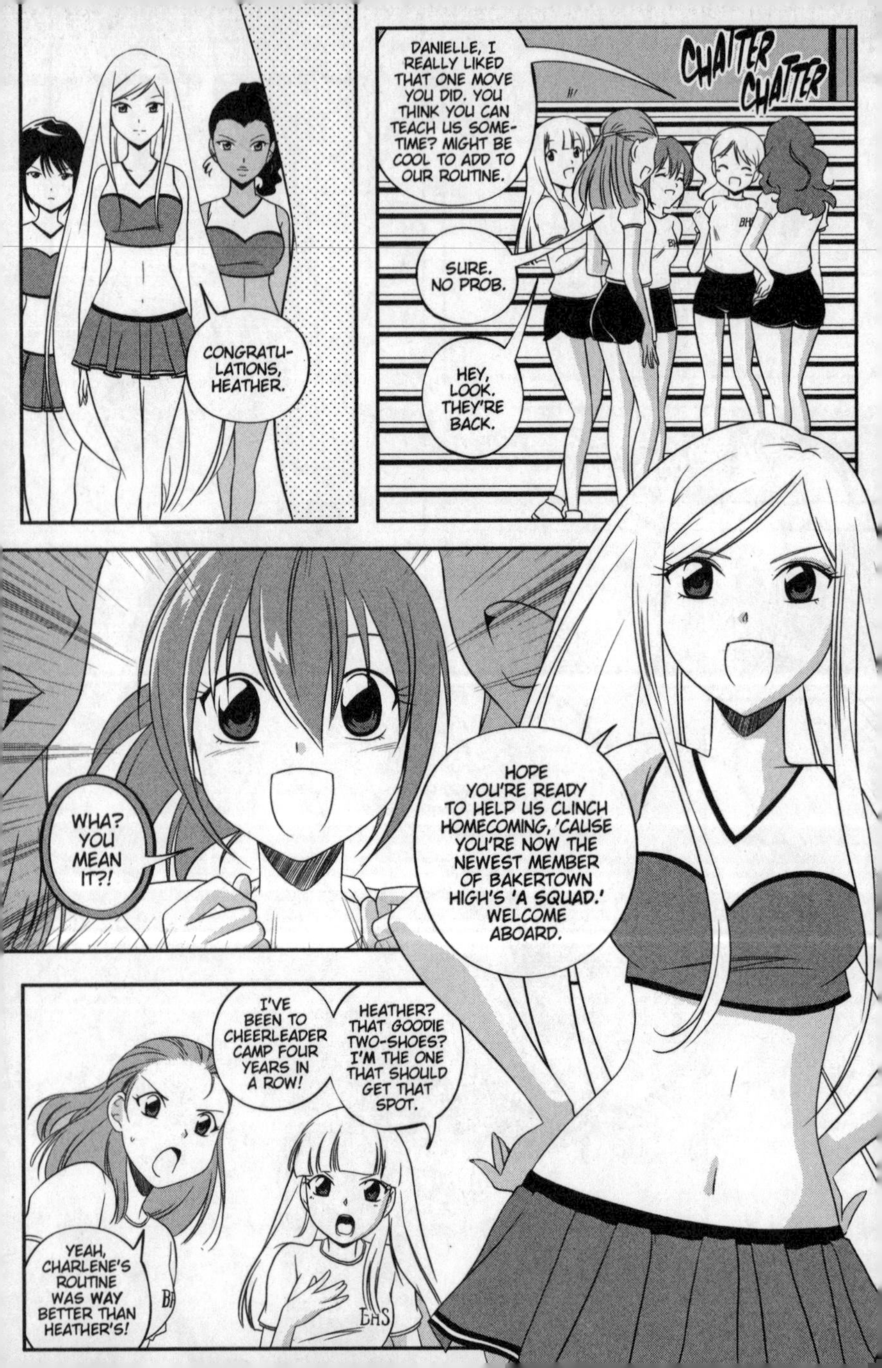
CHATTER CHATTER
DANIELLE, I REALLY LIKED THAT ONE MOVE YOU DID. YOU THINK YOU CAN TEACH US SOME-TIME? MIGHT BE COOL TO ADD TO OUR ROUTINE.
SURE. NO PROB.
HEY, LOOK. THEY'RE BACK.
CONGRATU-LATIONS, HEATHER.
HOPE YOU'RE READY TO HELP US CLINCH HOMECOMING, 'CAUSE YOU'RE NOW THE NEWEST MEMBER OF BAKERTOWN HIGH'S 'A SQUAD.' WELCOME ABOARD.
WHA? YOU MEAN IT?!
HEATHER? THAT GOODIE TWO-SHOES? I'M THE ONE THAT SHOULD GET THAT SPOT.
I'VE BEEN TO CHEERLEADER CAMP FOUR YEARS IN A ROW!
YEAH, CHARLENE'S ROUTINE WAS WAY BETTER THAN HEATHER'S!

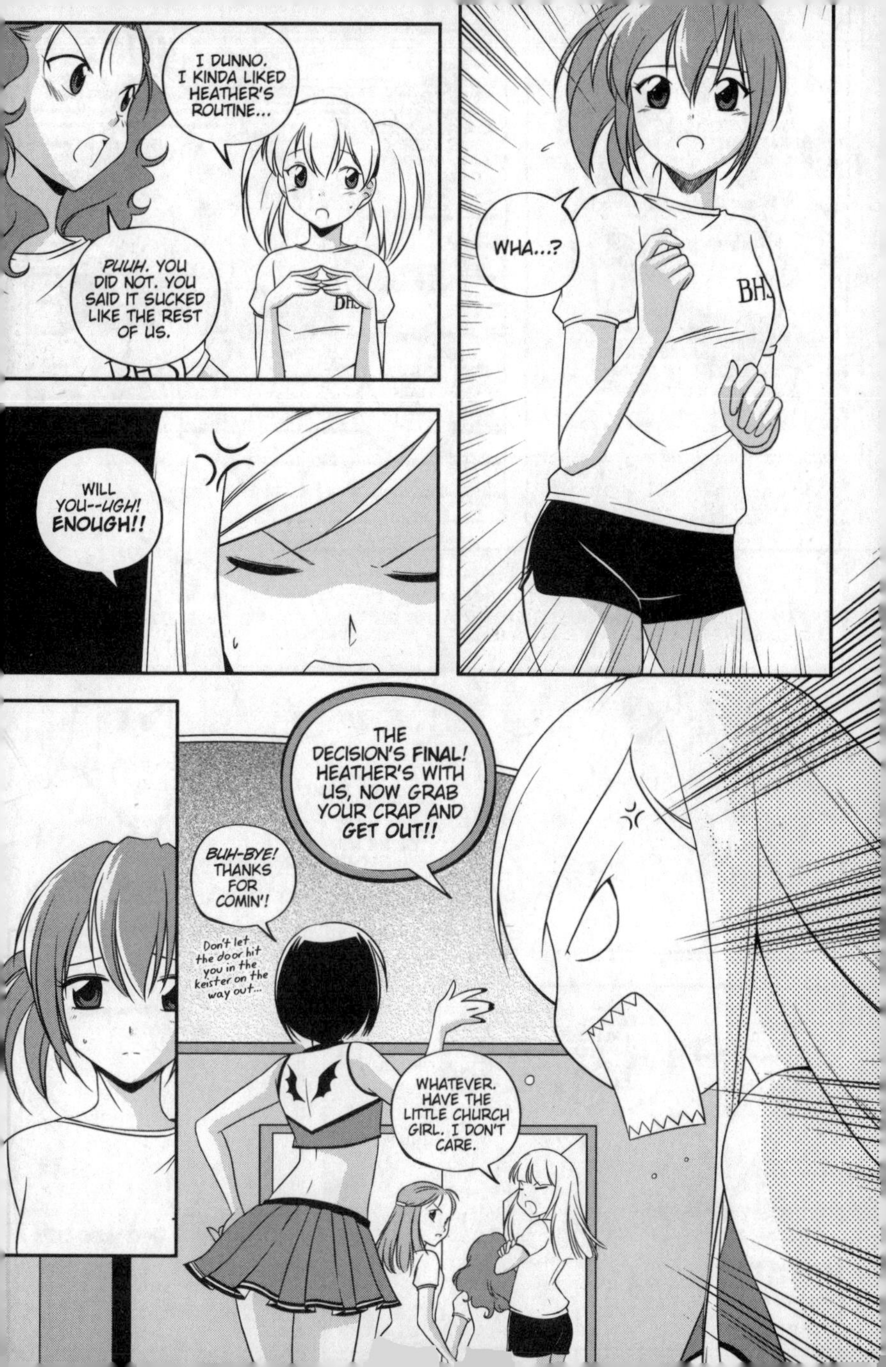
WHA...?
I DUNNO. I KINDA LIKED HEATHER'S ROUTINE...
PUUH. YOU DID NOT. YOU SAID IT SUCKED LIKE THE REST OF US.
WILL YOU--*UGH*! **ENOUGH!!**
THE DECISION'S **FINAL!** HEATHER'S WITH US, NOW GRAB YOUR CRAP AND GET OUT!!
BUH-BYE! THANKS FOR COMIN'!
Don't let the door hit you in the keister on the way out...
WHATEVER. HAVE THE LITTLE CHURCH GIRL. I DON'T CARE.

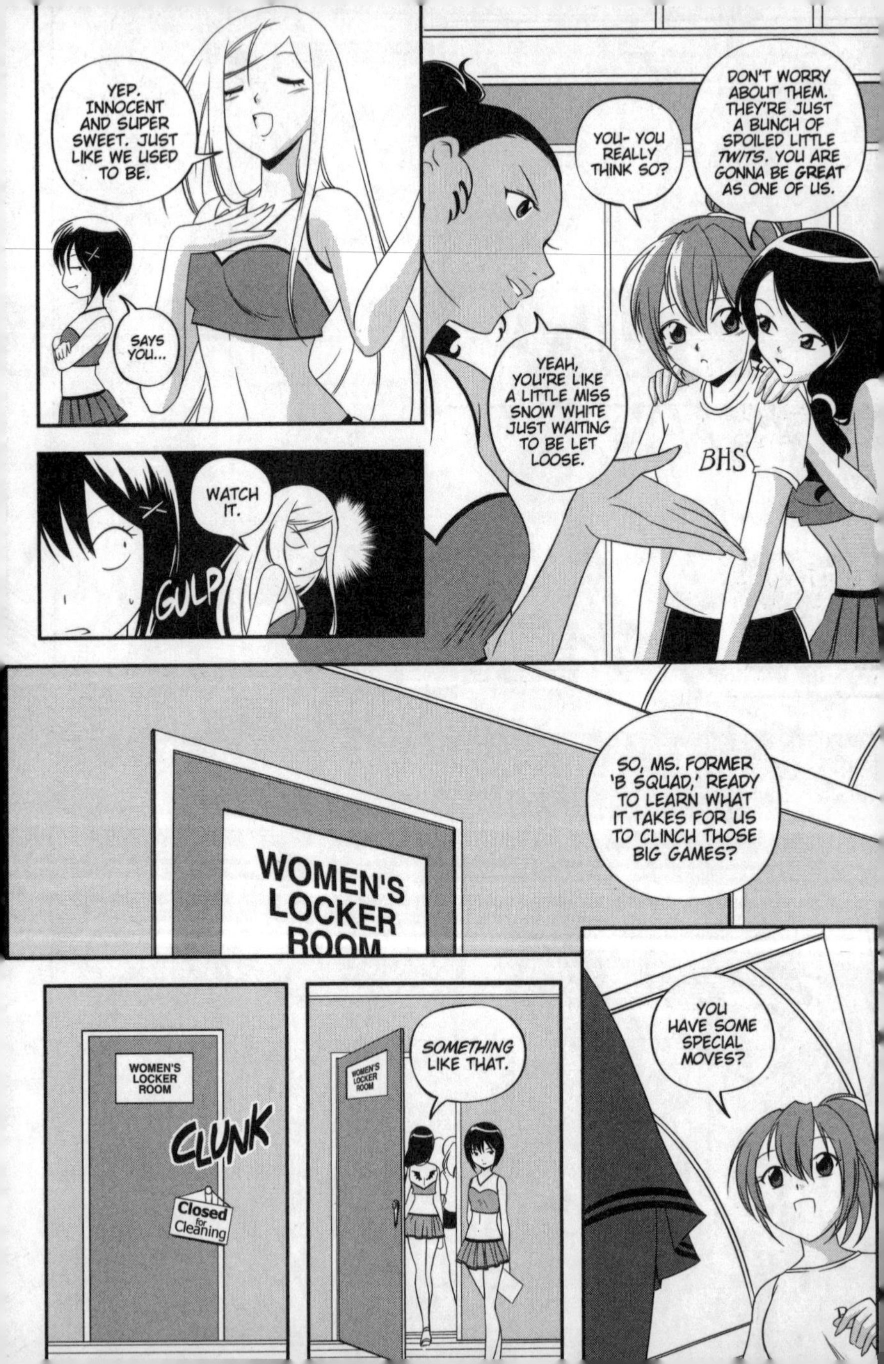
DON'T WORRY ABOUT THEM. THEY'RE JUST A BUNCH OF SPOILED LITTLE *TWITS*. YOU ARE GONNA BE **GREAT** AS ONE OF US.
YOU- YOU REALLY THINK SO?
YEAH, YOU'RE LIKE A LITTLE MISS SNOW WHITE JUST WAITING TO BE LET LOOSE.
BHS
YEP. INNOCENT AND SUPER SWEET. JUST LIKE WE USED TO BE.
SAYS YOU...
WATCH IT.
GULP
SO, MS. FORMER 'B SQUAD,' READY TO LEARN WHAT IT TAKES FOR US TO CLINCH THOSE BIG GAMES?
WOMEN'S LOCKER ROOM
YOU HAVE SOME SPECIAL MOVES?
SOMETHING LIKE THAT.
WOMEN'S LOCKER ROOM
WOMEN'S LOCKER ROOM
CLUNK
Closed for Cleaning

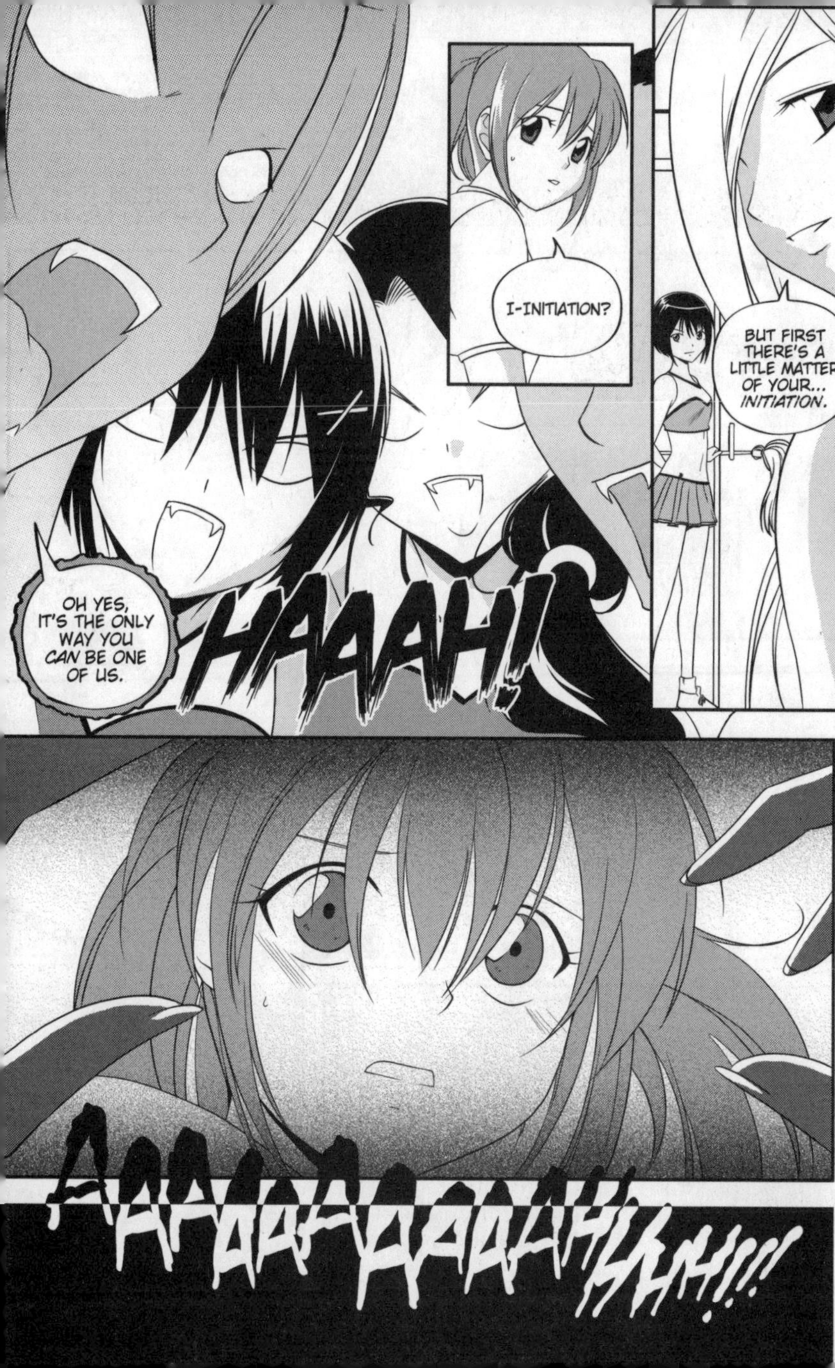
BUT FIRST THERE'S A LITTLE MATTER OF YOUR... *INITIATION*.
I-INITIATION?
OH YES, IT'S THE ONLY WAY YOU *CAN* BE ONE OF US.
HAAAH!
AAAAAAAAAAHHH!!!

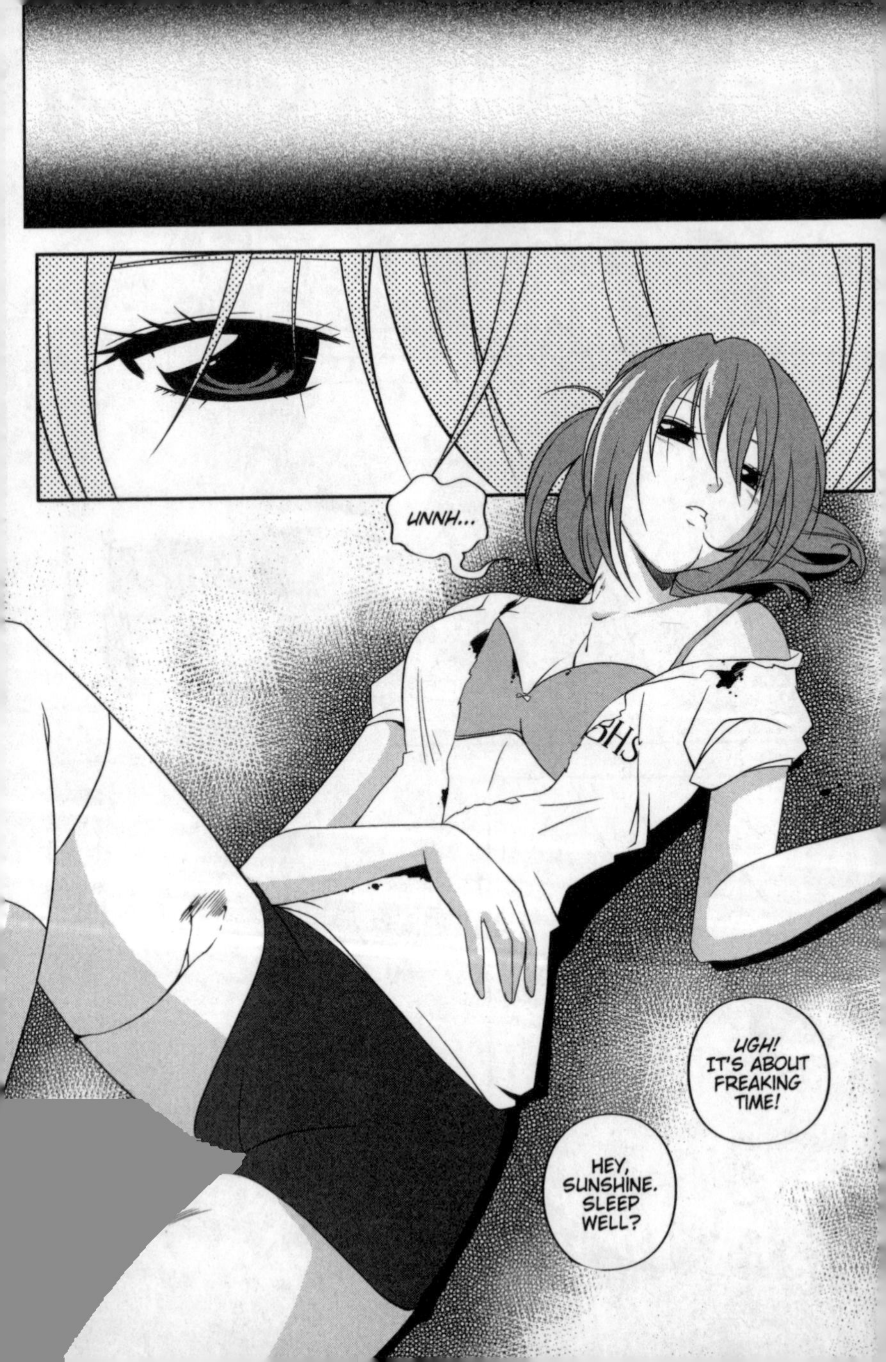
UNNH...
UGH! IT'S ABOUT FREAKING TIME!
HEY, SUNSHINE. SLEEP WELL?

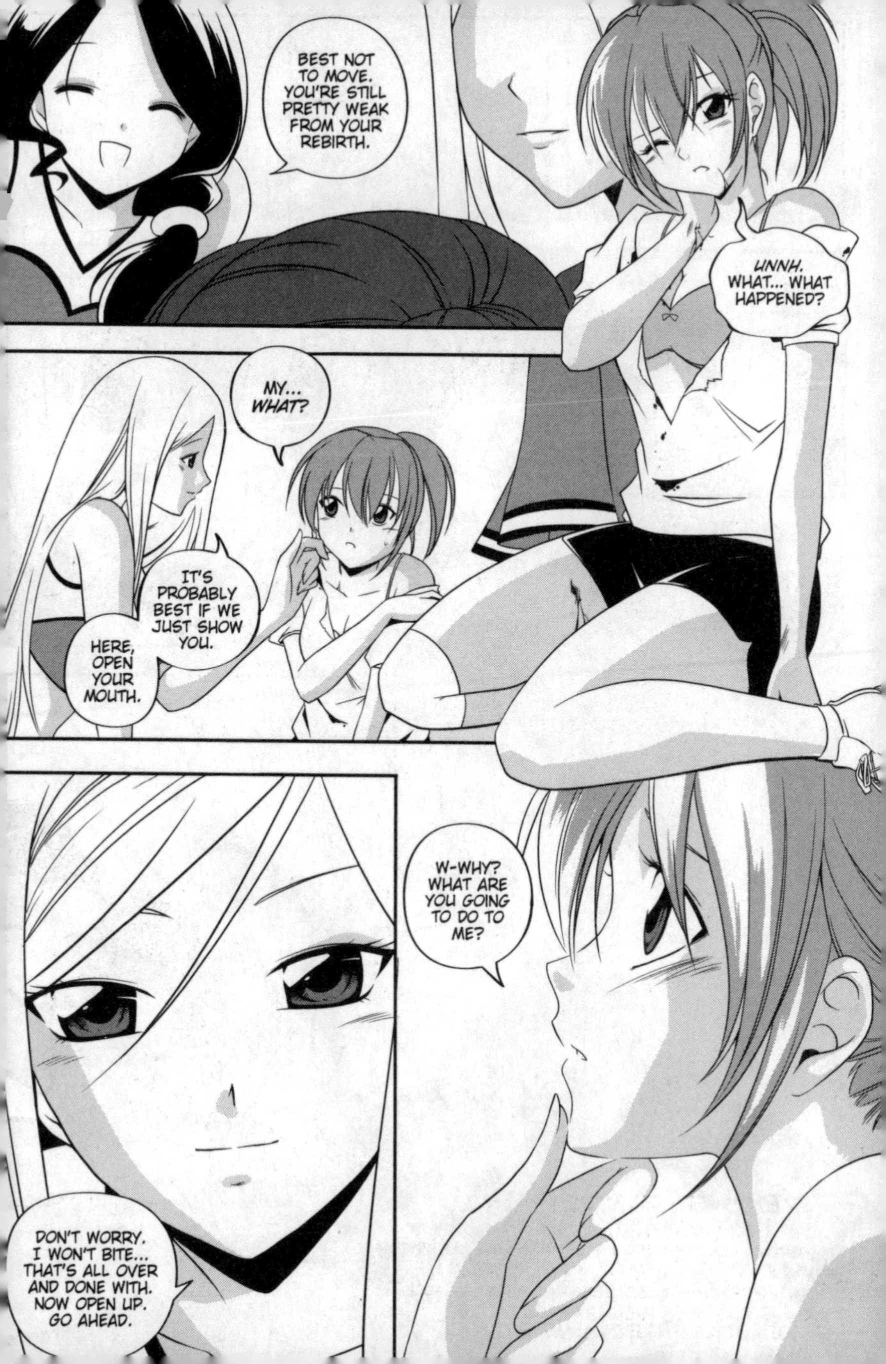
UNNH. WHAT... WHAT HAPPENED?
BEST NOT TO MOVE. YOU'RE STILL PRETTY WEAK FROM YOUR REBIRTH.
MY... WHAT?
IT'S PROBABLY BEST IF WE JUST SHOW YOU.
HERE, OPEN YOUR MOUTH.
W-WHY? WHAT ARE YOU GOING TO DO TO ME?
DON'T WORRY. I WON'T BITE... THAT'S ALL OVER AND DONE WITH. NOW OPEN UP. GO AHEAD.

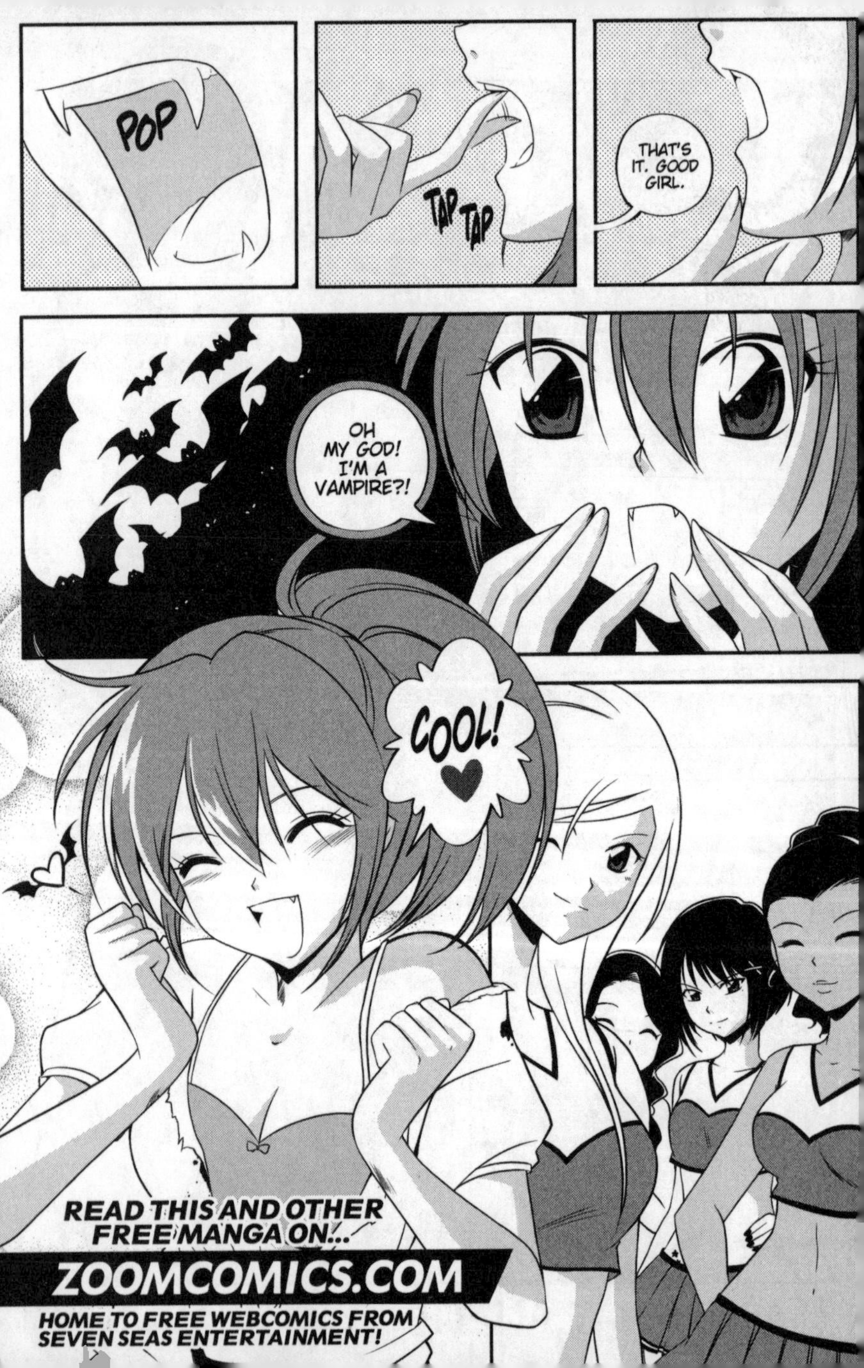
THAT'S IT. GOOD GIRL.
TAP TAP
POP
OH MY GOD! I'M A VAMPIRE?!
COOL!
READ THIS AND OTHER FREE MANGA ON...
ZOOMCOMICS.COM
HOME TO FREE WEBCOMICS FROM SEVEN SEAS ENTERTAINMENT!

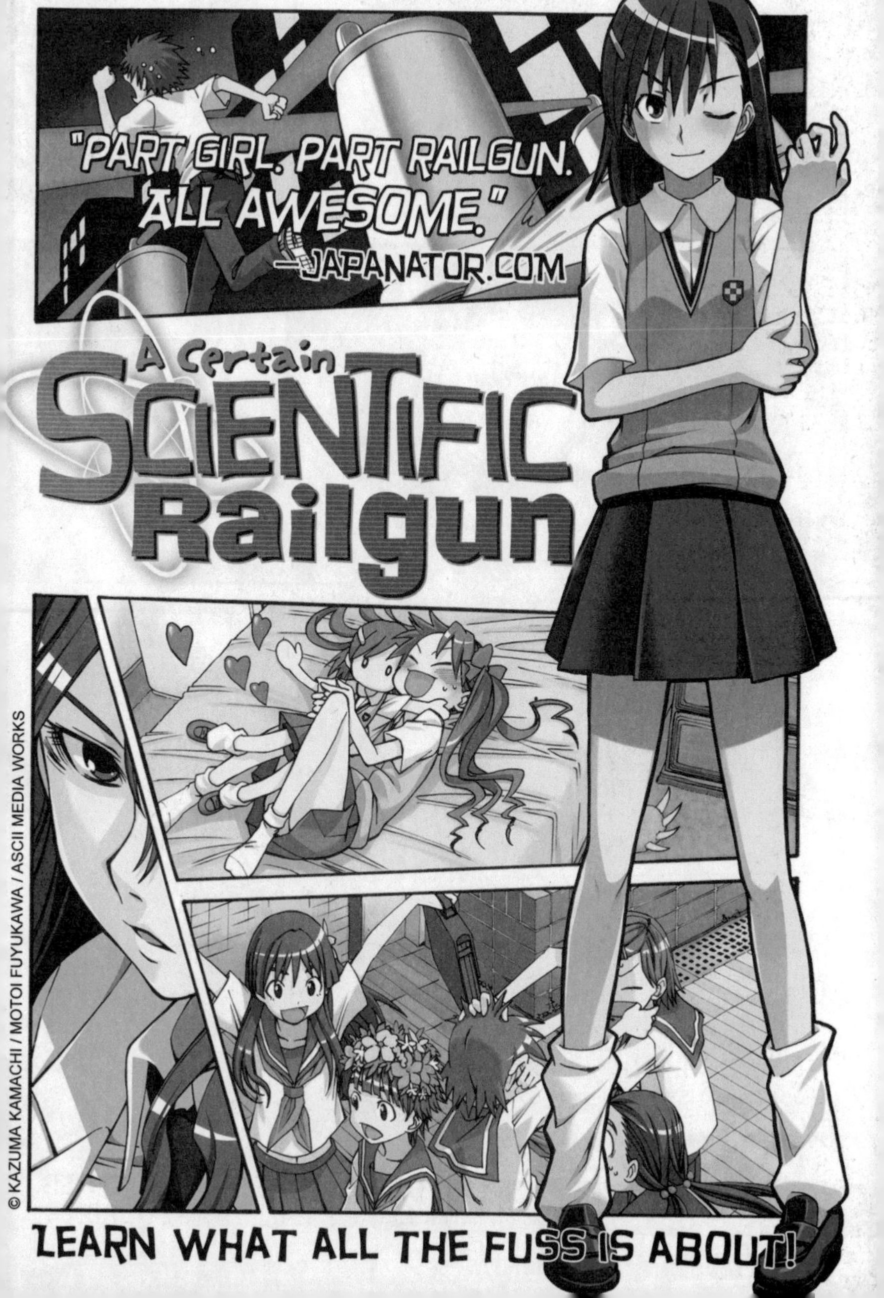
"PART GIRL. PART RAILGUN. ALL AWESOME."
—JAPANATOR.COM
A Certain SCIENTIFIC Railgun
LEARN WHAT ALL THE FUSS IS ABOUT!
© KAZUMA KAMACHI / MOTOI FUYUKAWA / ASCII MEDIA WORKS

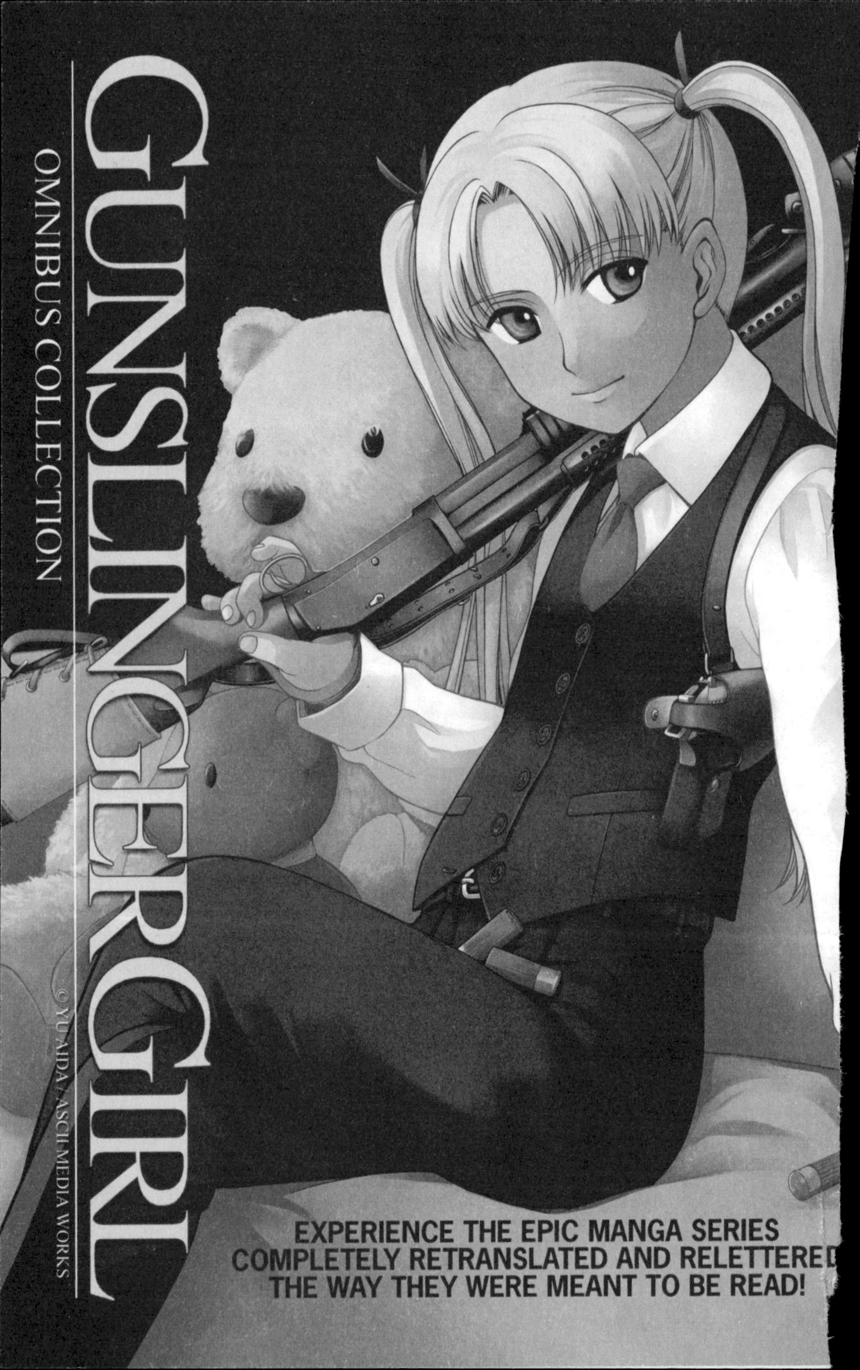
GUNSLINGER GIRL
OMNIBUS COLLECTION
© YU AIDA / ASCII MEDIA WORKS
EXPERIENCE THE EPIC MANGA SERIES
COMPLETELY RETRANSLATED AND RELETTERED
THE WAY THEY WERE MEANT TO BE READ!

Experience all that SEVEN SEAS has

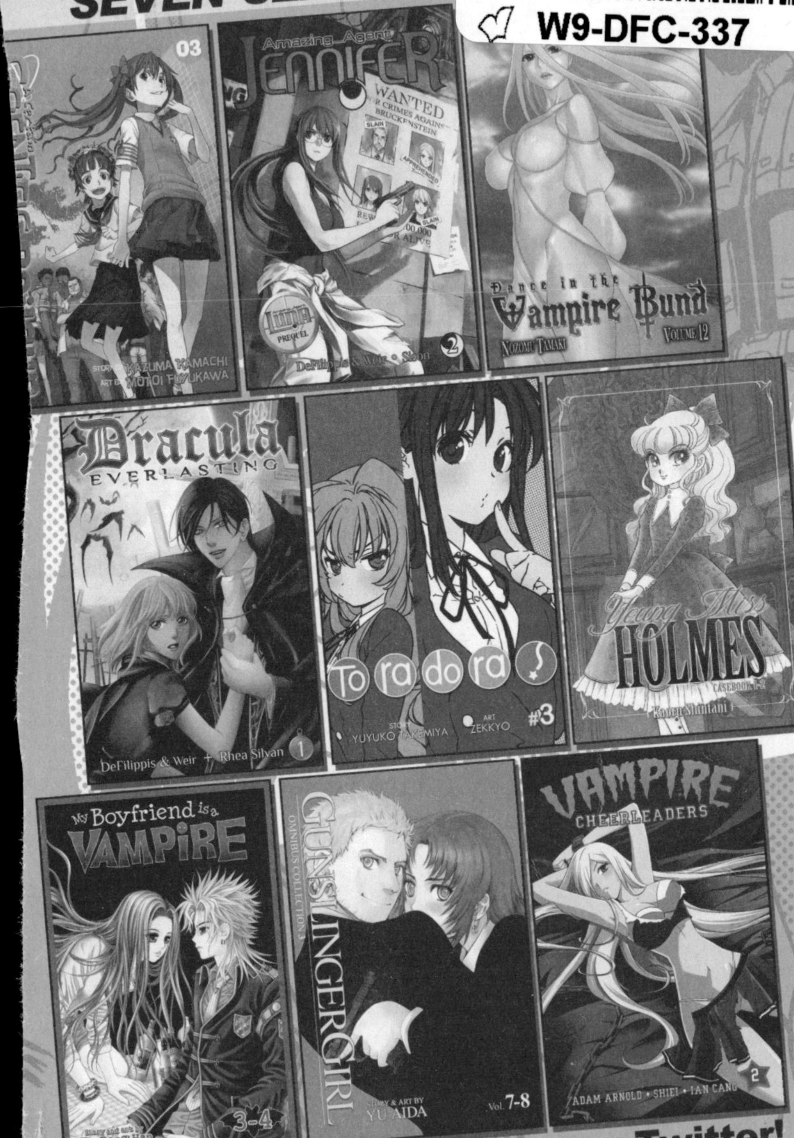
03
KAZUMA KAMACHI
Amazing Agent JENNIFER
WANTED
FOR CRIMES AGAINST BRUCKENSTEIN
SLAIN
APPREHENDED
LUNA PREQUEL
2
Dance in the Vampire Bund
Nozomu Tamaki
Volume 12
Dracula EVERLASTING
DeFilippis & Weir + Rhea Silvyan
1
Toradora!
STORY YUYUKO TAKEMIYA
ART ZEKKYO
#3
Young Miss HOLMES
CASEBOOK 1-7
Kaoru Shintani
My Boyfriend is a VAMPIRE
3-4
Yu-Rang Han
GUNSLINGER GIRL
STORY & ART BY YU AIDA
Vol. 7-8
VAMPIRE CHEERLEADERS
2
ADAM ARNOLD • SHIEI • IAN CANG

Visit us Online and follow us on Twitter!

WWW.GOMANGA.COM

WWW.TWITTER.COM/GOMANGA